THE GREATEST BOOK EVER WRITTEN

THE GREATEST BOOK EVER WRITTEN

Fulton Oursler

Triumph™ Books
Tarrytown, New York

TRIUMPH™ BOOKS Edition published by special
arrangement with the Estate of Fulton Oursler

Library of Congress Cataloging-in-Publication Data

Oursler, Fulton, 1893–1952.
    The greatest book ever written / Fulton Oursler.—Triumph Books
ed.
        p. cm.
    Reprint. Originally published: New York : Doubleday, 1951.
    ISBN 0-8007-3019-4 :
    1. Bible. O.T.—History of Biblical events. I. Title.
BX1197.O792   1991
220.9′5—dc20   91-13856
                                                                      CIP

CONTENTS

THE GREATEST BOOK EVER WRITTEN

PROLOGUE   The Story of Creation   15

BOOK ONE   The Beginnings
  Chapter 1   Adam and Eve   17
  Chapter 2   Cain and Abel   27
  Chapter 3   Noah and the Flood   32
  Chapter 4   The Tallest Building in the World   39

BOOK TWO   The Patriarchs
  Chapter 5   The Story of Abraham   45
  Chapter 6   The Story of Isaac   62
  Chapter 7   The Story of Jacob   65
  Chapter 8   The Story of Joseph   81

BOOK THREE   The Wilderness Adventure
  Chapter 9   The Story of Moses   97
  Chapter 10   The Escape from Egypt   109
  Chapter 11   The Ten Commandments   120
  Chapter 12   The Golden Calf   130
  Chapter 13   The Long Journey Ends   138

BOOK FOUR   The Story of Joshua
  Chapter 14   The Red Thread at the Window   149
  Chapter 15   The Conquest of Canaan   156

BOOK FIVE   The Rule of the Judges
  Chapter 16   The Stars Fight in Their Courses   165
  Chapter 17   Samson   179
  Chapter 18   Ruth   189
  Chapter 19   The Voice in the Night   196
  Chapter 20   Samuel and Saul   201
  Chapter 21   The Shepherd Boy and the Giant   219
  Chapter 22   The Witch of Endor and the Death of Saul   233
  Chapter 23   The Lament of David   240
  Chapter 24   David and Absalom   247
  Chapter 25   Son Against Father   252
  Chapter 26   The Death of David   260

CONTENTS

BOOK SIX   The Glory of Israel
   Chapter 27   Solomon   265
   Chapter 28   The Song of Solomon   273
   Chapter 29   The Trial on Mount Carmel   286
   Chapter 30   What Do You Here, Elijah?   296
   Chapter 31   The Strange Career of Elisha   305
   Chapter 32   The Singular Travels of Jonah   319
   Chapter 33   "I Despise Your Feast Days"   324
   Chapter 34   The Fall of the Northern Kingdom   327
   Chapter 35   The Little Angel and the Burning Coal   328
   Chapter 36   The Assyrian Comes Down   335
   Chapter 37   The Boy King   340
   Chapter 38   The Fall of Jerusalem   343

BOOK SEVEN   The Babylonian Captivity
   Chapter 39   Ezekiel and the Words of Isaiah   353
   Chapter 40   Why Must the Innocent Suffer?   360
   Chapter 41   The Handwriting on the Wall   365
   Chapter 42   The Singular Story of Tobias   377

BOOK EIGHT   The Return
   Chapter 43   Freedom at Last   383
   Chapter 44   The Story of Esther   389
   Chapter 45   The Building of the Wall   394

EPILOGUE   Between the Old Testament and the New   399
   Chapter 46   The Unwritten Years   399

THE GREATEST BOOK EVER WRITTEN

PROLOGUE

The Story of Creation

IN *the beginning God created the heaven and the earth.*

And the earth was without form, and void; and darkness was upon the face of the deep.

And the Spirit of God moved upon the face of the waters.

And God said, Let there be light; and there was light.

And God saw the light, that it was good; and God divided the light from the darkness.

And God called the light Day, and the darkness He called Night. And the evening and the morning were the first day.

And God said, Let there be a firmament in the midst of the waters, and let it divide the waters from the waters.

And God made the firmament, and divided the waters which were under the firmament from the waters which were above the firmament: and it was so.

And God called the firmament Heaven. And the evening and the morning were the second day.

And God said, Let the waters under the heaven be gathered together unto one place, and let the dry land appear: and it was so.

And God called the dry land Earth; and the gathering together of the waters called He Seas: And God saw that it was good.

And God said, Let the earth bring forth grass, the herb yielding seed, and the fruit tree yielding fruit after his kind, whose seed is in itself, upon the earth: and it was so.

And the earth brought forth grass, and herb yielding seed after his kind, and the tree yielding fruit, whose seed was in itself, after his kind: and God saw that it was good.

And the evening and the morning were the third day.

And God said, Let there be lights in the firmament of the

heaven, to divide the day from the night; and let them be for signs, and for seasons, and for days, and years:

And let them be for lights in the firmament of the heaven to give light upon the earth: and it was so.

And God made two great lights; the greater light to rule the day, and the lesser light to rule the night: he made the stars also.

And God set them in the firmament of the heaven, to give light upon the earth.

And to rule over the day and over the night, and to divide the light from the darkness: and God saw that it was good.

And the evening and the morning were the fourth day.

And God said, Let the waters bring forth abundantly the moving creature that hath life, and fowl that may fly above the earth in the open firmament of heaven.

And God created great whales, and every living creature that moveth, which the waters brought forth abundantly, after their kind, and every winged fowl after his kind: and God saw that it was good.

And God blessed them, saying, Be fruitful, and multiply, and fill the waters in the seas, and let the fowl multiply in the earth.

And the evening and the morning were the fifth day.

And God said, Let the earth bring forth the living creature after his kind, cattle, and creeping thing, and beast of the earth after his kind: and it was so.

And God made the beast of the earth after his kind, and cattle after their kind, and every thing that creepeth upon the earth after his kind: and God saw that it was good.

And God said, Let us make man in our image, after our likeness: and let them have dominion over the fish of the sea, and over the fowl of the air, and over the cattle, and over all the earth, and over every creeping thing that creepeth upon the earth.

So God created man in His own image. . . .

BOOK ONE

The Beginnings

Chapter 1 ADAM AND EVE

A D A M opened his eyes and looked into the face of his Maker. It was his first human act in the world as he stood, tall and straight and naked, his feet in the red earth. His dark eyes were full of wonder and a vast and perfect innocence. The beating of the first man's heart, the warm coursing of his blood, the strength of arms and legs, the breath of his lungs, the sweetness of woods and flowers in his nostrils, the wind in his reddish hair and its coolness on his bare skin, and the deep sense of comprehension of such things within his mind, all were mingled with a feeling of something greater, some spirit welling up in his soul, which could feel gratitude to this Presence before Which he was standing, thankfulness to the Lord God, the Father, Who had formed him from the dust in the ground.

Out of nothingness he had emerged in that first act of opening his eyes, coming from nothingness into space, one instant non-existent, the next being alive and looking into the face of his Maker, a countenance all wisdom and compassion and hope. In that unique moment when "man became a living soul," Adam could feel no fear. There was welcome for him in the Creator's steady gaze.

"Let us make man in our image, after our likeness"—so God had said. "And let them"—for He meant there to be many more like Adam—"have dominion over the fish of the sea and over the fowl of the air and over all the earth and over every creeping thing. . . ."

There were no questions in the first opening of the first man's eyes, questions that would plague his descendants. Not his need to ask, From whence did I come? Why am I here? Whither do I go when I depart? Adam had no need to formulate these simple and profound riddles which came from the fall, afterward; the modern sense of confusion was not born with him. It was the presence of God that reassured him and made him feel at home in the unknown. All the world, fresh from creation, was to be his domain; all perfection of beauty and comfort, with one restriction.

"You may eat freely of every tree in the garden but of the Tree of Knowledge of Good and Evil, you shall not eat, for in the day you eat thereof you shall surely die."

Looking at that tree, with its massive brown trunk and spreading greenness, Adam could realize that this command was mild indeed; a simple test, a token of obedience from himself, the created one, to Him who had given him life. God had put Adam at once upon his honor.

Left to himself, Adam looked around him. Everywhere heaven on earth stretched away, bland and smiling. In his eagerness to see all and know everything he stalked down the sunny paths, through the abundance of fruits and blossoms, among shady glens and close to running waters, on their way to some distant sea. Once he knelt before the smooth mirror of a pool and looked in, beholding himself and suddenly becoming aware that he was solitary; wishing—his first desire—that someone else were beside him, so that they could look together.

There was no one with him in the beautiful garden of the world; Adam was alone with mountains, rivers, oceans, forests, valleys, and lakes.

Should not this estate have been enough for Adam—to be formed by God as heir to the world? That awesome Will and Intelligence coming closer from abstraction to precision; veiling for His purposes the terrible might, the overwhelming majesty, that is His by nature, to be a smiling Father to this one creature; showing His tenderness, His hope in this unique experiment.

Why had God made Adam? The question did not nag Adam as it was to trouble billions of his descendants; the first man on his first day could never surmise that it would turn out to be so. He knew. Was it that God, too, willed to share His love? Did the Lord God hope to make creatures who could be His companions?

Man was no mere puppet whose strings were to be pulled this way and that by his Master. Instead he had been given something as precious as life itself, which was free will. God wanted him to be happy here, but through that extraordinary franchise of free will he could obey the rules or refuse to obey them; not an animated automatom but a potential companion, having free will to love or hate—and if he loved God and obeyed Him as a free agent, and not under compulsion, his potential companionship with his Maker would become a reality and he could be close to his Father.

For Adam it was a divine opportunity, and if anyone could have shown him then what his future, of his own making, would be like, Adam would not have believed that he could be capable of such folly. Tell him that the day would come—as it has long since arrived—when the Garden of Eden and all its luxurious beauty and happiness would turn into a blistered wilderness and Adam would have refused to believe the possibility of such a tragedy. Surely the four separate rivers that flowed around him would never dry up; the forests would never wither away, the fertile lands turn to sandy waste, ravaged with merciless heat. Adam would have said that such a tragedy would never —could never—come to pass; most certainly not through any doing of his.

God, compassionately watching his newly created man in the garden, said to Himself:

"It is not good that the man should be alone."

From distant reaches of the garden He summoned the lesser creatures that He had formed out of the ground: the four-footed beasts with soft, bright eyes and the green and yellow singing birds, all trooping in procession before thoughtful Adam, who stood at review beside God. And at the Father's suggestion, Adam gave names to the birds and the animals, the strangest naming party. His own name, Adam, meant the "red earth" and the "dust of the ground."

But the beasts and birds were not to be the only companions for Adam. Once again God dreamed the Creator's dream, making a new wonder for His creature.

A weakness stole through the thighs of Adam, unmanning him so that, to his own astonishment, he sank down into the cool grass and leaned his back against a boulder of gray granite. The dark eyes blinked uncertainly, then closed, and a deep sleep fell upon Adam, a dreamless catalepsy, his whole body unmoving as if the life had been taken from it.

Now the first patient in the world was fully under the initial anesthesia, ready for the original surgery. Painlessly asleep, he was as if he did not exist, while God, in ministering pity, laid hands upon him. Strange and wise, the ways of God, then as always. He could have clapped His hands like some enchanter in a fairy tale and made a new being appear. Or He could merely have thought His command and it would have been instantly performed by infinite and obedient forces. Instead, God's hands gently touched Adam's body with a deep and beautiful purpose. The man was now to have a companion formed of his own flesh and blood, bone of his bone—so close woman was to be to man, and man to woman, each part of each to be forever kin, like two notes of music yearning to be one note again, and even that whole note incomplete in an unresolved chord.

Shadows of late afternoon were deepening, as long, slanting rays of sunlight stole across the grass and flowers, and in the glade where Adam lay asleep a lavender haze promised the coming of twilight. Out of Adam's body, bloodlessly, painlessly, God drew his very substance; one of his ribs He took, and closed up the flesh again and of that rib the new creature was made.

Warmed in God's clasp, the fragment of Adam changed and grew in a swift, whirling metamorphosis of growth until she stood on small bare feet in the cool grass, while tender fingers touched her eyelids and she heard a Voice bidding her open and look.

Adam groaned heavily in his sleep. Half turning, he seemed to sulk for a moment in his half-awakened mood, then through blurred eyes he stared and saw the new creature. A cry burst from his mouth as love came at first sight to him and to her: the love of man and woman. Adam leaped up, joy in his shouts, the very voice of the human soul beholding its own completion, God's task well finished, for woman had come into the world.

Together they stood, Adam and his mate, delighting in seeing each other as if they had lived a thousand years together already, exultantly paired and glad; Adam in all his height and strength and power and she graceful and soft and kind and helpless, needing his might as he needed her tenderness. Eve he would name her, the mother of all living, and with Eve, let come what would, man need never again be lonely. God, standing by, smiled a blessing on this eternal fact.

"She shall be called woman," Adam declared, "because she was taken out of man." And in an ecstasy of prophetic vision he cried: "Therefore a man shall leave his parents to cleave to his wife and they shall be one flesh."

Before God they stood, knowing that they were man and wife in the first marriage. Of a sudden they were alone, the garden all theirs for their privacy.

There has been no happier marriage brief as was its paradise, since that little stay of Adam and Eve in the garden. They had more to enjoy than their countless descendants, for they had been born in a perfection of mortal powers, and every sight and sound, feeling and smell and taste was more intense to them, supremely satisfying. In God's full pleasure and approval their felicity bloomed; they existed in perfect bodies in perfect surroundings and had all the world to themselves.

Naked and unashamed, they were never satiated with each other. They had powers which those who came after them were never to know, except in fugitive hints to remind mankind of its lost inheritance; gifts of God which can transcend the ordinary limitations of time and space. Yes, and they shared a superior elevation, partaking of God's own life. Mysteries of existence were their commonplace possession; they had understanding without the need of toilsome, stumbling struggle toward knowledge; while there was not the beatific Vision, there did come to them habitually an instantaneous perception of the truth which in our days is only the occasional experience of saints.

As perfect man and woman, Adam and Eve knew each the thoughts of the other, as if without the need of speech. They had no fear of wild beasts, for Adam had been given dominion over them, and the wild animals did not hate or fear him. Nor did the man and woman ever stand in any danger from falling rock or trees or bolts of lightning; the ground was yet to quake and the volcanoes to belch their fire; the earth was at peace. The only fear of Adam and Eve was the fear of displeasing God, which was a part of their love for Him.

They did not misunderstand each other, and they were not bored. They lived in Paradise, for a very short but blissful time, and there was no excuse for the wickedness that they were to commit.

The time had come for the happy pair to be tested.

They were the only possessors of one priceless gift, superior elevation, with its glorious consequences—life and the choice of being trustworthy or not. Their free will was not a nascent power; not a privilege to be forgotten or to fall into disuse. All their continuing in the garden of uncountable delights depended on their making the right decision in their test.

So there came presently into the peace and quiet of their abode a handsome and plausible stranger. One afternoon he found Eve by a waterfall and accosted her. She looked at the intruder with frank astonishment. He was a tall and glittering creature, a part of him coiled in the grass but the rest of him, green with golden rings, rising like a graceful stem of some enormous flower, his cordial face its dark, ingratiating blossom. The stranger smiled at Eve and his voice was polite and interested, and with its own attractive music, sharp and clear against the mild splashing of the waters tumbling behind her.

"Is it true," the newcomer asked impudently, "that you are not allowed to eat of the fruits of these trees?"

Not so! Eve's expression revealed her amusement at such a question. She and Adam could take what they wanted from any bough in the orchard, with only one tree excepted.

"Which one?"

Eve told him, simply and without any resentment, that they were forbidden to touch the fruit of the Tree of Knowledge of Good and Evil, which was in the midst of all the others. To do so would be an act of disobedience to the Lord God, their Father, Who had given them everything, unstintedly. Adam had taught Eve her lesson with earnest care and now Eve told the stranger all about it.

"But why? What is the reason you can't eat that most delicious fruit?"

Eve's eyes, turning to the sky, seemed to be trying to find the answer in the white, fleecy clouds that rode invisible winds.

"All that I know is that we should surely die," she answered softly.

A chuckle sounded over Eden's treetops, followed by scornful and malicious laughter. The gaudy visitor threw back his head and opened his mouth, cackling as if his contempt for such prohibitions rose from fathomless depths within him. He shook his head, and the tears of his mirth ran, glittering and iridescent, down each side of his mocking face.

So that was how matters stood!

Clever indeed—the ruse that God had tricked them with. And the chortling stranger laughed once more, with insolent assurance.

Oddly, Eve was both repelled and attracted by him and his laughter. There was something frightening and yet monstrously daring in his effrontery. Japing at God's authority, he was bringing something new into Eden.

Taking a deep breath and a last chuckle, he said: "You shall *not* surely die."

And leaning forward, his cozening voice fell to whispering: could not Eve understand for herself why God did not wish either her or Adam to know too much?

"The day you eat the fruit of that tree, then your eyes shall be opened, and you both shall be as gods, knowing good and evil."

That was the reason it was forbidden them, the visitor solemnly averred: God simply wanted to keep the two of them in subjection.

Eve looked thoughtful. She felt a sense of limitation, as Adam had felt it; the stirring of active curiosity that, once roused, would not lie quiet. Until this caller had put the notion into her head, Eve had scarcely given a thought to the forbidden tree. Now she moved away from the stranger, dawdling a little as she went, her path a wide, unnecessary arc; she seemed twice about to change her direction, and her sauntering pace was leisurely. Nevertheless, moment by moment, she was coming ever closer to the forbidden tree.

At five steps distant, she halted, breathing in the deep, ravishing smell of its bark and leaves. Was this the odor of wisdom? Surely it must be a wonderful thing to be as wise as God. And clearly this fearless stranger was the most subtle and cunning of all the wild creatures of the garden; he reasoned out things so intelligently and so vividly too. But her reasoning was perfect too; she was equipped to defend herself against him.

Eve, are you afraid? Looking over her shoulder, she could read the question in the great, glittering round eyes. Then she saw him smile as he lunged back from her, golden rings flashing as he slithered up an oak tree and made his way with sure, small noises, off through the leafage and away into the forest, leaving her alone. There comes a time when evil has to leave us alone; the tempter is not allowed to stay at our elbow when we make up our mind.

The feeling was now like a thirst in the mind. Eve crept nearer to the tree, lifted her hand, and let her fingers curl around the cool skin of the golden fruit. One little tug was all she gave it, and the twig flew upward with a broken stem, the prize left moist and chill against her palm.

In one more ungovernable moment Eve lifted the thing to her mouth. She bit into it, her tongue tasting its sharp flavor, but now she would not spew out what she had bitten off, she had gone too far and was too proud to turn back, so she chewed the fruit and in its mastication was suddenly aware of an acrid, frightening sweetness mingled with bitterness. She shook her head in protest and her flowing hair rippled around her shoulders, but then she swallowed a mouthful of the pulp.

It was only a moment afterward that a shadow fell across Eve's flushed, excited face; the shadow of Adam who had returned to her, his footsteps unheard. In one glance he understood what his wife was doing.

Horror, sheer, downright, absolute, whitened his cheeks and darkened the deep eyes. Turning from her, Adam looked fearfully around, expecting on the instant the outraged appearance of God. But the garden was still quiet and they seemed altogether alone. When Adam looked at Eve again she was in command of herself, not waiting to be outfaced or reproved. Instead she swayed gracefully and smiled and told Adam of her visitor. Adam listened, saying nothing, but the more Eve told him the more disturbed he felt. With the rest of the half-eaten fruit between her rosy palms, Eve seemed to him, more and more, suddenly superior to him. He had greater strength than she, but she knew now much the more. She had dared to do a thing he had never thought of doing. She had eaten of the wisdom of Heaven while he had fed only on earthly food. She had swallowed that which would make her think herself God's equal. It was as if an abyss had opened up between them, an almost unbridgeable chasm. The thought was insupportable. The pain in his eyes was suddenly desperate. How does it taste, dear Eve?

With one rough sigh Adam received the remnant from her hands, opened his great mouth, and pushed the fruit between strong, white teeth. Diligently and rebelliously he masticated skin and pulp and core, staring down at her all the while, until it was all munched and the juice ran down his throat, and made him cough, even as he swallowed it.

And still it seemed as if they were altogether alone. Darkness was at its earliest with a stealthy spread of chill, creeping in with the young shadows, and bringing with it sadness that overwhelmed the lonely husband and his wife; a melancholy, a foreboding of something accusing and punishing and inescapable, surrounding them in the cold and gloom. They shivered and were grateful for the dark, only because they were somehow embarrassed to look at each other; it was as if they were stained by something sordid and ineffaceable. And then they heard the Voice of Eden calling from the darkness:

"Adam!"

The serene, ineffable composure of that Voice filled them with terror. They felt a great need to hide and to cover themselves, as if there was something shameful for God to see in what He had made, or what they had now made of themselves. They groped toward the thicket, reaching for leaves to cover with, and making no answer to that familiar hail. Under the whispering leaves of a spreading tree they stopped, to hear the Voice again:

"Where are you, Adam?"

From the depths of the thicket came the muffled answer of Adam, unknowingly blurting out his own indictment:

24

"I heard Your Voice in the garden and I was afraid, because I was naked, and I hid myself."

The silence then was itself a kind of sorrowful comment. But finally they heard the Voice in the same calm, unreachable tone:

"Who told you that you were naked?"

No answer to that. What answer could there be? The Voice persisted:

"Have you eaten of the Tree, whereof I commanded you that you should not eat?"

Cowering in the darkness, Adam knew that Eve was within reach of his hand. Even in his despair he knew, as clearly as ever before, that he feared God and loved his wife. Yet speaking treason to them both, his cry comes rolling down the ages, blaming God for giving him a wife and the wife for giving him the fruit. He was casting upon someone else, even the nearest and dearest, the responsibility for his own wrong use of free will.

"The woman whom You gave to be with me, *she* gave me of the tree and I did eat."

A long, shuddering quiet among the trees and the bushes and the nests of the birds, and even the waterfall, as Adam accused God and woman for what he had done; he seemed to say that he had no real culpability, but had been made a victim of conditions by his Maker and his wife.

Then the Lord God spoke to the woman:

"What is this that you have done?"

And Eve, too, now on trial in this terrifying ordeal of cross-examination, also tried to pass on the blame:

"The Serpent beguiled me," she answered defensively, "and I did eat."

As if turning His back upon the couple for a little while, God condemned the Serpent for his victory in Paradise, condemned him henceforth hopelessly among all other beasts to crawl on his belly and eat dust all his days. Between the Serpent and women yet to be born there would be enmity and the day would come when the head of the snake would be crushed under the heel of a woman.

Eve listened, wondering. She could not anticipate the far-off prophecy that lay in those words; could not guess how, after centuries of new opportunities given to men to show their purpose, God Himself would be born of woman to bring redemption into the world. But the stricken woman of Eden knew there was something of ultimate hope even in the condemnation of her.

Through all the subsequent gaudy history of men and women that must parade down the tumbling tomorrows, poet and seers and mystics and other guardians of hope were never to forget that promise made in the twilight of Eden.

Hearing Him pronounce the Serpent's doom and utter the mystical promise, Adam and Eve waited to know what their fate was to be. The situation baffled them. Why had God ever allowed the Serpent to come into their domain? To test them? Then why curse the Serpent for merely performing his duty? In these unanswered questions of Adam and Eve lay a mystery of good and evil, of infinite knowledge beyond finite comprehension. As years followed years and men continued to speculate on these enigmas, there would be told the history of the revolt among the angels, the fall of Lucifer through his pride, the chief of sins, and thus the creation of antagonism in the universe of opposition and of evil. In the exile of the fallen angel might lie the origin of the temptation that had come to Adam and Eve. But the first man and first woman did not understand these matters, nor will the last.

The malediction of God for the trespass of Eden was now, and with no delay, to alter the face of life on the earth. Having disposed of the Serpent, God turned again to Adam and Eve. They had been given fair trial and the first culprits among mortals would now hear the verdict, Eve first:

"I will greatly multiply your sorrow and your conception. In sorrow you shall bring forth children"—until that moment labor itself had not been conceived; this was the moment when pain was born—"and your desire shall be to your husband and he shall rule over you."

What was Eve thinking? Were her thoughts altogether cast down, or did she nourish a feminine reservation? Would she be ruled by Adam?

And for him, meanwhile, shattering words: an end to Eden, and to that priceless gift of superior elevation, so far as he and his descendants were concerned; an end of perfect happiness, a beginning of grief:

"Because you listened to the woman and ate of the Tree which was forbidden you, the ground shall be cursed to you and in labor and sweat shall you get your bread."

And then the final, most horrifying penalty:

"To the ground you shall return, for out of it you were taken. Dust you are and to dust you shall return."

This was no arbitrary punishment for some small or casual misdeed. The eating of the fruit was only a symbol of the breaking of a holy trust in the divine plan; the sin of pride by which angels had already fallen.

From now on, the old and priceless gift of superior elevation was lost. Man and woman were left to their own resources; they must work out their problems for themselves.

Death was in the world.

The darkness was almost complete and God was gone from the garden. Before the abandoned husband and wife, there dimly stretched away a road that led toward high and distant gates. Bent forward, hands covering their faces, they walked down the path and through the opening and they heard the clang of the vast gates, swinging shut behind them. Once only they looked back; once, one moment, appalled by the bleakness and barrenness they sensed in the scene all around them, beyond the doors of Eden, the dullness of the world that is ours compared with the Paradise that had been theirs, they looked over their shoulders toward their beautiful past. They could make out in the midst of the garden the gaunt, unwaving arms of the Tree of Knowledge of Good and Evil, and its shape was like a great blot on the sky, a distorted cross. In its shadow they had committed the original transgression of the world. Beside the Tree now they saw standing a new figure, an angel with a flaming sword, turning in every direction. But the garden was empty of God. Who would no longer walk its lonely paths, and before them was the savage earth.

Chapter 2 CAIN AND ABEL

FOR many long years Adam and Eve lived together in exile.

In those nine hundred and fifty years they had numerous children who in turn multiplied, until the sons and daughters of Adam and Eve, some at home, others wandering in every direction and to remote regions of the earth, peopled the world; so that before three centuries of Adam's life had gone by, there were a great many human beings earning their bread by the sweat of their brows, all sons and daughters of Adam and Eve.

But chief among them all were two men, two of that vast family; and few brothers were ever less alike than Cain and Abel. Their memories went back with father and mother, almost to the very gates of the long since lost and vanished garden. From earliest days they had grown up to help their parents, forever seeking a new home as they wandered by one of the four rivers that flowed from Eden. Their search lasted for years; the little group would settle at some favorable-seeming spot, remain a few years, and then, disappointed in crops or otherwise, would move on. Abel and Cain could both remember many such journeys, and remember, too, how they had helped Adam to dig and seed, water and harvest; learning to use their strength and brains to wrest a living from the soil. Often they had lived in caves and rocky grottoes, where they all felt safe from ravening wild beasts, over which Adam had no longer any control.

And with their father as their exciting model of what a man should be, the two boys tried hard to find new devices, invent expedients, were forever trying out new ideas in work. Adam's restless brain had devised for himself some simple tools of stone and implements of wood. And he had learned already how to make fire and Eve had learned to cook.

Around the fire and smoke on damp, chill evenings Adam and Eve would rest and tell Abel and Cain about how life used to be in the garden. They made no secret to their children of their disobedience. For centuries, by word of mouth, the record of their trespass was to be passed down through elders to the children, until with the invention of writing the whole story could be put down on dried sheepskin and so preserved. But in the beginning the tale was recounted to Abel and Cain by its two human actors, told under the stars, in the warmth of the blazing cedar boughs and the pungent incense of the smoke.

With strange feelings the two lads must have heard the facts of their life from father and mother. For they had been molded by the hands of God, but not so their sons, neither these two nor all the billions of others yet to be born. Life for Cain and Abel was not shaped from dampened dust nor taken from a dreamer's ribs. The seed had been planted and fertilized, nourished in dark secrecy, spreading and enlarging and reshaping its mother hostess, feeding upon her blood and bone, twisting and stretching close to her vitals, while it changed and grew until all was ready and Eve's first-born could be pulled, screaming with dismay, into the world.

Cain and Abel listened breathlessly every time the story was told to them around the home fires. And Eve never forgot what she said when Cain was born:

"I have gotten a man from the Lord!" Spent with pain and effort, she had uttered this simple magnificat. And she had named the baby boy, calling him Cain. Another year, and Abel had come to be his brother's companion.

From the very beginning there was bad feeling mixed with their playfulness. The two were ingenitally different. Cain was strong and far more powerfully built than Abel; the first-born had a fiery crop of stiff red hair, a thick neck, broad shoulders, and a tapering torso that his mother beheld with pride. Abel was slighter in build and in strength, his voice was softer and so were his eyes, greenish like his mother's.

It was Abel who was quieter about everything, thoughtful and serene; Cain never brooded for long, but let his emotions explode. If something troubled him he felt an uncontrollable desire to do something about it at once; he wanted what he wanted and when he wanted it. So from the beginning Cain and Abel did not understand or like each other very well. Perhaps Eve was a little tenderer to the younger one, although she loved them both. But Cain was jealous of every mothering attention shown to Abel; he must be given the same, and even more, or else he had a tantrum.

Cain seemed happiest when with his father, planting and reaping; he liked bodily activity. Fair seed fields bloomed under their care. Abel was not nearly so vigorous; he was gentle with the sheep whose flocks he tended. The first shepherd loved his work with a deep content. He loved to lie on a hillside and watch the sheep and wonder about God and how long it might be before the curse on his father and mother would be lifted; whether someday they might all go back to Eden together; in long hours of contemplation, man finding beauty and speculation, and growing as a soul.

At the family's night fires they would talk of ways to placate God and not passively wait for His displeasure to pass. They knew that all worship is sacred, but they thought of Him as somewhere far off in the sky, to which the smoke from their fires ascended. Those rising plumes of the smoke of burning cedars seemed like messages, as if the little fires of home were seeking to rise to find their way to the Creator. When the flocks multiplied and the harvests were plenty, it was an easy step to think of a burnt offering to please their offended God.

That was when they built earth's first altar. Stones were piled together to make rude tables in the fields, Cain, the farmer, piling up his vegetables and Abel bringing in his arms a choice fatling from his flock.

But it was in this very first public attempt at worship, the attempt at penance and reconciliation, that something even more evil was compounded.

They lighted their altar fires. Flames and smoke leaped bravely upward from Abel's offering, but not so Cain's; his fire gave but a feeble light, the flame smoldering, the smoke wavering and almost invisible in the sunrise. Why was this difference? Was he not Cain, the older, the more important one? Why should young Abel, moody, thoughtful, without the roar and strut of a strong man, be the favorite? Why did God show His preference for the dreamer against the man of action?

Cain's churlish, red-bearded face darkened. So, Abel's sacrifice was more acceptable to God? Jealousy and wounded pride looked through Cain's green eyes like madmen at a window. First envy and then murder were about to be born.

And not without warning. In the tense silence of Cain's dismay there came a Voice which neither had ever heard before, but of which father and mother had often spoken, the Voice of God speaking again to man:

"Why are you wroth? And why is your countenance fallen? If you do well, shall you not be accepted? And if you do not well, sin lies at the door, and unto you shall be his desire and you shall rule over him."

Awed at the Voice of which his mother and father had often told him, Cain should have fallen to his knees. But not he; his wrathy mind grew even angrier. So the Lord God thought his attitude was wrong! So he should subdue his feelings and rule over them, before worse than a divine snub happened to him? Well, the fact was that he had not been aware that he had not done well, nor that his life needed improvement!

Cain's bitterness rankled like poison, and violence gathered in his brain like a hurricane. Stone in hand, Cain came softly from behind his altar and looked down on Abel, kneeling in prayer. One mighty arm uplifted, one crushing blow and there it was, murder, bursting into the world, the second great sin let loose.

Like so many other murderers yet to be born, Cain ran away. He believed that he had only to escape the scene of his crime and he could forget what he had done and find peace, not knowing that to run and hide is already the beginning of punishment. When at last, many miles away, he sank down, panting and tired out, the haunted fugitive heard again the mysterious Voice:

"Where is your brother Abel?"

"I do not know," said Cain, and followed his lie with this inso-lence: "Am I my brother's keeper?"—a question which men in their folly keep on repeating today and still give themselves the wrong an-swer.

"What have you done?" God insisted. "The blood of your brother cries out to me from the very ground."

Cain stood mute, refusing to take the witness chair.

"Now," continued the inexorable Voice, "you are cursed from the earth which has drunk your brother's blood at your hand."

Then regret did begin to nibble at Cain's conscience. Surely he had never really hated Abel, his gentle brother; no, he had loved the lad, whose only offense was winning the favor of God, which was extreme provocation to anyone who so much desired to be pleasing to God. Perhaps he should explain to God. But the Judge had more to say:

"Henceforth, when you till the ground it shall yield you no return. A fugitive and vagabond you will be."

The thought of banishment filled Cain with all the fear of the un-known, and he cried out that his punishment was too great to bear. Homeless, he saw himself wandering over the face of an unfriendly earth.

"Everyone that sees me shall slay me," he pleaded.

Not so! Cain's fate was worse than to die; it was to live, to endure a lifelong burden of exile and remorse. God would see to it:

"Whoever shall slay you, on him a seven-fold vengeance shall be taken."

And then God set a mark on the murderer, a sign that at one fear-some glimpse set him apart from all his fellows, a marked man.

The wanderer sought his refuge in the land of Nod, and where was that? In Hebrew, the word "Nod" itself means wandering, and there are many who believe that Adam's eldest son got as far as India, or even China. There he made a few attempts to work some land, but nothing would grow for the runaway farmer. So Cain at last turned to an altogether different and novel idea; he built a few houses close to-gether and that highway collection of huts covered with leaves may well be called the world's first city—built by the first murderer.

The city had been built by Cain in honor of his little son Enoch. And what mystery is this, that Cain should have a son; a beautiful and wonderful mystery with meaning and hope for all who do wrong. Cain did have a son, because he had found a wife.

Somewhere the man with the mark upon him met a nameless

woman and she became his mate. God put the mark on Cain but there is no brand that can keep love away. For God Himself is love and women are the principal bearers of His mercy in this world. They habitually give their love to men who do not in any way seem to deserve it.

So Cain had a wife and family and was himself the ancestor of worthy descendants, among them Jabal, father of those who dwell in tents, and Jubal, father of those who play the organ and the harp, and Tubal-Cain, teacher of workers in brass and iron.

Chapter 3 NOAH AND THE FLOOD

WITH heavy hearts Adam and Eve watched how the world was going. Abel was dead and buried in the dust to which he had to return; Cain was lost to his parents, and far away. But the first mother and father were still alive, with many years still to be lived. Adam and Eve did not know that they would be allowed to remain alive for so long a time; more and more they wondered at the divine patience that tolerated the growing impudence of their sons and grandsons, great-grandsons and now countless descendants.

Before the world was much older Adam and Eve could see for themselves that the people in it, their own multiplying offspring, were as much like Cain as Abel; and they were forever making trouble for themselves and everybody else.

Not all the people hated God, nor declined to believe in His existence. There were some who did not find violence a pleasure, or murder the simple relief to complicated problems. But already, so early in our history, a decent man was like one diamond in a desert of sand.

There was Enoch, of course, who was a good man and "walked with God," and who was taken up by Him without having to die. This Enoch was the father of Methuselah, who would live longer than anyone else in the human race, and whose grandson was Noah, another simple-hearted and obedient man who was presently to play a decisive role in the story of mankind.

As good men are likely to be, Enoch and Methuselah and Noah were in the almost invisible minority. Another Enoch, born to Cain and his wife in the land of Nod, was much more typical of his times. One might suspect that Enoch took a perverse pride in his father's crime, since many years later one of his own descendants, called Lamech, was still busy boasting of that fratricide. There was an abiding perversity in such men; Lamech, seventh in the line of Adam, wrote a song to please his wives, Adah and Zillah, and the burden of his music was the death of Great-Great-Uncle Abel. In the parallelism of Hebrew poetry, Lamech chanted, once and then twice, repeating the thought in each line, of a killing he had done himself; he, too, had slain, as he declared it, in self-defense. And if, he lamented, passing up and down before the two women, his forefather Cain's crime was said to be avenged sevenfold, his own would have to be seventy times that punishment. The Song of Lamech, among the poetic creations of man, if not the first, repented of bloodletting.

To Adam and Eve it seemed as if with every wheel of the moon the people turned more to disobedience. They had lived to see their firstborn Cain follow Abel into the mystery of death, and thousands after him, and still they loved each other and continued to bring new souls into being, still hoping for more good than bad.

They were aghast at the rising flood of insolent wickedness that flowed from their original disobedience; horrified at changes in behavior that were becoming more and more fashionable. Strange beings now abounded, overgrown "giants" in the earth, who made perverted love to daughters of men, committing new sins of the flesh, and, as if the lesson of Eden meant nothing whatever, calling their male babies "The Sons of God."

In a thousand new caprices and inventions of evil those descendants outdid the original sinners. Speak to them of the Lord God and an incredulous mockery gleamed in their eyes as they looked up at an empty sky and laughed. In memory of Eden, Adam and Eve listened in vain for the long-silent Voice; they could almost sense what He was thinking: "I will destroy man and, with him, all living creatures that I have created."

It was the good life of one decent man that lightened the feelings of God and kept mankind going, and so it was to be again and again in centuries to come, with other lovers of the Father.

Noah was too simple and modest a man to dream that he had deep powers within himself, that he was chosen to take Adam's place as the true father of our race. Such an idea would have seemed ridiculous to Noah, who prided himself on his common sense and attended strictly to his own business. His name meant "rest," but in all the nine hundred and fifty years of his life—he was the grandson of Methuselah—he knew little repose and he had never heard of a vacation.

In a world where disbelief and violence were spreading like a contagion, bald and bearded Noah had remained a man of sturdy conviction. Yes, he would concede to his skeptical neighbors, it was quite true that God had not been seen, nor His Voice heard for a long time, beyond the memory of modern people. Nevertheless, Noah was serenely sure that, although long invisible and silent, God was still just and merciful. His faith made the mild, unshakable Noah unique; he lived with a fear of doing wrong and a wish to be reconciled with the Father.

So Noah, the carpenter and builder, worked hard with his hammer and nails and boards, building houses and carts. His three sons were his apprentices and worked with him, while his wife—legends say she was called Naamah, but her name is not mentioned in the Bible—cooked and swept and dusted and sometimes scolded her menfolk for being late to supper.

It was not far from Noah's six hundredth birthday when he heard the Voice:

"The end of all flesh has come before me."

At those words of doom Noah trembled. The end of the world—and Noah the last man in it to believe that he and his family were to be exempted from the general fate. But he was not left long in ignorance.

"The end of all flesh is come before Me," God told Noah. "The earth is filled with violence. Behold, I will destroy them, with the earth. Make you an ark of gopher wood——"

What was this? Noah was to build something? An ark? That was a new word, never henceforth to lose its divine significance. An ark of gopher wood, a tree very like our cypress. Noah soon understood that the ark of gopher wood was to be a kind of boat, to be divided into three floors, three hundred cubits or four hundred and fifty feet long, seventy-five feet wide and forty-five feet high. So the vessel was to be a big ship, about half the length of the *Queen Mary*.

"A window shall you make . . . and the door of the ark shall you set in the side thereof, with lower, second, and third stories shall you make it."

And the reason for this shipbuilding? There was coming ". . . a flood of waters upon the earth to destroy all flesh wherein there is the breath of life, from under heaven, and everything . . . shall die."

Only Noah and his loved ones were to be exceptions; they should ride safely in the ark, Noah and Naamah, and their three sons, Shem, Ham, and Japheth, with their wives.

Soon neighbors of Noah began to think the old carpenter and his folks had gone mad, at once and all together. For Noah promptly obeyed, even though he was a landsman with little knowledge of boats. He had his orders; he had been given exact measurements and told to pitch the seams from keel to roof, within and without. Stores of food for a long voyage were to be loaded, and—finally, dazing instruction to the obedient old landlubber—he was to drive on board two of every kind of creature, beast, bird, and creeping thing.

When Noah told the sniggering townsfolk that a flood was coming to drown the world and that he was building a refuge, they held their ribs with laughter. What nonsense to say that God had told him what to do. There was no God. Anybody with a grain of intelligence could see that fact for himself. Eat, drink, and be merry, for tomorrow we die and an end to us; it will be as if we had never existed. Did not Noah know that as well as everybody else?

The drunker they became the more they laughed—at the gopher lumber and the tools and the plans sketched out with a hog bristle on a sheepskin. Years passed, while Noah and his sons kept on tirelessly building the ark, and the people still laughed at the growing ship, and the growing zoo, enlarging week by week in a field behind Noah's house.

It was not easy for Noah to carry out his orders. He had to do triple work. First he must labor to feed and care for his family; he and his sons had to keep right on making a living. They also had to spend hours hunting for males and females, cow and bull, sow and boar, fox and vixen, and then to build cages for them, and feed them, and pay for their feed—and all the while they must get on with the building of the ship. But Noah, patient in his six hundred years, continued to carry out his orders literally, until at last the long boat was finished.

She was calked and wedged tight in all her joints and seams; she was seaworthy, and an asylum big enough to ride out quite a storm. But where Noah lived there was no water, no place to lower the ship, and the people laughed more than ever. But Noah knew that a flood was coming; although not even he had conceived the size of the deluge God was preparing. They thought the storm to come would perhaps last one day and one night. And then, just at dusk, it started to rain.

"All the fountains of the great deep were broken up and the windows of heaven were opened."

Flooding over the land, the waters were bringing death to the race —to the laughing people who, time and again, had heard Noah tell them of the rain of death that was on the way, and all others like them everywhere. With all his preaching—and this should console discouraged clergymen—Noah had made not a single convert.

Those scornful skeptics were not even slightly impressed when the heavy downpour began. They had seen it rain hard before. But for Noah the start of the storm was the signal for him and his family to herd the animals and other living creatures into the ark. At the end of the procession the family followed up the gangplank, and the hatches were fastened above them.

If by that time any frightened neighbors had tried to clamber aboard it would have been too late, because no one could brave the seas, swiftly coiling up from dry land, spilling over every barrier. Soon the high hills were submerged, and then the mountains. All flesh outside the ark was drowned.

Forty days the rain lasted nor was the end yet to be. For a hundred and fifty days the earth seemed a shoreless ocean on which alone the ark was sailing, without steering or destination, dependent on divine guidance and nothing else, and in all those months Noah's faith never wavered.

At last a wind came up and blew its drying breath upon the waters. It was in early autumn, the beginning of the tenth month afloat, when the watching family at the window beheld the tops of mountains upthrusting from the sea. Where were they? How far from home had they been carried? Where would they take up life again? Could they farm and build, resuming existence from where they had left off before the world was drowned? These questions filled their hearts.

Opening the shutters of the window, Noah released a raven, which flew about, a black-winged scout observing the scene. Next Noah set free a dove, but it could find no resting place and returned to the window sill. Patiently Noah waited another seven days, and then for a second time the dove was thrown into the air.

On this attempt they had not long to wait. Green olive leaf in its pink bill, the dove came flying back. It had found dry land and a living tree. That was a day for jubilation. The seemingly endless ordeal, the voyage into the unknown, was almost finished. To make absolutely sure, Noah sent forth the dove once more, and when, after seven days, it failed to reappear, the conclusion was irresistible—it could now live independently of the ark.

So on a day that was bright with sunshine the keeper of the ark grounded on a mountaintop, and Noah opened up the roof to air and sunlight. Their strange mooring was on the top of what we know as

Mount Ararat, five hundred miles from Noah's home in Mesopotamia. The rescue ship settled safely on the rocky height of the larger of two mountain peaks which today look down upon the frontier of Soviet Armenia.

Historians for a long time dismissed the Bible's circumstantial account of the ark and the flood, with its measurements and precise details, as a myth. Like the neighbors of Noah, they laughed at a peasant called Reskett, who climbed Mount Ararat on some rugged errand of his own, and stumbled across the remains of an old boat. A boat on a mountain peak! Could that petrified remnant have been part of the ark, retained there, as wood turned into stone, all these centuries? It would seem naïve to suppose so, when so many were so sure there had never been any Noah, ark, or flood.

But scientists have long since begun to consider the possible reality of a great flood which once drowned the world. Dr. Aaron Smith, on the basis of geological specimens gathered from the neighborhood, concluded that the whole Armenian range had once been covered by flood waters. Skeptics had also argued that if such a deluge ever really happened it was merely a local phenomenon, but this position has been largely forsaken. Reports of a deluge, by which the race of man was swept from the earth, are to be found in the traditions of all nations civilized or uncivilized. On this point the mythological testimonies agree among the Egyptians, Phoenicians, Chaldeans, Assyrians, Persians, Greeks, Romans, Goths, Druids, Chinese, Hindus, Burmese, Mexicans, Peruvians, Brazilians, the inhabitants of New Caledonia, and many islands of the Pacific. Among most of them the belief has always prevailed that a certain family was sent into an ark, a ship, a boat, or a raft, preserved to replenish the desolated earth.

But all the old tales differ in one great point from the Bible account. That is the covenant between God and man, which gives the story in the Book of Genesis a meaning, important to every individual.

The covenant was given as a promise to the human race, as soon as the ark's passengers were on dry land again and Noah had set up an altar of thanksgiving. On a broad flat stone he made burnt offerings, a simple act that was the best he could think of to show his feelings of gratitude. Moved to tenderness, God declared that never again would He curse the ground, nor would He smite human beings in watery annihilation again, although "the imagination of man's heart is evil from his youth. . . .

"While the earth remains, seed time and harvest, and cold and heat, and summer and winter, and day and night shall not cease," was the climax of the new assurance, promised in the smoke of Noah's sacrifice. As once long ago in Eden, so here on the bleak mountaintop the Lord God was close to man in mood and speech. His blessing was bestowed on Noah and his three sons. They were to repopulate the earth, but this time there was a new permission. To the eating of green herbs was added the consumption of meat. Until now Noah had believed that it was wrong to partake of blood, because blood, he reasoned, was sacred, the very source and substance of life. Now meat was added to his diet. But once again, and most solemnly, all men were warned against the shedding of blood of a man.

As a sign of His promise never again to destroy the world with a flood, God set in the sky an arc of ethereal colors, the rainbow of mercy. "I do set my bow in the cloud," He said, "and it shall be for a token of a convenant which I have established between Me and all flesh that is upon the earth."

So now, carrying out the command of God, Noah enlisted his three sons, Shem, Japheth, and Ham, to share with him the responsibility as founder of a new human race—but at this point the old builder made a curious restriction. Ham, his youngest son, was bluntly told that he and all his descendants were to be "the servant of servants" to his older brothers and to their generations.

Why, cried out Ham; what was the meaning of this? It was a rebuke, a penalty imposed upon Ham by his father for an offense he has committed soon after the flood. What had Ham done? Once he had come to his brothers, Shem and Japheth, and told them how he had beheld his old father naked as he lay on his bed, overcome with wine. The patriarch Noah had never forgotten that shame. He blessed his far more respectful sons because they had promptly hurried to his couch and covered his nakedness when told of it by Ham—all with averted eyes. Now Ham must stand back, while Shem, the eldest, was chosen to be the forefather of one ethnic group, which would become the Hebrews, the Shemites. The middle brother, Japheth, was to be the progenitor of another race which would become the goyim, or Gentiles. Ham was to be the seed of the peoples of Canaan, except for the Israelites, who were destined to conquer all the others, and father also of the dark peoples of Africa. Egypt was to be known as the "land of Ham."

So the family that had shared the experience of the flood and the ark now journeyed from the East until they came to dwell in the land of Shinar, later called Mesopotamia.

To begin the repopulation of the world, Shem had five sons, Japheth had seven, and Ham four.

Japheth's descendants became the most differentiated peoples of Indo-European stock—the Greeks, the Medes, the Celts, the Scythians, and a multitude of others. One descendant of Ham was the famous Nimrod; another, far more glorious, was Abraham of Ur.

But before the coming of Abraham there is looming another monument to the folly of mankind—the Tower of Babel. For no sooner were there new human beings propagating the world than proud ideas began to fill their heads, and they began to plan the tower and all its confusion for the future.

Chapter 4 THE TALLEST BUILDING IN THE WORLD

NOAH lived three hundred and fifty years after the flood; he reached nearly a thousand years, and he must have died a disenchanted man. For having seen the drowning of a world of scoffers, he had helped to beget a new generation of men and women, made in the image and likeness of God, and here they were, behaving just as wickedly as if no one had ever told them of the fate of their ancestors. Religious instruction seemed to have no effect upon them, and Father Noah must often have wondered whether, having once fallen in the Garden of Eden, human nature thereafter would remain forever incorrigible.

What made matters worse was that the new people increased more rapidly and became more numerous than the old, and they were everywhere on the march, exploring and pioneering, spreading out wherever they could find fertile land. Rivalries were springing up, groups in one place becoming envious of groups somewhere else; the seed of the idea of nations, and national greed for power and dominion, grew up like some deadly upas tree with far-spreading roots. In a small way warfare was already being waged, bloody raids, guerrilla attacks, by wanderers out of the Arabian desert pouncing down on peaceful settlers. These robbers bludgeoned the heads of gentler men and stole their women, and from this mixture of wild and peaceful bloods were soon to spring the Babylonians and the Assyrians with their great kings and lawgivers, Sargon I and the great Hammurabi.

The despoilers from the desert were brainy and competent men. Lacking the vision of faith, they nevertheless saw the necessity for order and peace, always, of course, on their own terms. They were the grand-descendants of Noah, through Ham, his punished son.

With skeptical eye old Noah watched the constant change around him. Wonderful as it all seemed, he could not call it progress. He realized the truth to which these fresh generations were blind and deaf —that the only progress the soul can make is backward toward Paradise. What mattered the codes and lawmaking; the perfection of battle weapons and farm implements; the cookery of cakes and pastries and the delights of confection; the checker games that people were learning to play and the excitement of betting on the results; and the songs men were singing to the harmonies of flute and harp, and something that resembled a clarinet?

Nor was Noah even impressed by the growing skill of planters and farmers, the harvest of grain and cereals, nor by the efforts of other kinds of men to carve little figures out of stones and bones, to paint colored images of men and beasts on walls. In the constant growth of agriculture and industry and art Noah saw also a great disproportion; some men did the hewing of wood and the drawing of water, driven and lashed by stronger men, shrewder men, who knew how to prosper through bullying their fellows.

Where then was the original design of God in the minds of men? Who wanted to win God's mercy and friendship and lift the curse of Eden's fiery sword? What of the great experiment of love and man's will, free and good, a dream in the heart of creation, the way to companionship with the divine?

The new race that Noah had helped to sire simply would not be bothered to think about such questions. And if Noah warned them, reproached them, tried to remind them, they shouted him down as an old fool. Their ridicule held a dangerous kind of laughter that Noah had heard before. Dying, the builder of the ark felt certain that once again, and before long, mankind would have another comeuppance.

All fear of God seemed to be buried in the ground with the body of Noah. Men took a heady pride in what they were accomplishing by their own efforts, as they imagined. They stood alone, and by their own cleverness, and they were proud of it. They were forever boasting to each other of their own greatness, and putting down the tale of their doings for their grandchildren to read in the latest invention, the art of writing, wedge-shaped script on tablets of clay and the scrolled skins of sheep.

There were smiths now, masons and carpenters, wavers and leather workers, traders and artisans, and builders of town walls and houses, palaces and fortresses, and even temples. For some poets and dreamers among them knew there was a missing essential in all the ferment, and of some perverted necessity they invented deities, results of their own imagining, and they shaped idols and altars for these false gods.

So it was in Egypt and in Babylonia; everywhere God seemed left without a friend on earth.

He had made a world, and He had given its people powers of body and mind surpassing all other living creatures, but no one remembered Him any longer, no one believed in Him. The old histories were told by the winter's fires and in the summer shade, not as urgent facts but as tales and myths, while tellers and listeners worshiped their invented gods who made no serious demands on the conscience. In fact men felt more and more as if they were themselves gods, superior to their own idols.

In a kind of frenzy of pride the descendants of Noah now decided to build a structure that should pierce the sky and show the rest of the world how great they were. Already the Egyptians had constructed a mighty pyramid at Gizeh, a stone monument with a square base, and sloping sides, meeting at the apex, a mighty structure that cast a shadow greater than any other thing. The Babylonians decided to out-top the pyramid makers.

They would make for themselves a ziggurat, which in the Sumerian language spoken by everyone in those days meant a pinnacle, the very, very highest. They had made smaller ones before but now, they decided to erect one supreme monument to be the utter wonder of the world, a man-made peak that would rise so high that it would penetrate heaven.

Because of this presumptuous undertaking, new grief was to come to men, a disaster never yet repaired, and still at the root of a great deal of misunderstanding and strife.

They were indeed presumptuous, these Babylonian builders, because they had many impudent ideas about their project. For one thing, some few remaining pious souls were troubled about the ancient history which all the others had discarded. And the reproaches of the few secretly disturbed many of their fellows. The memory of the flood would not down; it haunted men's dreams, even though they jeered and scoffed mockingly when awake. Why, some said, not build a shrine so high that it would stand, dry and safe, above all the flooding seas, if such a deluge rose against them? That was one reason behind the new plan. Others argued that since the gods they worshiped lived behind and beyond the clouds the tower would, in a way, make a bridge between earth and the sky, so that the gods could come down and visit men—and by the same first skyscraper men could walk up into heaven whenever they felt like it.

Other types of leaders saw something else in the proposed tower—a symbol of unity, of strength, of national force and power to overawe neighboring tribes and nations—and this notion·was the seed of another frightful urge in the fallen nature of man: to organize a group of people compactly, impose discipline among themselves, acquire might, and thus rule over their neighbors. The Tower of Babel was the original symbol of the forced unity and solidarity of man under one imperial government.

So the people, having built the city of Babylon, began next the erection of the breath-taking tower. It was dedicated to the glory and protection of the newest and most popular idol among their gods, a deity they called Marduk.

But while Marduk was to have the largest room, with a bed and table waiting for his visits, at the top of the tower there would be also six more rooms for six slightly lesser gods.

Human wisdom had never fallen so low as when the Tower of Babel began to rise so high. Nothing, it was clear, would curb mortal arrogance unless its present course was interrupted.

One blistering hot afternoon the blow fell. The bare-backed workmen were sweating up and down the ladders, carrying their hods of tiles and buckets of mortar, others with aching thighs and swelling throats dragged huge stones up the wooden ramps; hammers rang, bosses screamed orders and curses, every muscle was strained and every breath was labored, as the whole task was driven forward—until suddenly, instantly, without a moment's warning, all work came to a halt. Every voice was silenced, every hand was stilled.

An overseer had yelled a command to two workmen to turn a stone slab over. They had stared at him blankly and had not moved. Again he cried, with bloodcurdling oaths, but one of the sweating men, shivering as with a sudden chill, merely shook his head. The other opened his mouth and seemed to ask a question. But now the overseer stared in silence. What was it the man had said? The overseer knocked him senseless with a short club in his hand, breaking the fellow's skull. But violence did not help. The other workman fell on his knees and whined words that also had no meaning for his master. Neither could understand the other. And no one else could understand the man next to him. So it was everywhere, on scaffolding, walls, ramps, and crossbeams, among these thousands of laborers—a confusion of tongues. This man, that man, and the other man, each forgetting the language he was born to, suddenly cursed and entreated with a new vocabulary, a new grammar, a new idiom which no one else seemed to know.

Within five minutes the whole task force of the tower was a whirlwind of incoherent voices, betrayed into panic, helpless to go on.

"Behold, the people is one," the Lord God had meditated, "and they have all one language—and this they begin to do. Now nothing will be restrained from them. . . . Let us go down and there confound their speech that they may not understand one another's speech."

And therefore it was that by an unexpected act of the divine will the unfinished Tower of Babel had to be abandoned, a broken dream of pride and the birthplace of the basic languages which ever since have separated the thoughts and deeds of people and filled the minds of their neighbors with misunderstanding, suspicion, fear, and therefore dislike, all the result of pride.

Now each group must begin all over again to find its destiny. Would new friends of God appear among them, seeking to find Him, pray to Him in various languages, learn His will and perform it?

There would be a few such among multitudes of hardened men, but enough to save us all from annihilation.

The first of these servants of the Lord was one of the greatest men in history. His name was Abraham.

BOOK TWO

The Patriarchs

Chapter 5 THE STORY OF ABRAHAM

I n t h e midst of a world of heedless people Abraham was born in Ur, and his name and deeds were never to be forgotten.

As with most great souls, Abraham seemed to have no idea that he was important to God or his fellow man. Nor did he dream that he was one day to be put to a supreme test, reaching a height of decision without parallel before or since and thereby uncovering one of the great secrets of life and death, for those who have the discernment to grasp its meaning.

At no time did Abraham realize that he was one of the heroes of history. It was natural for him to deal with men today so that he would not fear to meet them tomorrow. Yet from earliest youth he was despised among his neighbors, because while gray-bearded Terah, his father, and his two uncles gave themselves to other gods, Abraham believed the history of Eden, kept to old ways, rejected false worship, remembering the Creator of Adam and Eve, the tales of lost felicity in the garden and the terrible experience of Noah. Terah was a direct descendant of the ark builder, and from one generation to another the family had passed on the traditions of the deluge, the drowning of many, the saving of the few, the bird with the green olive branch in its bill, the rainbow of heavenly promise in the sky. To the God of these events, the son of apostate Terah, Abraham, gave his worship.

But the people in Ur of the Chaldees—a Babylonian city on the west bank of the Euphrates northeast of the Persian Gulf—had no use for a stern deity; they wanted an easy old duffer of a god who would let men and women do as they well pleased, so long as they brought flattery to the altar and baked sweetmeats to the priests;

more, they wanted a war god and a money god to bring victory to their swords and spears and gold to their caravans.

The old true God of Abraham ruled the hearts of His people with strictness, rules, disciplines, punishments. So the people of Ur felt that anyone who would prefer the old God to the accommodating new ones must be mad.

Even Terah had not continued to worship the Lord God. When his little son was born he called him Abram, which meant "the father on high." Somehow as the child grew, he gathered the whole story of the past and recognized its truth. It was then nine generations since Noah, and Terah told Abram how he was descended through Heber. From that name would one day derive the word "Hebrews."

It was not easy to grow up comfortably as a pious lover of God in Ur, which was a city passionately devoted to trade and pleasure. The poor were urged to work by the whips of overseers, while the rich rode in gilded chariots; but, poor or rich, the people drank and bedded and gambled, while in palaces and in caravanserais musicians played on golden harps, crowned with bulls' heads, ornamented with lapis lazuli.

By the time Abram reached manhood it was no longer safe for him to remain in Ur. The people hated him for his faith. There is a legend that one of those who made life miserable for Abram was Nimrod. Religious persecution is not a new cruelty; the great hunter wanted the youth to bow down to Ur's principal god, whose name was Sin. When Abram refused, Nimrod lifted him up and tried to hurl him into a furnace, but then the fire would not burn.

In the city of Haran, four hundred miles from Ur, Abram and his old father settled, taking with them Abram's wife, a young black-eyed girl of the north and others. Sarai was the name of Abram's wife, a woman with an excess of life and eagerness in her eye, strength in her body, devotion in her heart, and a will of her own under the long black hair. Soon, as man and wife, Abram and Sarai settled down to attend their acres, feed their lambs, save their profits, and prosper on to a peaceful old age. So it was for many years. Neither expected any further adventures for themselves; their one great hope was for children. But at the years passed, and Abram was seventy-five years old, that modest ambition seemed more and more hopeless for all their nightly prayers—until the day came when the Voice spoke unto Abram.

That was a very great day in their lives. From where did the Voice speak? From the depths of a cave, the peak of a mountain, the hollow of a tree, or the chamber of the soul? From wherever came the sound of it, only Abram was there to hear, but he knew the Voice for what it was when he heard its first syllable—the same solemn yet loving Voice, with its tender tones, that once had sounded in Eden, and later at Abel's altar, and to Cain in the wilderness, and to Noah among his shavings and sawdust.

Now the Voice was speaking once more, and awe-filled Abram listened devoutly:

"Go forth out of your country and from your kindred and out of your father's house and come into the land which I shall show you. And I will make of you a great nation and I will bless you and magnify your name and you shall be blessed. I will bless them that bless you and curse them that curse you and in you shall all the kindred of the earth be blessed."

It was his obedience to that divine command, startled as he was, yet instant in his readiness, that made Abram the father of the Hebrew race. He made no difficulty about changing the whole course of his life. Not for a moment did he countenance in himself the slightest doubt about his supernatural experience. He had heard the Voice of Eden and he trusted in its divine authority, in all except, perhaps, the dazzling prophecy; it was hard to believe that he was to become the parent of a nation. There, surely, he must have mistaken the meaning. A whole race of people to spring from his wizened loins?

Nevertheless, and without delay, Abram packed his caravan and with Sarai on a donkey beside him set off on his unknown journey. Abram was the very soul and life, the living example, of that obedience whose failure in Adam and Eve cast us all out of Paradise. "God's will be done on earth as it is in heaven" was the spirit of Abram's prayer. Where was he going? He had no idea. But God would give them guidance. Their only company on their venture was Lot, Abram's young nephew, thirsty for any excitement, and with him Lot was yanking along a reluctant woman whose name history was never to remember; she is recalled only as Lot's wife. She was still a bride when the family set out, but already hard to manage, as Lot could tell you.

In the chill of dawn Abram led his party out of the sunset gate of Haran. His red woolen cloak was wrapped tightly around his lean shoulders and his hood was drawn down, almost hiding the silver in his beard. Behind him trooped a long train; Abram was not a poor man and he was traveling like a noble Bedouin chief, abroad with his wife and kinfolk and a long, cluttering line of men and maidservants, bondwomen and slaves.

Which way to go? It seemed to Abram that he was guided toward the southwest and that was the way they headed, until they came to a fertile but sparsely settled plain, all green and bland, a tempting region in the land of Canaan. But Abram would not linger, and refused to listen to the pleas of Lot's wife and her women; the caravan kept right on, marching upward toward the distant hills. Abram knew he would be told when to stop. And Sarai shared his faith.

Soon they came near to the pungent din of Damascus. Oldest of all living cities today, it was old even on the night when Abram led his weary caravan through its roofed and brawling streets. Here again Lot's wife wanted to linger; there were bazaars with silks and brocades of yellow and blue, silver and orange, perfumes and creams for the face and neck . . .

Onward as God has commanded; Abram would stop for nothing but eating and sleeping. They climbed up the northern slopes of the hills and came down to the open place of Shechem in Samaria, where men drink to this day from the well which his grandson Jacob was one day to find. This place of the well, where Abram and Sarai took their rest that night, is about halfway between Nazareth and Jerusalem. And there Abram heard the Voice again. It spoke to him at a moment when he had just been tempted to dally with false gods in a heathen region. Camel boys had pointed out to Abram a tree on a promontory at the tip of the mountainside, an awkward, ungainly, leafless old oak which spread wide its barren arms; an oracular tree, the natives declared, giving supernatural direction for all who appealed to it. But Abram shook his long gray locks; he looked at the sky, and standing under the infidel boughs of that tree, he made a prayer to the one true God. And as he waited, his great, bony hand on the trunk of the tree, Abram heard the Voice:

"To your seed I will give this land."

But Abram had no seed. And no sooner had he built an altar and settled his caravan than the Voice returned and told him to move on; he had not been promised that he could settle in this region but only that his seed was to have the land. Now God said to go and Abram went at once.

A towering man in his sleeveless cloak of brown deer's cloth, Abram led his caravan anew, in spite of grumbling in the ranks. Again he thought he had found his goal, when they reached the beautiful fields of Mamre, but no; like some witch's blight, famine settled with them, the worst in the memory of that smiling region—no rain in Mamre;

no dew, but only hunger drying up the soil. To linger in this beloved spot would mean starvation, now.

So Abram must get going again; across the blistering sands of the great desert, carrying plenty of water with him, and food, for they were all going to need both. On they trekked through the hot dust, passing a bleak mountain peak and never dreaming that on some distant night it would be the pulpit for the giving of the law: ten commandments on tablets shaped in lightning and thunder.

On they went in forced marches until they found themselves at the gates of Egypt. The sophisticated people of the Middle Kingdom stared at these outlanders as most garish and engaging curiosities. The king must see these strangers! The Pharaoh was kind; he fed them and clothed them with new garments. His eye fell with a gleam of desire on the tall and graceful Sarai. And why not? He did not know that she was the wife of another because in a moment of weakness, fearing that the Egyptians might kill him and take Sarai as a prize, Abram had said she was his sister. But when he told the truth the Egyptians still treated him kindly and kept Sarai at the king's palace within the shadow of the pyramids and the Sphinx. All seemed well for Abram and his people when suddenly a plague broke out on both sides of the Nile—and Abram was blamed for it, because of his lie about Sarai. The result was banishment; they were ordered out of Egypt.

Taking with them all their cattle, and the silver and gold they had accumulated during their stay in Egypt, they returned to Canaan, to the place called Bethel, resolved to settle down there. But that was easier said than done. As long as they were on their struggling way together, Abram and Lot had no trouble. But now that their goal was reached, the future before them to share in great abundance, Lot was dissatisfied. Perhaps his wife plagued him, but a greedy wife is no excuse for a grasping man. Trouble was growing, day by day; the herdsmen said there was not enough grazing to feed all the animals; and soon the pioneers were almost at each other's throats.

So Abram had to suggest that he and Lot part company, and he made the proposal with generous, warmhearted terms. The younger man could have first choice; let him take, as his share, whatever part of the land he liked, and Abram would be content with what was left.

And he actually made himself content, without grumbling, as Lot and his wife took, without hesitation, the very best for themselves: the fertile plain of the Jordan River, where their cattle and sheep would grow fat and numerous. And why not? The future belonged to youth. Or so it seemed then.

Alone, with less favored soil, Abram turned again to his own tilling. Now, he thought, he would have no more worries about his nephew and wife. With his altar and his crops, he and Sarai would live the rest of their lives in peace. And they did have peace for several quiet, enjoyable years. Watching the stars on chilly nights by his fire, Abram would sometimes wonder how Lot and his lady were making out. They had moved, as he had heard, to Sodom, a city by a busy inland sea, and were running their farms and flocks by stewards and underlings. How could they enjoy Sodom? Passing caravans transported ugly tales about the place. A spirit of evil pleasure seemed to possess its people; it was a far more degraded place than Ur ever was, if travelers were to be believed. Then one day came disastrous news.

Various kings with resounding names had gone to war in neighboring regions: Amraphel, King of Shinar and his allies, petty monarchs all, attacking the rulers of Sodom and Gomorrah and other towns, four kings fighting with five.

"And the vale of Siddim was full of lime-pits," and the kings of Sodom and Gomorrah fell there. Their cities were sacked, and the conquerors took Lot, Abram's brother's son, and departed.

That was tragic news for Abram.

No man loved peace more than he. It was a prodigious effort for him to leave his planting, sharpen swords and spears, recruit a company of 318 primitive soldiers, enfold Sarai in a weeping embrace, and march off toward Dan. Yet all this the old man forced himself to do; he led his men into battle, pursued the enemy to Hobah, left of Damascus and laid low the warriors of the petty kings, turning himself into something he had never expected to be, a conqueror of cities.

But all for one purpose only. He was a man under a noble necessity to live up to what he believed in. Abram broke the bolts on the cells where Lot was caged; he restored his possessions, and then went off to his own home, taking no loot with him, not so much as a souvenir of his victorious action.

That was very silly, his own troops thought. What kind of soldier is Abram, to lose the fruits of his victory?

But once again God came to him, saying: "Fear not, Abram. I am your shield and your exceeding great reward."

Abram knew peace in his heart and that was enough. On his journey home he received a blessing from a holy man called Melchizedek, who lived on a height of enormous black boulders, a wedgelike promontory called Salem. There in the area we know today as Jerusalem—Joru-Salem, "place of peace"—the old priest called to him. Melchizedek was both king and priest of that holy city, blessing him with bread and wine, portent of a Sacrament mighty in the centuries to come; he ruled and worshiped in the love and fear of Jehovah, the one true God of Eden. With trembling hands, withered with good works, Melchizedek made a sacrifice of bread, touched the gray locks of the kneeling Abram, and gave him blessing. As if by supernatural insight, Melchizedek recognized Abram as an instrument still to be used for divine purpose.

How right Melchizedek was would soon appear, for once again Abram was visited by God. As in a vision he came to the dreaming patriarch, and in almost reproachful tones reminded him that his seed was to be as the number of the stars. This time the slumbering Abram could not remain quiet.

He was an old man and he had no son. How, then, he protested, oh, merciful and awesome God, could he be expected to increase the world's population? Was it reasonable for him to hope for descendants numbered like the stars? Having no heir, he was willing his wealth to his steward Eliezer. Was Eliezer to be his propagator by proxy?

In stern tones God replied to Abram that Eliezer was not to be his heir. And the vision ended.

There was much for Abram and Sarai to talk about, after that celestial interview. Perhaps, Sarai reasoned, it was all only a dream. Abram blamed himself. While he had kept his disappointment a secret, never blaming his wife, he had been grieving in his heart for years. He wished so fervently for a son that now he must be seeking one in his dreams. But God spoke to Abram in visions and gave him promise and reassurance and Abram believed.

The realization of the depth of his grief was a shock and a sorrow to Sarai. The tears ran down her browned and wrinkled face, as they sat beside each other at the door of the tent and talked it over. The fault, she vowed, was hers, that she was barren; not Abram's, that he was sterile; of this she was convinced. Her sense of guilty responsibility was as sharp as was her jealous, possessive love of her huband—a distracted conflict for a good woman.

Why, she asked, should her pride stand in the way of his dream? Her husband should not have been made to look foolish in other men's eyes. He had a right to an heir in whose veins his own blood would flow. There was a way that it could be managed; a way that Abram would dislike and Sarai would detest, as one who must swallow an abominable drink. Yet, after all, the custom was socially respectable in their day.

"Take my Egyptian handmaid," whispered Sarai fiercely.

"Hagar?"

"Hagar. Take her to yourself and beget a child."

Now Hagar was a slave and could have nothing to say about the plan, one way or another. She was fiery and dusky with sultry eyes that slanted low and sidewise with invitation. She was abounding in energy and bounce, and was unmistakably fertile. The thought of her was not altogether tiresome to the troubled and conscientious Abram.

But Abram was allowed to be patient and silent no more. Once she had made the hateful suggestion, Sarai nagged Abram about it until one night, tired of listening, he went to the servant girl's tent.

Undoubtedly Abram believed that life would be just as pleasant with Sarai afterward as it had been before. He was the first—but not the last—to misunderstand wifely sacrifice, which can be wound up to a great pitch and then recoil dangerously.

From that day on, in the goatskin tents of Abram, life was a trial, and with every month of Hagar's pregnancy the tension became more acute. Those two women of Abram walked around each other like mortal enemies, saying nothing of their ill-will, speaking only when they had to. And every day Sarai grew more embittered, as Hagar became prouder of carrying Abram's child. The handmaid lifted her chin with a regal air, even while toting her pots and pans; there was pride in her eyebrows even when she bathed her mistress' feet. Hagar was a living indictment of Sarai's failure as a wife.

But when Sarai told Abram the girl was giving herself airs, Abram patted her old head and told her, like many another husband, that she was imagining things. Was it any wonder, then, that Sarai stormed and wept? Never did she blame herself, for not having trusted the vision of her husband and the word of God which he had received. The Voice had promised that Abram's seed should be plentiful; but Sarai could not wait for the divine fulfillment. She had decided to be the worker of God's will in her own way, and now she had done it, and hate was possessing her soul.

As day after day Sarai vented her spleen on Hagar, the handmaiden became so miserable that one morning she rolled a few things into a bundle and ran away. Fleeing the tents of Abram, she entered the desert and after trudging for hours across dry wasteland she came to a green island in a sea of gray sand; an oasis with palm trees and a merciful waterfall. And the Bible tells us:

> The angel of the Lord found her by a fountain of water in the wilderness, and he said: Whence came you, and whither will you go? She said, I flee from the face of my mistress Sarai. And the angel of the Lord said unto her, Return to your mistress. I will multiply your seed exceedingly, that it shall be not numbered for multitude. You shall bear a son, and shall call his name Ishmael. And he will be a wild man; his hand will be against every man, and every man's hand against him. And she called the name of the Lord that spoke unto her: You, God, see me.

She had heard, of course, of how the Lord God had come to Abram. But that He should come to her? It was almost beyond belief. But runaway Hagar was also obedient; she turned around and trudged back to the tents of her master. In spite of bullying words, scornful looks, the implacable hatred of the jealous old wife, she kept her prayer within her heart, telling no one what had happened at the desert oasis, and waiting in rugged patience for her child to be born.

Just as prophesied, he was a man child, and Hagar called him Ishmael, meaning "God Hears." With his first breath, Baby Ishmael had a harsh, indignant cry; but Abram was proud of his first-born. What man of eighty-six would not look fondly on such a brawling, scrimmaging, energetic infant? However, Abram was now discreet in his joy; finally he had learned that he had his wife to think about; and Sarai was always on edge.

For thirteen years Abram continued to be tender and uneasy, while Ishmael was growing up, a lad of remarkable strength and wildly impetuous, always eager for adventure and danger. They were years of strained truce in the household; Sarai still could not forgive the boy Ishmael for having been born, nor Hagar for having conceived him.

Abram was ninety-nine years old when he heard the Voice again speaking in the stillness before dawn.

Now, the Lord God declared, the time had come for a solemn covenant between them. As the father of many nations, Abram's name must be changed; no longer to be Abram, but "Abraham." His wife, too, must take a new name; from now on she must be "Sarah" instead of the original Sarai. Abram, in Hebrew, signified a "high father," but Abraham meant the "father of multitude." Sarai's name had meant simply "lady," her new one stood for "a great lady."

As a part of this covenant, every man child born of Abraham's strain must be circumcised when eight days old. The rite omitted, the child was to be outcast. But why these instructions about eight-day-old infants, to Abraham in his old age? Once again the miraculous promise; once again a son was prophesied, and, as if to remove all doubt, his wife, Sarah, the great lady, would be the mother.

"You shall call his name Isaac, and I will multiply him exceedingly."

All Abraham ever needed were orders; let the Lord God make known His will and he would go promptly and obediently to work. So, now, he told everyone that he and his wife had new names, and he set about circumcising the boy Ishmael, and every other male of the household. He even performed the same painful operation on himself, with a sharpened stone as an instrument.

And all the while there was in his heart a secret elation about a promise of which he did not speak to anyone. Not even Sarah was told of the latest promise.

But when would it happen, oh, dear Lord? The years continued to pass, husband and wife grew older, and there was not a sign of the miracle.

One day when Abraham sat bemused and alone at the door of his black-haired tent, three white-bearded strangers stood and hailed him. They were affable men and yet serious; they asked for nothing, told nothing of their business, but greeted Abraham with a charming show of courtesy. The brooding patriarch scrambled to his feet, returned their good wishes, and bade them enter his tent, be washed by his servants and fed by Sarah's cookery. While the visitors bathed, Abraham called to his wife; a calf must be dressed and roasted, and wheaten cakes baked on the hearth of the cook tent.

Finally the strangers, bathed, refreshed and well fed, leaned back against crimson cushions under a shade tree and began to ask Abraham about his family. Did he have many sons? Alas, there was only Ishmael. The three guests nodded, and stroked white and flowing whiskers. The oldest of them, who sat between his companions, he with the most serene movements and the brightest eyes, spoke in a soft, amiable voice, as with unfathomable casualness:

"Your wife, Sarah, will bear a child within a year."

Abraham was startled. These tidings must be miraculous; else how could these men have surprised his secret? All unaware, Abraham realized that he had been entertaining angels. More than angels; he felt

54

aware of the presence of the Lord, as if He could be present in three as well as one; strange mystery! He bowed low to the messengers from on high, not knowing what to say.

Wifelike, Sarah had been hiding behind a tent and listening to the after-dinner conversation. She to have a child at ninety? "After I am waxed old, shall I have pleasure, my lord being old also?" That was her bitter thought, and that was why wrinkled Sarah laughed silently, within herself.

At once the middle visitor stood up, and the others rose with him. The severity of his face seemed to say that he could see through camel's-hair tents and hear even laughter in the soul.

"Is anything," he cried, cupping white slender hands to his mouth and fronting directly toward Sarah, "is anything too hard for the Lord? . . . Wherefore did Sarah laugh?"

Sarah was so frightened that she burst forth with a lie: "I laughed not."

But the answer was implacable and beyond mortal contradiction. "Nay, but you did laugh."

From under the shade tree the three visitors moved off toward the highway, Abraham following, trying to apologize. But their smiles reassured him. They had other matters to confide to him. They were on their way to Sodom, about which Abraham had been hearing stories of increasing wickedness; a terrible punishment was coming to the city, it and all its inhabitants would be wiped out in one sudden blow of the divine wrath. And having told Abraham of the coming holocaust, the three angel messengers walked on, down the long purple road, and over the horizon.

Left alone, Abraham was shaking with anxiety. His nephew Lot lived in Sodom; Lot and his wife and their children. Plunging to his knees, he began to ask God for mercy:

"I am but dust and ashes, but will you also destroy the righteous with the wicked?"

If there were fifty good, decent men in Sodom, then the city would be spared, so the Voice answered Abraham, but Lot's uncle was not reassured; his frightened face, turned to the afternoon sky, told its own story. There might well not be fifty decent citizens in Sodom. What if there were only forty-five, forty, thirty, twenty, ten?

That same evening two of God's angels, still appearing as men, entered the gates of Sodom. Where would they look for ten honorable men in this mire of men's lusts and cruelties? They did not need to walk through the noisy, unclean streets to know that all the tales were true. The people of this place, as nowhere else, had given themselves over to unrestrained bestialities of pleasure and debauchery. Panderers screamed at every street corner, making their evil living by offering maids and men for cash to minister to the basest passions. It was a lewd and licentious capital where rammish men and wantons, tired of each other and of themselves, sought to invent ever new degradations and unspeakable vileness.

Hardly had the heavenly agents entered the gates than a man sprang up from the cool shadows of a corner and bowed before them. His name, he said, was Lot. Not Abraham's nephew? Yes, the same. He would like to offer the hospitality of his home to these farcomers. At first they demurred, but at Lot's earnest insistence they followed him to his house.

But even there, in the home of one who wanted to live uprightly, the visitors were not isolated from the evil that lay like a plague over the people. Suddenly, in the middle of night, there came a pounding on doors and windows. Drunken citizens of the town, having heard that there were handsome strangers in Lot's quarters, came from some tavern carouse, beating their fists on the oaken doors, and yelling lascivious proposals. That shameful night Lot showed great courage. Well knowing that his perverted townsmen might make him smart for opposing them, he refused to open the doors. At the top of his voice he called defiance to them, declaring he would rather see his own daughters violated than to betray the sacred laws of hospitality.

Angry screams came from the crowd. Plainly they were ready to batter down the tall doors and swarm into the dwelling, with murder in their hearts, for bloodletting was often a part of their orgiastic pleasure. It was an ugly situation. But when Lot turned back to his guests he was astonished to find them quietly praying and unperturbed. He was even more surprised when the hoots and jeers out of doors were turned to cries of fright, then groans and lamentations.

For while the angels prayed, a plague had fallen on the besiegers and every man of them was struck blind.

Then the celestial visitors told Lot tragic news. There were not ten decent men to be found in Sodom. The city was to be destroyed. When? Now! Immediately. Pack your things, Lot; bring your family and follow us.

Even then Lot had trouble with his wife. She did not want to leave. She did not believe that Sodom was going to be destroyed. What did these out-of-towners know, more than anybody else? It took a husband's rising wrath to make her obey, but finally, sullen and resentful, she chucked her jewels into the middle of a crimson scarf and tied it in a bundle. All the daughters did likewise; the earnestness of their father compelled them, even though two of the sons-in-law refused stubbornly to go along.

At last, when all was ready, Lot asked the strangers where they were to head for.

"To the mountains?" suggested the angels. But Lot declared that such a climb was beyond his strength. Could they not, instead, head for Zoar, a small town out of the danger zone? Consenting, the angels solemnly warned the whole party:

"But do not look back on what is to happen to Sodom."

It was the deepest hour of morning darkness when the little band set out on the road to Zoar. All was silent, except for occasional cries of wildcats and the barking of wolves. They walked without lanterns and more than once they stumbled; more than once wondered, too, if this were not a fool's journey. What was happening to Sodom? Apparently nothing.

Then suddenly it was as if a volcano exploded in the sky. There was a crash that seemed to rip the air and carry it away; for a moment no one in the party could breathe or move; they stood gasping and swaying, and the earth churned like water under their feet, and blood-red light seemed to set the heavens on fire.

The first explosion was followed by a long, roaring sound as if some upside-down crater were pouring brimstone and hot ashes down upon the city from blazing clouds. In their nostrils was a smell of burning, a rain of brimstone and fire. Almost deafened by the roaring, they could still hear in the distance, above the uproar of collapsing towers and tumbling palaces, screams of agony of hundreds and thousands of the people of Sodom.

"But do not look back," the angel had said. The temptation was acute, more to Lot's wife than to the others, because she had been proved wrong. Her mind resented being told what to do, anyway, and at last she defiantly turned her head around and stared at the fire-rent skies.

Now, lady of Lot, that you have stared at the fire-rent skies, turn back again, if you can. The lady of Sodom does not move. She stands there, neck twisted, looking over her left shoulder. In the dark no one misses her. They trudge on to Zoar, thinking she is with them. And meanwhile, whether from the mysterious rain of chemicals falling about them, or from the miracle of divine displeasure itself, by design, a most singular fate overtakes that unmanageable woman. The Bible tells us that she was turned into a pillar of salt.

Blocks of such salt, taken from the mountains at the southern end of the Dead Sea region—where Sodom was—are on display today in the Semitic Museum of Harvard University. One of them may even be Lot's wife herself. Who knows?

At sunrise, when Lot entered Zoar, fire and brimstone were still raining upon Sodom and its sister Gomorrah, the two wicked cities of the plain. Soon nothing was left of population and buildings except ashes and rubble. The melancholy evidence of the catastrophe persists until today in the ruins of the cities that once had flourished near the Dead Sea, then called the Salt Sea—the antique foundations now under lake waters, bitter as brine.

Early in the morning Abraham with heavy heart saw, afar off, vast billows of smoke rise as "smoke from a furnace." There had not been even ten good men in that region to turn aside the wrath of God. With joy he was to learn that his intercession had saved his nephew.

But it is not easy to dispel altogether an evil atmosphere, once it has been tolerated. The noxious influence of Sodom lingered in the hearts of Lot's two daughters. Their husbands had died in Sodom, and now father and daughters were living in an isolated spot in the mountains. No other men lived near by, and one night those two women made up their minds to an evil thing. They plied Lot, their father with strong wines, getting him drunk to bemuse and entice him.

Thus Lot became the father of his own grandchildren and no good to the world was to come from that crime against nature.

But meanwhile there was new strength and joy in the tents of Abraham. God's promise was being made good. Over Abraham and Sarah a curious, visible change was appearing. New youth flowed into the old man's veins and beamed in Sarah's dark eyes, making her once more desirable, even irresistible, to her husband. One night she lay in his embrace and conceived.

At the appointed time Sarah was delivered of the child of their old age; the boy baby seemed to glide peacefully into the midwife's hands, a peaceful person from his very beginning without the yelping of the newly born, a soul already possessed of patience and gentleness.

He was given the name God had chosen for him: Isaac, which means laughter. Abraham was jubilant. Surely now they could all be happy. Surely they should have been so. But Sarah was by no means happy.

At the feast they held at the weaning time Sarah took a long look at her stepson Ishmael. She did not like what she saw. For Hagar's son had grown to be an attractive, irreverent lad and the girls looked after him yearningly, even while he decided the solemnity of his elders.

"Cast out this bondswoman and her son," Sarah told her husband; "for the son of this bondswoman shall not be heir with my son, even with Isaac."

And so Ishmael and Hagar had to go. There seemed no end to Sarah's bitterness. Abraham would have resisted her, but the Voice returned to his heart with the guidance he so sadly needed; he was not to oppose Sarah's demand. Nothing that he could try would soften her jealous loathing for his first-born. Let hatred have its way, grievous though it now appeared; there was a destiny for Ishmael, who would father a great nation, as indeed, he did; he is still accounted the forefather of the Arabs.

Swallowing his tears, Abraham stood by the gate and pointed toward the road, ordering them away, mother and son, taking with them only some loaves of fresh-baked bread and a skin of water, as they walked toward the wilderness of Beersheba.

There they wandered until exhaustion overtook the tottering boy and he fell unconscious under a low bush. There was no more water in the skin bottle; none anywhere near. The weeping Hagar sat down a good way off because she could not bear to watch while Ishmael died. In that hopeless, abandoned hour Hagar once again heard the Voice that had reached her in the desert, long before, when she was still carrying her unborn child; the Voice that had sent her back to Abraham. Now the same Voice called to her with tender cadence:

"What ails you, Hagar? Fear not, for God has heard the voice of the lad, where he is. Arise! Lift up the lad! And hold him in your hand, for I will make him a great nation."

Hagar opened her eyes, the comforting Voice still echoing in her thoughts, and saw before her a vision calling herself and her son back to life and hope—a well of water that was no wilderness mirage but a reality, near at hand, to which she could rush and dip out a saving draught for the senseless boy under the bush.

From then on Hagar knew that she and Ishmael were under God's protection. Soon they found shelter, friends, and a chance to make their own living.

In the wilderness of Paran, to the south of Canaan, Ishmael grew to manhood, becoming a champion archer and marrying an Egyptian girl like his mother.

Abraham hid his grief at the separation and found his consolation in Isaac. Was there, he would ask, ever another such son born to any man?

He found in that laughing, tender child new life, new joy, a fullness of purpose and a reason for living. The old man's heart was set on Isaac to the exclusion of all other thoughts. Their companionship was constant and each delighted in the other. Abraham told his son the great tales of the past, so that the boy could have drawn a map of the Garden of Eden; could repeat what Adam and Eve and the Serpent had said; trace with a twig in the dust the profile of the ark and the façade of the abandoned Tower of Babel.

In his father Isaac beheld a man with whom he identified himself, wanting only to be like him, and Abraham saw in the beloved youth the reality of long-denied dreams and disappointed hopes, ultimate proof of God's tender care for His own. Isaac's growing years were full of placid happiness, which seemed as if it would never end. And with all at peace, Abraham, too, contentedly assumed that all would continue to go well with him and his family. Why not? Did he not sacrifice yearling lambs to the Lord, the altars of fieldstone running with blood as the smoke rose from burning faggots? Regularly Abraham thanked God for His goodness and implored His continued blessings. What, then, had he to fear?

Thus the patriarch was taken by surprise one windy afternoon as he trudged alone across a brown and fallow field and suddenly heard the Voice of the Lord God speaking for the first time since Isaac's weaning feast:

"Abraham!"

The old man halted in the wind-swept field, exclaiming:

"Behold, here I am."

"Abraham! Take Isaac, your beloved son, to a mountain which I shall show you in the land of Moriah. And there offer him for a burnt offering."

What were these words the old man heard? Oh, Voice of Almighty God—You cannot mean what I have heard? My son? My Isaac? My dearly beloved against whom I have never once lifted my hand—Isaac to be burnt like a beast on the altar! I am having a nightmare.

The command was no illusion; Jehovah, the Creator, the one God, the true God, the only God, had spoken to His most obedient servant Abraham. Now, having learned to love his little boy with a love deeper than the springs of the desert, Abraham must ask himself a question:

Do I love God more than anything else in the world? Or do I love Isaac more than I love God? Old Abraham, more than any of his fore-bears, more than faithful old Noah, even, had seemed to love his Creator perfectly. But now he was being tested as no mortal, before or since. His long wait for his son to be conceived and born was a part of that test; his separation from Ishmael doubled its sharpness; the happy years of his growing up increased the force of his love. Now, would he obey?

For the rest of that day and night, frowning Abraham brooded and walked alone. At dusk he waved away his bowl of milk and his wheaten loaves, pacing in the darkness outside his tent. But when the night was blackest he shouted his orders:

"Up by dawn! Isaac and two menservants—we go to a distant place."

They loaded a pile of faggots on the back of a young gray ass and set out. Three days they traveled across the ripening, golden plain of Mamre and on and up into the thickly wooded hills. In all that time there was no talk between father and son. Abraham's browned face was like a mask of stone and the deep gleam in his eyes was like a fire in the depth of a cave.

At last the boy Isaac dared to break the silence.

"If we are going to worship," he remarked, "behold the wood—but where is the lamb?"

Abraham closed his eyes and groaned as he answered:

"God will provide a lamb for a burnt offering."

The boy said nothing else. No reason had been given to him for this sudden departure to a new and distant altar. Nor could it have entered into the boy's head to suppose that these faggots were being fetched to burn under his own body or that his father carried in his sleeve a knife with which to cut his throat.

At a clearing near the mountaintop, when a natural plateau stretched right and left for quite a distance, Abraham bade his servants remain. Then Isaac loosened the thongs of the asses and loaded the firewood on his own back, as he trudged after his father, still higher until they reached the bald, deserted patch of level land on the very peak of Mount Moriah. Both were panting and out of breath, but Abraham did not dare to rest for fear that all his terrible resolution would forsake him; even now he wanted to scream out against this fiery and bloody sacrifice.

His palsied hands could hardly lift the stones with which to fashion the altar, but Isaac helped him. Why must he give up his healthy son, his good and decent son? Abraham and Isaac, alone together, were the first to be tormented with this dreadful requirement; first but not the last; countless millions since have shared Abraham's agony, making ready for the dearly beloved to be sacrificed on another altar, raised to war, whose commands must also be obeyed.

Isaac saw how his father was quaking. Something was wrong; his question flew back again; where was the sacrificial lamb? The broken heart of Abraham was reflected in his helpless eyes; one glance was Isaac's answer. The boy's cheeks turned white, his eyes rolled back; then, obedient son of obedient father, he held out his hands. His wrists were tied with strips of pliable leather, feet and ankles bound, and still not a word between them. The boy was a prisoner, bound fast beyond hope of escape, and now the old man lifted the young body, so warm, so yielding, and laid him on the mound of faggots piled on the altar. A jerk of the arm, a clutch of fingers around a flashing blade, and there it is, quivering high in the air, the knife in Abraham's hand.

It was then the Voice spoke:

"Abraham! Abraham!"

"Lord, here am I," faltered the old man.

"Lay not your hand upon the lad, neither do you anything unto him; for now I know that you fear God, seeing you have not withheld your only son from me."

Abraham heard no more. Through eyes streaming with tears, he beheld a ram caught by the horns in a thicket just beyond the pile of stones. The beast for the burnt offering was waiting for him there.

Shaken and yet uplifted, the two men descended from the mountaintop together, the smoke of the sacrifice rising from the altar behind them high toward the morning sun. They knew then, as never before, that if a man gave all to God he received God in return, and that is all in all.

Chapter 6   THE STORY OF ISAAC

His terrifying experience seemed to deepen and emphasize the gentleness of Isaac's nature. People did not expect great things of such a quiet, gentle soul. With the flowing on of time, he became more and more a friendly man, extraordinarily gentle, a peacemaker, and certainly not even his doting father guessed that he was to live the longest of the patriarchs, or that centuries afterward, such would be the luster of his fame that the prophet Amos would call his name a synonym for the whole history of Israel.

And ever closer he drew to his father. When Sarah died—she was one hundred and twenty-seven years old and hers is the only woman's age the Bible reveals—Isaac walked with his arms around Abraham, on the long climb to the cave of Machpelah, which was the mother's tomb.

For a while Isaac was the constant companion of the lonely widower, but he was astonished one day when Abraham began to reproach himself for selfishness toward his son. How old was Isaac? Forty! Well, he should have been married long before this. Once that idea was fixed in his brain, Abraham seemed to think of little else. He called for his steward, Eliezer.

"Eliezer! Isaac must have a wife and you must find her for him. He must not marry one of these Canaanite women. Pack for a long journey, Eliezer. You are going back to the land of my youth, to Haran in Padan Aram, to find there a wife for my Isaac."

For that mission Eliezer had no liking at all. Eliezer was a bachelor. Suppose he fetched home some girl that Abraham did not like? At least let him take Isaac along to help pick the lass. No; Abraham was stubborn on the point; he was sure the Lord God would send an angel to guide the steward's choice. No one could argue against Abraham's faith, so without more delay Eliezer organized a caravan.

Outside the city of Ur the moody Eliezer stopped at a well, called Lahai-Roi, where at the gloaming time women of the neighborhood came with green jars, and red and yellow, to draw water. Prayerfully the messenger from Abraham waited; he was hoping for guidance when a damsel appeared and began to fill her pitcher, her long dark hair parting on her shoulders as she leaned forward. Eliezer was stunned with her beauty.

He approached her diffidently:

"Let me drink a little of your pitcher of water, I pray."

"Drink, my lord," she said. At the same time she offered to draw water for all his thirsty animals. Her name, she told him, was Rebekkah.

It seemed to the excited Eliezer that Rebekkah would be an ideal choice for Isaac—but he could judge only by beauty, by her politeness. How could he know, as if by divine guidance, that she was the woman he should choose?

"Whose daughter are you?" he asked next.

"Bethuel is my father's name. He is out in the fields but my grandfather, Nahor, the head of all our family, is at home."

Her grandfather Nahor! Eliezer laughed for joy. Abraham had been right in saying there would be guidance in their quest. Nahor was no stranger; he was Abraham's own brother. Isaac and Rebekkah were cousins. And that relationship was not frowned on; indeed, it was still regarded as an advantage.

Reaching into his capacious sleeve, Eliezer unfastened a bag tied to his wrist, and from it he drew golden earrings and a pair of bracelets for the dazzled Rebekkah.

Theirs should have been a happy marriage, for Isaac and Rebekkah loved each other, but to their sorrow no children were born to them.

It seemed impossible for Isaac to beget; in spite of constant prayers and eager young passion, Rebekkah did not conceive. For many childless years she and Isaac lived in his father's tents and under his father's authority, as was the tribal law. But while the kinfolk gossiped about Rebekkah's barrenness, old Father Abraham was unfailingly kind to his beautiful daughter-in-law. Often she would sit beside him at the door of his tent and look up hopelessly at the living stars and sigh. For a while he would seem not to notice her melancholy as he mumbled on boastfully with family news. News of *his* children. In extreme old age, after so many fruitless years, the widower Abraham had married again, taking for his wife Keturah, and by her he had already sired six young ones. Of these children he would talk, and before long he would also tell her about his Ishmael, left-handed problem son of Hagar, the bondwoman. Wild Ishmael showed no love for his father, although he was living at home, and had been, ever since Sarah's death. Ishmael was not happy in his family reunion; he frankly told his friends that he was waiting only for the patriarch's death so that he could go back to the desert with a band of fierce followers, of whom he was to be chief.

In the wilderness Ishmael had once been known as a "wild ass man" and now he yearned to resume his old marauding, freebooting existence; Ishmael still and forever the opposite of half brother Isaac, who was so quiet and peace-loving. Abraham clucked his tongue over his desperately begotten son, wishing he were different and yet loving him as he was, which is a way with fathers.

Hearing Rebekkah sigh one night, Abraham patted her shoulder:

"Have you forgotten, Rebekkah, dear child? My Sarah was ninety-five years old before your Isaac stirred in her womb? And for many more years Isaac was our only one? Yet God has promised us that our descendants are to be as the stars of heaven!

"Be patient," he would croon to her. "The Lord will reward!"

The kind old gentleman died at the age of one hundred and seventy-five years. Having seen many changes in the world and obeyed the one true God through all of them, he lay down in his tent, crossed his enormous bronzed hands, and closed his eyes, knowing that he was shutting out one world only to find in another the countenance of the One Whose Voice had been his law.

Abraham's funeral was Rebekkah's darkest hour. She wailed inconsolably as she stood with Isaac and Ishmael in the torch-lit gloom of rocky Machpelah, the cave where Abraham's body was laid to rest beside his Sarah. They were burying the patriarchal chief of their family, but they could not dream on that sad day how great was to be the fame of that good and faithful man.

To our own day and hour, Jews and Christians alike praise in poetry and song this servant of the Lord God who was unfailingly ready to listen to the divine Voice and unfalteringly ready to do what he was told. In the young history of mankind he played two heroic parts, for he was founder both of a race and a religion. Father of the Faithful and Friend of God he is called, even by Arab Mohammedans, who consider him, through his exiled son Ishmael, their first ancestor. And when men speak of heaven and all its joys they utter the ancient phrase for such felicity, "In Abraham's bosom."

For no other man has history reserved such reverence as for this early farmer, the father of Isaac and the grandsire of Jacob and Esau. He became grandsire because, when all hope seemed over, Rebekkah bore Isaac not one son, but twins.

Chapter 7   THE STORY OF JACOB

THE twins came as the result of moonlight and songs, back in Rebekkah's old home, at Nahor, not far from the well of Lahai-Roi, where Eliezer, the steward, had found her long before. Once Abraham was gone, Rebekkah had insisted on their moving. She was a self-assertive, middle-aged woman now, with a commanding look in her still lovely eyes; her maidservants learned to obey her without dawdling.

But one night, as she sat with Isaac at the door of the tent in a world that seemed all made of silver light, Isaac noticed her tears, and comforted her tenderly, admiration in his eyes. That mystical night Isaac implored the Lord God to send them a child, then fell asleep in the midst of the prayer. And it was as if the night grew sweeter all around them; his body and hers felt a strange renewal and exhilaration; and before long Rebekkah knew the living truth.

There was indeed a commotion in her womb; not one but two children were being nourished there, and they seemed to tumble about as if wrestling in the dark. Women friends who had already borne twins assured Rebekkah that they had never known such prenatal violence. Only the nurse, Deborah, tried to soothe the alarmed Rebekkah, but Isaac's restless wife told him that she, too, had heard the Voice, speaking in her heart:

"Two different nations are within you. And one shall be stronger than the other as the older shall serve the younger."

And when the two boys were born the second came into the world clutching in his tiny hand the heel of his brother, as if trying to hold him back, and get ahead of him.

From their birth, the brothers were to be rivals. Far from being identical twins, each was a startling contrast to the other.

The first-born was given the name of Esau, which meant red, because his body was crimson when he was born, under a growth of thick and dark hair. His brother's skin was a gentler pink, and as hairless as the palm of his hand. Because he had seized his brother's heel the second-born was given the name of Jacob, the word signifying a "Wrestler" or "One Who Supplants."

It was the rugged Esau who grew up to be his father's favorite. With his love of hunting and all vigorous activity, his careless, jolly ways, and independent but generous ideas, Esau was unlike the kindly, quiet and meditative Isaac; theirs was the attraction of opposite natures. Esau would come back from the chase and regale his doting father with tales of adventure and bold exploits. And always he brought home meat for his father and often cooked it for him.

Quite otherwise was Jacob. Seemingly, the good-looking lad had no adventure in him; he was content to be a shepherd and a farmer with time to think. From earliest childhood Jacob was adored by Rebekkah, and she dominated him, meanwhile watching her other twin with critical eye. Esau, perhaps, she thought, was too much like his uncle Ishmael.

When she and Jacob were alone together they talked of secret matters. Because Esau was the first-born, by law and custom he had what was called the "birthright," the most important dignity and authority a man could inherit. But it was also a great moral responsibility, a sacred obligation imposed on every first-born son. With it went priestly privileges in the family, the necessity of deciding all disputes wisely and with prayer, leading the group in serving God. But was Esau, the first-born, a priestly man? Obviously not.

All Esau wanted to do was to chase wild beasts and tell wilder stories. Only by accident, by just a few unimportant minutes, had Esau been born first. But by natural ability, and the need for real leadership of their group, Jacob felt justified in believing he should have the birthright. If by some decree he should be able to get it, everybody would be better off, including Esau, who had no desire to be bothered with responsibility.

Such were Rebekkah's ideas. She knew perfectly well that her husband did not share them. In Isaac's eyes, Esau was the ideal first-born son, a man among men. As for thoughtful, studious Jacob, he was a splendid boy, but no leader. And Jacob knew what his father thought of him; as a result of preliminary hints by Rebekkah, the aged Isaac had bluntly spoken his mind. He would not change the order of nature, no matter how superior Jacob might seem in his mother's eyes. The birthright belonged to Esau, and Isaac refused to take it away from him. But Rebekkah did not lose hope.

Thanks to her endless talk about it when they were alone, the birthright became the most important goal in Jacob's life. By good means or crooked he meant to have it; his mind was a witch's brew of desires and resentments, as he stirred a potful of lentil stew one day over a fire of twigs in the open field. Suddenly a shadow covered his hands: Brother Esau looming up exhausted after a long, unlucky hunt. The red-haired brother threw his enormous body down on the ground, as if to shake the earth; he would rest here awhile before going on home; good-natured green eyes looked hungrily at the red beans simmering in the bubbling water, and mighty nostrils sniffed their delicate fragrance.

"I'm famished," Esau groaned in mock despair. "May I have some of the bean stew?"

Jacob shook his head. There was just enough for one—and he, too, was famished after having worked all day. Esau must walk several miles more to the home tents where he would certainly find supper.

"But I am hungry now, my brother. I would give all I own in the world for a dish of that pottage."

Jacob looked up, suddenly startled, pale and shrewd. All that Esau owned in the world?

"Brother, I mean it—I am starving!"

Jacob's fingers interlaced. Well—how about selling the birthright? Esau laughed when he heard. Why not? Who wanted to be the family leader anyway?

"You must swear," Jacob stipulated eagerly; Esau must never say later that he had looked upon the bargain as a joke.

"I swear."

Hardly believing his ears, Jacob piled a dish with lentils, and in his exuberance added bread and wine until the hunter's ravenous appetite was satisfied. When the strange meal was over Jacob ran home to tell his mother, and the rejoicing Rebekkah danced around the tent as if she were a girl again and no gray hairs in her head. This was the thing she had longed for.

But nothing must be said to anyone! Least of all to Isaac. Let the aging man live the few years left to him, never knowing what had happened. When he was gone, then Jacob would be the heir to the land and the herds and the storehouses and the treasure. And Esau would be happy, too, because he would not be tied down with duties; he could roam where he liked and no one the worse off.

It did not hurt her schemes that Esau chose a wife among the alien Hittites, a tribe of infidels, as she reminded Isaac; their women would turn any man from the true faith.

Was Isaac disappointed in the marriage of his favorite son? If so, he kept it to himself. He spent much of his time now sitting in silence; more and more he was showing his age, especially in his sight, so far gone that human forms had become as dim shadows to him.

One day the old man called Esau to his side:

"Take, I pray you, your weapons—your quiver and your bow—and go out into the field and take me some venison; and make me savory meat, such as I love, and bring it to me that I may eat, that my soul may bless you before I die."

Rebekkah heard that conversation with deep excitement in her conspiratorial mind. She knew how important were those closing words of Isaac; next to the birthright, the most precious family possession was the father's blessing, reserved only for one and considered to impart a special sanctity and power. By one trick Jacob had gained the birthright; by another he must take the blessing also.

That was how Rebekkah came to plan a most famous imposture, a historic masquerade, the beginning of disguise and impersonation and acting and all hoodwinkery.

"I have been shown the way," she whispered to herself, as if giving thanks for this swindling idea. Finding Jacob in the field, she instructed him in what must be done before Esau returned from the hunt.

"Pick two of the best kids," she said, "and I will prepare a fine dish for your father; he will never know the difference and you shall get the blessing."

Jacob shuddered at his mother's boldness. Did she seriously expect him to kneel before his half-blind father and pretend to be Esau, to extract the blessing by false pretenses? But, Mother—Father Isaac can tell the taste of his favorite venison from mere goat's meat.

Rebekkah waved aside her son's timidity, his skepticism, his conscience even; she was there to wheedle, to coax, even to bully him.

But, Mother—even if Father cannot see Jacob, he can touch him. Jacob is not the hairy man that Esau is. Then he will be found out—and cursed, not blessed!

Rebekkah smiled, as if secretly she rolled some sweet beneath her tongue.

"Then upon me be your curse, my son," she replied. "Now go and fetch me the young goats, quickly."

While Jacob went off to do as he was told Rebekkah made ready to cook an imitation of stewed venison. She considered herself a cunning hand with herbs and sauces; let dotard Isaac detect the difference if he could.

To meet Jacob's other objections she had still more elaborate deceptions to prepare.

From an old cedar chest she took out some of the clothing of Esau. It smells like him, she thought, making a grimace with her nose. Soon Jacob was dressed in Esau's garments, but his mother was by no means through with him; the best was yet to come. She took the skins of the slain kids and cut them into strips winding and binding them with loving care around the neck of Jacob, and around his wrists and even his fingers. Now Isaac, feeling in the dark, would find smooth, hairless Jacob very shaggy.

"Be bold," said his mother. "Imitate that rumbling voice of Esau. Take this dish. Now go to your father."

As he approached the bedside of Isaac, bowl of goat stew in hand, Isaac lowered his voice as deceptively as he could and muttered: "Father, here I am."

"Who speaks?" asked the doddering old man. Eyes dull and blear, he peered dimly at the son kneeling beside him. Which one was he?

"Esau, my father. And I have brought the tenderest venison."

FULTON OURSLER'S GREATEST

"So soon?"

"The Lord helped us. Shall I get you wine?"

For some obscure reason Isaac sensed that something was wrong. Or was his imagination playing tricks?

"Come closer," he said, "that I may feel if it is truly Esau."

Jacob, full of misgiving, could hardly move his legs, but he came forward and let his father's hands ramble up his arms and around his hands.

"Are you satisfied, Father?" he asked after that long tactile examination.

Isaac seemed deeply perplexed.

"The voice is the voice of Jacob but the hands are the hands of Esau," he stammered. "Tell me, are you my very son Esau?"

"I am, Father," lied Jacob, wishing himself well out of the predicament.

Not altogether guileless, even in second childhood, Isaac murmured:

"Come nearer, and kiss me, Esau."

As he received his son's kiss the purblind Isaac inhaled deeply, smelling the odor of Esau's cloak. That seemed to settle all doubts; the smell of the hunter's clothes was unmistakable.

"Bring me venison, my dear son," he called happily.

"Bless me, Father?"

The old man laid faltering hands on the wrong son's head and blessed him:

"God give you of the dew of heaven, and the fatness of the earth, and plenty of corn and wine. Let people serve and bow down to you. Be you Lord over your brethren, and your mother's sons bow down to you."

Solemn words that, in the belief of those days, could never be recalled, never rescinded, once uttered as now, with heaven and earth as witnesses. Shaken to the soul by the immensity of his deceit, Jacob left his father's side. Each remembered word of the blessing was already fuel to a burning conscience. Now that the thing was done he avoided returning to that strong, determined woman, his mother; instead he climbed a lonely hillside where he could tear the false hair from his head and his hands.

Meanwhile, Esau returned with a roebuck that he had slain; prepared the meat as his father liked it best and brought a bowl of pottage to him with a loud and playful proclamation. Half asleep, Isaac sat up in alarm, trembling from head to foot.

"Who are you? Who are you?" he called.

"I am your son, your first-born, Esau."

And now Isaac knew the truth and his withered old body trembled. "Your brother. He has stolen the blessing away with false pretenses," he mourned, and father and son wept together over Jacob who had now twice supplanted his twin. Old Isaac was almost incoherent as he tried to console Esau; his pride had suffered a deadly blow.

"Bless me, also, O my father," pleaded Esau.

With shaky voice and hands Isaac blessed Esau with a prophecy: the day would come when he would break his brother's yoke from off his neck. Even so, hate filled Esau's heart; to himself he swore to wait until his father's death; "then I will slay my brother Jacob."

Rebekkah guessed the vengeance that Esau was planning; but she did not realize his patient resolution to wait until Isaac's death. Calling Jacob to her tent, she urged him to leave in the night, and at once, for a visit with relatives in Haran, her girlhood home. "Tarry with them a few days," she counseled, "until your brother's fury turn away."

Jacob went, and Rebekkah was never to see him again in this world.

Like Cain after his killing, fleeing from the scene of his crime, so Jacob ran from his swindle, seeking to lose his fear in distance. His punishment, too, had started already.

On his journey from Beersheba Jacob "lighted upon a certain place because the sun was set" and laid himself down under the open sky, with a stone for his pillow. Thousands of years later, there would be men who believed that a certain red sandstone block was that same stone on which Jacob laid his head and dreamed. That would be the coronation stone, once stolen from Westminster Abbey—the Stone of Scone, of destiny. And now Jacob dreamed and the dream was of seeing a ladder set up between heaven and earth, and on the rungs of the ladder angels ascending and descending. More wonderful still, Jacob heard for himself the great Voice which had spoken to his grandfather and his father; the calm, deep Voice first heard in the lost garden, identifying the God of Abraham and Isaac, and making him astonishing promises.

"The land whereon you are lying, to you I will give it. . . . Your seed shall be as the dust of the earth . . . and in you shall all the families of the earth be blessed."

At this divine good news, the heart, the very conscience, of Jacob was stunned. God knew everything. He most certainly knew how Jacob had betrayed his brother and his father, lied, connived, cheated.

Then why these benignant and generous promises?

Jacob was a man of destiny and this encounter in a dream was his first glimpse of his future. Puzzled as he was, he still did not surmise that God may forgive His erring children, but the pain of disobedience lasts on for a long time.

Jacob awoke from his dream in a chill sweat.

"Surely," he said to himself, "the Lord is in this place and I knew it not."

Jacob was afraid. He took the stone which had been his pillow and set it upright, as a memorial pillar, anointing it with oil, and naming the place Beth-el, which means "the House of God." He felt hopelessly unworthy and conscience-stricken, ashamed of what he had done, as he dedicated not only the spot where he had seen the vision and heard the Voice, but himself as well, consecrated henceforth to the service of the Lord, Who in that miraculous dream had proven Himself kind and merciful beyond the comprehension of men.

Resuming his flight, Jacob at last reached the region of Haran, and like Eliezer before him, he joined some shepherds resting near the well. A large and heavy rock lay over the mouth of the well for removal only when water was drawn. Did these shepherds, perhaps, know one Laban, son of Nahor? Jacob inquired. They did; if the stranger would look yonder he would see Laban's daughter Rachel coming toward them with her father's sheep.

Even from that distance the eyes of Jacob danced at the sight of this maiden. He forgot that he was an outcast, a runaway from his own brother's vengeance. Rachel's face was kind and lovely; her long black hair fell over both shoulders as she walked with sturdy strength and yet gracefulness of movement, as if her body moved to inaudible music. Her father's ashen crook was in her hand as she prodded the gray flock of waddling, fat-tailed sheep.

Smiling at her, as if in welcome, Jacob sprang gallantly at the rock across the top of the well. It was large enough to call for several men, but Jacob seized it alone. Groaning, the blue veins in his forehead ready to burst, he shoved the stone aside by his own single strength and turned back to smile again; by a show-off wave of his hand he invited her to water her animals in peace.

She stood amazed, twice as beautiful in her astonishment, so entrancing a figure that Jacob embraced her and cried, with tears in his eyes:

"Your father and my mother are brother and sister."

Uncle Laban welcomed the wandering Jacob cordially. His manner was so natural and sincere that the runaway from Isaac's favor never for a moment doubted his good faith, but felt wholly in the family. With his own flesh and blood, what had he to fear? It still did not occur to him that his brother Esau might have asked the same question.

Uncle Laban was all friendliness; he did not even pry into Jacob's affairs or ask uncomfortable questions about why he had left home. Together they worked in the fields where Jacob did his full share so well that, after a month, Laban offered him a permanent job. "Tell me," he urged, "what shall your wages be?"

Jacob stammered his answer: he would like to take one of Laban's daughters as his wife.

"Now he had two daughters; the name of the elder was Leah and the younger was called Rachel.

"Leah was blear-eyed; Rachel was well favored and of a beautiful countenance."

And Jacob loved Rachel; and said, "I will serve you seven years for Rachel, your younger daughter."

Rachel, mind you—not Leah! Leah was plain, and for all her yearning sighs, she was so large and powerfully built that the earth might tremble when she strode out from her tent on a fine morning. Jacob was for Rachel and Rachel was for him—Rachel who every day seemed to him to grow more beautiful.

So the compact was made, and for seven years Jacob labored for Laban, but at last those seven years neared their end, and Jacob demanded Rachel for his wife. His uncle Laban smiled at him like a father and agreed to arrange at once for the wedding feast.

By custom, the bride would be heavily veiled when she was turned over to the bridegroom and so it was at Jacob's wedding. But what skullduggery was here? Next morning when Jacob looked by daylight into the face of his bride an incredulous groan broke through his lips. This woman whom he had married was not Rachel, but her older sister Leah, who had long been withering on the stalk.

So it fell that Jacob, who had stolen his father's blessing by trickery and used his brother's hunger to wheedle his birthright, was now betrayed out of seven years of the hardest labor of his life, hoodwinked and married off to the wrong woman, the one with the red-lidded eyes.

In a frenzy of wrath, Jacob towered over the complacent Laban. All the uncle's answers were ready. Did not Jacob know—everybody else did—that in the land of Nahor a younger daughter must wait until the older finds a husband? Anyway, the substitution was not as tragic a matter as Jacob seemed to think. Why not give Leah a week of himself, as required by tribal custom, then marry Rachel also? Would not that be acceptable—to have the two of them? In this poorly populated part of the world plural marriages were not uncommon.

The heart of Jacob seemed to rise from the grave of his hopes. An impetuous embrace sealed the bargain; it was done, and not until then did Jacob notice his uncle's wily smile. Laban softly called Jacob's attention now to another absolute and unchangeable custom of people here in Haran: as Isaac's son had worked seven years for Leah, so he must work seven more years for Rachel, although he could take her immediately.

His own medicine was bitter in Jacob's mouth, but he knew he deserved it all.

Two sisters with the same husband was not an unusual triangle in those primitive days, but no more workable then than now. From the very start of the arrangement life became a contest between the older and the younger sister. Leah was miserable because of Jacob's preference for Rachel, but she was not discouraged. At her every opportunity she showed herself smiling, adoring, tender, yielding, flattering, and soon Jacob began to feel that she was a pleasant companion. After all, why should he blame Leah? She had to obey her father in making the marriage. And even Heaven itself seemed to smile on Leah's efforts—she was first with child; the beautiful and passionately beloved Rachel was bearing no children for her husband, but dulleyed Leah gave him four sons, one after another: Reuben, Simeon, Levi, and Judah.

To the tearful Rachel it was cold comfort to remember how Sarah and Rebekkah, Jacob's mother and grandmother, were for so long afflicted with barrenness. Confronted every day with her sister's four romping brats, her ears deafened with their shouts at play, Rachel was becoming a neurotic woman.

"Give me children or else I die," she screamed at Jacob.

"Am I in God's stead?" he retorted. "It is His will and we must abide by it with patience."

But Rachel, beside herself with envy and jealousy, remembered Sarah and Hagar.

"Take my handmaid, Bilhah, that she may have your children that shall be mine also," she proposed, and Jacob realized by the look in her heartbroken eyes that she and her sister were mortal enemies now.

Two sons of Rachel's handmaid were sired by Jacob—Dan was one and Naphtali the other. Oddly, in those two years, meanwhile, Leah had not conceived again, while by proxy Rachel was giving sons to Jacob. But Leah was not one to endure this situation for long. What one sister could do, another could imitate. Rachel had given Jacob boys from her handmaid, Bilhah; but Leah, too, had a pretty servant —Zilpah! Two can play at the same game; actually Leah persuaded Jacob to marry the pert little Zilpah, and she bore him two children, Gad and Asher. Leah had other sons—Issachar and Zebulun, and a little girl named Dinah.

In those years of heartbreak Rachel had begun to believe that there was no more hope for her. She had tried every trick, every device, and all had failed. Her sister Leah was triumphant, even though Jacob had loved Rachel first and still loved her the more. But not one of his many sons had come from her own womb. There was no helping that. But finally it came to Rachel that Sarah and Rebekkah had doubted the promises of the one true God, and the longer they doubted the longer they had waited. Perhaps she should learn a lesson from those long-buried women.

Walking alone in the twilight, Rachel implored the God of Abraham and Isaac to hear her prayers. . . .

"Jacob," she cried to her husband one day, "thank God with me. I shall bear you a child. And I am going to name him Joseph."

Now it was of mystical significance, although Jacob did not realize the fact, that he had twelve sons—an important number to those who read symbols in mathematics—twelve sons, twelve tribes, twelve months, twelve apostles—the future would hold many significant twelves. The twelve lads of Jacob's loins were all to be cast for significant roles in dramatic tomorrows—Reuben, whose name meant "Son of Vision"; Simeon, "Hearing"; Levi, "Joined"; Judah, "Praise"; Dan, "Judging"; Naphtali, "My Wrestling"; Gad, "A Troop"; Asher, "Happy"; Issachar, "A Hire or Wages"; Zebulun, "Dwelling"; Joseph, "Adding"; and finally, Benjamin (who was not yet born), "Son of the Right Hand."

But while Jacob did not understand the high destiny of his twelve stalwarts, he was enchanted by the birth of Rachel's first child, and he loved Joseph as he had never loved any other. The bright eyes of the baby Joseph, looking straight up at him as if already he beheld wonderful things to which others were blind, evoked a passionate tenderness in Jacob's heart. He wanted to show the boy Joseph to his father, back home.

Isaac still lived in Beersheba, although restless, anxious Rebekkah had long since been laid to rest. Twenty years had come and gone since Jacob had run from home, and now the tents of his father began to haunt his memory.

But leaving Laban now was no easy matter; he invented excuses, quoted old agreements, prepared new bargains. The swindled Jacob was tired of being rooked.

"Return to the land of your fathers," was the word spoken by the Voice of the Lord God in Jacob's heart. "And I shall be with you."

To his two wives Jacob confided a secret plan. He reminded them of how again and again their father had cheated him, changing his wages on any excuse. Rachel and Leah encouraged their husband. Legally, Laban might be able to make it difficult for them to go, and so they planned to vanish without warning, watching for a good chance. And so they did, one day when Laban was far off, shearing sheep. Gathering all their possessions, Jacob and his wives with all their children, servants, animals, and goods fled in the direction of Mount Gilead.

It was a journey stalked with fear. Wrathful Laban pursued them; Brother Esau, with old vengeance in mind, waited for them. But all the fears vanished like the mists of morning. In a bivouac of his vindictive pursuit Laban was warned by a dream that Jacob was under some special providence, and when he overtook his son-in-law he prepared a covenant of love and peace between them. Together, all rancor gone, they gathered a heap of stones, with a big one for a central pillar, as witness to their compact, the historic treaty of Jacob and Laban, that made Gilead a debatable borderland, but which also gave the world a prayer it can never forget, the protection these two long-hostile men asked together:

"Mizpah; The Lord behold and judge between us, when we shall be gone one from the other."

The story behind this beautiful word "Mizpah" is often misunderstood. The interpretation of the name is not the beautiful one of blessing but an ugly assertion of Laban's continuing distrust of Jacob. For in effect he said: "If you shall afflict my daughters, God is witness"—as if to threaten Jacob: "I will not be able to watch you, but God will watch you. So beware!"

As for Esau—who would have inherited Isaac's great estates, if rid of Jacob—he did not lift hand against the brother who, twenty years before, had stolen the blessing after extorting the birthright. Not willing to live in constant anxiety, Jacob sent messengers on ahead to his wronged twin, asking that bygones be bygones; to Esau who was marching this way with four hundred wild followers. Gifts fit for a desert prince went with the messengers: two hundred she-goats and twenty he-goats; two hundred ewes and twenty rams; thirty milch camels with their colts, forty kine, twenty bulls, twenty she-asses, and ten foals.

Waiting for his brother's answer—peace or war, kinship or vengeance—Jacob was too restless to sleep. Alone, and apart from his caravan, he walked by the brook Jabbok, to pass the moonless night in prayer and supplication, so he hoped. But in the darkness he felt the figure of some stranger, barring his way. Not a word was given or taken. Without a sound and immediately they came to grips, Jacob and the unknown challenger, wrestling, might and main. Hour followed hour and still they struggled; all night the contest continued in silence and darkness. Not until the first arrow of light in the east did the unknown antagonist give up the fight and gasp for mercy.

"Pray let me go," the unknown pleaded, just before sunrise.

"Not until you bless me," replied Jacob; for something within had told him this wrestler in the dark was no mortal, but some celestial messenger.

"What is your name?" asked the stranger.

"Jacob."

"Hereafter you shall be called Israel," declared the challenger in authoritative tones, as if he had a divine right to change Jacob's name. "For you are a prince of power with God and with men, and have prevailed."

"And what is *your* name?" cried Jacob.

The question was never answered. With uplifted hands the stranger blessed Jacob, now to be called Israel, then disappeared in the morning mists. Profoundly stirred, and feeling he had seen his Maker face to face, Jacob named the place Peniel, which meant "The Face of God."

A mysterious business, that contest between mortal and immortal. Had Jacob actually wrestled with some angel? Whatever had been the truth of that mystery, it was also certain that Jacob had also wrestled that night with his own fears, the littleness of his old life, his scheming nature and his desire to get the best of everybody else—and he

77

had overcome the weakness of his character, downed it, thus making his conscience master of his fallen nature. When any man can do that he may well believe that he has been close to God.

Out of that strange duel in the woods Jacob came like a new man, a different person—and one immediate proof of the change was the absence of all fear of Esau's vengeance. Calmly he proceeded to lay his plans so that, if he must fight, he would be well prepared. With complete composure he watched a cloud of dust approaching far down the highway; soon he could see Esau riding at the head of a galloping column, Brother Esau on a swift camel, red hair flying in the wild wind, one arm held out, high and eager, vast palm exposed in friendship. The twins embraced.

Twenty years had worked soothing changes in Esau. Bland and magnanimous, he seemed to toss old grudges over his left shoulder, while he touched hand to heart, as the Easterners do to this day, and declared that he had long ago forgiven all offenses. Only with reluctance was he persuaded to accept his twin brother's gifts and peace offerings; they were not at all necessary, he insisted.

After the cleansing and healing of this old and open wound, the brothers parted again in perfect harmony, Esau going ahead to Mount Seir while Jacob pitched his tents at Shechem, in Canaan. Yet harmony between the brothers was to be followed only by tragedy in their lives.

First there was the odious thing that happened to Dinah, the only daughter of Leah. In spite of her mother's watchful eyes, Dinah managed to wander away from the resting caravan. One twilight she met a handsome young man who told her he was Sichem, son of Hemos the Hivite, princeling of a heathen tribe living thereabout.

There was uproar in Jacob's camp when Dinah's seduction became known; the ire of Dinah's brothers was frenzied; they wept and they swore vengeance. It was almost impossible for Dinah to persuade them to listen; Sichem, son of Hemos had decent intentions, so his messenger wanted to assure the clan; he was in love with Dinah and was offering honorable terms of marriage.

At this news the outraged brothers dissembled. With great cunning they asked if this impetuous heathen would submit to God's commanded rite of circumcision. The answer was prompt; indeed, the lover would be circumcised; he would do anything to win Dinah for his bride. He would dedicate himself to his wife's God.

But Dinah's brothers grew still more cunning. One circumcised

78

Hivite was not enough. Sichem's father, Hemos and his uncles, brothers, cousins, nephews, all the males in his presumptuous tribe, would also have to be circumcised and dedicated.

That was difficult. Sichem could answer promptly for himself; the others he would have to convince. Nevertheless, he would try; he was an enthusiastic youngster, eager to set himself right with the whole world. Soon he was back to announce that for the sake of peace all the male Hivites were willing and waiting to be circumcised.

This was not the end of the matter but the real beginning. A plot all the while had been hatching in the minds of Dinah's brothers, Simeon and Levi, who were consumed with a craze, a very lust, for reprisal. They had no conscience about their vengeance; to them the seduction of the innocent Dinah would justify any return; they meant to glut their ire. For an uncircumcised heathen youth to betray a daughter of the line of Abraham, Isaac, and Jacob was beyond all atonement, except by death; it made no difference that promises had been made to Sichem and to all the Hivites. Breaking one's word, to an outlander, simply did not matter. If to kill one enemy is sweet, why not take a hundred?

So Simeon and Levi waited for the mass circumcision. They waited even longer until the second day's fever would surely weaken and lay low Sichem, Hemos and their fellows, until their brows burned, pulses raced, eyes blurred, and a hot fatigue held them down sprawling and in pain. Then with massacre in their hearts Simeon and Levi fell upon the whole tribe and killed them one by one.

They boasted of this infamy.

"Shall Hemos deal with our sister as with an harlot?" they demanded self-righteously when Jacob denounced them. He declared that their bloodthirsty deed was as "a stink" to his name. The family honor was vindicated, so they reasoned, not realizing that they had stained that honor, so that men would recoil from their treachery forever after.

To his dying day Jacob held it against these offending sons; in his very last blessing he was to say: "Simeon and Levi are brethren; instruments of cruelty are in their habitations. . . . Cursed be their anger, for it was fierce; and their wrath, for it was cruel: I will divide them in Jacob, and scatter them in Israel."

In pain and humiliation—not without some fear, too, that neighboring tribes would arise in rage to avenge the scurvy treason played upon the Hivites—Jacob decided to seek the counsel of God in the most sacred place of his remembrance, in Bethel, where, as an outcast, a fugitive from Esau, his twin, he had laid his head on a stone and dreamed of a ladder that bridged earth and heaven. Now he raised a new altar at Bethel and again he heard the long-absent Voice speak to him, reassuringly, with a new promise that Jacob would inherit the land so long ago promised to Abraham and Isaac.

But who could be joyful, even with such a prophecy, when Rachel, still dearer than all others to Jacob, was pale and tottering these days? With child once more, Rachel lived in an unfamiliar mood of melancholy, as if she harbored a dark forecast in her thoughts. No tenderness of Jacob could cheer her; she seemed lonesome for her old mid-wife Deborah. When word came that Deborah was ill, she packed and set out to find and comfort her. The road she traveled on that brief journey is now a highway close to Bethlehem, and many call it Rachel's road. Slowly Jacob's cart was climbing the heights, when suddenly Rachel was seized with violent labor pains. In agony she reached the side of Deborah, where one sick woman tried to help the other.

But when Jacob, following after, got to them, Rachel was dead. The mourning Deborah held a boy child in her withered hands.

"Did she name him?" asked Jacob, when evening had come.

"Almost her last words were 'Son of Sorrow,'" the midwife told him.

"Nay," cried Jacob, his own ideas prevailing even in his woe. "Nay, he must be called 'Son of My Right Hand'—he shall be Benjamin."

Jacob's misfortunes seemed complete when he at last reached the tents of Isaac his father, only to find him, too, at the point of death. He had reached home just in time. The gentle Isaac had lived one hundred and eighty years.

Almost two centuries had passed since Abraham had laid him on the altar and stood ready to set fire to the kindling.

Esau and Jacob, old men themselves now, but both completely reconciled and liking each other, stood side by side as their father's body was laid in the grave.

Now Jacob came into his long-delayed inheritance. He had the power and use of his stolen treasures, the blessing and the birthright —and they seemed to him of no importance at all. He was the patriarch, the all-powerful head of his family—but his life seemed a finished book, with the rearing of his motherless son Benjamin a postscript to the past. Soon, he felt sure, his own long life would be reaching its close.

Though he was, indeed, in his maturing wisdom, coming ever closer to God, Jacob did not dream that greater adventures, greater sorrow, and greater joy were yet to come and that these latter-day events were all bound up in one son of his twelve, in the eleventh of these sons, Joseph.

Joseph was a dreamer, and that made most of the trouble.

Chapter 8 THE STORY OF JOSEPH

T H E first trouble was that Joseph, the dreamer, was the favorite of his father, and the others were envious. When he had been the smallest and youngest of the family everybody had spoiled Joseph, but now that he was growing to manhood—and Benjamin was the youngest, and he the one to be spoiled—his brothers thought that Joseph gave himself airs. Then his brothers began to hate him. Why did not Joseph come out to the farm lands and do his work along with the others—roughen his hands, and sweat with the rest of them?

Daily the ten sons of the unloved Leah and the bondswomen, Bilhah and Zilpah, tending thousands of sheep and cows on the plains and hills around Bethel, rehearsed their grievances. Rugged and storm-bitten men, battling the sudden whims of weather in that country and vigilantly on watch against wolves and thieves, their work was a constant strain on muscle and nerve. Why was Joseph spared?

Sometimes, on his own account, Joseph would take a notion into his head to spend a day in the fields with them. But his coming there would not be as a brother among brothers or even as a man among men. It was more like ten hostile strangers meeting with one imperious coxcomb.

At such times there was, in the give and take among Jacob's sons, no badinage, no friendly raillery; not as far as Joseph was concerned. They knew that he could think faster, come up with more ingenious reminders and solutions of little daily problems, and bring to any question a readier understanding than they, but this superiority only exasperated them. Long before manhood, Joseph had outstripped them all—and harrow and alas, he knew it.

Many a meal that began in tranquillity ended in a brawl, just because of Joseph. If this seventeen-year-old lad had only had the grown-up wisdom to conceal at least half of his cleverness, if he had allowed his brothers to keep a better opinion of themselves, things might have turned out differently for him and for them. But Joseph, in his inexperience and simplicity, seemed, to his brothers, to show off before them, and they loathed what they thought was his conceit. Besides, he was forever boring them with tales of dreams that he had, visions in which the whole family bowed down to him while he lorded it over them all. And to take such talk from a stripling, who showed a finical attention to the way his bushy black hair was dressed and parted and oiled and wrapped about his handsome young head, was getting to be unbearable. What's more, Joseph was careful about the cleanliness of his body; such overniceness, his brothers decided, was an insult to their own unperfumed persons; Joseph's manners made them feel like boors.

But it was Joseph's coat—the pride of his heart, a coat of many colors and with long sleeves, indicating a man of leisure—which embittered them most. The brothers knew that their father had given the gorgeous garment to his favorite, loved more than all the others because he was the first son of his old age. Very grand the lad was in his coat of many colors, the popinjay!

One fragrant spring day, when the brothers were grazing their animals near Dothan, miles from home—they had been away a week—Jacob sent Joseph out of the vale of Hebron to see if all went well. Feeling full of himself, with all the importance of an ambassador plenipotentiary, the youth, in his elegant coat of many colors, came singing through the fields. Soon his brothers heard his song, spied his gay, telltale coat. Often they had complotted to injure Joseph but until this morning it had been only talk.

"Behold, this dreamer cometh," said one brother to the others. "Come now, therefore, and let us slay him, and cast him into some pit, and we will say some evil beast has devoured him and we shall see what will become of his dreams."

As Joseph approached, singing and striding confidently toward them, Reuben entreated his brothers to show moderation; in fact he had already decided in his own mind to come back secretly and rescue the prisoner, if they did throw him into a pit. They wanted to kill Joseph but Reuben persuaded them to dispose of him so that he could be left to live or die without the stain of murder on their hands.

Gaily as a peacock in spring feathers Joseph greeted a ring of glowering faces:

"I must tell you about the dream I had last night in Shechem———"

Three brothers seized him and forced him to the ground. Hand over his mouth, knee in his stomach, they stripped him. Then, with three more brothers helping, they lugged him off to a place not far from the highway, and heedless of his cries for mercy, they dropped their victim into a deep pit.

"And we shall see what becomes of your dreams. . . ."

Those mocking words reached Joseph in the darkness below. Why must he dream? And why tell others of his dreams? It was too soon for Joseph to know that these were prophecies that came to him as he slumbered; for all his youthful self-sufficiency he did not guess that was the divine purpose to make him an instrument in the process of salvation. Later Joseph was to be regarded as a foretype of the Messiah, his singular story a kind of preshadowing of the shape of things to follow, from Bethlehem to Calvary.

And so Joseph was abandoned in a pit with no food or water in it. His brothers marched off with their cattle and sheep, putting distance between themselves and the pit. But the farther they journeyed the less they talked among themselves. In silence they sat on the grass to eat the noontime bread and cheese; the meal over, and still in silence, they separated for various grazing fields, Reuben going farthest away of all. But a few, dawdling over last morsels of the lunch, saw presently the approach of a company of Ishmaelites coming from Gilead, on their way to Egypt, with transports of balm and of myrrh and dried fruits and spicery. Judah, most forceful of the ten brothers, he from whose name the word "Jew" was to come, now spoke up:

"What profit if we slay our brother and conceal his blood? Let us sell Joseph to these merchants."

There is no question that they planned to sell Joseph into captivity. Morally they were guilty of the crime which they did not actually get a chance to commit. For while they were arguing among themselves some Midianites happened along and stole a march on Joseph's brothers. These Midianites drew and lifted up Joseph out of the pit and they sold him to the Ishmaelites.

Twenty pieces of silver—about twelve dollars in American money—was the bargain they struck for selling their prisoner into bondage.

As the caravan moved on the captive and enslaved Joseph looked over his shoulder and saw his coat of many colors left lying behind him in the dust.

What story would they tell at home? Jacob was not gullible; he had practiced some trickery in his own time, and old though he was, he would be suspicious. Strange how human beings will often rush headlong into crime and then try to think up ways to escape after the deed is done. If Jacob were to learn the wicked truth he would raise an army to rescue his favorite son from the Egyptians. Let him, instead, think of Joseph as dead; that was the safest tale to tell. To convince the patriarch, to calm him in his sorrow, they concocted a wild-animal tale, of how a ravenous wolf had eaten poor Joseph—and by killing a kid of the goats and dipping the coat in the blood, they stained it rusty red and carried it home as a piece of evidence.

Jacob tore at his own cloak, put sackcloth on his loins, and mourned inconsolably; he wept until he had no more tears to shed.

Not knowing the truth, deceived as he had once deceived, Jacob could not realize the ironic revenge of the years, measure for measure. His sons were hoodwinking him as grievously as he had practiced fraud on doddering Isaac, to gain a fraudulent blessing.

To none of his large household would Jacob talk now, except only his youngest, Benjamin. That smiling other son of Rachel became his comfort, the treasure of his bitter grief.

Almost as soon as the camel train reached the borders of Egypt, Joseph was put up for auction in the market place of a boundary town —a brawling, clamorous place, crowded with hawkers and cadgers of every kind of merchandise from dried beans to human beings. Here was an old woman offering melons, her daughter peddling sweetened water in a bloated gourd, yonder a herd of water buffalo for sale to farmers. Drums were beating, bells ringing—a hubbub of market-day crowds, jostling, stinking, ready for anything. Standing on a block of granite, Joseph was surrounded by slave buyers, who pinched and measured him, felt for his muscles, until he finally caught the eye of one of the important ministers of the Egyptian government, Potiphar, an officer of the ruling Pharaoh.

The caravaners haggled with Potiphar, who was rich; here, indeed, was a great prize, undoubtedly an emir's son from afar. But Potiphar paid little heed to their sales talk; all Bedouins were liars, but he liked the looks of the young captive and paid the price.

Before that day was over Potiphar was certain he had a bargain in his young slave.

A complete transformation had come over Joseph; he was patient, reconciled to his fate, obedient. In all his gay and insufferable young arrogance Joseph had never imagined that his brothers did not love him. Were they not all of the same flesh and blood? Was not the family the strongest tie of all? Even when they dropped him into the pit he had thought that they were frightening him, trying to teach him a lesson. But now, thanks to their undeniable hatred of him, their malevolence, he was a slave in a strange land. He decided to make the best of it, and he faced his master with a cheerful air. In all the varying fortunes of the future Joseph continued to take what fate brought him with a steady eye.

Thus Joseph, the Hebrew slave, was a faithful and dutiful prisoner; in willingness and intelligence he outshone all of Potiphar's other servants. As the years sped by he was promoted again and again; within ten years he had actually become overseer of Potiphar's house. And still, with every day that passed, he seemed to become more efficient, relieving his master of domestic cares and responsibilities. Moreover, not one of the workers under him had anything but praise for the able and kindly alien executive.

"And Joseph was a goodly person and well favored.

"And it came to pass . . . that his master's wife cast her eyes upon Joseph; and she said, Lie with me."

For a long time Joseph had been aware that Potiphar's wife had been watching him tenderly. More, he had heard the gossip of palace guards about other dalliances of Potiphar's wife. With the utmost sang-froid she invited her husband's slave to bed, and the distracted Joseph replied:

"Behold, my master know not what is with me in the house, and he has committed all that he has to my hand;

"There is none greater in this house than I; neither has he kept back anything from me but you, because you are his wife: how then can I do this great wickedness, and sin against God?

"And it came to pass, as she spoke to Joseph day by day, that he hearkened not unto her, to lie by her, or to be with her.

"And it came to pass about this time, that Joseph went into the house to do his business; and there was none of the men of the house there within.

"And she caught him by his garment, saying, Lie with me: and he left his garment in her hand, and fled, and got him out. . . .

"And she laid up his garment by her, until her lord came home.

"And she spake unto him according to these words, saying, The Hebrew servant, which you have brought unto us, came in unto me to mock me:

"And it came to pass, as I lifted up my voice and cried, that he left his garment with me, and fled out.

"And it came to pass, when his master heard the words of his wife, which she spoke unto him, saying, After this manner did your servant unto me; that his wrath was kindled.

"And Joseph's master took him, and put him into the Prison, a place where the king's prisoners were bound: and he was there in prison."

So now the fame of Joseph, Hebrew slave whose name had been so fair, was a scandal in Egypt, his character slandered by every camel boy at the watering trough. No one had any sympathy for Joseph any more; he was an outcast among outcasts, condemned to a reeking jail. But there in prison the love of God found him; there Joseph's true direction, his divine guidance, took possession of his life.

Even the flint-eyed keeper of the prison found himself irresistibly drawn to his new inmate. Indeed, before long the jailer gave him charge over all the other prisoners. Even with the convicts his popularity was astonishing, because he was kind to innocent and guilty alike; he was interested in their experiences and even listened while they told him their dreams.

In those days every Egyptian believed in the mystical nature of dreams. Joseph would explain the meanings to troubled prisoners, and so often was he proved right that they began to look upon him with awe. That was what he was about one winter afternoon when the door of the wardroom was unbolted with a clanging of irons and chains, deafening roars and curses, and two wretches were shoved in:

"Murderers! Assassins! Dogs!"

There had been, so it seemed, a conspiracy to poison the mighty Pharaoh, and these cringing, frightened men, chief butler of the court and the king's chief cook, were being thrown into prison on suspicion. A thousand deaths by slow torture would be their sentence, if guilt could be proved. Neither a detective nor any man's judge, Joseph welcomed them as if they were innocent men; he made them as comfortable as he could, and soon they were asleep.

One morning, as Joseph came into the warden's room, he found the butler and the baker sitting with pale faces and trembling with fear. What was wrong? The two murder suspects had experienced frightening nightmares. Would Joseph tell them what they meant?

"Tell me the dreams," said Joseph. "Do not interpretations belong to God?"

The cook and the butler knew nothing of God. They knew only the Egyptian deities and star gods, celestial cats and bulls, and solar disks worshiped in the labyrinthine temples at Luxor, up the Nile. But though they knew he was a man of different faith worshiping the only true God they entreated him to listen to their dreams. The butler told this fantasy:

"From a three-branched grapevine that budded and ripened at once, I pressed wine into Pharaoh's cup and gave it to him, and he drank of it. What can it mean? That I am guilty and will be put to death?"

Quite the opposite, good butler, so Joseph declared; within three days the frightened functionary would be restored to royal favor.

"And then, remember me," pleaded Joseph. "And speak that I may be released from this place."

The butler was garrulous in his assurances; he would speak up for Joseph before Pharaoh.

Next the chief baker launched into his recital of mental adventures in sleep, ending up with what had impressed him most:

"And from these three white baskets on my head, which contained various baked meats for Pharaoh, the birds ate, and they consumed everything that was in the uppermost basket. I woke in fright."

Joseph remained silent.

"Is my dream an evil omen?" quavered the baker.

Alas, yes. Joseph candidly predicted that in three days judgment would be given against the baker; the dream meant that he would be hanged, and the birds would eat his flesh.

As Joseph the diviner of dreams had foretold, so everything happened. Within seventy-two hours Pharaoh celebrated his birthday, feasting his servants and granting amnesty to certain chosen prisoners, while putting others to death to make his holiday more enjoyable. The butler was restored to his place in the palace but the baker was hanged from a tree.

Did the chief butler remember and petition Pharaoh to free his friend?

The baker was dead, his bones plucked clean, and the butler was back on his old job, but for two more years Joseph remained a prisoner.

The years of Joseph's imprisonment came to an end at last, and with bewildering suddenness, all because the great Pharaoh himself found his sleep invaded by weird phantoms and intimidating visions. A series of repeated nightmares of the king threw the court into gloom.

A melancholy fellow in golden robes, trimmed with disks of emeralds and rubies and pearls, his crown of diamonds awry over his right ear, the Pharaoh walked his vaulted aisles in glowering silence. Some evil fate portended in his visions and he was frustrated because all the numerous company of royal astrologers and necromancers and thaumaturges, his sand diviners and analysts of dreams, magicians, wizards, conjurers, and interpreters and conjecturers of inexplicable phenomena quailed before his throne as they confessed that their arts, their charts, their spells and charms and conjurations still left their brains blank when they tried to explain the king's bad dreams.

Night after night the visions came to haunt the sleeping ruler; in the full and in the dark of the moon they plagued him as he lay in the coolness of his bedchamber, with pool and palm tree and nesting birds, royal head tossing on a silken pillow, over a bolster of alabaster, his brow fanned by perfumed slave girls waving branched peacock plumes.

The news was spreading through the kingdom of Pharaoh's double dream: seven fat cows being eaten up by seven lean ones; and again seven full ears of corn devoured by seven thin and blasted ones. The people were afraid for their ruler and themselves. In this atmosphere of deepening national alarm the chief butler remembered Joseph, the interpreter. He prostrated himself before the royal presence and told of his prison experience. Half an hour later the warden told Joseph that Pharaoh had sent for him. But Joseph was not alarmed; only the night before he himself had known a dream, like one of those old, haughty visions of eminence that had thronged his mind when he was young, back in Beersheba; arrogant phantasms of the mind's eye that had so infuriated ten envious brothers. Joseph had seen a palm tree, exceedingly tall, its gray stem springing from earth toward heaven, its broad boughs spread like a green halo far above, and yet this stately palm tree could lower its head from the clouds and bow before a mortal man, before Joseph, before himself, the dreaming prisoner, as if acknowledging something secret and splendid.

Unfrightened in the vastness of palace walls and painted monoliths, whose capitals were lost in shadows far above, Joseph faced the black-bearded Pharaoh all fox and lamb on the gold and blue enamel throne, and bowed with uncompromising politeness. He listened intently to the story of the lean and the fat kine, the voluptuous and the shriveled ears of corn, twenty-eight in all, the healthy devoured by the ill.

He did not look like any magician they had ever seen; he wore no star-embroidered robe, carried no mystic rod, nor was he muttering incantations. Clad in a felon's robe, he stood, head bowed, eyes closed in meditation, deep as prayer. Then:

"There is no one who can expound my dreams," said Pharaoh, impatient at the silent figure. "Now I have heard that you are very wise at interpreting them."

Joseph opened his eyes and his answer disclaimed all credit for any supernatural powers:

"Without me, God shall give Pharaoh a prosperous answer. . . . God has shown Pharaoh what He is about to do."

Who was this God? The deity worshiped in this prisoner's homeland. The king looked uncomfortably about him. Well, what was He about to do?

"There will be seven years of plenty in the land, and seven years of famine to consume them utterly, unless careful measures are taken."

The assurance in the voice of the handsome slave carried conviction. Deep within him the king felt aware that this young man was inspired. He recalled stories told of former famines in Egypt, although in these days it was fertile beyond all other lands, and the Nile ever faithful in its yearly overflow.

"Tell me, Hebrew, what must be done?"

"Now, therefore, let Pharaoh choose a wise and industrious man and make him ruler over the land of Egypt, that he may gather into barns the fifth part of the fruits in the years of plenty, and let all the corn be laid up under Pharaoh's hands and be reserved in the cities, in readiness against the famine which is to come."

The king's smile at the prisoner was itself a royal appointment. The troubled monarch was convinced.

"Can we find such another man," he demanded, "that is full of the spirit of God? Can I find one wiser than you? You shall be over my house and all the people shall obey; only in the kingly throne will I be above you."

And the king took a ring from his own hand and gave it to Joseph, and put on him a robe of silk, though not of many colors, and a golden chain around his throat.

Joseph was thirty years old that day when Pharaoh proclaimed that he was made governor and gave him a priest's daughter to be his bride, and named him, in the Egyptian language, the Savior of the World.

Now the fat years were on the land, and one might have believed from all the abundance of harvests that there would never be a famine. The earth brought forth so much corn that Joseph's servers grew weary. Day and night he kept them busy, bringing in the sheaves, garnering food that they did not need and could not possibly eat, and building more granaries to store the surplus. Joseph was carefully executing his plan to save for the future; let the worst befall, Egypt could feed the world.

But at the end of seven years, true to the king's recurring dream, the Nile failed, and drought swept the country, the worst scarcity ever known. From all the lands around came reports of dwindling, vanishing stores of food. Joseph's name was in every hungry mouth; he distributed the stored-up food and let it be known there was enough for everybody. Other countries came begging bread from Egypt and they, too, were fed.

And word of this generosity reached even to distant Canaan, where aging Jacob still lived with his eleven sons.

There no one had had the foresight to fill the bins against the uncertain future. Misery was everywhere; herds and flocks were dying off, ruin and death creeping closer.

"Why are you careless? Why do we starve?" Jacob demanded of his sons. "There is plenty in Egypt. Go down there and buy corn. Wayfarers have told me that the Egyptians have a magician who grows corn in great houses of stone."

He sent them all packing, except his beloved Benjamin, too young for a long, dangerous journey. Mounting their asses, the ten brothers started off, and without misadventure reached the delta of the Nile. A few days later they appeared at the governor's palace, where they bowed ceremoniously to the floor, in homage before the bearded prime minister, whom not one of them recognized.

Indeed, not once had any of the ten brothers dared to lift eyes to the face of this awesome official, who had the power to sell them food, or to withhold it, life or death. There was a great silence in the audience chamber as the principal officer of the mighty Pharaoh looked from one to another of the kneeling supplicants, counting them. He knew them, every one. These were his blood brothers who had cast him into a pit and who had said: "We shall see what becomes of his dreams."

Through an interpreter, for he chose to act as if he could not speak Hebrew, Joseph listened to their appeal with a pretense of suspicion and rough asperity.

"You are spies. You have come to view the weaker parts of our land," he objected through his interpreter. "Tell me about your family and your lives."

Humbly, Brother Judah began the tale. He told about Jacob, their aged father, and his twelve sons—one, alas, dead these fifteen years, the youngest left at home, ten others here before him. Their cattle had roamed a hundred hills, but now faltered and fell with hunger. Their intimate recital seemed to make no impression on the stern-visaged official. He said:

"Nevertheless, unless you bring your youngest brother here, I shall look upon you as a lot of spies. And you shall be in prison until what you say is proved true."

Confounded but helpless, the ten were taken to jail, and kept there for three days. Why was the prime minister playing cat and mouse with them?

"I fear God," Joseph sent word to them through the interpreter. "Therefore, I will let you go back laden with grain. But one of you must remain as hostage until you bring me that youngest brother to prove your trustworthiness."

For a few minutes he turned his back on his brothers and they talked in their own language—"We deserve to suffer these things because we have sinned against our brother"—and Reuben reminded them how, on that long-ago day by the pit, he had warned them. They could not know that the governor with his back turned to them was their Joseph, nor that he understood every word that they spoke, nor that the tears were running down his cheeks.

It was Simeon who was held as hostage, while nine brothers departed from the land of pyramids. Not without hope they left; all might yet be well, and they took note of wonders to describe to Jacob and Benjamin: the carved gods with heads of birds and animals, and the living horses which they saw for the first time; it was the Semite Hyksos, of whom the present Pharaoh was one, who had introduced horses into Egypt.

But travel wonders were suddenly put out of mind by a discovery they made when about halfway on their journey home. In readjusting the packing, they found in each brother's sack of grain the exact sum of money that had been paid for it tied in the mouth of the sack. What to think and what to do? Was this a trick to convict them of dishonesty? Would they be overtaken by pursuing Egyptian guards and yanked back to prison or worse? All the rest of the journey they kept looking fearfully over their shoulders, but they were not pursued.

Home at last, they poured out the whole alarming story to their father. Jacob began to bewail Simeon, left behind in a foreign prison, and he was horrified at the demand that his dearest Benjamin be also taken to Egypt. The old man refused to let him go; he was obdurate.

But the famine showed no sign of relenting; it grew worse, and soon Jacob and his large household found themselves once again eating husks. Then Judah made a proposal.

"Father, I will be surety for Benjamin. And all the blame will be mine now and forever, for whatever may happen."

Jacob had to yield. Take double money with them, was his advice, as well as the amounts which were in the sacks last time. Return the money with fair words, explaining it as an oversight not of their contriving. They should take gifts also—a little balm and honey, and storax, myrrh, turpentine, and almonds. And take your brother and go to the man. And may Almighty God make him favorable to you.

With a sad heart Jacob watched his sons depart, and he was left alone. . . .

Once again the brothers, ten of them this time, bowed low before Joseph. With a catch in his throat, Joseph noted that Benjamin was among them, Benjamin, his brother by the same mother. Clapping his hands, he called for his major-domo and instructed him to take the petitioners away.

"To my own home," he said, "and get ready a special noonday meal."

What now? The brothers suspected a trap. Entering the door of the prime minister's house, they began nervously explaining to the steward who met them that they were returning the cash left inadvertently in their former sacks. But the man waved them aside. Their God, he said, must have done it, for he had kept their payment in his accounts. The steward fetched water and they washed their feet, while he saw to feeding their animals.

Promptly at noon Joseph drove home in his gilded chariot, second only in magnificence to that of Pharaoh. Hardly had he greeted the brothers when they began to press on him the gifts they had brought, from their father. For the first time Joseph smiled. He inquired kindly about the health of the patriarch and then about their own welfare. Looking intently at Benjamin, who stood uneasily before this great man, Joseph found himself looking into the eyes of Rachel, his mother, and he turned hastily and left them all, because his tears gushed out.

Seated, a little later, for the noonday meal, Joseph remained alone in his eminence, while the brothers were placed below his table, off to themselves, for it was considered an abomination for Egyptians to eat with foreigners; Joseph was playing his masquerade to the last detail. Secretly he ordered the steward to see that the brothers' sacks were filled to overflowing. He also told them to put the money in the sacks as before, and to place a precious silver cup, his own special pride and delight, at the top of Benjamin's sack.

"But say not a word of this," he abjured the steward.

Homeward toward Canaan the eleven brothers started the next morning. That inscrutable and unpredictable prime minister had bade them a most courteous farewell. Yet only a short distance out of the city they were overtaken by the steward, who accused them of stealing a priceless drinking vessel from his master. Of course all the brothers swore their innocence and were unanimous in declaring that if one of them was guilty he should die, and the rest be made bondsmen.

Confidently they opened up their sacks. There was the money, as before! Worse, there was the silver cup of Joseph, lifted by the steward from Benjamin's sack. Pack up your opened bags again, and load your donkeys; back to Egypt!

In half an hour they stood again before their persecutor, the agent of the king, and his stern and sorrowful face seemed to charge that all foreigners were liars and thieves. What could they say for themselves?

In half an hour they stood again before their persecutor, the agent Judah was spokesman, Judah pale with a new emotion, an attack of conscience that now afflicted all the brothers. What did it matter that they were innocent of the charges against them? While they had not embezzled the purchase money of their food, and most assuredly had not stolen my lord's silver cup, still who were they to protest; they who deserved much worse, being guilty of an older and deeper wickedness? For their long-unrepented misdeed the punishment was upon them. They had been ready to sell a brother into Egypt as a slave and now would themselves be taken into Egyptian bondage. It was just.

But Joseph shook his head. He did not want them as slaves. He would not have them! All but one of them could go back home, unmolested, to that poor dear father, Jacob, now called Israel, of whom they had told him. Only Benjamin, the youngest, Benjamin, last born of Jacob's seed, Benjamin must remain behind, as the minister's servant.

Judah stepped forward, fell on his knees, and held out his hands in supplication.

"If then, my lord, we return to our father without the lad, who is all in all to him, he will surely die. . . . Therefore, my lord, I pray you let me, Judah, remain here as slave to my lord, and Benjamin go back with his brothers. I could not bear to see the evil that would smite my father if his youngest son is taken from him."

One could have heard a bird stir in the egg. Joseph rose from his gilded chair. And now it seemed as if a mask dropped from his face, and he spoke in the Hebrew tongue.

"I am Joseph! Tell me that my father is alive."

The abased sons of Jacob stared up at the governor, open-mouthed incredulous.

"Come near to me. I am Joseph," he repeated. "Your brother whom you sold into Egypt."

But they remained speechless, cataleptic in their fear.

"Now, therefore," Joseph went on tenderly, "be not angry with yourselves, that you sold me hither. For God sent me before you to preserve life for us all. So it was not you who sent me hither, but God. Haste you and go up to my father and say, come down unto me, tarry not."

And Joseph fell upon his brother Benjamin's neck and wept.

As time is reckoned, it was a bright day in the year 1700 B.C., or thereabouts, when Jacob, watching the long road, spied the returning procession of his sons. At their tale of Egypt he was lost in amazement and ecstasy. Joseph alive! And a mighty governor in Egypt. Twenty asses loaded down with food and rich gifts sent him by that ruler who was his favorite son. His other sons all clad in fine raiment, finer than the forgotten coat of many colors they had once abominated. And Benjamin showed his father three hundred pieces of silver that Joseph had given him, just for himself. And now they would all be together.

But first Jacob insisted on going to Beersheba, and there, at the altar of old memories, the patriarch offered sacrifices to the God of his grandfather and his father. And there, in the night, after long years of silence, Jacob heard the well-remembered Voice:

"Fear not to go down into Egypt, for I will there make of you a great nation: I will go down with you into Egypt, and I will also surely bring you up again; and Joseph shall put his hand upon thy eyes."

So in the four-wheeled wagons in which Pharaoh had sent them home the sons of Israel brought their father to Goshen, at the gates of Egypt.

' And with Joseph clasped to his heart, the old man cried:
"Now let me die, since I have seen your face."

But Jacob, called Israel, still had many more years to live, years of
peace and prosperity that followed the hard times of the famine. Sev-
enteen years passed happily over Jacob's hoary head, surrounded by
swiftly multiplying kindred. But the end at last drew nigh, and Jacob
had a private talk with Joseph.

It was a singular deathbed interview. Drawing nearer toward the
other world, Jacob was once again the principal actor in a distorted
scene of blessing. First he bade Joseph swear that he would bury him
with his fathers in Canaan. Then he sent for Joseph's own sons,
Manasseh and Ephraim, and the old hands were raised to bestow the
patriarchal benediction. But Jacob, dim-eyed as his outwitted father
long before, first touched the heart of the younger son, Ephraim.
Nothing that Joseph said would correct the old man; he would not listen, but, filled with some curious certitude, he brought his favor upon
the younger, and not the legitimate heir.

"The angel which redeemed me from all evil," Jacob murmured,
"bless the lads."

The years were to prove that the dying Jacob had seen into the future, for Ephraim, the younger, was the leader, a charter of surpassing
worthiness; and Ephraim would give kings to ten tribes and become
the ancestor of Joshua, who one day would bring the people into the
Promised Land.

Then Jacob called for all his sons to hear him. One after another,
he blessed them according to their due, praising their virtues and
abilities, and warning of their defects and weaknesses. Of Joseph he
said:

"His arms were made strong by the mighty God of Jacob, and by
the Almighty who shall bless thee with blessings of heaven above,
blessings of the deep that lieth under, blessings of the breasts and of
the womb . . . unto the utmost bounds of the everlasting hills; they
shall be on the head of Joseph . . . fruitful bough, even a fruitful
bough by a well, whose branches run over the wall."

Then, gazing with faltering eyes up into the faces of the twelve
sons, Jacob raised both hands. These sons of his were the twelve tribes
of Israel, blessed just before Jacob's life came to a peaceful close.

Israel as a national concept began to be a reality at Jacob's
deathbed.

The body was embalmed by the Egyptians, as if Jacob had been a highborn noble of their own. Then the twelve sons carried the mummified body to the burial cave in Machpelah, where Abraham and Isaac and Rachel, the beloved, were buried.

And once again the brothers lived through years of peace. There was anti-Semitism in Egypt, even then, but all the relatives of Joseph were popular and beloved.

Profoundest sorrow filled Egypt when at the age of one hundred and ten years Joseph followed his father in death. His body, too, was embalmed, and laid away in a nest of elaborate coffins; his body may be preserved even until these times, but if so, it is yet to be found. The very souls of the Egyptian people grieved at the passing of their great outlander, slave and convict who had governed them as one inspired with divine wisdom. They vowed never to forget him.

Centuries went rolling by, four hundred years, while the descendants of Joseph and his brethren begat more descendants in increasing multitudes and there arose up a new king over Egypt—the Pharaoh Seti I—and he knew not Joseph.

But Pharaoh was worried about the thousands of Jews living in his kingdom. His thoughts were preparing a bitter time for the twelve tribes of Israel.

BOOK THREE

The Wilderness Adventure

Chapter 9 THE STORY OF MOSES

PEOPLE were now spreading by millions all over the face of the earth. In the Far East the Hsia dynasty had come to power and was laying the foundations of a Chinese empire. The Aryan invasion was sweeping down the snowy mountain passes of northern India, and on green islands in the Aegean the culture of the Greeks was beginning. Pyramids were already built in Yucatán, while within the upmost circle of the north, in a land not then obliterated as now with polar ice, men and women were loving, hating, inventing arts and crafts. The world was being populated. The Lord God had seen the struggles of the patriarchs to overcome their fallen nature; men so devout in yearning that they could hear the Father's Voice speak in their hearts. The plan of creation could never be without friends on earth while men such as these lived and died.

But now Israel needed a new leader, for the Jews of Egypt were in a sorry case.

The latest Pharaoh and his advisers were looking askance at the prosperous descendants of Jacob's twelve sons. And the tongues of the envious mob were clacking like the bronze sistrums, shaken in the rites of Isis. Public opinion was rising like a typhoon.

Calling together his councilors and administrators in a special conclave on policy, Seti, the Pharaoh, reviewed the population problem. Slaves in the kingdom, captives from conquests of hundreds of years before, had continued to multiply, and now dominated the labor market. However, these serfs could be held under control; the real trouble was from the Hebrews, who were freemen, not slaves nor the children of slaves. Long before, they had been legally allowed to settle in Goshen; and by now they were a nuisance. In four hundred years they had been increasing themselves to a degree that threatened the safety of the nation. Also their pernicious loyalty to old religious notions was notorious; at best they gave only lip service to On (Zoan) and Avaris and other current Egyptian deities.

So now Seti, the Pharaoh, standing oracularly in golden robes of state and wearing a crown ornamented with a golden cobra with ruby eyes, spoke to his wise men in words of some such meaning as these:

"These people of the children of Israel grow bold. Let us be wise in time. Should war come again, as it will with the Hittites, the strength of these Hebrews might be added to that of the enemy, and then we could be overcome. Such strength must be used for our own benefit, not against us."

The sovereign man-god, as he proclaimed himself, paused to give weight to his words, then proceeded:

"I have planned two treasure cities to be called Pithom and Raamses. Their walls shall be from six to ten feet in thickness of fine brick, and they shall add glory and protection to our land. Though I may not hope to equal the great works of the immortal king Khufu, who raised the Great Pyramid, or to rival the everlasting monuments of Thutmose, I shall follow their example in keeping rivers of sweat flowing. These descendants of aliens, still in our midst, shall be set to building my new cities. They shall have no time for anything else but long labor and little sleep. The birth rate will soon fall. Thus they will be made to pay us back somewhat for our enduring hospitality."

No one in the courtroom allowed himself to remember that the aliens had continuously paid for their benefits by forced labor and in heavy taxation, since the earliest days. At once the orders were issued against the Jews, a draft into prolonged servitude. They must toil with brick and mortar, they must haul blocks of granite and dig waterways, and all for mere sustenance.

Never before had the sons of Israel known such taskmasters. With whip and bastinado, the helpless people were goaded on to more and more efforts. Yet, inexplicably, the harsh devices failed; the Hebrews did not wane in number; more and more of their babies were born, and their love increased under affliction.

To the Egyptians the vital statistics seemed a downright insolence. In the growing Hebrew birth rate they read a deliberate purpose to breed in spite of oppression. When the figures were carried to Pharaoh he roared across the throne room, demanding to have brought before him two of the leading midwives, Shiphrah and Puah. Shoved into the royal presence, they collapsed to their knees.

"Hereafter," Seti commanded the trembling crones, "it shall be your duty, and that of all the other midwives, to destroy the boy babies born to Israelite mothers. Let not one of them live an hour. See that all midwives know what to do"—an early attempt at genocide.

"It will be done according to Your Majesty's divine will," murmured the midwives. What else could they do but dissemble? But even so, they were good nurses accustomed to the tender handling of women in childbirth and their newly born. Were they now to turn killers? At the risk of their own lives they failed to carry out the inhuman edict. A year later, when Pharaoh demanded to know why there were still little boy babies in Hebrew families, the midwives had an excuse. Did not his godlike royalty know that Hebrew mothers often delivered their own babies?

So Pharaoh issued a new fiat. Every Jewish man child born thereafter must be cast into the river, no matter who delivered it. From such an edict there was no appeal whatever, and it went into immediate and retroactive effect—and terror reigned in many houses.

A new Hebrew boy had just been born when the murderous law was proclaimed. The father and mother were of the tribe of Levi, and they had a beautiful daughter, whose name was Miriam, and an older boy called Aaron. Amram, the father, had just been called from home to toil in the new city of Pithom, when the child was born. Could Jochebed, the mother, and little Miriam throw the new boy baby into the Nile?

Instead, they contrived to hide the child safely for three months, but then they learned that Pharaoh's inspectors were beginning to search all dwellings. So Jochebed thought of another plan to save her child.

Weaving a tiny basket of wattled reeds, Jochebed made it waterproof, coating it inside and out, with bitumen and pitch. Then she lined it with downy cloth and finally laid her son, fast asleep, inside the basket. Softly she fastened down the light cover of woven papyrus stalks, and carrying the small burden to the brink of the broad, green river, Mother Jochebed launched the basket and its precious cargo among the shallow flags and rushes, close to shore. Then she ran away, that distracted mother, not knowing that her eight-year-old Miriam had followed and watched and remained behind, hidden in the swamp to be a sentry over the floating cradle. When sunrise was not two hours old Miriam saw an unusual sight, a princess at her bath. Lovely Bithia, daughter of Pharaoh Seti I, came down to wash herself, attended by her tirewomen; came to the reedy bank of the Nile and found the basket and child in the bulrushes.

All bedizened with feathers and gems even at that early hour, Bithia

wept with compassion, understanding at once that this was a condemned baby, whose mother was trying to save him.

"This is one of the Hebrews' children," she said. "I will call his
name Moses because I drew him out of the water."

Then Bithia saw she was not alone with her tirewomen. Out of the
tangled reeds appeared the pale and watchful little sister.

"Does the noble lady want me to fetch her a Hebrew nurse?"
Miriam asked. "I know where there is one."

"Go!" said Princess Bithia. "Bring her home to nurse the child and
I will pay her wages."

Thus the daughter of Seti I defied his commands and rescued a
despised Hebrew baby from death and, even while taking him as her
own son, hired his real mother to attend him, and teach him of his
people, of Abraham, Isaac, and Jacob. And thus Moses found not only
a name and protection and a court education, but also an indoc-
trination of the God of his people and their adventures back to the
Garden of Eden.

It was well that this was so, for Moses was destined to be one of the
few truly great men of history; seldom has human nature ascended so
high, or shone so brightly, as in the personality of Moses. He was to
lead his people out of bondage, give them their law, and bring them
to the doorsteps of the Promised Land.

Again and again Heaven made it clear that He was God's chosen
man. Not only did he receive the Ten Commandments on Mount
Sinai; he expanded and catalogued and interpreted and expounded the
whole complicated code of Jewish law as the Bible sets it forth in the
Books of Exodus, Leviticus, and Deuteronomy. To this day the vast
compilation of Jewish discipline is called by his name, the Mosaic
Law. What men feel about this hero from the bulrushes was best expressed by Michelangelo in a magnificent statue. Strong, determined,
wise, and yet humbled by his respect and worship of God, the figure
of Moses emerges in marble, the strength and wisdom and courage of
mankind at its best; that was Moses.

As the adopted son of a princess, Moses was given all the advantages of the Egyptian elect. From private tutors he went on to the
University Temple of On, the most celebrated center of learning in
that day. There he was taught astronomy, philosophy, metaphysics,
and the secret lore of the priests, all amid an imposing atmosphere of
vast and awesome temple architecture.

An avenue of sphinxes led from the riverbank to the university with
its lofty red granite obelisks at the entrance, some of them one hun-

dred and fifty feet high. The painted courts and carved cloisters formed a panorama of history, with religion the main theme: colorful scenes of fantastic gods and their adventures, a crowded pantheon. And what a contrast, in his searching, acquisitive mind, to the one God his nurse-mother had taught him to love—the true One, the only One!

Once graduated, Moses, under the aegis of his foster mother, the princess, was welcomed in court; an anomaly never commented upon, a young Jew in high life, no longer thinking seriously about religion or anything else, but enjoying royal pastimes, as if he were born to them, even while his own people groaned under the inflexible Egyptian cruelty.

But not for long could Moses relish the palace way of life. Soon he realized that its people luxuriated in idleness and loose pleasures, thanks only to the toil and pain of an army of slaves, many of his own blood. Egyptian aristocracy thought no more of the poor and helpless than of refuse and rubbish. Seeing that arrogance, and feeling more and more a kinship with his own race, Moses began to absent himself from the court. He preferred to meditate while roaming the countryside in solitary exploration. The power and obstinacy of the Nile fascinated Moses, and the way clever Egyptian engineers were coaxing its waters into man-made channels and irrigation ditches. Now they were busy on a new series of dams, and Moses stood and watched the workmen, goaded at their derricks in the blazing sun. He saw a Hebrew laborer, feeling exhausted, crawl into a freshly dug trench and lie there for a moment resting. But the gang boss appeared, spied the prone figure in the shadow, and shouting to him to stand up, began beating the man's naked back and stomach with a whip of copper-headed thongs.

Sudden rage erupted in Moses' soul, a blind fury, as irresistible as it was unexpected. Leaping upon the overseer, Moses broke the man's neck.

After burying the body of his victim in the sand, Moses, aghast at his own violence, returned home to struggle with his conscience. He had saved one life but he had taken another in consequence, and the mystery of the balance tormented him.

The next day he faced the very same problem again, when he found himself interfering in a quarrel between two Hebrew workmen, and one of them asked:

"Who made you a prince and a judge over us? Do you intend to kill me as you killed the Egyptian?"

So his bloody deed was known. Before long, in a land swarming with spies, it would come to the ears of Pharaoh. Moses must flee Egypt at once.

That same night Seti I heard of his murdered overseer and ordered Moses to be seized and put to death.

But Moses was already gone, hastening through darkness into desert country, heading first eastward, then south across the heights toward the blue, deceiving waters of the Bitter Lakes. Crossing the lakes, he fled on down the coast of the Sinai Peninsula, in the general direction of the copper and turquoise mining region.

And what talk there was in Seti's court of adopted children and how they are likely to turn out!

Ultimately the fugitive reached the land of the Midianites, two or three hundred miles across the desert, at the head of the Red Sea.

Moses, the future leader of the chosen tribes, could have gone to no better place to seek peace for his mind. In Midian he could try to forget the decadence of the Nile civilization, and invite his spirit in the bland quiet of open country. But a practical and immediate question plagued him in the midst of peace: he had brought little money and had only scant possessions—how was he to live?

Weary from his long journey, Moses sat resting at a well on the Midian frontier and slaked a long day's thirst, when there suddenly appeared seven maidens coming toward the well to water their flocks. Moses rubbed his dusty eyes and gave a low cry of admiration. These were seven extraordinarily beautiful girls. They did not see him, but chattered gaily among themselves, as they filled the troughs for their sheep. But several shepherds rushed at them as if to drive maidens and sheep away from the well.

"Hold!" cried Moses, and, though one against several, held them off while the girls finished their tasks. Maidens and rowdy shepherds were equally astonished; Moses, rising up among them, was like an apparition. But the shepherds were far from stupid; in Moses' travel-stained apparel they recognized the garb of a gentleman, a man of power; they were struck, too, by the authority of his tone, so they drifted off in one direction, while the girls herded their flocks the other way, hurrying home to tell Jethro, their father, of the handsome stranger who had come to their rescue.

Thus it happened that Jethro, the priest, made Moses welcome in Midian and gave him one of his daughters, Zipporah, whose name meant "A Little Bird," to be his wife. And Moses thought he would live and die with her, happily, peacefully, in the misty blue and gold valleys lost from the great world.

Time brought them two sons, Gershom and Eliezer, and when they grew old enough to understand, Moses loved to tell stories to his boys of the long ago, of his youth in the university and in the topmost midst of the luxury and wickedness of Egypt.

So "forty years" had sped by—a phrase often used by the Hebrews meaning not a precise reckoning of years but an indeterminate number. Forty years of uneventful home life, of wandering with flocks over the hilly slopes of the Midian country. Moses never tired of its contrasting rich pastures of grass and bare, bleak, rocky scarps and heights. Especially the sky-piercing mountain called Horeb, or Sinai, exerted an ever-compelling charm and thrill upon his imagination. For to Moses it seemed as if the mountain was the very dwelling place of the Lord God, the majestic peak looked like God's throne. But Moses had no premonition of a distant but coming storm, nor of his climb to the peak of that mountain and his own transcendent experience there. That time was still far off.

The Pharaoh died but after the coronation of Rameses II the condition of the Israelites only sank from bad to worse. With great fanfare the new Pharaoh proclaimed a building program: by the toil of enslaved workmen he would build a lofty temple, with a forest of towering columns, and still another temple to be hewn out of a sandstone cliff above the waters of the upper Nile, at the place known today as Abu Simbel, between the first and the second cataract. Colossal statues of the king must be hewn, mighty works to the glory of Rameses II, the most chuckleheaded shilly-shallier of the dynasty.

For years the children of Israel had been praying for the death of the Pharaoh Seti I; but now that the prayer was answered, tidings came to Moses by passing caravans, reporting the litany of afflicted people:

"They flog us! They flog us! They starve us! But there is One above Who will punish them!"

As he tended flocks on the lower slopes of the sacred mountain Moses looked often upward to the peaks, so remote, seemingly so stern, and prayed for justice. And one peaceful twilight, when the air was noisy with the drowsy quarrels of the birds, the herdsman beheld a remarkable phenomenon. A thorn bush suddenly burst into flame before his eyes; the fire burned bright and red in the midst of the bush, but the bush was not consumed.

The astonished Moses took a step forward but halted when he made out a misty figure appearing in the heart of the fire. A Voice, not of this earth, a Voice he had never heard before, came out of the burning bush:

"Moses, Moses, draw not nigh hither. Put off your shoes from off your feet, for the place whereon you stand is holy ground."

The Voice of Eden, the Voice that had spoken to Adam and Eve and the Serpent, to Cain and to Noah, to Abraham, Isaac, and Jacob, now clearly rose from the bush that was on fire. In fear and trembling, Moses covered his face, palms darkening his eyes.

"I have surely seen the affliction of my people which are in Egypt," said the Voice. "And I have heard their cry by reason of their taskmasters. And I have come down to deliver them out of the hand of the Egyptians, and to bring them up out of that land unto a good land and a large, unto a land flowing with milk and honey; unto the place of the Canaanites.

"Come now therefore, and I will send you unto Pharaoh, that you may bring forth my people, the children of Israel, out of Egypt."

That was more than the stricken Moses could believe.

"Who am I, that I should go to Pharaoh? And that I should bring forth the children of Israel out of Egypt?"

Said the Voice of the Lord God:

"Surely, I will be with you; and this shall be a token unto you that I have sent you; when you have brought forth the people out of Egypt, you shall serve God upon this mountain."

"But if I say to them, The God of your fathers has sent me to you, and they say, What is His name? what shall I say to them?"

And God said:

"I Am who Am. He said: Thus shalt thou say to the children of Israel: He who Is hath sent me to you."

And so it was; henceforth the Lord God of Abraham, Isaac, and Jacob was to be known as Yahweh (Jehovah)—I Am who Am, which, further interpreted is: "He who causes to exist what comes into existence."

Falling on his face at the utterance of the holy name, Moses listened spellbound to further instructions. Going down to Egypt, he was to gather together all the elders, the wise counselors of the enslaved people. First he must convince them and win them to his mission. Then he would be ready to ask for an audience with Pharaoh.

Moses, even while prostrate in awe, was troubled in his soul. Wonderful, his commission was—to demand freedom for his people from the king; freedom to depart into the wilderness and find a new home for themselves where they would be free to worship the one true God —but how was it all to be managed, even with Jehovah's help? How were the thousands of the children of Israel to be provided for? Equipped, financed, provided for in their pioneering? They had no possessions to sell or pawn; in their poverty they owned nothing.

But the Voice replied to these unuttered questions. Moses was not to fret himself; the Egyptians owed more to the Israelites than could be paid back in a hundred years, and they would be mysteriously influenced to give of their own food and goods—even their golden ornaments—when needed. Moses must trust.

Trusting Jehovah, but not himself, in this tremendous task, Moses again objected:

"But who will listen to me? They will not believe me when I tell these things."

"What is that in your hand?"

"A rod."

"Cast it on the ground."

When the little staff lay on the ground it suddenly began to squirm, a living thing: a serpent. And Moses shrank from it.

"Put forth your hand and take it by the tail," commanded the Lord. And bending down to do so, Moses saw that the serpent had become a rod again. As if that test were not enough to drown his skepticism, the Lord told Moses to thrust his hand into his bosom and when he withdrew it knuckles and thumb were leprous; a second thrust and the hand was healed.

Power for himself to do these wonders was promised Moses to convince those who would doubt his message. If such signs failed to win credence he was to pour water of the Nile on dry land where it would be changed to blood. Such mysteries would greatly impress the people, Moses knew. But he also felt sure that the wonder-loving Egyptians had glib tongues and would try to talk him down.

"But I am not eloquent, O my Lord; I am slow of speech."

"Who has made man's mouth? Have not I, the Lord?" thundered the Voice from the burning bush. "Therefore go, and I will be with your mouth, and teach you what you shall say."

Not Abraham, not Isaac, not Jacob had ever shown such reluctance to trust and to obey the divine will. Still patient, the Voice told the slow-tongued Moses that his brother Aaron would join him and be his spokesman, but—

"You shall speak unto him, and put words into his mouth. And he shall be your spokesman unto the people: and he shall be, even he shall be to you instead of a mouth, and you shall be to him instead of God."

What more could he want, this uncertain Moses? The fact was Moses did not yet know his strength, as an instrument of divine power. He heard the last words of the Voice, bidding him:

"Take this rod in your hand, wherewith you shall do signs."

Then everything instantly changed.

It was as if Moses had been in heaven and now was back on earth, standing alone. Gone the solemn silence that had lasted for so long; now he heard again the familiar sounds, buzz of insects, bird calls, and the bleating of lambs. Gone the mysterious fire; the thorn bush, no longer flaming, shuddered gently, unsinged, all green and bright in the gloaming wind. Had it all been a dream? Moses, a humble man, could not believe that God had chosen him.

Lying on the ground, fallen from nerveless fingers, lay the rod of Moses. Had that staff actually been a serpent for a few seconds— Moses picked it from the ground. Something in the feel of the gnarled wood made his palm tingle; it felt alive, what seemed dead wood.

With the least possible delay, Moses, taking his wife and their two sons, set out for Egypt. When he arrived in the delta city of Tanis, Moses noted many changes made during the forty years of his absence. Most disturbing was the unhappy air, not only of enslaved Jews, but of the Egyptians themselves; even nobles, carried in gilded chairs, looked furtive and sad. Rameses II was a tyrant over everybody.

Of course Moses, too, was changed. He was eighty years old now and silver-gray, and Aaron, his brother, was three years older. As promised, Aaron had met up with Moses in the desert and his enthusiasm for the great project was heartening.

Secretly from Tanis an appeal was sent to the elders of Israel, asking them to meet the brothers, to hear a supernatural message. Would they come to the underground conclave? Moses had his doubts. By now they were a cynical lot, those enslaved leaders of slaves; they had waited for God's help for so long and had known so many bitter disappointments. But most of them came to the clandestine convention.

With stern faces they listened while Aaron, mouthpiece for his brother, spoke with passionate eloquence and performed signs of breath-taking wonder. But some said afterward that it was the silent presence of Moses, a natural leader, that inspired their feeling of devotion. Convinced in spite of themselves, the elders promised to arrange a larger meeting.

Such a conventicle would be difficult, but there did exist an underground system—as always among the downtrodden. So not long afterward a large crowd of Israelites assembled in their place of worship, and the words and wonders of Aaron were repeated. Hearing the news that the one true God of their fathers had commissioned these brothers to redress their wrongs, they began to beat their breasts and to prostrate themselves in prayer.

"Go unto Pharaoh," they cried. "Tell him of our Lord God, and that we are in His hands and you are the ministers of His will."

Upright and disdainful on his golden-lion throne, his slim body clad in jeweled arrogance, Rameses II stonily regarded the two gray-bearded Jews.

Like a deaf man, he heard the tale of a burning bush and a Voice in the flame. Then he called for a perfumed brazier as if to fumigate the throne room of superstition brought there by these two witless fanatics. What they were calmly asking for was nothing less than the ruin of his dream—his building program that was to blazon his fame to the ends of the earth forever. Did these two fools think that any ruler in his right senses would give up so profitable an asset as enforced labor?

"Who is this Lord that I should obey His voice to let Israel go? I do not recognize Him, neither will I let Israel go."

Moses whispered in the ear of his brother, and Aaron spoke again:

"We pray you let us go three days' journey into the desert and sacrifice to the Lord our God. Or there may be pestilence—or the toll of the sword."

Rameses was at once in a passion. Did these wretches dare to threaten Egypt, so that his laborers might be released for a desert holiday? Idlers, they were. Their burdens would be made heavier. Go now, Aaron and Moses!

That same day the infuriated Rameses issued orders that thereafter straw be withheld from Israelite brickmakers, but the output of bricks must not be diminished an iota. Bricks without straw! How? The lives of the brickmakers were already miserable enough; they can be seen depicted at their perspiring toil in a wall painting of the tomb of one Rekhmises, displayed in the Egyptian section of New York's Metropolitan Museum of Art. And in the British Museum there are actual bricks from Egypt, still showing the straw that was a part of their composition under the manufacturing process then in vogue.

How could the Jews make brick without straw? It was a necessary portion of the process. They knew no other. This order of Pharaoh must be the malice of a madman.

As they were hustled out of the throne room Moses and Aaron knew that they had failed. But they had perfect faith, far more than the oppressed people whose leaders they now were. As soon as life grew harder to bear—and before long they were being beaten with whips because production of bricks was falling off—these slaves turned on Moses:

"Only hatred have you brought upon us," they wailed, denouncing him as with one voice. "You put a sword in Pharaoh's hand to smite us! So let us alone, that we may obey the Egyptians."

"Have you forgotten the Lord?" asked Moses.

"Why did the Lord not change Pharaoh's heart when we petitioned for mercy?"

Alone in prayer, and in deepest humility, Moses himself questioned the one true God:

"Why is it that since I have come to Egypt to do as I was bidden nothing but evil has come of it? The children of Israel are not delivered from bondage, and I know not what to do or say."

Within his soul Moses heard the Voice reply:

"Now shall you see what I will do to Pharaoh: for with a strong hand shall he let them go, and with a strong hand shall he drive them out of his land."

"Greater than all the kings of the earth is the Lord God, there is no strength equal unto His," murmured Moses.

"Say unto the children of Israel, I am the Lord, and will bring you out from under the burdens of the Egyptians, and I will rid you of their bondage, and I will redeem you with a stretched-out arm, and with great judgments.

"And I will take you to me for a people, and I will be to you a God; Lord your God, which brings you out from under the burdens of Egypt.

"And I will bring you in unto the land, concerning the which I did swear to give to Abraham, to Isaac, and to Jacob; and I will give it to you for an heritage. I am the Lord."

But the children of Israel were too low in spirit to take fire from Moses' glowing story of this latest interview. They were at the bottom of human misery and they had no more hope. They were the absolute slaves of that Rameses II whose gigantesque statue portrait they were hacking out from black rock; not one but four statues of the Pharaoh are still there, and each one sixty-five feet high. A mighty ruler, this Rameses II—and he did not believe in the one true God, who was the Father of the slaves. Pharaoh had crushed hope and faith out of the children of the one true God and they wanted no more of Him, nor of Moses and his supernatural messages.

Chapter 10 THE ESCAPE FROM EGYPT

MOSES again sought counsel, but God insisted he must not be discouraged. It was his job to continue his campaign in spite of the hostility of his own people; he would have to save them from themselves as well as the Egyptians:

"When Pharaoh shall speak unto you, saying, Show a miracle for you: then shall you say unto Aaron, Take your rod, and cast it before Pharaoh, and it shall become a serpent."

Which was what did happen. In the hostile atmosphere of the throne room, and before the arrogant king and his court, the two Israelites bowed, and Aaron's wand miraculously turned into a snake. But there was no awe, only laughter, as Pharaoh's court magicians bent double with their mirth. After all, they cackled, this is an old and familiar feat; these Hebrew brothers must think we are simpletons. And the Egyptian sorcerers threw down their own wands and they, too, became snakes.

But all sniggering and mockery ended abruptly when the rod-serpent of Moses and his brother swallowed up the others.

With an irritated wave of the hand Pharaoh dismissed Aaron and Moses, while his eyes turned balefully toward his disconcerted court conjurers. For a long time he had suspected that they were no more than sleight-of-hand performers, their alleged miracles only tricks of skill. Now, in defeat, they stood glum and fearful, as the king swept silently out of his throne room. For many a long hour he sat alone, fretful and weary.

Why had he not ordered those two Hebrews put to death? Why did he go on granting them hostile hearings? Why did he permit them to plague him with their appeals?

Once the brothers came suddenly upon him at his daily bath in the river, to repeat their demand that he let the Israelites go from under his rule. Else, Moses had the audacity to warn him, the river of his bath, and all the waters of Egypt, would be turned into blood, as by one stroke of the rod.

Pharaoh scoffed at the threat, and the immediate result was frightening even to Moses and Aaron. On that day, river, stream, and pond, everywhere in the land, turned red and stinking with dead fish. The people were anguished with thirst, and all over Egypt they began to dig in the ground, seeking new wells and springs of unpolluted water. Nevertheless, Pharaoh remained obstinate, sure that the blight would pass, which it did; within seven days the bloodlike waters turned clear.

So the king felt he had lived through the worst.

But not yet! There came a second plague, and frogs covered the country outdoors and indoors, infesting yards, stables, bedrooms, and kitchens, even the kneading troughs of the royal bakers. This time the surly Pharaoh sent for Moses and Aaron:

"Entreat the Lord your God that He take away the frogs that pester our lives—and I will let your people go that they may sacrifice unto Him."

Moses did not trust the word of the king, but he acted as if he did, giving him the benefit of the doubt.

"Appoint the hour and it shall be done," said Moses, hoping that a release from the plague, arriving on schedule, would be wonder enough really to impress the tyrant for good and all.

"Tomorrow."

So be it! So be it, Pharaoh, that you may know that there is none like unto the Lord our God.

And Rameses, the Pharaoh, should have been startled, and to the very roots of his soul. For what Moses promised, God fulfilled for him. On schedule, the plague ended. Frogs that failed to reach the waters died throughout the land; millions of dead ones had to be gathered into heaps and burned. For days the land stank with their corruption.

But the Pharaoh, Rameses, was the least impressionable of all men. The minute the nuisance was abated he abandoned his word. Why, indeed, should he release an army of laborers just on account of a horde of frogs that had come and gone? Aye—his ministers agreed. The Jews would not be allowed to go into the desert and worship. Even as Pharaoh so decided, the Voice of God was speaking to Moses and Aaron again:

"Stretch out your rod, and smite the dust of the land that it may become gnats."

Now, everywhere in Egypt, man and beast were tormented by insects. No wonder that Pharaoh began seriously to distrust the power of his court magicians. He thought of sending to foreign lands, seeking more powerful sorcerers to best these plagueful Jewish brothers. Or perhaps he might hire the brothers themselves, the two to serve him with their astonishing capacity—he could pay them to forget all about their enslaved people. But that attempt would be only a last resort; it might even be suicidal to keep such men of power too close to himself.

There never was such a whirligig of scares, and broken promises, before or since. When Moses rid the kingdom of vermin the king again denounced his own pledge—and so it was with a whole succession of afflictions:

Biting swarms of flies that got into eyes and ears and mouths of all except the children of Israel; boils breaking out on the bodies of the Egyptians and their beasts; and then a prolonged storm of unheard-of violence; hail with thunder and lightning, bringing general ruin except in Goshen, where the Jews lived; everywhere else the tempest drowned animals and crops; and next, when clear blue heavens rolled again over Egypt, an onrush of clouds of locusts, droning and buzzing, filling the air and consuming all that which had escaped the hail—the wheat, the rye, and the leaves and fruit of every tree. At last Rameses' advisers took courage to ask:

"How long is this man Moses to wreak his will on us? Let the Israelites go! And serve their powerful God!"

Testily, obstinate Pharaoh recalled the brothers and seemed to give in:

"By all the gods of Egypt, you may go into the wilderness, but I must know how many and who."

"All of us," said Moses, refusing any compromise. "Young and old. Sons and daughters. And our flocks and herds, for all must participate in the sacrifice and the feast."

The gorge of the king was rising again; he would have liked to have Moses hanged by the heels in the market place.

"So be it," he agreed grimly, meaning to keep his word no more now than before. But this time the Lord God did not wait. He commanded Moses to use the rod of power at once and call up an east wind. Before next day's noon a gale was blowing from off the desert and the air was darkened with a new mass of ravenous brown insects. Everything green and edible began to vanish as Pharaoh sent his swiftest chariot drivers scurrying everywhere to round up those two implacable Hebrew brothers.

"Pray forgive my sin again," he begged. "And entreat the Lord your God once more——"

Once more through the long-suffering patience of God, Rameses was granted a reprieve. A strong west wind came and blew all the insects like chaff into the Red Sea. Not one insect was left. That should have settled everything. But alas, no! Pharaoh's changeable spirit reverted to its incorrigible obstinacy. There would be no royal permission for the children of Israel to leave.

Promptly, as if God were tired of this traitorous liar, darkness spread over all the land, all of it except Goshen. In a blackness like a vast hole in the earth the Egyptians found themselves lost. No sunrise, no moonrise, no meridian glare, but three days of impenetrable darkness. While many ordinary folk remained fearfully in bed, messengers of Pharaoh with torches of knotted pine lighted their way to Moses.

"Go! Go! Go!" the king cried when once more Moses stood before him. In the wavering light of the torch-lit throne room his frightened face had not yet lost his cunning. He still wanted to bargain. "Take old and young—but your flocks and herds shall stay behind."

"No," said Moses. "We require sacrifices and burnt offerings."

"If we refuse?"

"Then," replied Moses solemnly, "consider what I shall say with all your mind and heart: the Lord God will take all the first-born of the Egyptians, and the first-born of all their beasts, and they shall die together overnight."

With a snort of rage Pharaoh arose, his reddening face and bulging eyes frightening to witness.

"Get you gone! And take heed never to see my face again, for on that day you shall die!"

And Moses answered:

"It is wisely spoken that we meet no more."

Leaving Pharaoh, thus fairly warned of the tenth and most terrible of the plagues, Moses hastened back to the elders. There was, he told them, no time to lose. They must begin at once instructing the Israelite people just what they must do in preparation against the certain coming of their deliverance from bondage. He urged every Jew in

Egypt to believe him; the time would not be long, and much was to be accomplished. In secret, children, cattle, goods must be made ready for immediate flight. Meanwhile they would all be wise to solicit gifts of useful articles, as well as ornaments of gold and silver, which would be valuable for trading in the long journeyings that would be before them.

Asked for such contributions, the Egyptian neighbors in Goshen were generous. They, too, had come to esteem Moses as a great leader, as, indeed, had many of the other inhabitants. Later some of them were to cast in their lot with the departing Israelites.

By now the Hebrews trusted Moses completely. Without protest they accepted a change he ordered in their calendar; thereafter the time we know as April was to be their first month of the year. And now he gave a confidential command for every household. On the fourteenth evening of April a male lamb without blemish was to be killed and eaten, after its blood had been sprinkled on the lintel and doorposts of the house of every Jew in Egypt.

"None shall go out at the door of his house until the morning," Moses further ordered. "For the Lord will pass through to smite the Egyptians; and when He sees the blood upon the lintel and on the two side posts, the Lord will pass over the door, and will not suffer the destroyer to come in unto your houses. And you shall observe this thing for an ordinance to you and your sons forever."

The Lord would not smite the Jewish first-born, the angel of death would pass over their houses—this was the sign and meaning of the "pass over."

In awe and worship the children of Israel promised to obey the instructions. There were other important duties they were taught, particularly as to the last meal they were to eat in Egypt, the passover meal that was forever after to be a memorial of deliverance from bondage. A thousand years later the passover meal would become the occasion for a new testament of grace, the blood and the wine, the real presence, the Holy Communion—passover, passion, resurrection.

All these great events of the soul began with the first paschal meal, as ordered by Moses while he talked with the leaders of the Israelites. The flesh of the lamb must be roasted, and eaten with unleavened bread, and the first azyme, the Jewish parched loaf, must be eaten with bitter herbs. If any morsel of it be left, it must be burnt up before morning. In case of need, neighbors were to share their lamb. Whatever the group, wherever and forever thereafter, until the real and ultimate Pasch of the Last Supper, the ritualistic and memorial meal should be eaten only when all the eaters had first dressed, as if for travel, shoes on, staff in hand.

At midnight, April fourteenth, death seized the first-born of the Egyptians. The boy firstlings of high families and low, from the golden palace of Pharaoh to the lowliest hovel of the slaves, all alike withered suddenly and died, alive one moment, gone the next—and soon lamentations and maledictions were echoing and re-echoing everywhere throughout the land.

"Let the children of Israel go!" was the haunted cry of woe. "Let them go!"

And Pharaoh Rameses II was convinced at last; to him this man Moses seemed indeed deipotent, possessed of some godlike power. There must be no more equivocation; Rameses that passover night was as frightened as the feeblest beggar in his kingdom.

Not even waiting for dawn, Pharaoh rose from his bed and commanded Moses and Aaron and their host, all six hundred thousand of them, to get out at once. Officers, dragged from sleep and cursing, cracked their whips and yelled to round up the slaves and drive them beyond the border, with their belongings and their cattle. Hebrew women had to rush away, carrying on their backs their kneading troughs, their dough still unleavened.

In spite of the dark hullabaloo, the children of Israel were joyous. It was four hundred and thirty years, even to the day, since their forefathers had come down into Egypt, and now they were going home again.

The sun was high up and so was the heart of Moses as with brave step and proud he marched and danced at the head of the long column, intoning prayers of thankfulness as they filed through the gates that breached the walls of the capital. With them the elders were carrying sacred relics including the four-hundred-year-old bones of Joseph to be buried anew when they reached the Promised Land.

Under supernatural guidance, Moses shunned the short route toward Palestine, for that way they might encounter armed garrisons or be attacked by bandits. Instead, Moses led the host in a southerly direction. When time came to rest they pitched tents at Etham, with the yellow vastness of the Arabian Desert shimmering in the distance.

For the first week all was pleasant. But as the days passed the sun grew hotter and the nights colder with the icelike piercing desert wind called the sarsar blowing in their faces, freezing to the bone. The people complained. They were also beginning to be afraid, like escaped prisoners feeling homesick for cells and chains. Suppose they were to perish in the desert. How could they be sure of the right way when there was neither path nor signpost but only emptiness? The answer came from Heaven:

"And the Lord went before them in a pillar of cloud by day and a pillar of fire by night."

That was a queer sight—a moving pillar of white vapor, moving ahead with gliding speed, showing the route to be followed. And when, because distant springs must be reached before they could bivouac and night had fallen, they must march in darkness, the cloud-white column changed into a tall plume of fire. They could follow that supernatural torch, on and on through the night, until their watery goal, their oasis, was reached. This pillar of cloud by day, of fire by night, was a continual reminder to the people of the supernatural guidance under which they journeyed, and upon whose direction they must depend, rather than upon their own plans and schemes.

Reaching the water's edge at last, they pitched their tents to rest for a season. This was the Red Sea, named for a sedge plant with long grasslike leaves that stained the tides a dull crimson. The pillar of cloud and fire was gone, and now the people began to wonder how they were ever to get across the Red Sea. In boats? If so, where were the boats? There was also a growing rumor, a report spreading like a contagion, that they were not safe, and never would be, until they could get across those roaring waters, out of the reach of possible pursuit by the Egyptians.

Why did not Moses do something about it? Should they just sit there and wait to be taken again?

Even as the weary, distrustful Israelites sat and speculated, Pharaoh and his chariots were already coming after them in hot pursuit. Once again mighty Rameses had changed his mind. The moment his Jewish slave laborers were gone he wanted them back, and with his army he was rushing to overtake them.

There was now to occur one of the most extraordinary events in human and superhuman history.

Looking inland from the coast, the Hebrew campers saw distant swirls of dust and caught the gleam of spears. Terrible fear spread among them. Tongues began to clamor for appeasement, for going back:

"Are we to die in the wilderness like dogs? Why, oh, why

did we ever leave Egypt? Did we not say to Moses, let us alone that we may serve the Egyptians?"

For forty years they were seldom to leave off doubting and distrusting and repudiating their amazing leader, this Moses who had led them out Egypt; who would give them laws, rule them through difficult and bitter years, and lay the foundation of their religion, the greatest human figure in their history. They were too close to him to take his height.

"Fear not," Moses assured them in their panic. "Stand still, and see the salvation of the Lord, which He will show you today. The Lord shall fight for you. Hold your peace!"

Even while he spoke the guiding pillar of cloud appeared again, descending between the encampment and the approaching chariots, still a few miles away. For the rest of the night it remained in that strange position. Twilight having fallen, Moses stretched the rod toward the waters of the Red Sea.

And the Lord God sent upon them a strong east wind with a rushing sound like the noise of wings. The wind came to divide the waters of the Red Sea, making a pathway of dry land for His people's feet. Through walls of water on either side, the Jews followed their pillar of fire in the darkness through the deep, safely to the opposite shore.

Meanwhile, in the morning watch, when the army of Pharaoh broke camp and started to drive forward in furious speed, the Lord impeded the wheels of their chariots to such maddening extent that the drivers shouted to turn back, protesting that God of the Hebrews was invincible. But their captains forced them on, prodding their own drivers with arrow points.

And the Lord God spoke again to Moses:

"Stretch out your hand over the sea, that the waters may come again upon the Egyptians."

Moses raised his rod, just as the first Egyptians came hurling themselves down to the shore. When the Egyptian soldiers and chariots were out in the midst of the divided sea, the walls of water suddenly tumbled and collapsed, countless tons of water spilling upon the army of men, horses, and chariots, drowning all.

And Moses, standing with all his people safely on the farther coast of the sea that had swallowed up the last of the Egyptians, began to sing a little song:

"I will sing unto the Lord, for He has triumphed gloriously: the horse and his rider has He thrown into the sea."

Voice rising as he went on singing, he rehearsed all the signs of grace and power and favor that the Lord God had vouchsafed to the children of Israel, and he prophesied future blessings for their welfare. Soon the melody reached the people and they began to sing with him responsively, until Miriam, the sister of Moses and of Aaron, seized a timbrel in her hand, and the women followed her example. They struck the timbrels and they danced on the sand, while Miriam repeated the opening words of her brother's song:

"Sing you to the Lord, for He has triumphed gloriously: the horse and his rider has He thrown into the sea."

Now indeed, Moses thought, their troubles were all behind them.

On into the wilderness of Shur the great migration moved. Again the people complained, suffering cold by night and heat by day, and laid low by the recurring simoon—the hot, dry, exhausting wind of the desert.

Their way lay southward, following the gray sandy line of the coast. For three days they had no water to drink. They gave feeble cries of relief when at last, reaching a place called Marah, they came to glittering well pools of cool, inviting water. But the drink was bitter, unfit for human consumption, and remains so today; the Arabs and their camels will swallow none of it. In their raging thirst the Israelites turned against Moses again. Why had he brought them to these treacherous wells, in this abandoned spot, unfrequented by human beings? "At least in Egypt we never once knew thirst!"

Moses felt himself led to a curious tree. He stripped off some of its bark and dropped it into the wells, thus sweetening the bitter water, so that the people could drink their fill. Gratified but still tired and sullen, the wanderers were reluctant to push farther into the desert. Suppose that even more bitter water lay ahead? Or no water at all? With grim faces they followed Moses, meditating revolt with every step—until he brought them to Elim, with its twelve famous wells of sweet water, and seventy palm trees—a little taste of Paradise.

From this oasis it was even harder to get them going again. The wilderness called Sin (after the old moon god of the Babylonians) was a forbidding stretch of gray and yellow waste between Elim and Sinai. But Moses promised the people they were more than halfway to their goal, which was the Mountain of God, where everything would be made clear.

With regretful backward glances at Elim they trekked on behind Moses and into the sands of Sin. Blazing day succeeded blazing day. It was slow and painful plodding and food was growing scarcer. By the middle of May, a month after they had left Egypt, they began fresh complaints. Would that they had died in Egypt when they had at least a bit of bread in their stomachs! Did Moses and Aaron intend to kill them with hunger? Was plenty of water a substitute for bread?

The Lord God spoke to his harassed servant Moses:

"I will rain bread from heaven for you; and the people shall go out and gather a certain amount every day."

And afterward He spoke directly to the assembled people from a cloud of glory, addressing them through Moses, as his mouthpiece:

"At even you shall eat flesh, and in the morning you shall be filled with bread; and you shall know I am the Lord your God."

The meat they fed on was the flesh of quail; thousands of birds miraculously began to fall each evening into their midst. And a strange nourishing dew dropped like hoarfrost in the morning and hardened into a honey-flavored bread.

"Look, it is manna!" cried the marveling Israelites.

"Yes, this the bread which the Lord has provided," Moses told them. "And he commanded that you shall gather it each morning for six days, but on the seventh, the holy Sabbath, there shall be none to gather; therefore on the sixth you shall gather twice as much against the Lord's Day."

And so thereafter, during the long wanderings of these volatile and distracted and refractory people through the wilderness, they were never hungry again. They ate of what the region could provide them, or what they could buy, but when harvests failed and no barter was possible they still had their fill, with manna to sustain them.

Traveling southeastward, the wandering people encountered new trouble when they pitched their tents at Rephidim. Their skins of water were exhausted and no sign of spring or pool anywhere to be seen. Past blessings all again forgotten, the murmurs arose:

"Give us water."

"Why did we ever leave the Nile?"

"Have we been brought all these weary miles only to die of thirst—we, our children, and our cattle?"

But Moses, as always, turned unfalteringly to the Lord, and the answer came instantly. He was to take his rod in hand, and calling elders and people together, smite with it a certain rock to which he would be led. They all gathered in front of a great, dark boulder, and Moses towered before them.

On the slab of granite he smote twice with his rod of power—and himself was startled and amazed at the instantaneous result. Almost before his hand was lifted water began to trickle forth from a fissure in the rock, and the trickle became a flow, clear and cool and sparkling, a silver fall in the desert sun, pouring forth with a bubbling song, like a newborn spring, gushing more plenteously, as if enough to fertilize the whole desert.

As the emigrants plodded once more across the land from Rephidim they were attacked, again and again, by outposts of a fierce tribe of Amalekites, descendants of Jacob's brother Esau. The Amalekites kept making little forays in the rear of the Israelite ranks, falling upon stragglers and making slaves of them.

"Choose your men of valor and go out against these wicked marauders," Moses said, addressing one of his younger men, a coming leader, he felt sure, whose name was Joshua. "And while you wage battle I will stand on the top of this hill with the rod of God in my hand."

"The Amalekites shall rue the day," predicted Joshua, who had already shown himself a fearless warrior and true believer. Swiftly the young captain organized a fighting force and confronted the raiders, themselves eager for combat and spoils. With frenzied war cries the foes rushed together and clashed in the midst of sand and rocks, while from a distant height civilian Israelites watched the ebb and flow, retreat and advance.

Most often they fixed their eyes on three figures upon the topmost hill overlooking the battlefield, where Moses stood with Aaron and Hur, who was Miriam's husband, at either side of him. Whenever Moses lifted up his rod the advantage would be with Joshua and his fighters, but if he let down the rod, even a little, the Amalekites would begin to get the best of it. Hours were passing without decisive victory, and the arms of the aging Moses had grown tired and numb. Aaron and Hur persuaded the old leader to sit on a stone, while they took turns holding up his hand with the rod in it. And so it was, until at sunset victory came to the forces of Joshua. The enemy was routed.

Soon Mount Sinai, the appointed place of the Lord God, as He had specified to Moses a year before, rose before them in desolate and awesome majesty. The region at its base was fertile and pleasant, compared to the wastes they had traveled over, and besides, Moses felt himself at home here, where he had spent forty happy years. There was a joyous reunion with his wife Zipporah and his two sons, and his father-in-law Jethro, the priest of Midian.

To his family Moses told his story: his adventures with Pharaoh, and how ten plagues had devasted Egypt, the deaths of the first-born sons and the Passover; the parting of the waters of the Red Sea for the safe passage of the Israelites and the drowning of Pharaoh's army; the pillar of cloud and of fire.

No one could have been prouder of his son-in-law than Jethro, but he was distressed to see how many people harassed and overwhelmed Moses with their problems and troubles. Childlike, they turned to their leader for everything; all day long he had to sit, listening, advising, judging, until exhaustion forbade more.

"Laws and ordinances can be taught the people," Jethro declared, "and the ways of righteousness explained by able men that you shall choose and instruct. Use men of truth, hating covetousness. Place them, according to their abilities, over groups large and small. They shall be judges, and you their final authority."

Before Jethro left for his home in Midian he saw the practical application of his advice: judges were chosen to render advice and decisions, with Moses appealed to only in the most difficult causes and disputes, himself the first supreme court.

Fortunately that relief gave Moses more time to seek the help of the Lord God on Sinai, for the stupendous events that loomed not far ahead.

Chapter 11 THE TEN COMMANDMENTS

THE people liked their place of latest encampment and wanted to stay there. It was a fair land, with springs both deep and sweet; herds and flocks could pasture well; a good place to settle down. But Moses, keeping his own counsel, went off, mysteriously up the mountain fastnesses with its solemn solitude.

Upward the white-bearded leader was clambering; an urgent impulse was drawing him breathlessly ever higher up the Sinai steeps to revisit the spot where a thornbush had burned and was not consumed. What God had promised then—what had seemed impossible—was accomplished; the children of Israel were no longer slaves in Egypt.

He must thank God on the spot where he had received his commission.

As he labored nearer to the top of the mountain Moses could make out, near his right hand, the aerie of some gray and bloated predatory bird, standing guard over enormous eggs and flapping her wings against the sun and the wind and the immensity of distance all around them. He could stagger up only a few steps more when he heard the Voice:

"Moses! Moses!"

"Here am I, Lord," gasped Moses.

"Thus shall you say to the House of Jacob, and tell the children of Israel:

"You have seen what I did unto the Egyptians, and how I bare you on eagles' wings, and brought you unto Myself. Now, therefore, if you will obey My Voice indeed, and keep My covenant, then you shall be unto Me, above all people, a peculiar treasure; and you shall be unto Me a kingdom of priests and an holy nation. These are the words which you shall speak unto the children of Israel."

The Voice ended and Moses knew he would hear no more that day. Raising himself from the stony ground, on which he had fallen prostrate, Moses gazed around at the far horizon, the gracious prediction of the unearthly Voice still ringing in his ears:

". . . you shall be unto Me a peculiar treasure . . . you shall be unto Me a kingdom of priests and an holy nation."

And with that divine promise to confide, Moses turned and started back; all the way down the mountainside he was in such ecstasy that his body seemed without weight.

Once again in camp, he immediately called a meeting of the elders. Mighty and solemn the message sounded to the weary desert wanderers. The children of Israel were to be the chosen people of the Lord forever. But they must so live that they would be an example for all the nations of the earth. At once the elders realized the dangers and difficulties in this divine singling out, how vast a burden it might prove. Who could fail to recall the faults and weaknesses of the sands? They could be stubborn and wayward and stiff-necked.

Why had the Lord God chosen them over all the others? And why did God need a covenant with creatures that He had brought into being and whom He could destroy, as with the thought of one second? Moses could not answer the questions; all that he could do was to hold fast to conviction and faith; he had been before, and would be again, in touch with the Voice of universal truth. The intrepid leader told the wanderers that he felt secure and at peace; moreover, that his own guidance was at once personal, intimate—and divine.

All this Moses first told the elders, but next morning at daybreak the trumpet was sounded for general assembly; the people came running from the tents to learn the news. When Moses delivered to them the purport of Yahweh's message from Mount Sinai a shout rose as from one throat:

"We will do all that the Lord desires!"

The face of Moses beamed with pride and joy.

"Blessed be the name of the Lord God," he said fervently.

Aaron and Hur went with Moses to the foot of Mount Sinai, but there he parted from them, waving them back, as he resumed his solitary climb upward. Brother and brother-in-law promised to return and await Moses at dusk in the same place.

On this climb Moses did not have to go far, however, before the Voice called to him. The leader of the Israelites told his news; the people were grateful and would make a new covenant, to serve the Lord God. Then came a new divine proposal:

"Lo, I shall come unto you in a thick cloud, that the people may hear when I speak with you and believe you forever."

For such extraordinary manifestation the people would have to be prepared, and the Voice gave clear directions. They were to wash their bodies and sanctify their thoughts. For two days they must indulge in no sensual pleasures. On the third day the Lord God would appear at Mount Sinai in such a way that all would be made aware of His presence. But care must be taken that none of the Israelites should come too near to the mountain. The limits of approach must be made clear.

Trespass by these excitable people on the sacred ground which Yahweh would occupy would mean death.

All of these rules were explained by Moses when he got back to the encampment. The elders agreed to draw the boundary lines and issued strict warnings.

It was encouraging how little disorder there was, as the great hour drew near. The throngs foregathered at appointed places on the plain from which Moses led them in solemn procession to the foot of the Mountain of God—but at a careful distance behind the boundary lines.

Again there rose a prolonged blast from the trumpet; in the slow dawn it had an eerie sound. Then suddenly the mountaintop blazed with fire. Clouds of black smoke bloomed over the great rocks and filled the deep ravines. What was happening? Why such an uproar, louder than any heard since the winds roared over Noah's roof? And why the flame and smoke, to terrify thousands of men, women, and children at the base of Mount Sinai? Why, Moses?

Moses knew the character of his people, their volatile emotions, their susceptibility, "the hardness of their hearts."

And God knew what would impress them.

So lightning split the dark sky, and thunders seemed to tumble heaven, and the quaking earth shook while cattle and sheep pranced across the meadows. The children of Israel clung speechless, one to another, while Moses again toiled up Mount Sinai—"altogether on a smoke because the Lord had descended upon it in fire."

And then the Voice of the Lord called to Moses. He was commanded again to warn priests and people not to trespass on holy ground, across the barrier lines. But the assembled Israelites showed no sign of surging forward. Rather, they shrank back and listened, as the Voice addressed Moses as leader of the people, who were trustees of the future for all mankind:

"I am the Lord your God, who has brought you out of the land of Egypt, out of the house of bondage.

"You shall have no other gods before Me.

"You shall not make unto you any graven image, or any likeness of anything that is in heaven above, or that is in the earth beneath, or that is in the water under earth; you shall not bow down yourself to them: For I the Lord your God am a jealous God, visiting the iniquity of the fathers upon the children unto the third and fourth generation of them that hate Me; and showing mercy unto thousands of them that love Me, and keep My commandments.

"You shall not take the name of the Lord your God in vain; for the Lord will not hold him guiltless that takes His name in vain.

"Remember the Sabbath day, to keep it holy. Six days shall you labor, and do all your work: But the seventh day is the Sabbath of the Lord your God: in it you shall not do any work, you, nor your son, nor your daughter, your manservant, nor your maidservant, nor your cattle, nor any stranger that is within your gates; for in six days the Lord made heaven and earth, the sea, and all that in them is, and rested the seventh day: therefore the Lord blessed the Sabbath day, and hallowed it.

"Honor your father and your mother; that your days may be long upon the land which the Lord your God gives you.

"You shall not kill.

"You shall not commit adultery.

"You shall not steal.

"You shall not bear false witness against your neighbor.

"You shall not covet your neighbor's house, you shall not covet your neighbor's wife, nor his manservant, nor his maidservant, nor his ox, nor his ass, nor anything that is your neighbor's."

The Voice spoke again, of more detailed rules for the Israelites, supplementing the great edicts demanding purity of worship, righteousness, justice, good will, and brotherhood. A restatement of the code of behavior already written in the human heart had come to mankind.

Of the divine orders, none impressed the recent slaves of Egypt more than the injunction against false gods: the absolute command against worship of images and idols. From the early days of their forefathers, as modern excavations prove, it had been the custom and practice of some of the people to possess household images, wear charms and amulets, and rely on other symbols. That was because Mesopotamia, Canaan, and Egypt had presented a choice of innumerable deities, and it was hard for a simple folk to conceive of an invisible God with no concrete representation. Such a spiritual conception had been beyond the grasp of many. They would have to look to Moses, friend and instrument of invisible Jehovah, for guidance in this revolutionary idea.

Moses would expound the tremendous import of the Ten Commandments, as a personal code for each man, yet universal, the foundation for an ideal society and harmony between heaven and earth.

Later Moses would give them an additional commandment:

"The Lord our God is one Lord: and you shall love the Lord your God with all your heart, and with all your soul, and with all your might," adding another later which One greater than Moses was one day to quote: "You shall love your neighbors as yourself. On these two commandments hang all the law and the prophets."

The children of Israel, having received the Ten Commandments, were still far from their Promised Land. And meanwhile Moses was receiving more and more of a long list of regulations for the people to follow, rules insuring health and safety for body, mind, and soul; ordinances for religious worship and laws to govern the social life of Israel. Moses must be ready to record these rules when the time came. And in the midst of making the code of the covenant, for the first time there began to dawn in the minds of the fretful wanderers the idea that God is to be loved, rather than merely feared. This conception was full of ennoblement and added exciting interest to all that was happening.

An altar of unhewn stone was to be erected; unhewn because any tool lifted upon it would be as pollution. Nor should any Israelite go up to the altar by steps. These were rules amplifying the basic law given to Moses from the hand of God. The first fruits were to be given to the Lord God and three sacred holidays were to be observed yearly: the Feast of Unleavened Bread, or Passover; the Feast of Harvest, otherwise called the Feast of Weeks, identical with Pentecost, to be observed on the fiftieth day of the Passover, another commemoration of delivery from Egypt, and the Feast of Ingathering, or Tabernacles.

When the Promised Land of Palestine finally came into possession of the Israelites, they were to allot its produce to the poor every seventh year.

Human servitude must be limited. Laws would be required for the rights of servants under bond to a master; the slave could be bound to the proprietor for six years only; in his sabbatical year he must be free to go.

Justice was also to be watchful over what was done for the widow, the orphan, and the stranger. Their rights must be upheld; the poor must receive help, kindness, and consideration.

Even any enemy must fairly dealt with.

False reports were to be forbidden, as well as lending support to irresponsible mobs.

Usury was to be prohibited, and decent rules enforced for borrowing and credit.

Spiritualism, traffic with ghosts and mediums, and what passed for phantasms of the dead, all must be avoided as a spiritual pestilence.

The divine clauses ring with beauty and authority:

"If a stranger sojourn with you in your land you shall not vex him; but the stranger that dwells with you shall be unto you as one born among you, and you shall love him as yourself, for you were strangers in the land of Egypt: I am the Lord your God.

"And if you sell aught unto your neighbor, or buy aught of your neighbor's hand, you shall not oppress one another, but shall fear your God, for I am the Lord.

"Regard not them that have familiar spirits, neither seek after wizards, to be defiled by them."

Crimes against life and property were to be codified, and penalties exacted for murder, theft, burglary, arson, and all kinds of trespass. Likewise, injuries to or from animals, as of an ox, were to be carefully weighed and released. The law of retaliation (*lex talionis*) was to be enforced for any physical injury: "an eye for an eye, a tooth for a tooth, hand for hand and foot for foot."

This regulation of exact justice, far from being arbitrary and cruel, represented an immense ethical precision. Until Moses received the law from Mount Sinai, men set no limit on vengeance; one could have an eye for a tooth, if powerful enough to take it. Not until many more centuries of struggle would the full new dispensation come, the emphasis on mercy as a part of the divine law, and a duty of the redeemed.

Seduction of a virgin must bring her wifehood from the man who deceived her.

In all human relationships a high standard of justice was to be maintained, under the governance of a righteous God, Who had brought to His chosen people an ethical code immensely superior to any lawmaking in the world, including the statutes of King Hammurabi of Babylon, who had thought up a good code of his own and then ascribed it as divine law, as the gift of Shamash, his sun god.

The black stone monument of Hammurabi, presenting his code of law—six feet high it is, with its figures, the king and the god, on top—may be seen in all its three thousand years of dignity in the Louvre Museum in Paris. One cannot find anywhere the tablets of the law of the one true God which Moses was soon to receive. But Hammurabi's black diorite boulder with its three hundred paragraphs of legal pronouncements on commercial, social, domestic, and moral life is a dead thing, although prepared, as itself it declares, "That the strong might not injure the weak, and the widow, and that the widow and the orphan might be safe." A stone of dead letters is Hammurabi's wonderful code, but the Commandments of the Lord God of Israel remain potent in men's minds today, imperishable.

At no time did Moses speak as one with a superior mentality, laying down the law. He was conspicuous for his humility, his patience, and his obedience. That obedience of Moses was based on the deepest spiritual understanding.

In the Book of the Covenant which he drew up, as if under dictation, the children of Israel were to be solemnly exhorted to render obedience if they would be brought into the land promised their fathers. An angel of the Lord would go before them, as earlier the cloud by day and the pillar of fire by night had guided them through the wilderness. Various enemies they would find resident in the promised land of milk and honey—Amorites, Hittites, Perizzites, Canaanites, Hivites, and Jebusites—but all these would be driven out, little by little.

Having descended from Sinai, and the presence of Jehovah, Moses wrote down all these clauses and injunctions of a Book of the Covenant, every last syllable. And a little later, as the Lord God had enjoined him, he invited Aaron and his two sons, Nadab and Abihu, together with seventy elders, to accompany him up the Mount a certain distance, where the covenant was to be celebrated and sealed.

Again calling people from tent and field, Moses addressed them, first having built an altar under the soaring head of Sinai, and erected twelve pillars of stone to represent the twelve tribes. When he had finished his speech outlining the details of the everlasting agreement they cried out in a unison of vows:

"All the words which the Lord has said will we do."

On the new altar of commemoration were now sacrificed burnt offerings and peace offerings, until the air was filled with their roasting savor. Taking blood of the sacrificial oxen, Moses sprinkled it on the altar; then after reading aloud the written words of the covenant, so that no ear should miss a word, and once more receiving the assent of everyone, he sprinkled the remaining half of the ox blood upon them, saying:

"Behold the blood of the covenant which the Lord has made with you."

And the people bowed and worshiped.

The ceremony of the pledge being over, Moses and Aaron and seventy invited elders went up Sinai a little higher still and then sat down to feast. The table was spread with meats and bread, and an array of dainties such as were never seen before against those frowning rocks. Thanking the Lord God for His goodness, the elders for the first time caught a glimpse—or believed that they did—of Yahweh's robes, clear and beautiful as heaven, sweeping over a pavement of shining sapphire. There was no time to decide which was truth, which fancy, for suddenly the Voice called again to Moses:

"Come up to Me into the Mount, and I will give you tables of stone, and a law, and commandments which I have written; that you may teach them."

At once Moses withdrew from the group. He signaled his young captain, Joshua, now his minister, to walk up a ways with him that he might have a parting word; he also instructed Aaron and Hur to take over his authority with the people until his return; he could not foretell how long he would be gone. But Moses certainly did not suspect that he was to be gone "forty days."

Soon Moses bade Joshua farewell. His climb became steeper as, staff in hand, he forged on up toward the clouded summit. From below, where the people still watched intently, his moving figure growing ever smaller in their sight, the glory of the Lord seemed to suffuse the peak of Sinai, with color and quiet, and Moses vanished in the clouds. Spontaneously the whole gathering began to chant an ancient hymn, which went back to the days of Jacob and Joseph.

For forty days and forty nights Moses communed with Jehovah in the heights, neither eating nor drinking in all that time, but listening to words that, now in final form, would mold a nation, a world. As the weeks passed and no word, no sign, came from Moses, the children of Israel grew lonely and restive. Without their leader they felt rudderless. Aaron and Hur tried earnestly to keep up their spirits, but the wisdom and force of Moses were missing.

When will Moses return? That became a daily question, nagging, unanswerable.

Meanwhile the Lord God had inscribed His Ten Commandments on two tables of stone. Thus they might be preserved and revered for ages. In addition He gave full instructions to Moses for the construction and furnishing of a tabernacle, a specially designed tent to be a sanctuary, a place for worship. This would be the first church in the world.

The people would share the cost, according to their means, their possession of valuables; a tax on the people would pay for its maintenance; everyone twenty years old and over was to contribute regularly, with a half shekel of "atonement money" required as "a ransom for his soul unto the Lord."

Within the tent-sanctuary, in the uttermost sacred part of it, was to be placed another new thing in the world, an object to be called the ark of the testimony. This large ark box would be made of acacia wood, and within it the Commandment stones were to be kept. The covering of the ark was to be of pure gold. Moses received most precise instructions as to the architecture, the designs, and the furnishings, the inner and the outer shrines, the great court, the table of show-bread, an altar for the general worship, the unfailing light of a seven-branch candlestick made of a talent of pure gold; fine linen and a laver, incense, and anointing oil.

In the midst of the cloud, as Moses communed with God, the law was established and the visible symbol of it all was the Tabernacle in the wilderness.

In the innermost chamber, the Holy of Holies, the ark of the covenant would be set up in awesome silence and simplicity: a coffer of wood, covered entirely with plates of gold, about three feet nine inches long, by two feet three inches in height and width. Beside this reliquary for the tables of the law would be set a pot of manna, and Aaron's rod from Egypt. Within a golden crown, surrounding the top, was to be placed the mercy seat, a plate of gold, with figures of two cherubim on either side, bending down in adoration, wings extended. Here in the Holy of Holies the divine Presence would rest, and God Himself, and alone, light the sanctuary. Into this place none but the high priest might come—and even he but upon one day in the year, the day of solemn atonement.

The whole frame of the Tabernacle was to be enclosed by a tent of black goat's hair, and two other coverings, one of ram's skins dyed red, and the third of fine furs.

The Tabernacle was to be the very soul of the people. Egypt and Babylon might build their multiplied temples and altars with all their marble height and splendor but Israel alone would house the one true God in a simple sanctuary that was to be transported with them on plain and hill, carried through valleys and across rivers, their ever-present help in time of trouble.

Aaron and his four sons were to be the appointed first priests. Their garments of office were minutely designed: robe and embroidered coat, mitre and girdle; breastplate and ephod, and the Urim and Thummim—"lights and perfection"—all must be cunningly fashioned and jeweled. Aaron was to be high priest. He and his sons were to be consecrated in holy ceremonies, fully set down, and other rituals performed.

The children of Israel were being organized and directed in a way of life that, if followed, would bring them happiness and harmony under divine care.

Eager to get it all started, mind filled with laws and ordinances, Moses received the two tables of stone in his arms. But he was greatly alarmed when he heard the Lord say:

"Go, get you down; for your people, which you brought out of the land of Egypt, have corrupted themselves."

Already? In such a little absence?

Already! The people were even then straying away from the Sinai precepts. Gently and fearsomely Moses pleaded their cause:

"Turn, O God, from this fierce wrath against your people. Remember Abraham, Isaac, and Israel, your servants, to whom it was sworn that their seed would be multiplied as the stars of heaven, and that they should inherit the land of promise for ever."

Bold beyond all bravery—that a mere man should remind the Lord God of the past and of the promised future of the house of Abraham, Isaac, and Jacob! There was no answer; the Voice remained silent, as the unhappy Moses left the Eternal Presence, his arms weighed down with the tablets of stone.

Never before had it seemed so long, so heartbreaking—the journey down from Sinai.

Chapter 12 THE GOLDEN CALF

WHAT had happened was that in the long period of absence and waiting the children of Israel were losing patience and becoming afraid. Where was Moses? Why did he remain away? As the moon waxed and waned, darkened, and waxed again, the people began complaining to Brother Aaron. Had he no news of his long-lingering brother? Had a fatal accident befallen him? Could it be that God had decided on keeping him to Himself? Surely, mere commonplace, ordinary people had by now been forgotten.

There were murmurs about seeking advice and solace from the forbidden heathen gods of other tribes and peoples. It was then that young Joshua, the captain, perturbed and uneasy at the growing discontent, left the camp, without a word to Aaron or anyone else. Intensely loyal to Moses, he took up a solitary post on the lower reaches of Mount Sinai, and there he watched and prayed. But still the days passed without a sign and revolt was coming to a boil:

"We are deserted!"

"Give us a god which shall go before us!"

Hearing these insistent cries, Aaron's staunch faith was shaken at last. In sheer despair he blurted out words: "Bring me your golden earrings, everyone—that I may see what can be done."

To the anxious people, this command was a happy augury of some new and wonderful thing. They well remembered Aaron's rod of magic, used so successfully in earlier trials. Now, once again, Aaron would do something prodigious. So they broke apart their earrings and heaped golden fragments before him.

"Now give us a god to go before us!" they chanted.

But Aaron, facing them, did not hold up his wonder-working rod; his hands were empty. Dolefully, for he knew this was an act of apostasy, he cast the broken trinkets into a circle of fire. As the gold melted and ran in the fierce blaze, artificers and workers in metal came forward and pulled the mass of melted gold out of the flames, working it, molding it, so that as it began to cool and harden everyone could see that it was taking on shape, the crude form of a calf of gold.

This little eidolon of a beast Aaron then fashioned with his own tools into a more realistic likeness. He knew—and so did they all—that the calf, or bull, was one of the chief symbols of heathen Canaanite worship. Before the eyes of all, the brother of Moses had made a calf in golden blasphemy.

Entranced with the golden image, the people screamed:

"These be your gods, O Israel, which brought us out of the land of Egypt!"

And even Aaron, carried away by the general frenzy, hastened to have an altar put up before the golden calf in all its yellow glow.

"Tomorrow is a feast of the Lord," he shouted.

It was a moment of complete spiritual blindness for Aaron, a very decent man. Like many another appeaser and compromiser, he was actually thinking it possible to combine the adoration of the one true God of Noah and Abraham, Isaac, and Jacob with the paganism of the desert tribes and all their hideous practices. Never was any man more self-deceived.

The people danced jubilantly before the new altar. There was a defiant sense of relief in their wickedness; the long vigil of waiting was over; they had a god to placate, now, a glittering golden calf.

Next day they celebrated with burnt offerings of oxen and peace offerings of sheep. In eating and drinking they forgot their fear of Yahweh, and their convenant with Him, giving themselves up to gluttony. Some of the celebrants spread wide their arms and wheeled themselves about in frenzied circlings of song and dance, to the clash and whine of tambourines and stringed instruments; others in their excesses leaped naked, up and down, screaming at the top of their throats.

It was at the very height of this Canaanite orgy that the figure of Moses came into view, clambering down from the slope of Sinai.

The heart of Moses smote him; once more the all-knowing Lord God had told him the truth. The people could not hold out. Backsliders again! At the foot of the slippery mountainside Moses beheld the self-posted sentinel, clear-eyed, faithful Joshua. What was happening? Captain Joshua could not answer.

Moses strode toward camp, the precious tables of stone carried on his shoulder. On their granite surface the finger of God had graven the law—even the law forbidding idolatry to the beloved, the chosen people. Yet already, the calf of gold.

Enraged beyond all self-control, Moses raised his hands above his head and hurled the two tables of stone, the graven laws of God, over the nearest cliff. A shudder racked his huge body when he heard the crash far down in the abyss; the ruin of law and order, breaking into fragments.

Rushing on into the very midst of the corybantic renegades, Moses reached out mighty hands toward the golden calf itself, ripped it from its pedestal, and hurled the thing into the altar fires. Cries rose from thousands of witnesses; cries of grief, of fear, of conscience.

But even the most frightened of those thousands was not prepared for the chastisement of the outraged Moses. Ever since the exodus from Egypt he had been most patient in spite of their weaknesses, failings, treacheries, backslidings. But now they stood and watched, while at his stern order the golden lumps of what had been the idol were taken from the ashes, cooled, and ground to powder. Then the shining dust was mixed with water and the guilty sons and daughters of Israel were forced to drink the golden liquid to the last drop.

"Surely, we will all die!" they moaned.

Meanwhile Moses went searching for his brother Aaron. Him he blamed as the one most responsible for this reversal to false gods. As if he were a stranger, Moses demanded:

"What happened?"

Aaron wondered himself; how had he ever led such wickedness? Brokenly, he tried to explain the atmosphere which fear had created among them all—these people who now stood shivering in their nakedness.

Moses turned to the frightened multitude, the setting sun bronzing his weather-beaten face and turning the hairs of his beard to gold.

"Who now is on the Lord's side? Let him come unto me," he called.

In instant response the sons of the tribe of Levi gathered around him, their action signifying grief and repentance for their pagan folly. Moses commissioned them as his deputies to go looking for the guilty instigators, who had led others astray—and to kill them on the spot. None was to escape the penalty and none did. Many met instant death that day.

Weary with blood and anger, still heavy of soul, Moses climbed again to the mountaintop on the following day and begged forgiveness for his irresponsible, wayward people:

"If not, blot me out of Your book."

In spite of their transgressions, Moses forgave and loved the house of Jacob; he was willing to lay down his life for the twelve tribes of the twelve sons. But Jehovah would have none of such nobleness:

"Whosoever has sinned against Me, him will I blot out of My book."

So Moses was not allowed to offer himself as a scapegoat. Instead, let him attend now to the decision, the penalty. Moses was to continue to lead the children of Israel toward the land flowing with milk and honey that had been promised to their forefathers. But from now on everything would be different; no more pillar of cloud and pillar of fire; no longer would God be with this stiff-necked people.

When Moses, grim and helpless, stumbled down the mountain once more and, facing the whole people, delivered to them this fearful message, a howl of sorrow arose. With ashes in their hair, the Israelites mourned and entreated. They put off all their ornaments of pride and humbled themselves, prostrate, face down in the gray dust. Without the sure hand of guidance from God they would all be as straws in the wind. Would Moses, too, now desert them? Would God desert Moses? It was an hour of sheer, downright, utter despair.

Meanwhile, outside the camp, as if feeling himself already apart from them, Moses pitched a temporary Tabernacle, which was fortunate, for at once the people saw over the goatskin tent a miraculous plume of mist and smoke, a sign that God was still to be near them a little and that He and Moses were still together. Believing that even at that moment the one true God was in there talking with Moses, the congregation rose up as one person and, still standing at a great distance, worshiped God in the sincerity of contrite hearts. Touched deeply by this spectacle of mass repentance, Moses pleaded for renewed grace. What could he do? He was at the end of thought, his soul spent.

"Oh, this people have sinned a great sin and have made them gods of gold. Yet now, if You will, forgive their sin, if not—blot me out."

So Moses had pleaded, unavailingly. But now, as he entered the Tabernacle, the Lord spoke to Moses, "face to face, as a man speaks unto a friend," declaring:

"My presence shall go with you, and I will give you rest."

And Moses was speechless with gratitude when the Voice in great mercy bade him hew two new tables of stone to replace those broken, and promised that He would write on them once again, His laws with His fingers.

The soul of Moses soared with praise as he tooled all the next day, making duplicate tables of shining, polished granite. Heavy as they were, he carried them swiftly upward to the secret recesses of Sinai. There the Lord of infinite patience wrote His Commandments a second time.

And now a strange thing happened.

The Israelites, waiting anxiously far below, saw the white-robed, bearded Moses coming down to them; and saw that his face was lit with a rainbow radiance, from orange to violet and colors never before seen by men, so blinding that they had to lower their eyes. They were afraid to approach close to him until he veiled his shining countenance.

All because the glory of the Lord was shining through His servant.

And the people looked with veneration at the tables he held up before them. Hopeful news, O Israel! Those of willing heart were to bring offerings of whatever they had to contribute to the building of the new Tabernacle, to be of gold, silver, and brass, the finest wood, and rich stuffs. The reconciled Lord God would dwell in the Tabernacle and would be with them wherever they went.

Once more the irresponsible yet chosen people were fully restored to God's favor—the past, and not themselves, blotted out. Eagerly they came forward with gifts, more than enough; Moses had to restrain them in their generosity. Under the inspired craftsmanship of Bezaleel and Aholiab, the Tabernacle was laid out, its outlines and proportions traced in the silver work sheet of desert sand. Expert carpenters and builders soon raised the Tabernacle in the wilderness of Sinai, so cunningly was it constructed that it could easily be taken apart, broken down, as we say, and carried on journeyings.

By spring, a year after they had escaped from Egypt, the Tabernacle was ready for worship. After the initial ceremonies, the pillar of cloud appeared again, descending and covering the tent of the congregation. Thus the people knew that the glory of the Lord filled the Tabernacle.

Moses had also received and now published in most minute detail the various statutes, ordinances, and laws that were to govern the religious and secular life of the people henceforth—that they "shall be holy for I, Yahweh, am holy." These multiple injunctions of conduct and thought were all summed up in a few final words:

"You shall not hate your brother in your heart; you shall surely warn your neighbor, and not increase sin because of him. You shall not take vengeance nor bear any grudge against the children of your people; but you shall love your neighbor as yourself."

A month after the completion of the Tabernacle word came from God, addressing Moses, that the children of Israel must be counted: the first census in the world.

The tribes were also given instructions on their position and order of march; they were to start again for the Promised Land. Special responsibility was laid on the tribe of Levi, whose members must take full charge of the holy things in moving and placement as the multitude traveled northward in the direction of Canaan. Why, muttered some of the malcontents, was one tribe set apart for the service of the Tabernacle? To reasonable men, the cause was clear enough; being separated from secular affairs and living close by the Tabernacle, they could give to their vocation complete attention. Though there was considerable grumbling, the preparations went forward.

When all was in readiness for resumption of the journey, the Voice commanded Moses:

"Speak unto Aaron and unto his sons, saying, On this wise ye shall bless the children of Israel, saying unto them: The Lord bless thee and keep thee; the Lord make His face to shine upon thee: and be gracious unto thee: The Lord lift up His countenance upon thee and give thee peace. And they shall put My name upon the children of Israel; and I will bless them."

It was on the twentieth morning of the second month of the second year that the cloud lifted from off the Tabernacle—expected signal for breaking camp, for going onward, and, incidentally, for being counted. Excluding the Levites, it was calculated that there were now in camp 603,500 men over twenty years old—a formidable and almost unmanageable force.

Silver trumpets were blown as the tribes, in prearranged orderly ranks, moved out toward the wilderness of Paran, the ark of the covenant being borne in front. And the cloud by day and the pillar of fire by night once more guided their course.

Surely, thought the wanderers, the Promised Land would soon come to view; and all hunger and thirst were trials left in the past, but not so. When they camped at a place called Taberah, thousands were hungry and thirsty again and bitter complaints were heard against Moses. Food was scarce, the daily manna monotonous and tiresome, and water hard to be eked out, drop by drop.

"Who shall give us flesh?" they complained. "We remember the fish which we did eat in Egypt freely; the cucumbers and the melons and the leeks and the onions and the garlic."

Moses took his trouble to the Lord in prayer and God answered him instantly:

"Gather unto me seventy men of the elders of Israel, and they shall bear the burden of the people with thee."

When the seventy elders Moses had chosen met for counsel they seemed singularly inspired; they discussed their problems eloquently and with good sense and the spirits of all were lightened. Even two unchosen elders, Eldad and Medad, not of the seventy picked by Moses, also felt the wave of inspiration, and began to prophesy, not going to the Tabernacle but orating in camp. This presumption alarmed Captain Joshua so much that he adjured Moses to forbid them.

"Are you envious for my sake?" smiled Moses in reply. "Would God that all the Lord's people were prophets, and that the Lord would put His Spirit upon them!"

Moses was a very great man.

A great man, a great servant of the Lord, but with weaknesses and family difficulties just like anyone else—as in the matter of his brown-skinned wife. Moses had married an Ethiopian woman, and this dark intrusion into the family circle infuriated his sister Miriam as well as Brother Aaron. Why should a man who could have such a twilight romance as that be considered the exclusive messenger of God? Did not Jehovah also speak to the people through the sister and brother of Moses? The answer to this impudence was not delayed.

"Hear now My words," thundered the Voice. "If there be a

prophet among you, I the Lord will make Myself known unto him in a vision, and will speak to him in a dream. My servant Moses is not so, who is faithful in all Mine house. With him will I speak mouth to mouth, even apparently, and not in dark speeches; and the similitude of the Lord shall he behold.

"Wherefore then were you not afraid to speak against My servant Moses?"

The cloud vanished and the Voice ceased. And in the same instant a terrible fact became visible. The face of scolding Miriam, chief offender in the family dissension, was seen to be ghost-white now— with her hands and wrists—a ghastly change in that once beautiful skin. All in a sudden instant Miriam had become a leper.

Overcome with horror and remorse, Aaron begged that his sin be forgiven him and that the stricken Miriam be purified of her disease. And Moses, too, called on the Lord, interceding for Miriam.

"Let her be shut out from the camp seven days and after that let her be received in again," was her sentence.

And so the campers dawdled perforce at Hazeroth, and Miriam had to endure her banishment, until her leprosy was healed.

Forging north again into the wilderness of Paran, the people arrived at Kadesh-Barnea, where they found abundant springs, green fields, and peace; the pillar of cloud rested to show the next place of settlement.

Kadesh-Barnea was a pleasant oasis. While all the thousands took rest and ease by the pleasant springs, word came from the Lord to Moses that he must not wait. They were now not far from the southern boundary of Canaan and Moses must hasten to select leaders of the tribes, excepting always those of Levi, and send them as spies to "search out the land" of Canaan and report back what they found.

Among the pioneers chosen by Moses to spy on Canaan and its inhabitants were two of his most skillful aides—Joshua, of the tribe of Ephraim, and Caleb, of the tribe of Judah. Theirs was to be a hazardous mission; they crossed the frontier and got as far as Hebron, where the giant sons of Anak dwelt.

After "forty days" of close observation they returned, carrying with them clusters of purple grapes so big and heavy that two men toted them on a staff across their shoulders; also great green figs and golden pomegranates.

But the tale of the adventurers was full of terrifying facts. Yes, the land did indeed flow with milk and honey; its hillsides and meadows gladdened the eye. But its cities were walled and strong in defense, and the men of the land were of formidable stature, some of them actual giants.

"We were as grasshoppers in their sight," said the scouts, with vivid exaggeration. The returned explorers, all except Caleb, were doubtful of waging a successful campaign against such entrenched and fortified enemies.

Where, then, were the children of Israel to go? Had they marched all this distance in vain? Emotional as ever, the people wrung their hands and wept—and turned on Moses.

"Would God we had died in the land of Egypt, or would God we had died in the wilderness!" they lamented. "Has the Lord brought us here to fall by the sword, our wives and our children to be made a prey? . . . Let us make a captain and let us return unto Egypt."

Moses and Aaron were stunned at the readiness of the people to wilt and recant, after all the heavenly favor that had been shown them.

"Let us make a new captain and return to Egypt!"—the chorus swelled, intent on insubordination, stirring up treason.

Moses and Aaron fell on their faces and began to pray. Thus far had God brought all of them, in perfect safety. But their fright of the future was so acute that in their hysteria they began to pack their baggage ready to rush back into the chains of Egyptian slavery.

Chapter 13 THE LONG JOURNEY ENDS

THIS moment was the point of the greatest crisis in the history of the people and it completely altered their future.

Moses and Aaron, the bearded old brothers in travel-worn robes, lay prostrate on the gray earth and prayed despairingly, while Joshua and Caleb tore their clothes. What unspeakable folly! Why were they so unstable? Joshua and Caleb with him, stouthearted and resolute men, tried to calm them:

"Why do you fill yourself with doubts? Have faith in the Lord. He will bring us into the land of milk and honey. Neither must you fear the people of Canaan. They have no defense against the Lord, and He is with us."

"Stone them! Stone them!" screamed the frightened crowds. They were actually stooping to pick up the stones, they would have murdered all four, Moses and Aaron, Joshua and Caleb, had not the glory of the Lord fallen then in the form of glowing firelight upon the Tabernacle. The bright, unlikely spectacle of quivering flame and light silenced the people suddenly and now all of them could hear the Voice:

"How long will this people provoke Me? I will smite them with the pestilence, and disinherit them, and will make of you, Moses, a greater nation and a mightier than they."

For the second time God was offering to lift up Moses above all men because of his constant love and devotion; with him alone to begin once more. But again Moses, whose heart was great, as was his thrilling and selfless love for his people, pleaded for God's mercy. By no assent of his would the tribes ever be wiped out. Even though their transgressions were many and perverse, he still had hope for them. Moses loved God and his neighbor never more than in this extraordinary hour.

"Pardon, I beseech You, the iniquity of this people according to the greatness of Your mercy, and as You have forgiven this people from Egypt even until now."

The plea came from the very depths of Moses' being. Moved by a good man's prayer, God declared He would not punish them with pestilence, nor would He disinherit them. Nevertheless, the rebellious and disbelieving children of Israel had to pay a severe penalty for their present defection. They must be made to learn, somehow. The decision was that all the tribesmen who were twenty years of age or more were forbidden ever to see the land of promise, to which they had now and at last drawn so near. Instead, they must continue wandering in the wilderness until forty years were passed, and by then all of them would be dead and gone.

They had feared, in their hysteria, that the growing new generation would be "a prey" to the foe. Now they learned that these little ones alone would become the happy inheritors of the new land.

Dire tidings, these. Profoundest grief overwhelmed the Israelite host. They had journeyed so far and it had all come to nothing. Would not ashes of repentance, perhaps, or prayers and sacrifice placate the Lord God and obtain a reprieve? Or, better—perhaps some brave audacious action undertaken against Canaan would win favor from the Lord. Yes! They would attack the enemy, the abhorred Amalekites. In an upsurge of enthusiasm which they mistook for inspiration, the mob shoved the protesting Moses and Aaron over and away out of hearing, as they began to plan their campaign. Shouting to them hoarsely, Moses warned them that they would fail, because God would not be with them. Quiet, Moses! We know what we are doing!

Unthinking as ever, they prepared themselves for battle and promptly laid siege to a hill occupied by Amalekites and Canaanites. Bravely, it is true, they faced a sortie by the foe. But complete defeat was the bitter reward.

Would the children of Israel never, never learn? A dozen times, a hundred times, God might have been expected to drop His hopes forever, in His disappointment with His chosen flock. Even in their sincere contrition, their most earnest desire to make amends for their sins, they still could not learn the simple lesson of unquestioning obedience.

Moses sighed. He well knew the character of his people: a strange, provocative compound, an inner conflict of reason and emotion that was forever going on, as if it were a fever in the blood itself. Moses was near to complete despair. And it was at this time of all times, and in spite of their defeat in battle, that the people rose in outright rebellion, solely out of the childish spite of malcontents, grown jealous of Aaron and his sons. Why had they alone been given the priesthood? It was favoritism, nepotism, the troublemakers decided. Aaron had no right to be high priest anyway; had he not made an idol, a calf, out of molten gold? Yet he was rewarded with holy office. With talk like this, four ringleaders—Korah, Dathan, Abiram, and On—stirred up enough grumbling to bring two hundred and fifty other men of important standing in the assembly, all conspirators, to confront Moses with their dissatisfaction.

"Why do you and your brother Aaron lift up yourselves above all the congregation?"

Moses felt very old and tired, but he heard them through their long, insulting challenge. The Lord would decide the matter on the morrow, he promised, if they and their followers would bring censers containing fire and incense, and stand in the door of the Tabernacle. He remained quite unruffled, even when he observed sons of Levi standing brazenly before him with the other rebels. Had they forgotten that it was their tribe, the sons of Levi, that had been chosen as a priesthood, to be close to the Lord? Sending them away, Moses fell on his face in prayer.

Gathered at the Tabernacle the following day, they heard Moses call to heaven for judgment—punishment for himself if he were guilty of misusing the power entrusted to him; obliteration for those who accused him, if they lied.

As the people stood and watched they were herded out of danger and just in time. For where they had just been standing the ground opened, swallowing up the four leading conspirators and their families while the two hundred and fifty men who had joined with them, coming there with lighted silver censers, were instantly consumed by fire.

It was a stupendous demonstration and should have convinced every delinquent one of them. But no! Despite even this dramatic judgment, some still persisted in finding fault and nourished resentment against Moses and Aaron. The patience of the Lord was so tried again that He sent a plague upon them, which took many lives before it was stayed through the intercession of Moses.

To settle all dispute about Aaron as high priest and the sons of Levi as the chosen caretakers of the Tabernacle, the Voice bade Moses bring the twelve princes, leaders of the tribes, to the Tabernacle and in their sight lay a rod on the altar.

"The man's rod, whom I shall choose, shall blossom," said the Lord.

It was done and before the eyes of the twelve the rod of Aaron bloomed like a bough in spring, and not only blossomed but also turned into almonds. The censers of the two hundred and fifty rebels slain in flames were now to be beaten into plates for the altar and the rod of Aaron must also be preserved there, all as a perpetual testimony against perverse critics. Aaron was personally addressed by the Voice:

"You and your sons and your father's house shall bear the iniquity of the sanctuary: and you and your sons with you shall bear the iniquity of your priesthood."

Thus all the burden of responsibility for worship in the Tabernacle was delegated to Aaron and his descendants. They were to be given no land and must depend for their support on the tithes of the population; ten per cent of what the people had must go to the priests, for their education and all their other beneficent works.

For a long time the children of Israel remained camped at Kadesh-Barnea, and Miriam died there. But the time came when Moses told them they must continue their onward march, even though the older ones knew now they would never lay eyes on the Promised Land. Before setting out, Moses sent messengers ahead to the king of Edom, requesting safe passage through his country. In no way would his people be molested or his property used by the Israelites on their journey to Canaan; and money would be paid for any goods or service. Peaceful as this overture was, it drew from the King of Edom only these words:

"It is forbidden you to pass through my territory, or I will draw the sword against you."

Not wishing to invite war with the powerful Edomites (those wild descendants of Esau), Moses led the Israelites on a long, roundabout route, safely skirting Edom. When the first stop was made at Mount Hor, the Voice spoke to Moses:

"Aaron shall be gathered unto his people: for he shall not enter into the land which I have given unto the children of Israel, because you rebelled against my word. . . ."

Under divine orders, Moses conducted Aaron and his son up the mountain and into a deep ravine where he divested the father of his priestly garments and put them on his son Eleazar, as his successor. After this ceremony, performed in the silence of the hills, Aaron closed his eyes to the light of day, and Moses left the body of his brother there. The new high priest returned to the multitude that had watched their ascent of Mount Hor and told them the news. And the people who had reviled him and revolted against him mourned Aaron for thirty days.

Now this was their fortieth year of the wilderness and what had they learned? Actually, of the things of the spirit, of a proper relation between God and man, they had learned virtually nothing, although they had been taught a great deal. Once, on their renewed journey, they were attacked by the Canaanite king of Arad and his armed horsemen but this time, instead of relying on their own power as warriors, they entreated help from God and so defeated Arad's leader and his experienced campaigners. Their prayer for help was a hopeful sign, but they did not live up to it.

Footsore and weary, they trudged on their way by the frothing shores of the Red Sea, and again, as of yore, they grew bitter and rebellious. Their complaints, only muttered at first, soon mounted to a din. Once more they talked about going back to Egypt, until fiery serpents suddenly appeared among them, death in their fangs. Then, as usual, the people cried:

"We have sinned against the Lord, and repent. Pray take away these serpents from us!"

That was why and when the Lord God instructed Moses to make a serpent of brass as a symbol of their sin, and to set it high on a pole. Those who had been bitten could look upon it and be cured.

Relieved of the plague of serpents and all its fears, they pushed on with renewed vigor, pitching their tents next by the brook of Zared, where abundant water flowed out from a well. Now they were on the edge of the Promised Land itself, with Mount Pisgah, opposite Jericho, already in plain sight.

But to reach their long-deferred destination they would have to pass through the land of the Amorites, and once again Moses tried the peaceful way. Messengers were dispatched to King Sihon, but his instant answer was to send his army. And to a devastating defeat. Sihon lost his land to the Israelites, and all his cities fell into their hands.

It was the first great triumph for the wilderness wayfarers.

But more was to come at the will of the Lord God. The seasoned Israelite warriors fought and conquered King Og of Bashan, whose kingdom was one of giants, his own bedstead being twelve feet long. All hearts were lightening now; some of the tribes of Israel were given parts of the conquered land and Moses told Joshua there were to be even greater victories ahead, because they would all trust not to their valor alone but to help from above. Indeed, the general rejoicing also raised some furtive hopes in the heart of Moses for himself. They were so near their goal now, all the prospect was smiling before them —could not the doom laid upon Moses perhaps be lifted, the banishment from ever entering the Promised Land rescinded? Moses asked the God he had loved and served so long to let this bitter cup of punishment pass from his mouth untasted. The answer was final: from the top of Pisgah, Moses might drink in with his eyes the verdant beauty of the Promised Land but "you shall not go over this Jordan," said the Voice.

This famous Jordan was so called because it came from the old word "Jord," which means something that flows down or comes down. In the midst of the river, miraculously ceasing its flow until all was done, Moses was soon to arrange that "stones of memorial" be set up, like the twelve pillars of Sinai, so that his forgetful people, when at last they came into possession of the Promised Land, might have a continual reminder of their covenant.

It was at this time that Balaam had his famous colloquy with an ass.

The children of Israel had marched until they reached the plains of Moab, near Jericho, where they set up their black goatskin tents, now numbering thousands, on the east side of the river Jordan. The move, a clear threat of coming invasion, was a signal for King Balak of Moab to call in his counselors. Already his scouts had reported what the soldiers of the Israelites had done to the Amorites.

"Now shall the company lick us up as the ox licketh up the grass of the field," Balak reflected. In great trepidation he sent for Balaam, his adviser, and the elders of Moab and Midian waited on the seer and gave him the king's message:

"Come, I pray you, and curse these strangers for me that I may prevail over them, for they are mighty."

Now it happened that Balaam was an independent character. His answer to the king of Moab was that in prayer he had been forbidden to curse the children of Israel. But King Balak demanded that Balaam come and stand before him, and when, as to that order, Balaam asked in prayer to be shown what to do, he was told to obey the royal summons, and powers outside himself would control his tongue.

Such a restriction irritated Balaam, but he mounted his ass and set off. On the stony road to Moab his ass suddenly balked and turned aside, for in her path she had seen an angel of the Lord, sword in hand, but invisible to Balaam.

Much as the exasperated fellow urged and stormed, the beast would not budge, not even when he beat her, but in the confusion the ass crushed Balaam's foot against a wall on the side of the road. Now really hot with anger, the rider rained harder blows than ever on the miserable animal.

But in the midst of the uproar the angel, still unseen by Balaam but still wholly clear in the sight of the ass, drew so close that the beast fell down in fear. Still her master increased the flailing of his heavy staff, until suddenly the ass began to speak; the Lord had given her speech:

"What have I done that you have smitten me three times?"

"Because you have made a mockery of me," answered Balaam, still furious in the midst of his astonishment; his rage was more than his astonishment at the unnaturalness of an animal asking questions. "And if I had a sword in my hand I'd kill you."

"Have I not been ever faithful and obedient since the first day?" rejoined the ass. "Have I ever done aught to deserve this treatment?"

"Nay," admitted Balaam, cooling down and beginning to look wildly about him. This was gruesome! Then, suddenly, the angel made himself visible to the bewildered man, and added scathing reproaches to those of the abused animal; he told Balaam he was perverse and headstrong, and that the poor ass had saved his life.

Remorseful and ashamed, Balaam offered to retrace his steps, if that were the best course, but the angel told him he was free to go on to Moab, and added:

"Yet you must speak only the word of the Lord."

King Balak greeted Balaam his adviser with promises of highest honor for the service to be rendered. But Balaam gave him no assurance in return. All that he would say was that his loyalty was to the Lord God, Who would direct his tongue. This faith satisfied the heathen Balak, and he led Balaam to a hilltop. There he got a full sight of the Israelites and their thousands of black tents. Seven altars were built on the spot for burnt offerings, all at Balaam's orders, and after the sacrifice he cried aloud:

"How shall I curse whom God has not cursed? Or how shall I defy whom God has not defied? Who can count the dust of Jacob? Let me die the death of the righteous, and let my last end be like his!"

Wroth, but still bent on having his will, Balak took Balaam to another hill, where seven more altars and sacrifices resulted in the same cry:

"Behold, I have received commandment to bless, and I cannot reverse it. It shall be said of Jacob and of Israel, What hath God wrought!"

The words he spoke still echo in men's minds when they are in the presence of the wonders of God.

Undaunted, for the third time the king of Moab escorted Balaam who would not curse Israel to a very great height, hoping there for better luck, and the performance was repeated in every particular. Seeing the encampment of the invaders on the far horizon, Balaam hailed them:

"How goodly are thy tents, O Jacob, and thy tabernacles, O Israel! His kingdom shall be exalted. Blessed is he that blesses thee, and cursed is he that curses thee."

Thwarted and enraged, Balak shouted:

"Flee back to your place! I thought to bestow honors upon you, but the Lord held you back from them. Begone!"

"What the Lord says that will I speak," insisted Balaam. "There shall come a star out of Jacob, and a scepter shall rise out of Israel. Out of Jacob shall come he that shall have dominion."

Balak could do nothing to alter the inevitable, and now he realized it.

But while the future was clear and full of brightness, the leadership of the incomparable Moses was almost over.

Even as he felt the end draw near, the tired old leader was saddened
again at the treason of many of his followers. Many of them were already wooing foreign women of this region, lying with the heathen,
and when the aliens were reluctant, being true to their own religion,
consenting to accept their false gods. Such apostasy meant bloody
clashes among themselves, defilers slain, corpses hanging on the walls
of the tents to warn the others, and finally, with their leader on the
brink of the grave, the need for making war on the Midianites.

"Avenge the children of Israel of the Midianites," the Lord commanded Moses. "Afterward you shall be gathered unto your people."

A thousand men from each tribe were assembled, armed with weapons, and with trumpets to blow. Under the order of Moses they
marched against the Midianites, destroying utterly all the males of the
enemy, together with their five kings. Tremendous was the booty they
gained of beeves, asses, and sheep, as well as gold and silver, and other
valuables. Of these, the proper portion was consecrated to the glory of
God, who had put another victory in their hands.

The task was almost over. There was yet to be taken a census of the
children of Israel. Several more such censuses would be taken, including that historic counting of the people, a thousand years later, when
Augustus Caesar was on the throne of an empire yet unborn, and
Mary was to be delivered of her child in a stable, and the wicked children of the earth were to find a new dispensation.

By this first census it was found that all of the older generation,
condemned not to enter the land of promise, had already passed away,
with the exception of Caleb and Joshua, and Moses himself. So the
inheritors of the land of milk and honey could now proceed to complete the long journey.

To Moses the Voice spoke again:

"Get you up into the top of Pisgah and lift up your eyes westward
and northward, and southward and eastward, and behold it with your
eyes: for you shall not go over this Jordan.

"But charge Joshua, and encourage him, and strengthen him: for he
shall go before this people, and he shall cause them to inherit the
land which you shall see."

Moses promised instant obedience, and heaved a long and gratified
sigh. The wilderness wandering was over. Behind Moses and his immi-
grants lay those forty years of tribulation, but never entire despair, for
were they not also forty years of miracles? What memories of God's
attendant care were those miracles to a faithless people: the parting of
the Red Sea, the sweetening of the waters of Marah, the burning

bush, the feeding with manna, water flowing from the rock at Rephidim.

But the greatest miracle of all had been God's love in the face of the way the wanderers had behaved themselves. Please God, they would do better in this beautiful Promised Land!

As God had instructed him, so Moses now spent most of his time with Joshua, instructing him, until the captain had absorbed all the teachings, then, on his own birthday, Moses, of the long-ago bulrushes, commanded that the people come together to hear his message—a song that was a very paean of farewell.

Long he spoke before them, while the mountain that was his pulpit seemed to burn with heavenly fire. For the young people that were now to go on, into the Promised Land, the old leader rehearsed the history: the bondage in Egypt, the wilderness wanderings, the lessons on Mount Sinai, the covenant and the law, all the many instructions, warnings, and predictions, with a new covenant to be entered into, after the conquest of Canaan, which was to be their divine heritage.

And the voice of Moses rose in a grand song, which began:

"Give ear, O ye heavens, and I will speak; and hear, O earth, the words of my mouth . . .

"But if you shall seek the Lord thy God you shall find Him, if you seek Him with all your heart and with all your soul . . . the Lord has chosen you to be a special people unto Himself, above all people that are on the face of the earth . . . that man doth not live by bread only, but by every word that proceeds out of the mouth of the Lord. Hear, O Israel! The Lord, our God, is one Lord. . . . And now, Israel, what does the Lord require of you but to fear God, to walk in all His ways, and to love Him, and to serve the Lord with all your heart and with all your soul?

"Lay up these words in your heart and in your soul, and bind them for a sign upon your hand. Who shall go up for us to heaven and bring it, that we may hear it and do it? Neither is it beyond the sea, that you should say, Who shall go over the sea for us and bring it, that we may hear it and do it? But the word is very nigh unto you, in your mouth, and in your heart, that you may do it.

"See, I have set before you this day, life and good, and death and evil. I call heaven and earth to record this day that I have set before you life and death, blessing and cursing: therefore choose life, that both you and your seed may live, that you may love the Lord your God, and obey His voice, and cleave unto Him for He is your life, and the length of your days. I am a hundred and twenty years old this day;

I can no more go out and come in; be strong and of good courage. Fear not, nor be afraid of them, for the Lord your God it is that does go with you; He will not fail you, nor forsake you. Fear not! And as your days, so shall your strength be."

Praising God, and beseeching their devotion, Moses cried:

"He is the Rock, His work is perfect: for all His ways are judgment: a God of truth and without iniquity, just and right is He. . . . Rejoice, O ye nations, with His people: for He will avenge the blood of His servants, and will render vengeance to His adversaries, and will be merciful unto His land and His people."

Then Moses, having blessed the tribes that had listened entranced to his story and his song, struggled up from the plains of Moab to the top of Mount Pisgah from whence he could look down on the city of Jericho. As friend to friend, the Voice pointed out to Moses all of the beautiful inheritance of Israel. And the Lord God said:

"This is the land which I sware unto Abraham, unto Isaac, and unto Jacob, saying I will give it to your seed."

On that broad scene, in his one hundred and twenty-first year, Moses closed his eyes forever. And God saw to it that he was buried in a place in the mountain, but where, no man ever knew. Never was there to be seen again on earth a prophet like him, whom the Lord knew face to face.

In this secret burial there was a fresh instance of divine wisdom. So great a man was Moses, having lived so close to God, that most likely the great merits and fame of the Hebrew lawgiver and leader would have led the people to elevate him above mere mortals and to establish an idolatrous temple over his tomb.

Far below the peak of Pisgah, on the plains of Moab, the children of Israel wept for many days. But in the midst of their sorrowing, Joshua was filled with the spirt of wisdom imparted to him by the immortal Moses, and now by God Himself.

Joshua must take up the burden that Moses had laid down.

BOOK FOUR
The Story of Joshua

Chapter 14 THE RED THREAD AT THE WINDOW

It was Joshua, intrepid general and brilliant military strategist, who conquered the land of Canaan and made it reasonably safe for the children of Israel. At the start he had the connivance of a Canaanite harlot whom he never beheld, and before his victory was complete, by divine power, the earth itself had to be halted in its turning, and the sun and the moon to stand still for him, until his most desperate battle was won.

Joshua had to wage war against fierce barbaric little kings with stubborn armies and the strife lasted many a year. Nor could victory ever have been accomplished without the steady counsel of the Voice which, of all the secrets of life, is the most important and the most often ignored or forgotten. That forgetfulness was one of the reasons, if not the principal cause, for the long-drawn-out campaigns; whenever the Israelites listened to their God, the one and the true, all went well; when they turned away there was disaster.

No sooner was Moses dead and his body mysteriously buried than the same supernal, faithful Voice spoke to Joshua:

"Arise, go over this Jordan, you and all this people, unto the land which I do give them. As I was with Moses so I will be with you. Be strong and of a good courage; be not afraid, neither be you dismayed: for the Lord your God is with you whithersoever you go."

Those words, spoken to Joshua, have outlasted him by thousands of years: God's encouragement, not only to the old general in a strange land, knowing that the green grasses of the fair fields below and beyond them must soon be turned to scarlet with the blood of his own

149

followers, but to every man and woman who must face an unknown and dangerous future.

"Be strong and of a good courage; be not afraid, neither be you dismayed—"

They are like the sound of a father's voice leading a son in the dark.

It was a great moment to the grieving host when they were reassured; they would not be forsaken—their one true Lord God, unfailing source of help, would speak—and had already spoken to Joshua.

Here was a new leader to be trusted and every tongue respected his name with satisfaction, a name of many fashions and distortions; some called him Hoshea, others Oshea, or Jehoshua, Hehoshuah, and Jeshua—all variants of the name which, in Greek form centuries later, was to form the name of Jesus.

Under Joshua's command the first move was to march from Moab, where Moses had died, down to Shittim, the valley of Acacias, soft blooming little greens that grow beside the tumbling Jordan. Now they were not far from the vanished foundations of ruined and wicked old cities, of all that was left of Sodom and Gomorrah, while around them lay volcanic dust and desolation and deposits, pillars of salt, and the savage depth and spread of the lowlands, far under sea level; this haunted region of furnace heat and barren land, piled over with red rocks and blue boulders and yellow clay, poisonous in the nostrils— the long, blistered shore of the Dead Sea.

Yonder they must go now, to the point, seven miles off, more or less, where the rushing river entered the bitter lake, after its long descent from the Lake of Galilee, or Kinneret, as men called it then, as they say Genessereth even to this day. At this juncture of dead and living waters, drink of death and of life, they were to cross into the Promised Land.

The people were happy, now they were on the march again, for to their simple minds it already seemed as if their hardships and trouble were behind them, and forever. Some members of the tribes of Reuben, Gad, and half the full number of Manasseh were left behind, for they had been given the fertile lands on the eastern side of the river. For the others there stretched away on the other side the riches of the Promised Land; all that seemed left for them to do was to cross the Jordan and claim every square mile for their new home.

But that consummation was not to be peaceably accomplished.

The land was already well populated; its cities were crowded with Canaanites, fed by their farmers tilling amiable and ever prodigal fields and meadows. The farmers were a sturdy and resolute lot, always ready, so reports ran, to march to war whenever brawn and ferocity were needed. Moreover, the city-states were walled and fortified, and governed by clever kings, warriors all, and when their defenders sallied out to battle they rode in iron chariots, the latest and most improved weapons in their hands.

How strong were they in numbers? How ready their will to fight? Before he could plan a campaign Joshua had to know such facts as these, to match the estimates against the potentials of the children of Israel.

They were a poor, struggling people, still in the psychic throes of achieving nationhood and in vital need of all the food and manufactures to be had in the land of milk and honey. Canaan was not a large country, roughly six thousand square miles, which is a third less than the size of the American state of Vermont. But Canaan had mountains of grandeur, gentle hills and smiling valleys, wide plains, abundant springs, and a seacoast. Furthermore, it was the enviable caravan link between the empires of Mesopotamia and Egypt, in whose trade there was great profit.

Joshua had to know the facts. That necessity was why he sent out two of his most trusted men, to swim spring freshets of the foaming green of the Jordan, and to penetrate into the nearby city of Jericho. The two spies were to find out what they could, and pray to God to help them get safely back to Joshua with their report.

In those days there lived in a house on the wall around Jericho a woman of ill repute. Her name was Rahab, and her disreputable establishment was a one-room affair over an abutment, a kind of buttress at the end of the inner wall, looking on the bridge that ran down from the city gates.

It was to Rahab's door—directed there by a leering peddler of fruit juices in a goatskin bag—that the two spies of Joshua came and asked for lodging. Lifting the spangled curtain at her window, Rahab pushed back the hinged window sash and looked the strangers down and over. Then, swaying her voluptuous body until all her bangles jingled, she opened the door and stood there, smiling, hands on hips.

Never had these innocent spies, born amid desert wandering, unacquainted with city ways, seen such a woman before. Her face was painted, her lips, and even the lobes of her ears. The hard eyes, greenish like jade, were surrounded by dark circles crayoned with intense black paste. The stuff of her flowing robes was of a silken texture unknown to her callers, and dyed in stripes of red and green and yellow; jewels were in her ears and golden bracelets and silver bands on arms and wrists; so on her ankles, the ornaments making a *cling-clong* sound as she walked. And by the way she smiled at them the young spies understood the unfamiliar fact that Rahab was one who would have carnal traffic with any and all who came to her with cash in hand.

The spies had been provided with cash and with gold but they wanted only a lodging for the night.

Rahab smiled, as one who saw more than she would tell. Enter, strangers. Here is bread and milk and honey—Israel's first taste of that food of the new land, promised so long, long before. Rahab treated her guests as if she knew the two young men were not ordinary strangers. She guessed what they were precisely: agents of a mysterious and distrusted horde of strangers from no one seemed to know where, encamped over beyond the Jordan. Everybody in Jericho had been talking about them for days, ever since they were first discerned coming on from the direction of Moab. Out of the desert, rumors and wild yarns had come before them, tales of how the God of these wanderers performed miracles for them whenever necessary. Was this true?

Rahab's eyes were bright with curiosity and fear. The two spies knew now that all Jericho was living in terror of coming invasion. This would be great news for Joshua.

Then suddenly there came a fierce knocking at Rahab's front door: soldiers of the king striking the panels with their spears. Discovery! The two spies, as one, lowered their trembling voices and whispered:

"Help us quickly! Where can we hide?"

Amid the thudding blows on the door, Rahab, the first woman under-cover agent, proposed her historic bargain. Well she knew that her house was watched by the secret police of the king, full of suspicion of all outlanders. Always she had herself been loyal to the throne of Jericho, but now everything was different. There was an army on the other side of the river, ready for an attack. The God of that army was all-powerful and always to be counted on; so the spies had just told her.

"Promise me that when your soldiers come," whispered Rahab huskily, "they will spare me and my family—and I will hide you."

Under a mass of dried flax stalks piled on the roof Rahab hid the two Israelites, while she lied to the blaspheming soldiers at the door. Yes, she admitted, two men answering the descriptions had been in her house. But now they were gone. Better hurry on into the city and find them. And she chuckled when they believed her and darted off into the narrow and coiling streets.

As soon as it was safe the young spies came down from the roof to thank her but Rahab was still intent upon her bargain.

"Give me a token that we shall be unharmed," she urged, "since I have shown you kindness."

What token? One spy lifted from the sleeve of her dress a scarlet cord.

"Place this around your window," he told her. "Our soldiers will know to look for it. And you will be protected."

Then, and not before, between the dark and the daylight, Rahab let the men down from the wall by a rope. Their bargain was faithfully kept by the troops of Joshua. When the city of Jericho was reduced to cinders and hot ashes, only Rahab the harlot and her kinfolk were spared.

But that rescue was to be possible only after an extraordinary act of faith by the Israelites and the fulfillment of one of God's most remarkable promises.

The plans for invasion were started as soon as the two elated spies returned from the house of the harlot and made their report.

"Certainly, the country is ours for the taking," they said. "We know that the people faint because of us!"

Joshua, too, felt the thrill of conviction. He gave orders for an early march in the morning. Moreover, the Voice had already given him mysterious instructions—the strangest orders ever received by a besieging commander, before or since. Only a man who placed complete trust in God could have accepted such advice. But Joshua, stouthearted in his faith, took the Voice seriously, literally, and proceeded to carry out the orders.

The people followed him, heading westward for the riverbank. The ark of the covenant was borne by the Levites in advance of all the others by many rods, a fixed distance of holiness. Ahead of the men of war, went the women and the elders, and the wide-spreading flocks and herds. The impressive procession reached the brink of the flooded Jordan at nightfall.

But there the swift turbulent water, spilling over the banks, gave them pause.

"How shall we cross? Where is the ford?"

"Tomorrow the Lord will do wonders," Joshua promised. "The living God is among you and without fail He will drive out from before you the Canaanites, the Hittites, the Hivites . . ."

At sunrise priests bearing the ark set their feet in the Jordan. And suddenly its rushing waters seemed to cease, to flow no more, backing up its arrested mass to the north and remaining solid and unmoving while dry land appeared for the children of Israel to cross over in safety. To commemorate this act of God, so like that of the Red Sea passage forty years before, twice twelve stones were selected by representative men of the tribes. The dozens of holy rocks were heaped up, one pile in the river at the feet of the priests, and the other twelve set up in Gilgal, where they encamped on the other side, memorials to God's power.

This was a strange and brooding time in the career of Joshua and all the Israelites, a time of wonder and an imminent impression of greater wonders to come. How was it that there fell from the sky no more of the manna on which they had come to depend? No more manna could mean only that they would need it no more; they were at the threshold of a land overflowing with bounty. It must be so! And who was the stranger with drawn sword?

Joshua had never heard or seen such a creature before. Yet one night, all of a sudden, there he was, undeniably, blade uplifted and glittering in the moonlight, on Joshua's lonely stroll.

"Are you for us, or for our adversaries?" challenged Joshua.

"As captain of the host of the Lord am I now come," said the stranger, and Joshua knew by the very accent of the voice that this was a supernatural visitor whose tones were like echoes of the Voice of God. At once Joshua prostrated himself.

"What does my lord say to his servant?"

"Loose your shoe from off your foot; for the place whereon you stand is holy."

It was from this celestial apparition that Joshua received his precise instructions by which the fortified, seemingly impregnable city of Jericho was to be overthrown:

"You shall compass the city, all you men of war, and go round about the city once. Thus shall you do six days. And seven priests shall bear before the ark seven trumpets of rams' horns: and the seventh day you shall compass the city seven times, and the priests shall blow with the trumpets. And it shall come to pass, that when they make a long blast with the ram's horn, and when you hear the sound of the trumpet, all the people shall shout with a great shout; and the wall of the city shall fall down flat, and the people shall ascend up, every man straight before him."

Curious and yet redoubled assurance this was, that God was with Joshua as He had been with Moses. When Joshua promised to obey, and looked up again, the mysterious stranger was gone.

Jericho was well prepared for a siege. Powerful though its fortifications were, the area of the city covered only about six acres, and its population little more than fifteen hundred. But it was surrounded by two high walls, the outer one six feet wide, the inner wall double that width. It had only one gate, the one near Rahab's house, looking east.

Joshua ordered that the ark of the covenant be paraded behind seven priests with rams' horns, all in accordance with his mysterious instructions. They persevered for an entire week in what seemed to them an inexplicable charade. Day after day a long procession marched around the walls of the beleaguered city, the ark held high in the general silence; once around, on six days, but on the seventh day a change, exactly as specified. It must be seven times around on the seventh day, while the warriors marched to the fore and the silence ended.

First quiet, broken only by the muffled tread of priests and warriors, carrying the ark around the city. Then suddenly the tart sound of a tantara, a quick succession of notes blown on trumpets made from the horns of beasts, and Joshua's powerful bellow for all to hear, within the city as well as out:

"Shout! For the Lord has given you the city. And it shall be accursed. Only Rahab the harlot and all that are with her in her house shall live."

Loud blew the trumpets. The war cry of the Israelite people resounded to the skies. And then the never-to-be-forgotten miracle as the walls of Jericho came tumbling down.

They fell flat to the earth, those mighty walls of such great thickness, as if smitten by an atomic blast. Under the fronds of palm trees the Israelites marched over the ruined walls and took possession of the city, in which only one exempted woman and her disreputable household were spared.

In our day the ruins of the broken walls have been unearthed; the catastrophe proved, even to skeptics, to have been an established fact. Materialists who find no proof that God personally instructed Joshua, and who can see no sensible reason to believe that prayers and processions, blowings of rams' horns and shouts to the sky could ever produce the destruction of a city, now examine the fragments of the tragedy and conclude that, naturally or miraculously, but certainly mysteriously, the defenders of Jericho were indeed wiped out, all of a sudden.

The enemy and his animals were destroyed; only his silver and gold and vessels of brass and iron were preserved and consecrated to the Lord. The soldiers' loot and booty were forgone, as a thank offering.

So Jericho was no more, and the wanderers were in the Promised Land, and very set up with themselves for having won such a tremendous victory, forgetting the Promiser. They felt well able to go on, without supernatural assistance, to the full conquest of Canaan; they considered themselves powerful warriors indeed.

It was not strange, then, that suddenly they were stopped short.

Chapter 15 THE CONQUEST OF CANAAN

Now Joshua was to have a taste of the troubles that Moses had known: the disobedience of the people he had to lead, their readiness to stop worshiping God and worship themselves, or even the idols of strange tribes; their sudden panics, their everlasting childishness that was like one persisting malaise of delinquency.

The lost battle of Ai was an example. Flushed with the victory of Jericho, they all became very full of themselves, as an invincible host. Why not attack the next city immediately? Pounce on the king's city of Ai and exterminate it, with all its inhabitants. The inhabitants were fewer in Ai than in Jericho; it could be taken without the loss of a single Israelite.

Against the sober judgment of less impetuous minds, and without bothering to make one prayer to the Lord God, the hothead soldiers decided to attack. Not far from Bethel they assembled and threw themselves at the city gates—only to find themselves met by an inferior force that nevertheless fought with strength and ferocity. Shrieking with rage, the heathen foe flailed at the Israelites, who fell back in terror, turning their back to Ai and its defenders and running away.

At this degrading spectacle, Joshua rent his clothes. Barefoot, he stood with the elders, the rulers, and ran ashes through his long gray hair.

"O Lord, what shall I say when Israel turns her back before her enemies?" Joshua cried in woeful prayer.

Had these people no stability, no hope of holding on to the lessons of past experience? Like Moses, Joshua bitterly asked himself if they would ever, ever learn. Walking outside his tent in the moonlight on the night of their defeat, Joshua was hailed by a messenger with even more disturbing news.

The gold and the silver they had taken from Jericho was gone, booty sacredly put aside for the glory of God. It was then Joshua began the first detective investigation of recorded history, first official police inquiry into the malfeasance of man. And, as later sleuths were often to find, Joshua encountered a wall of silence. No one would talk. No one would denounce his fellow.

But Joshua broke that wall of silence as he had tumbled the walls of Jericho, by appealing to God and reminding his people of their disloyalty, which had just cost them a battle. Now another sin against Yahweh cried for exposure; it must be requited quickly, for the safety of all.

And next, a cry of remorse. There was a casting of lots and as this indication fell, one soldier looked guilty. The same man stepped forward from the ranks and threw himself on the ground.

"I did it," he wailed. "My name is Achan, a soldier of Judah."

Might Heaven forgive him, he begged, as he laid bare his conduct. He had never been a good man, although he was a good fighter. But in all his career he had never before attempted such a flagitious, wicked deed. Sly and avaricious, he could not get the gold and the silver cups and plates and candlesticks out of his mind's eye, nor a certain garment, a prince's robe of purple stuff with green and yellow fringes on the sleeves.

And now the wretched man confessed that the candlesticks and cup and also the robe were hidden in the ground under his tent. The agents of Joshua dug up the evidence, the proof of the impious theft, and by general acclaim Achan and his whole family were stoned to death. Their bodies were burnt that day in the valley of Achor.

When they had applied this vengeance the people felt better; as if by punishing one exemplar they had purged and acquitted themselves. Relief surged through the congregation, the general conscience at rest.

And Joshua heard the Voice again, directing him how to go against Ai. A strategy of ambush was planned, in which some Israelites were to bait the enemy with false flight, duplicating their former retreat, while others of the host were to lie in wait to smite Ai suddenly.

The operation was a complete success, and it was Ai's turn to be destroyed and leveled. Hanged on a tree, the king of Ai swung lifeless in the wind.

With Jericho and Ai wiped out with bewildering quickness, fear of the irresistible Joshua and his host spread throughout the land of Canaan. Kings of other settlements began to propose alliances to each other, joining together in preparation to repel aggression. By now they were certain that Joshua meant to conquer the whole region. And, as they were heathen, having no faith in the God of Israel, and denying His authority to dispose of their property by giving it away to His chosen tribes, they were determined to resist to the death.

At that time there was a city called Gibeon just a few leagues over the hills, with a local king whose people were called Gibeonites. He was a strong friend of the king of Jerusalem and should have stood with him, and with other kings, in the alliance against the oncoming armies of Joshua. But the stealthy-minded king of Gibeon thought up a masquerade by which to hoodwink Joshua and outwit him with trickery. His intention was simple enough; his country lay directly in the path of Joshua's march. With Jericho and Ai before him, the city of Gibeon knew what to expect—obliteration, death to the king and every man, woman, and child.

But the king of the city of Gibeon had heard a wonderful rumor about these invaders. They believed in the sacredness of a man's word, of a promise once given. They might fall away from their ethical ideas now and then, but such was their code. If Joshua could be tricked into giving his promise the Gibeonites might be spared.

So Gibeon's king decided to deceive Joshua by making believe that this tribe was really settled at a far distant place, not in his path at all, nor in his sphere of interest. Surely, then, they need not quarrel.

Joshua's simple soul, they felt sure, would never suspect their subtle intention; and of course they had no idea that God would talk to him and give him all necessary counsel; they would have laughed at such a notion, for to begin with, they did not even believe in God. So dressing themselves in threadbare garments, putting on worn-out shoes, and providing themselves with moldy bread, as if they were at the end of a long journey, they stood at the flaps of Joshua's tent in his camp in Gilgal.

"From a very far country, your servants are come, because of the name of the Lord, your God, for we have heard the frame of Him . . . now therefore make you a league with us."

Accepting their story, Joshua made a league of peace with the people of Gibeon sworn to from that day forth. With the signed sheepskin, the shabby outlanders departed for their "far" country, which soon was discovered by Israelite spies to be only a few leagues over the hills.

Hoodwinked! But there was the treaty; the sworn oath of friendship prevented any violent retaliation; the pledged word could not be violated.

"Let them live," said the princes of Israel to the cheated Joshua. "But let them be hewers of wood and drawers of water unto our congregation."

And so it was, although the Gibeonites piteously pleaded their fear, their danger, and that deception was the expedient thing for them to try. The sentence remained. Forced labor, with apparent moral justification, had come into the world.

Even as slaves, as hewers of wood and drawers of water, the Gibeonites were not safe. They, who should have stood with their own kind, were now serfs of the newcomers, while the five kings of the land planned its defense.

Particularly wroth was the king of Jerusalem. He was called Adoni-Zedek, and Adoni-Zedek was incensed at the weakness of the king of Gibeon, hitherto his friend. As a result he called a conclave with four other Philistine kings of the southern region to inflict a bloody punishment upon their lily-livered friends. With their united strength they could take Gibeon as a prize of war for themselves, and with Gibeon in their pockets, they would confront the infesting Israelites.

Seeing the approaching hordes of the five kings and their armies, the disarmed Gibeonites screamed for Joshua. Five armies were not to be taken on lightly, Joshua knew, but the heard the Voice:

"Fear them not, for I have delivered them unto your hand."

Gathering his forces together, Joshua then marched from Gilgal, while it was night. Dawn found them on the field of battle, before the armies of the five kings dreamed that they were near. Fury added to surprise, the Philistines, lifting short, sharp spears, came charging, hurling the javelins fiercely and swinging spiked war clubs and broadswords. Soon the fields were made crimson with the blood of Israel and of the five kings and their cohorts, red plains under a burning sun.

Joshua deployed his troops, spreading them out in his carefully plotted line of battle, but the enemy was fierce and fighting for survival; this was to be no easy triumph.

Hours and hours passed, and the fighting went on and on. The five kings and their minions showed astonishing and tireless valor. But gradually, as more hours passed, with no letup in the fury of the conflict, the Philistine leaders began to realize that something was wrong, something fantastically weird and strange hung over this battle.

How long had the armies been fighting? Hour upon hour. True—and where is the sun but still high in the heavens, still the golden ball of noon. When will it set, when will gloaming come, when will night cover us so that we can rest? Not for a long time, O royal five! For this is a disputed day in history, whose mystery will challenge the credulity of men forever. They will never cease to wonder, with the five bewildered kings, at the undiminished daylight. Never since, indeed, has there been a day like it, when in the presence of his enemies Joshua found a unique power bestowed on him by the Lord, as the battered general stood on a hill and called to the sky for help, that his enemies might not rest and re-form their lines:

"Sun, stand thou still upon Gibeon; and thou, Moon, in the valley of Ajalon."

The sun and the moon to stand still! What a thing to pray for! We moderns could tell him: "This boon, Captain Joshua, cannot be granted to you; it is impossible for the sun to stand still upon Gibeon, or anywhere else, and equally impossible for the moon to halt in the valley of Ajalon. Impossible, brave, eager, trusting Joshua, simply because, in the sense that you are speaking and praying, the sun and moon do not move at all—so how can they stand still for you? It will take science thousands of years to realize this fact of impossibility, but they will learn, someday—and will know, therefore, that while you may have prayed for such a thing, it was an unanswered prayer for an impossible thing."

So the realist would say to Joshua, and the more he knew of astronomy the more positive he would be. But the five kings would tell the modernists another kind of story. The five kings lost the battle. Their people were massacred because sunset was retarded, the light of heaven kept burning, with no opportunity to rest, while the Israelites continued to pour in more and more reserves, hacking away with no thought of stopping short of victory.

Overhead the sun stood stubborn and still, pouring down heat and light, and over the vale of Ajalon men saw the moon in silver refulgence, hanging steadily in the eastern sky. "Is this not written in the book of the just? So the sun stood still in the midst of heaven and hasted not to go down the space of one day. There was not before or after, so long a day."

Across the field of that sublunary battle the five kings sent messengers to one another, calling attention to the tall figure of Joshua like a man of bronze, as he stood on the hilltop as if directing the very sun itself. Nothing, they agreed, surely, nothing could be done against a magician of such power.

Time to retreat, now that time had been subject to a human master. Demoralized, the combined five armies that had invited battle fled in defeat and confusion, leaving the field of carnage to the Israelites.

The five kings—as has often been a royal practice even in our times —tried to save themselves from the fate of their subjects. They hid themselves deep in caverns, amid the limestone damp and bat-flown galleries of a cave at Makkedah. But the agents of Joshua found them there and yanked them back into the still lingering light of the evening. The monarchs fairly crawled before Joshua, those once proud kings of Jerusalem, Hebron, Jarmuth, Lachish, and Eglon.

"Put your feet on their necks," Joshua yelled to his captains, which they did, though with a certain awkward hesitation. Never before had they seen kings treated as worms underfoot. But Joshua said:

"Fear not, nor be dismayed, be strong and of good courage: for thus shall the Lord do to all the enemies you fight."

The five kings were hanged to trees. At sundown their bodies were cast into the cave in which they had hidden and boulders were piled at its mouth.

Battle after battle now, and victory upon victory. By the waters of Merom another alliance of northern kings was broken and their power finished off. Thirty-one petty kings fell before Joshua and his warriors in that long, unremitting campaign, until the strongest part of the land of Canaan was in the possession of the Israelites and the Voice told Joshua it was time now for him to rest.

In his heart Joshua was grateful to the Voice for the word. He was getting old. The people must consolidate their gains, digest their booty, distribute the conquered lands, and begin their cultivation.

There were nine and one half of the tribes of Israel waiting for their portion of the new home land: Reuben, Gad, and half of the tribe of Manasseh were not counted, for they had already received their shares on the other side of Jordan. Now all the others were given their shares, except the tribe of Levi, which was devoted to the service of the Tabernacle. In lieu of a portion of land, the Levites were given, as a gift in perpetuity, forty-eight cities and suburbs by their brethren of each tribe; and the support of the Levites was to come from the Tabernacle monies and offerings.

Finally Shiloh, a city which was in a wide valley surrounded by verdant hills, some twenty-five miles north of Jerusalem, was appointed the center of worship. There the Tabernacle was to be built and consecrated as the soul of Israel.

At last the tribes were at rest, and ready to work their land of milk and honey, which the Lord their God had given them. And aging Joshua, feeling his end was not far off, called for all Israel to stand before him in Shechem, where he might remind them of the favors of the Lord and their bounden duty to love Him in the future. Like Moses before him, he rehearsed all the wonders and works that had been done for the children of Israel since Abraham's journey to Canaan "from the other side of the flood."

And Joshua lifted up his eyes and said:

"Choose you this day whom you shall serve. Now therefore fear the Lord and serve Him in sincerity and in truth: and put away the gods which your fathers served on the other side of the flood, or the gods of the Amorites, in whose land you dwell: but as for me and my house, we will serve the Lord."

The people chanted:

"God forbid that we should forsake the Lord to serve other gods."

Joshua warned them:

"If you forsake Him and serve strange gods, then He will turn and do you hurt, and consume you."

"Nay, we will serve the Lord," they insisted.

"You are witnesses against yourselves," he warned them.

"We are witnesses," they vowed.

Then Joshua set up a great stone under an oak near the sanctuary of the Lord for a witness to their pact, and that day he knew his work to be finished. Not long after, Joshua, the son of Nun, died, and he was buried in Mount Ephraim. Likewise, the bones of Joseph, which had been carried out of Egypt, were laid to rest in Shechem, in a plot of ground once bought by his father Jacob for a hundred pieces of silver.

But who was to rule now in Israel? Serving as a committee, the elders, the wise old ones of the tribes, did very well for a while, after the death of Joshua. The people and the land were at peace. Who among them would have dreamed that they were soon to reach the darkest age of their history?

BOOK FIVE

The Rule of the Judges

Chapter 16 THE STARS FIGHT IN THEIR COURSES

F R O M the day that Joshua was laid to rest until a night when a child called Samuel heard the Voice and answered it, the people of Israel were ruled by their own elder statesmen—in the time of the judges. It was a time of repetitious cycles, of history regurgitated—Israel falling into wickedness and calling down punishment upon itself; Israel repenting, again promising to be faithful, whereupon God would call a new personality to be leader and a judge, to deliver the people into freedom and to give them still another chance.

These judges, whose careers are related in the Bible's book of that name, were unrelated, unchosen by the populace, springing up by divine call in crisis. Their history makes up the chronicle of fourteen administrations, wise and foolish, brave and craven, including great figures like Gideon, Abimelech, Jephthah, and Samson.

No sooner was Joshua buried than the old senseless cycle of sin and repentance began. It had been planned to go on and complete the conquest of Canaan. Now that divine goal was put aside, while the children of Israel made friends with the Canaanites, compromised and fraternized with them and tolerated their heathenish way of life, until, with the passage of the years, they began to forget the Lord God, their promises to Him and His promises to them. The Ten Commandments were largely dead letters in the public conscience; every day the people violated the prime ordinance of the ten by bowing to the strange, false gods—Baal and Ashteroth, imaginary powers at whose altars they sacrificed, whose help they besought, so that, when war overtook them again, they went down to defeat.

These were turbulent times with the whole land in violent agitation, fearing always that war and extermination were near. One said "Do this," and another, "Do that," and Israel again fell into the anguish of disobedience; one day, brazen with contumacy, with incorrigible obstinacy toward a God in heaven Who had been tender and merciful; the next day, penitent and contrite. Not a pretty nation, but the best God had to look to for the hope, not yet relinquished, that had been born with Adam and Eve in Eden.

It was the judges, imbued with grace, who saved the great hope and kept it going on the earth, during those years of waywardness. By their efforts tribal solidarity, at least, was maintained in the midst of a cynical apostasy. Thus the judges did their best as spiritual leaders of a fickle population; they did very well indeed in preserving the political and economic life of Israel.

There was Othniel, younger brother of Caleb, who served forty years. Wise and strong as Othniel was, he could not keep the people true when the yearning to commit sin, as sanctioned by false theologies, brought them to their knees in idolatry before lifeless images. And after Othniel, Ehud, the second judge, for eighty years prescribed righteousness, but all too often his voice was drowned out by the noise of orgiastic revelry. Then came Shamgar, a man of physical might, a giant in height, whose shoulders and arms and thighs were humbling to behold. He controlled his temper as day after day he saw the Philistines, pillage and plunder in their hearts, make forays into the peaceful towns of Israel—riding in on marauding expeditions, robbing, kidnaping, and killing. But one day Shamgar lost his patience and he is remembered for the fact that in one day he slew six hundred Philistines with a ploughshare.

But it was the fifth in the long judicial line who earned the brightest niche in history. That was the time of Deborah, first woman to be touched with the finger of divine appointment as a leader of men—tall, dark-eyed, lovely Deborah, anticipating St. Joan, glorious Deborah was both judge and general.

No one guessed beforehand the role that Deborah was going to play. She lived as a prophetess in the hill country of Ephraim, and the people came to her for advice. At this time, Barak, the son of Abinoam, of Kedesh-Naphtali was governing the land.

So matters stood when another great danger threatened the people. They were in one of their long sprees of idolatry when word came that King Jabin of nearby Hazor was purposing to attack and lay Israel low. Already he had begun to assemble an army of Canaanites under the command of fierce and redoubtable Sisera, who was King Jabin's military expert. And when Sisera said he was ready for action the army under his leadership boasted nine hundred chariots of iron.

It was when this awesome threat overshadowed the people that Deborah really emerged.

As, centuries later, Joan was to hear voices calling her to destiny, so Deborah was suddenly, incomprehensibly, selected to be the one to save the people from enemies, within and without.

So Deborah turned her back on her tents on the hillside. Leaving children and home and all other duties, she trudged down to the center of things and faced the elders and told them she had talked with God and had a message for them.

What thing is this? The elders stared in frightened incredulity, as they nervously milked their beards. But Deborah was not to be outfaced by scared old men. She insisted on talking to Barak, the judge, face to face.

Inspired by God, and "as a mother of Israel," Deborah urged Barak to take ten thousand men and to go into battle against the terrible Sisera at Mount Tabor—centuries later the scene of the Transfiguration—near the river Kishon. This assault, she declared, was the word, the urgent command, of the Lord.

"Not unless you go with me," replied Barak, who was neither coward nor jester; he sensed a power possessing this prophetess that in the time of battle might bring him victory.

"I will surely go with you," promised Deborah; and then she warned him: "Notwithstanding, the journey shall not be for your honor. For God will sell Sisera into the hand of a woman!"

Two women, as it turned out.

Sustained by the fire of faith that God had told her what to do, Deborah marched along in step with the Israelite host against the combined forces of the Canaanite kings.

That historic clash was immortalized in the glorious Song of Deborah, one of the precious literary legacies from those far-off times. The Song of Deborah records the high tide of the furious battle waged on the great plain of Esdraelon, over against Mount Tabor. Barak's ten thousand men were augmented by thousands from various tribes of Israel, help from the whole nation. Even so, the armies behind Deborah were pitiful in number and equipment against the enemy in his iron chariots, the tanks of that day, yet inspired Deborah knew no dismay. Dark eyes glowing, hair flying behind her, she shouted to Barak and his men:

"Up! For this is the day in which our God has delivered Sisera into your hands. Is not God gone out before you?"

A new, mysterious strength of will and of muscle seemed to flow suddenly, warmly, through the ranks of the Israelites. They surged forward, and presently they were hacking and struggling with the Canaanites in hand-to-hand battle. Their fate did look desperate, too, until assistance came pouring from the skies in a blinding torrent of rain. Like the trap of Napoleon at Waterloo, the rain made a bog for the chariots of Sisera. And while they struggled, tangled and trapped, the ten thousand men of fighting Israel smote them from all sides.

Later, when the battle was over and won, and all the people were called together, convoked to give thanks to the one true God, Deborah hymned her victorious song:

> "They fought from heaven:
> The stars in their courses fought against Sisera."

While the charioteers were mired in mad confusion their great general, already tasting a defeat more bitter and disgraceful than he had ever feared, deserted his own chariot and ran away. Fleeing across fields without direction or goal, Sisera was stopped by Jael, an Israelite woman, the wife of Heber, friendly to King Jabin. With a smile and uplifted hand, Jael offered the battered wanderer the hospitality of her tent.

"Give me a little water to drink," Sisera pleaded, "for I am thirsty."

But Jael gave him cool milk instead. With womanly tenderness she sympathized with his aches and pains, his exhaustion, and coaxed him to go to sleep. She covered him with a blue blanket when finally he did lie down.

"If any inquire of you, I am not here," he cautioned sleepily, and sank into slumber. For a few minutes Jael waited, warily watching his breathing until it became deep and quiet and regular.

Then Jael took a big wooden nail, a spike used to anchor the tent ropes, and deliberately drove it into Sisera's temple, beating the point right through his head with a mallet.

Not a sound from dying Sisera then, except one short final spasm. Jael stood proud and alone with her motionless victim. She had broken the sacred law of hospitality but she did not care. For her heart was with the cause of the Israelites. And Deborah, judge and general and prophetess, would sing of Jael and her desperate hammering:

"Blessed above nomad women shall be Jael, the wife of Heber; the wife of Heber, the Kenite."

But while Sisera lay with his spiked head on the ground, his mother at her palace window kept peering through the lattice of woodwork with crossed bars, anxious for her son's return. She did not dream that he had lost the battle. He had promised, with a fond smile, to bring her pretty spoils, including the fine needlework of Israelites, which she coveted. Thoughts of his death were farthest from her mind. Had her son not gone forth with the greatest army ever seen in Canaan?

But soon she would hear Deborah sing:

"So let all Thine enemies perish, O Yahweh!
But let them that love Him be as the sun
When he goeth forth in his might."

After that decisive battle in which a farm woman led the troops on to victory for the first and only time in the records of Israel, there were forty years of peace, while the loving and forgiving God, the one, the true, once more expunged from the present all records, all consideration of their misdeeds, as if they had never been.

But, eventually, the same old pattern: more wickedness, then retribution—hordes of old enemies from outside the borders of Canaan, the cruel, the detested and relentless Midianites and Amalekites, descending in a bandit scourge upon the peaceful countryside until the crushed Israelites fled from the fields of milk and honey and hid themselves in caves.

From those damp galleries of refuge in rush-lit dimness of a limestone labyrinth they turned, as usual, miserable and shameless, to the Lord God, once more imploring His help. And would God again forgive them? They had no priest, no judge, no leader left to which the wise, consoling Voice of old could now speak.

But suddenly out of one unclouded afternoon the angel of the Lord appeared to a man named Gideon. At no time had Gideon ever thought of himself as a political or spiritual or military leader of his people. All that, he might have said, was quite out of his line; he, Gideon, a general and a priest and a directed instrument of the will of God? Nonsense! Any average man would have the same sort of feelings today. For Gideon, the son of Joash, was a businessman and a farmer and he was well to do. In spite of the gangster raids of the Midianites and the Amalekites over so many bloody years, Gideon had not abandoned his farm, his far-spreading grapevines, his wine press, and his livestock. By one stroke of shrewdness after another Gideon was still there, still selling his produce, putting aside a decent profit and keeping his family in comfort.

One day as he was threshing his wheat he heard the voice of an angel appearing before him and addressing him in somber, majestic accents:

"The Lord is with you!"

In another thousand years a voice would speak that same assurance, in hailing Mary, the peasant girl of Nazareth.

"The Lord is with you," the Voice declared, and added an incomprehensible compliment: "You mighty man of valor!"

Gideon, tall, sun-browned, black-haired, and strong, stood in the midst of his wheat and chaff and in bewilderment lifted the back of his hand against his eyes. Man of valor? He, Gideon, had no experience in war. And this Voice was speaking as if, through him, the God of Israel was addressing the people.

"But the Lord has forsaken us," he protested, only too well remembering how Israel had deserved to be deserted. But the Voice replied:

"Go in this your might and save Israel. . . . Surely I will be with you. And you shall smite the Midianites as one man."

"But give me a sign," begged Gideon, unable to believe or fully to grasp his sudden commission. But even as he was pleading, he brought out food for his visitor and spread it on palm leaves laid across a rock that would serve as a table. The sign that came then convinced Gideon.

The angel merely touched the victuals with his staff and they instantly broke into bright crackling flames—dates, milk, and roasted kid all eaten up by the miraculous fire. When Gideon looked toward the visitor again there was no one standing there—the messenger was gone, leaving nought but the ashes of a meal he had not tasted.

Gideon knew that he had been truly called to be the new leader; he must proclaim himself such, with all the authority of an Eastern suzerain ruling over a wide domain; knowing nothing whatever about government, he felt himself invested with paramount authority, chosen to save Israel. Striding back into the settlement, Gideon headed straight for the ring of gray boulders which was the place of worship, the altar of heathen gods.

The people saw him stand there with arms uplifted, as if in divine entreaty. They heard his unaccustomed voice, raised for the first time in public address, calling them all toward the circle. And as they rushed to see and hear, full of curiosity as always, herding together around the ring of boulders, they found themselves in front of a man transformed from a peaceful farmer to a veritable judge over their sins, a man driven by conviction into an ecstasy of authority over them and obedience to the Lord God.

Before their amazed eyes the big and simple man fell upon the symbols of their treason with passionate violence. Swinging cudgels, he pounded away at the boulders of the false altar, until the granite crumbled and the stone fell apart; he made havoc of that altar of Baal, even though it had been erected by Joash, his own father, and he cut down the *asherah*, or sacred pole of the heathen idol, and used its wood for fire in a burnt offering to the one, true, invisible God upon a new altar that he built in front of them with his own hands. Not in nearly a century had there been such zeal for God seen in Israel.

The people were astounded, outraged by the audacity of young Gideon. A cry went up that he be put to death; how far from their God now were these Israelites in their devotion to Baal!

However, Joash, thoughtful and influential father of Gideon, refused to be stampeded into giving up his own son for a death sentence.

"Let Baal defend himself," argued Joash; if Baal was a real god, now was the time for him to assert his divinity. It was that challenge which resulted in Gideon, son of Joash, being thenceforth called Jerubbaal, which name meant "Let Baal contend."

Baal, of course, did nothing whatever to show his resentment at the wreckage of his altar. No one heard his voice, no one saw him, a disillusioning silence and emptiness for the people. They began to regard Gideon respectfully as a fearless fellow who had apparently put Baal in his place. And when now they got word that savage Midianites and allies were already massed for battle in the valley of Jezreel, it was natural for them to turn to Gideon.

The world today fears the atom bomb no more than did the Israelites dread the coming onslaught of their enemies. They were sure it would mean total destruction; it would devastate their fields, depopulate and lay waste what cities they had left. Wicked and idol-worshiping cowards, now they were all frightened and full of their familiar remorse. They were willing to do anything Gideon asked of

them: renounce their sins, abjure the Baalian idols—there was no ab-
negation too severe to get back into God's grace; no self-deprivation
too severe to promise; and no tomorrow of second thoughts rose in
their minds; they meant what they said while they were saying it, if
for no longer.

If ever Israel needed a champion it was now, they wailed. And
Gideon, having heard and obeyed the Voice, was no longer retiring or
doubtful; he took command at once. Quickly he had gathered together a force of thirty-two thousand men on the slopes of a mountain, which overlooked the enemy encampment.

And at this point there came a profound and mystifying test. Suddenly the Voice spoke again, ordering Gideon to reduce his men to a
handful of three hundred picked soldiers, a command without example in the history of warfare. What other general on the eve of battle
would listen to God and disarm himself at the very whisper of the
Voice? Gideon did that.

From the eminence of the mountain, where he could overlook the
armored might of his foes, he turned back to his own troops and bade
them retreat, ordered them off, demobilized and sent back to their
home tents without hurling one spear at the enemy. Such was
Gideon's faith in God, such his obedience. Three hundred valiant
men remained with their general; an army of three hundred and one,
if God is not numbered with them.

The people of Israel were aghast. Had Gideon lost his mind? His
very method of choosing his three hundred seemed to them as frightening evidence of insanity. For Gideon had picked his men through a
peculiar test of the manner in which the soldiers drank water while
kneeling at the edge of a stream. Those that lapped water from their
own hands were the ones to be chosen. All this, he declared, was done
according to the order of the Lord God, who would now show for all
time that a few men, imbued with His power, were equal to any out-
numbering of heathen antagonists. And by sheer force of will Gideon
compelled the people to go along with him; he told them he did not
try to understand God; he sought merely to obey.

What exactly was he planning? The people were demanding an answer. Yet, if he told them, Gideon's plan of action would appear quite
as preposterous as his test of the lapping of the water. He was preparing his strategy on a dream recounted by an enemy soldier! When he
heard of that vision of a cake of barley bread falling upon a tent and
overturning it, slight though its weight was, Gideon pounced on the
dream as the idea for the campaign. At least that dream was its seed.

Calling his force of chosen men, Gideon divided them into three companies. To each man he gave a trumpet, together with an empty jar, or pitcher, in which there was to be set a torch, a bough of a tree, oiled for quick lighting.

Deployed strategically in the darkness, the three hundred with their trumpets and lights were to listen and wait for Gideon's trumpet. That brazen sound would be the signal. Then all three hundred must blow their trumpets, making the loudest, most earthly blasts possible, mingling the trumpet notes with maddening yells, and at the same time lifting their pitchers with blazing torches. And they were to shout:

"The sword of the Lord and of Gideon!"

Silent as painted figures on a wall, the three hundred men took their positions in a circle around the sleeping camp of the enemy. Unmoving, noiselessly, they awaited the call. An hour of black quiet—and then the sudden blast of Gideon's horn. Like an echo a thousand times amplified, their trumpets screamed in answer, their broken pitchers flamed with tongues of fire, wild voices screamed and yelled, and to the enemy it seemed as if a numberless horde of demons had fallen upon the bivouac. The Israelites ran amok with their swords, shouting the war cry: "The sword of the Lord and of Gideon."

Awakened by what seemed to them an overwhelming superiority of numbers, the Midianites scrambled up into panic. Wildly disordered, they fled toward the Jordan Valley, snatching up what they could of their weapons and possessions. It was mob terror—sheer, downright, absolute fright; the sole thought, escape.

Dawn showed Gideon and his three hundred men still in hot pursuit of Zeba and Zalmunna, the fleeing kings of Midian, and their thousands of men, all scared witless. Rounded up at Karbov, miles away, and putting up no resistance, these two kings were slain, after being exhibited to the elders as prizes of war. The special display was because those same elders had doubted the Gideon leadership and tried to confuse the people.

Now Gideon was the hero of heroes. Thanks to his courage in trusting the divine counsels, the raids and persecutions of the Midianites were over. Enormous booty captured after the battle would make up many old losses. All Israel was buoyant with joy, the people so delirious that their elders actually approached Gideon with the offer of a crown.

"Rule over us," they urged. "You and your son and your son's son also."

"I will not rule over you, neither shall my son: the Lord shall rule over you."

Really there was an old, ingrained prejudice in Israel against kingship, and Gideon's wise refusal was in line with their deepest feelings. They were well in hand for forty years during which Gideon remained the chief and judge.

But with his death, his calm, righteous influence was dissipated. It seems incredible, but the Bible says it is so that, as of old, the Israelites again reverted to the forbidden worship of Baal.

Their promises were just as frangible as ever, vows just as easily broken.

Gideon had left behind him seventy sons. As soon as their father was in his grave they began to wonder if one of them should not succeed him, even though Gideon himself had renounced a successor.

Sixty-nine of the sons merely speculated on the matter, but the remaining one, bolder and more practical, acted. His name was Abimelech and he had the mind of a natural conspirator. Let his brothers argue; Abimelech left them to their disputations, while he set out for Shechem, where his mother's family lived. There he won the support of his relatives in his ambition to rule, and they furnished him with funds. With this money he hired assassins who quietly, skillfully, and promptly killed sixty-eight of his brothers, who had lived together and who died together in Gideon's old homestead in Ophram.

From this vicious, wanton slaughter only Jotham, the youngest, managed to escape. But everyone believed he was also dead. Remaining in hiding, Jotham was forgotten, while the citizens of Shechem voted bloody Abimelech to be their king. They had no idea that Jotham had taken himself to the top of Mount Gerizim and there told a most meaningful fable to a gathered multitude of indignant mountaineers.

In Jotham's parable, perhaps the first fable ever to be told, the trees were looking for a king. But none of the trees would consent to be king, preferring to follow their own fine, natural uses—shade and fruit for man, housing for birds. However, the bramble consented, in all its vanity and thorns. Now, said Jotham, Abimelech is that bramble, and if my brother prove to be the wrong choice let him be consumed by fire!

Finishing his fable, and leaving them to think it over, Jotham fled again to a secret place where his brother Abimelech could not lay hands on him.

In the end Jotham's fable had a great effect on men's minds. Soon, between Abimelech, the human bramble that would be king, and those he would make his subjects, there was deep dissension, and at Shechem many Israelites took to the hills, became the first bandit-revolutionaries, and under the guidance of a tough adventurer called Gaal they worked night and day to overthrow the Abimelech government.

When these guerrillas felt they had grown strong enough Gaal baited Abimelech as an upstart usurper, daring him to fight it out. This foolish challenge was accepted. Abimelech, with all the resources of entrenched power, swooped down to besiege Shechem, until the harried population seized Gaal by shoulder and rump and shoved him out through the city gates, a sacrifice, an appeasement, a peace offering to Abimelech.

But the pretender, though son of Gideon, was without mercy. He continued to pound his battering-rams against the walls of Shechem, to toss over his burning torches, to raise his escalators and send his soldiers up and over, every one with massacre in his soul.

Men, women, and children fell in that general slaughter, and those who escaped the first onslaught—perhaps a thousand men and women of all ages—were packed like salted fish in the city tower.

"Firewood!" yelled Abimelech.

Everywhere the invading soldiers turned to the urgent task of cutting down the fair green trees. Blood lust unslaked, Abimelech himself wielded an ax, felling oaks and tamarisks and pines, piling the logs higher and ever higher, around the tower with its thousand captives—and then setting fire to the heaped-up fuel.

All the thousand were cremated; all died in one red torture of malodorous and consuming bonfire.

When, by nightfall, the flames began to die down, Abimelech groaned aloud. His pleasure was receding and the letdown infuriated him—let them take another city immediately so that they could have another such ghastly revel of fire and death, without a day's delay. On to the next town, which was Thebez.

Nor could Thebez resist the military machine which Abimelech hurled upon its tiny army. The rams battered their brick and mortar, the flaming casts fell over the wall, the boarding ladders went up—all was as it had been in Shechem, even to the thousand leftovers, jammed into the city's tower.

But here the story changed.

Some nameless Israelitish heroine acted in God's name that sad morning; some daughter of the old faith, who knew her heritage from Abraham to Joseph and to Gideon. How she could have dragged such a thing along with her and not be seen, no one knows, but she had a broken millstone under her skirt, and she waited to use it until bloody-fingered Abimelech, with scorched eyelids from coming too close to his pyre of enemies, came within her view. She waited until he was under her position at the parapet of the tower. And just as he was giving orders for more tree felling, more log piling, more oil smearing to make the timbers burn, that unknown Israelite maid, or wife, or widow, or whatever she was, leaned over the parapet and let the broken millstone fall from her hands, and it struck the pretender's skull.

Abimelech tumbled to the ground and lay there with a crack in his head from which there wormed its way a living scarlet thread.

The frightened people, long since sickened by his abominable cruelties but not daring to protest, now stood around the fallen terror in a breathless circle to watch him die. Hours passed, as he lay as one already dead, but eventually he opened his eyes to the light of noon, the sun at its topmost glare and heat, and he knew that his life was finishing.

"Draw your sword," he gasped to his armor-bearer. "Slay me! That men may not say that a woman slew me."

His rolling eyes upturned in savage hatred toward the tower from which that brave woman had dropped the broken millstone.

Then the sword fell——

The children of Israel believed now in Jotham's fable. The fires of the thorn tree, set to devour human life, had destroyed Abimelech.

They knew now—or so declared—that they should never have followed the pretender in the first place, nor should they have forgotten all the patriarchal and judicial teachings of the past. Yet, with Abimelech dead, they soon fell into error again, continuing their idolatrous ways. No longer relying on the God that had chosen them, they were prey to more raids, more maraudings, kidnapings, murderings, arsons, rapes, and finally full-fledged war, waged upon them by the Philistines and the Ammonites, savage enemies, both. Finally the greedy Ammonites decided to kill all the Jews in the Promised Land, to be rid of them forever.

The time had come for a new champion to save the people from extinction. And, as always, one appeared. There was a man among them whose name was Jephthah. He was the leader to which the old men of the tribes turned, asking that he rule over them in their peril and be ninth of the judges of Israel.

Jephthah stared at this nominating delegation as if he doubted his senses. Were they actually asking him to become their temporary governor, virtually their dictator until the foe was beaten off—he, the son of a harlot mother? He who all his days had been scorned and cast out, as illegitimate, the trash of townspeople? Denied his father's house because of the scandal of his birth!

"Come, Jephthah, and be our captain," the people insisted. They knew of his reputation in his own fields for courage and wisdom.

"Once you hated me," he reminded them. "And now you seek me in your distress?" He eyed them coldly but shrewdly. "If the Lord deliver the enemy into my hands, will you elect me your head?"

"Yes," the elders swore, as God was their witness.

Jephthah lost no time in organizing the Israelite men of war for a battle that would draw the enemy's fangs. But meanwhile, during the secret preparations, Jephthah tried persuasion with the king of Ammon. That arrogant monarch would not talk peace at all, insisting that the children of Israel had stolen his land, and he intended to regain it; his resort to arms was final.

In his great eagerness for victory Jephthah made a foolish vow. He promised the Lord God that if he won the battle he would offer up as a sacrifice whatsoever creature greeted him from his house after his return as conqueror.

Victory was his. The Ammonites proved powerless; their soldiers fell like wheat before the reaper's stroke. Twenty of their cities were taken, and the Ammonite military strength was destroyed.

Every drop of his blood surging and singing with his triumph, Jephthah returned to his home in Mizpah. The bar sinister of his origin was blotted out in glory and victory. But wait! Who was that coming to meet him from his door? A girl with timbrels, dancing—his daughter, his only child, prancing and singing to celebrate her father's victory.

She was a teen-ager, full of a very young girl's glee and extravagant love for her father. Her face was glowing with joy as she strutted toward him in a dancing pantomime of congratulation, all sprightly and gay, leaning her head far to one side and clanging her platelike metal disks high above her bosom, as she hastened toward her father with a blithe, rhythmic welcome.

Then she saw the horror in his eyes.

"Alas, my daughter!" he moaned as he rent his clothes. "I am bowed down to earth in grief. For I have promised the Lord a sacrifice of the first one to greet me from my house!"

The girl stood silent for a long moment. She thought upon the news of doom. But when at last she spoke it was as if Jephthah were the child, not she:

"Do to me according to that which you have promised the Lord, as He has given you victory over our enemies."

"Oh, that I might die instead of you," wept Jephthah.

The terrible fate of Jephthah's daughter is not unique although it seems to be so. There are such tragedies every day in every year—suffering and separation and death falling on the innocent. Men and women cry, as Jephthah's dancing child might well have cried:

"Why should this happen to me? What have I done to deserve it?"

It is the divine teaching that the meek, those who, like this young girl, can accept the worst and still believe in the goodness and mercy of the Lord God, shall inherit the earth. It is not easy to believe this statement without the gift of faith, but it is true. The nameless daugher of Jephthah did not wait or bemoan her fate as did her far less spiritual father. Already, in her mind, she was preparing to die.

The gift of two months more of life she asked him for and he agreed. At least he would have her with him for those two months, as he reckoned—but his reckoning was wrong, for the girl took companions of her own age and went into the mountains. There for two months they prayed and meditated on the mysteries of life and death. Calm and beautiful, the doomed maiden then came back to her father, who had to keep his vow though his own life would be made void because of it. So Jephthah put his own child to the sword.

His daughter's example of obedience unto death was an unforgettable lesson in Israel. But Jephthah's example was also unforgettable—for the general had made a tragic and horrible moral blunder. He never should have made such a vow in the first place and, having made it, he never should have kept it.

Because of her fate, the maidens of the race instituted the custom of yearly withdrawal four days to lament the passing of a shining soul.

But could the Israelites learn obedience to the Heavenly Father even by the example of Jephthah's daughter? The next years were to give strange answer.

178

Chapter 17 SAMSON

F o R some years following the death of Jephthah—he soon followed his daughter into the grave—the children of Israel fell back into disorderly habits, and three judges, one following the other, could not influence them.

In those days the tribes were trying to be all things to all men and to their gods. Nowhere among them was clear vision or purity of faith any more. Let Micah of Ephraim stand as a general example; Micah who built himself a private altar on his estate, a sanctuary, elaborate and with all the ceremonial properties, yet on that same sacred altar to God he also raised a forbidden molten image, and hired a Levite of Bethlehem to officiate at a service that included and tried to meld both, the one true God and Baal! And that Levite willingly complied.

It was a dark period—dark as any before or since—when "every man did that which was right in his own eyes," with few knowing right from wrong.

Meanwhile the Philistines more and more began to dominate the Israelites, enslaving so many of them that they were as badly off as their ancestors had been before the exodus from Egypt. The Philistine power was growing, so that they were able even to oust the tribe of Dan from their portion of the Promised Land, forcing them to quit their inheritance and settle in a northern part of the country.

These non-Semite Philistines were a sea people who had come from the Aegean regions of what we know as the isles of Greece. They arrived seeking fresh territory and settled along the Mediterranean coastal plain, building five important cities—Gaza, Ashkelon, Asdod, Ekron, and Gath. Each of the five cities had its "lord" or "tyrant" who ruled independently, but they all united in action for the common welfare, in offense and defense. Ultimately the name of "Philistia" was given to Canaan, "Palestine" as the Greeks made it.

The Philistines were inventive, and among other secrets, possessed the priceless formula for making iron, which had already revolutionized agricultural implements and weapons of war. Aware of past conquests, the·Philistines determined to keep the Israelites in check by threat and aggression, and decided to begin against Judah and southern Israel.

But while they were making their farseeing political and military plans a baby was born who was to become their great affliction; he was to be the thirteenth judge of Israel, unique in that dynasty of magistrates as a lone champion, strongest of all the warriors of history—and a huge, lumbering giant of a man, marked for tragedy.

Samson was the son of Manoah of Zorah of that defeated tribe of Dan, already evicted and living on new-found land farther to the north. Like the mothers of some other Bible great men, the wife of Manoah had been a barren woman until an angel of the Lord made himself known to her and announced that she would conceive. Her child was to be consecrated to the service of the Lord God; he was to be brought up a Nazirite, which meant that he was not to taste wine or unclean food, and his hair was never to be touched with a razor.

Brought up in this severe fashion, Samson grew to be the strongest man ever to walk the earth. Often his parents worried about how their son would use his enormous physical powers. Father and mother were wise enough to realize that his full-blooded body must contain a sensuality that was as urgent and intensified as were all his other physical appetites. Samson, they saw, had too much of everything, except self-control, and they tried to teach their son how to master his most compelling feelings and be lord of his passions.

Thus in boyhood and youth Samson was made to live a religious life. He actually felt close to the Lord God and even believed that he was to have a divine mission to inspire the people by heroic deeds. They were going to need heroism, for the crafty Philistines were already shrewdly at work infiltrating themselves into the daily life of the wavering Israelites. Their peaceful penetration, backed as it was by reports of growing military preparedness, troubled the elders deeply—and thus caused division between themselves and their children. For the young people were attracted by these persuasive outlanders. Even Samson liked their company—more, he horrified his parents by announcing that he had fallen in love with a woman of the valley, a Philistine girl from Timnath.

To the old folks it was unthinkable that their Nazirite son, dedicated to the service of the one true God, should be drawn to one of an enemy and heathen race, people who respected neither truth nor honor, and followed disgusting false gods of fertility and sensuality.

What kind of influence would a woman of such people exert on their giant son, brought up in such simplicity? They could not surmise, "they knew not," as the Book of Judges reports, "that it was the Lord, that He sought an occasion against the Philistines."

"Is there no daughter of Israel to please you?" his parents pleaded.

"None," replied Samson in the finality of youth. "I must have the beautiful Timnite for my own, and you, Father, must get her for me."

He did not believe his adored one cared anything about the religion she had been born to. He was sure she would join him in the worship of the one true God. Anyway, he wanted this girl more than anything else in the world.

So the parents, heavy at heart, yielded to their strong-willed son and set out on the long walk to Timnath to begin business negotiations with the family of their son's inamorata. Behind them by an hour or so followed mighty Samson himself, his shadow flooding the yellow road. At the loneliest part of the journey the young giant heard a hissing noise, smelt a sudden tang of wild flesh—and there came flying down from a crag in the rock, claws extended, mouth slavering, the fiercest of mountain lions. There was less than a second's warning; Samson must act instantly or the teeth of the beast would be buried in his throat. Almost automatically he raised his incredibly large hands, caught the springing beast as if it were a bundle tossed to him, and with one unhesitating movement pulled the long-toothed upper and lower jaws apart.

Limp, broken, and choked with a fountain of blood, the lion lay helpless in his grasp, while Samson methodically ripped off its legs, broke its bones, and tore open its middle—then cast it to the ground under the center of the wheeling crows and ravens.

This experience Samson considered a good omen from on high. He washed the blood from his hands and face and resumed his journey, resolved not to tell his parents, or anyone else, what had happened. Perhaps the strong man did not want to boast. Or perhaps some wise influence cautioned him to silence. He was, at any rate, to be glad that he kept his adventure to himself.

At the home of his ladylove in Timnath all was going well. The old folks of both families got on with each other and arrangements for the marriage were made without a hitch. Indeed, the Timnite family were glad to have an alliance with a man of such renowned strength. The Philistines had giants in their own armies, but there was none like Samson. Cherishing a lock of the slain lion for luck, Samson returned home with his father and mother to await the date set for the wedding.

"Did you not think her wonderful?" he asked them.

His parents changed the subject. The persistent racial prejudice could find no exception. With a resigned but sullen air they made ready for the wedding feast.

On the journey back to Timnath, Samson had a childlike curiosity to look again at the bones of the lion he had torn apart with his bare hands. So, slipping off by himself, still telling his parents nothing, he went alone to the spot. The carcass had been undermined by jackals and crows but a swarm of bees and their store of honey filled the opened stomach. This strange discovery Samson felt certain must be regarded as a sign. Perhaps the honey might hold some magic virtue to win over his parents to his bride.

Gathering a portion of the honey, the bees being not at all hostile, Samson shared the sweet with his mother and father, saying nothing of its source.

Soon, however, Samson forgot his worries about the attitude of his parents in the frantic excitement of the wedding. The marriage rites were brief, but the wedding feast was to last seven days. Stories, music, and riddles were to accompany lavish eating and drinking. These customs were new and strange to Samson; he felt more and more ill at ease. Among the guests were thirty young men, all old friends of the bride. She was very popular, as even Samson's parents could see. But these blades of the past assumed a vaguely superior air, as if to outshine the bridegroom. Sophisticates they were, and elegant, and Samson, to them, was a simple boor, all body and no brain.

Samson, nevertheless, tried to take them good-naturedly. But finally their boasts of worldly experience and knowledge began to nettle him. Wine already had loosened their silly tongues, but Samson was cold sober; because he had been dedicated to the God of Israel, no drink except water might pass his lips. Some of the heady youths twitted him. What kind of bridegroom was he not to take a drink at his own wedding? Did he not know that a bridegroom ought to match each cup drunk by the company? Even amidst such raillery Samson managed to keep his temper, until the clique of the thirty male friends of the bride tried a new tack. Was he good at riddles?

This favorite form of entertainment had been going on, and Samson had neither answered any of the conundrums nor propounded any. That was when Samson got angry. These foreigners considered him a nitwit. Samson smiled fatuously like a child borrowing adult indulgence.

"Look you," he said. "I will grant these thirty gentlemen of quick wits and speech seven days to guess my riddle—and wage thirty changes of garments on the outcome."

That was a real challenge. Samson's parents looked deeply worried; they knew their giant among men had neither skill nor practice in this intellectual pastime. But Samson, as if by some inner spiritual counsel, persisted. He knew beforehand, without knowing how he knew, that the thirty mocking young Philistines would neither guess the answer—nor pay the promised forfeit. Then he would have a just reason for breaking with the Philistines and that schism, he foresaw, was soon going to be necessary.

Seven days' time to answer a riddle! Thirty changes of garments the stake! The young men winked and nudged.

"Lo, a riddle to outriddle all riddles!" they gibed. "Tell it to us."

Said Samson:

"Out of the eater came forth meat, and out of the strong came forth sweetness."

Puckered brows and whispered conferences brought no solution. Every answer they gave was wrong. After three days of guessing, the clever young men of Timnath became alarmed at the prospect of having to pay the wager to this Israelite lout. It would bankrupt every profligate one of them. On the seventh day, when they must lose or win, they called Samson's bride to a private corner.

"You must get the answer to the riddle out of Samson," they warned her. "Or everybody will think it is a scheme of yours to rob your wedding guests. And what's more, unless you help us, we will set fire to the house and burn you up in it."

Fully aware how ruthless the young Philistines could be, and perhaps sorry also for the humiliating position Samson had put them in, the bride promised her old friends to wangle the riddle's answer out of her dolt of a husband. As yet he had told no one what it was, not even his mother or father. Therefore Samson was thunderstruck when the lovely creature patted his cheeks with her cool soft palm and pleaded with him for the answer. Why did she want to know? Well, she argued, if he truly loved her, he would share all secrets with her, his adoring wife. For an hour or more she coaxed and cajoled, relaxed warmly in his arms, and wept until Samson, born to be weak with women, capitulated.

Leaving him with moist kisses, herself with the secret, the bride hastened to her thirty men friends and gave them the answer. When the last day's feasting was resumed and wine flowed, and all the wedding guests were together again, the spokesman of the thirty said:

"What is sweeter than honey? And what is stronger than a lion?"

The company cheered and toasted the winners; no mere bumpkin

Israelite, they chortled, could ever outsmart a Philistine. Samson morosely walked outside. He knew exactly how he had been hoodwinked and betrayed. Alone he strode toward the nearby town of Ashkelon. He stalked through the gates, killed thirty Philistines with his bare hands, and lugged their garments in his arms, back to the wedding feast, where he paid his debt.

Nor did Samson tarry. In grim silence mother, father, and giant son made the long journey home together, all resolved to think of the false Philistine woman no longer. But Samson still could not get her out of his veins. He resolved to humble himself, to appease his bride. He would take her a prized kid as a peace offering. There is no doubt that Samson was still in love with the Philistine woman.

But now, to his surprise, she was his wife no longer. In Philistia as everywhere else, a deserted bride was a disgrace. So according to the Philistine custom the father of the bride had taken legal steps to save his child from humiliation—his jilted daughter was now the bride of a sympathetic friend, one of the thirty.

"I thought you had hated her," the father said. "But she has a sister who is younger and fairer than she. Take her to wife instead."

Like a curse was Samson's answer:

"From this day I shall be blameless in what I do against the Philistine; for I will do you evil."

Clearly, the massacre of the thirty men of Ashkelon had been weighing on his conscience. But no more! An idea was blazing through his brain as he turned his back on the woman's father and walked away.

It was harvest time, and the crops stood ready for reaping. With skill and endless patience the big fellow hid himself in the field, while he performed the fantastic feat of trapping three hundred foxes. He joined their tails, each pair tied together, and fixed a firebrand in each knot, and lighted the standing corn. Soon Philistine harvests were burnt up beyond all salvage, and with them the vineyards and olive groves.

And, as usual, violence begot violence; the Philistines punished the Timnath father and daughter by burning them alive. Then they pursued Samson but only to their death: the mighty Israelite turned and slaughtered the pursuing posse; he smote them hip and thigh; he scattered them like chaff.

When all the bloodletting was over, Samson hid himself on the top of a lonely rock called Etam, in a low ravine, far from his home.

Even in the wilderness of sand and granite, with buzzards and scorpions his company, Samson could not keep back the world. His mortal enemies, the Philistines, marched across the frontier; their army threatened the people of Judah with death by the sword unless the giant arsonist and killer was captured, safely bound, and delivered to them. Three thousand Judeans marched into the desert and gathered at the base of the high rock where Samson stood alone.

"Have you forgotten that the Philistines rule over us?" they shouted to him.

The strong man heaved a sigh at the littleness of the human spirit. But what did it matter? Upon their promise not to harm him, he let them bind him with windings of rope and fetch him prisoner before the overlords of Philistia.

They carried him to Lehi, where assembled Philistines hurled insults and curses upon the big man, until suddenly the roots of Samson's hair tingled; he felt the thrill of some divine power descending upon him. One stretch of biceps and thighs and the ropes that were tied and retied around his body burst like thread.

Spellbound with fear, the Philistines watched that feat of muscle and power. They remained still awed and silent while Samson stooped to pick from the ground a curious object, a monstrous weapon, the whitened jawbone of a dead ass. Who could have foreseen, only five minutes before, that a thousand Philistines would be slain by a single man, swinging a donkey's jawbone?

So much did the Philistines dread him that their generals in council refused to wage any more war on the Israelites, as long as they had the giant to fight for them!

"Let us waylay him in the dark," one said to another, "when his God is not with him." They decided to be crafty and wait. And meanwhile Samson became a judge in Israel and served for twenty years.

But the time came when Samson brooded on the inertia all around him. He felt deeply despondent. Oh, if he were only another Joshua, or a Gideon! Well, he was not; he knew that he lacked their brilliance, their qualities of leadership. Why, then, should he waste his wonderful vitality in despair? Why not enjoy life? So Samson, drawing away from God, was attracted again to Philistine women, for to him they were always diverting and gay. One night in Gaza he paid a visit to a courtesan, not caring a straw whether any of his friends knew it or not; let anybody try to interfere with sullen Samson.

Perched at an antic angle on his head that night he wore a black sheepskin cap from under which his hair poured down over his shoulders in an ebony torrent. He was easily recognized; some of the Philistines of Gaza saw him go into the woman's house and promptly decided that the time had come to trap him. Locking the city gate with extra bars, a company of them lurked in the darkness ready to pounce on the giant when he sought to leave town, probably at midnight or later. They meant to overpower him, knock him senseless, dismember him, and send his bloody parts to several chief cities to be hung on public walls as exhibits in festivals of rejoicing that the most dangerous man in Philistia had been done away with.

But again the Philistines underrated Samson. When they saw him coming, a lantern in his mighty hand, they rushed up and threw themselves at him. But the great body did not go down; Samson shoved the conspirators aside, lifted the city gate with its brazen posts deeply embedded in the earth, pulled the whole thing free into the air, slung it across his shoulders, and carried it to the very top of a hill, and from there, without an extra breath, he tossed it down toward his assailants.

"But we'll destroy him yet," they promised one another after he was gone.

On all his comings and goings they continued to keep a watch. Knowing that women were his besetting weakness, they were delighted when at last reports came that Samson was smitten again. This time it was the beautiful Delilah from the valley of Sorek, a siren who with her first glance had made the big fellow her slave. It was rumored that this man, thewed as with iron, who could strangle an ox with one arm, was like wax in the soft and perfumed fingers of Delilah.

Without delay a committee of Philistine princes and elders waited on the woman. They exulted at the sight of her, for her sensuous body was indeed fashioned to betray a man's soul.

The Philistine elders looked at each other, raising shaggy brows, and came directly to a business proposal:

"We want to find out the source of the unparalleled strength of Samson. There have been others as tall, as broad, as thick—but never another one so strong.

"Deceive him and learn of him wherein his great strength lies and how we may be able to overcome him, to bind and afflict him; which, if you shall do, we will give you, every one of us, eleven hundred pieces of silver."

If she could discover the source of Samson's strength Delilah would be rich.

But Delilah, too, underestimated Samson. She considered all men weaklings. But Samson was no weakling; he was not easily persuaded to tell his secret. Delilah's sudden curiosity, her persistent cajoling, awakened bitter memories of his Philistine bride and her treacherous entreaties about the secret of his riddle. There was no mystery, he told Delilah; he was born to be strong, just as she was born to be beautiful. Ah, but there were many secrets of beauty. To build a body like his must require a special regimen, or else some supernatural direction. Tiring of her coaxing, Samson gave her a series of wrong explanations; once he told her that if he were bound with seven cords made of sinews and green withes, not yet dry, he would be weak like other men. So it became a sort of game between them. When she had bound him, according to his recommendations, Delilah would call aloud, as if summoning his enemies to pounce on him, and then Samson would instantly break his bonds like cobwebs. Of course Delilah had never given the real signal to her cohorts, realizing that the fly in her web was not yet caught. At last she desisted in a fruitless game and fell back on tears and tender reproaches.

And Delilah said to him: "How do you say you love me, when your mind is not with me? You have told me lies these three times and would not tell me where your great strength lies.

"And when she pressed him much, and continually hung upon him for many days, giving him no time to rest, his soul fainted away and was wearied even until death.

"Then, opening the truth of the thing, he said to her:

"The razor has never come upon my head, for I am a Nazirite, that is to say, consecrated to God from my mother's womb; if my head be shaven, my strength will depart from me."

Should she believe him or not? He certainly seemed convinced of its truth. And Delilah remembered that the fops and dandies and other weaklings of the world were forever going to barbers and getting their hair cut.

"Shorn of my hair," declared Samson, "I would be as weak as any other man. Now you know."

Delilah veiled her eyes, not to let him see the scorn she felt for him. Dunderhead! Blockhead! You are your own executioner, you mighty dunce, to betray yourself for seven drops of water falling down a woman's cheek. Already she was hearing in her mind the clink of blood money.

Cannily she took herself to the Philistine committee that had hired her and demanded payment before she revealed Samson's secret. Agreeing, they warned her that her life would be forfeit if her information proved false. Thus, in mutual distrust, they put their heads close together and presently Delilah had a new assignment.

Dressing herself that evening as for a high festival, in purple and cloth of gold, her face painted, her ears, fingers, wrists, ankles, and toes bedight with jewels, Delilah greeted Samson as if he were a royal guest. The warmth of her greeting, her mood, excited him like a potion. What a lucky man he was to possess this most desirable creature!

That night Delilah outdid herself in attention to him, singing his favorite love tunes and preparing a special fruit drink he liked. The air of the room was drowsy with perfume, and the music of dulcet strings was a lullaby.

Samson grew sleepy, just as Delilah had planned.

"Couch your head in my lap," she suggested, "and forget the world and its cares."

And soon Delilah lulled the big fellow to deep sleep. Making sure that he was indeed lost to the world, she signaled to someone unseen. In a moment a little man hopped into the room, a razor gleaming in the lamplight. With the touch of a ghost, the dwarfed barber had Samson's head shorn of its seven locks within five minutes and never a flutter of the victim's eyelids. As noiselessly as he had appeared the dwarf vanished, grinning, arms laden with the hair of the sleeping giant.

At once Delilah began to pummel the sleeper.

"Awake, awake, the Philistines are upon you, Samson!" she cried, her voice now harsh and strident.

Samson felt a chill on his head. His hand, rubbing his skull, brought home the truth to him, even as a dozen Philistines crowded over him. With hot irons they put out the eyes of the betrayed man. Then they took him, blind, helpless weakling, back to Gaza, through the very gate he had once lifted and which was now restored.

All the city screamed with glee at the sight of him. There before them, bound with fetters of brass, the once mighty Samson was set to grinding corn and he was whipped if he lagged.

The elated Philistines busied themselves for weeks in preparation for a great sacrifice to Dagon, their god, a thanksgiving feast that would be a national festival. Thousands gathered for the celebration at the green granite temple. Eating and drinking and love-making were untrammeled and wild. When the revelry had exhausted the devices of fleshly pleasure, there arose a cry for Samson to be fetched in as a target for their sport. Blind and ragged, he was dragged from his prison and placed between the two main pillars of the temple, an object of derision and scorn, a stolid fellow, impassive and dull; why had they ever been afraid of him?

"Behold the mighty muscles that grind but corn for pudding!" the people laughed.

When the tide of mockery was at its height Samson muttered to the lad who had led him there:

"Put my hands on the pillars of the house that I may lean upon them."

"Look, he faints!" yelled the watchers.

But Samson was not fainting; he was praying. Aware that during his servitude of the last few weeks his hair had grown to some length again—and that he might also find more grace in humility—he beseeched the Lord God with all his soul:

"Remember me, I pray you, and strengthen me only this once, O God, that I may be avenged for my two eyes."

Through his body coursed again the old thrill of power. Taking hold of the two great pillars that supported the temple, he bent to flex his muscles against their enormous solidity.

And, as the world has ever since remembered, he gave one great push with both his arms—one concentrated effort—and cracked the pillars, pulling the very foundations loose, breaking open the roof and splitting the beams and rafters so that the temple itself was ripped apart, the stones and masonry falling on the drunken revelers—death upon them all, the blind giant destroyer among them.

Thus the ending of a pitiful life that might have been truly great.

Chapter 18   RUTH

IN the troublesome latter days, when judges still ruled in Israel, another famine blighted the land and the people were hungry. With no Joseph to foresee and prepare for their needs, no grain had been stored up in bins; and everyone had to shift for himself as best he could.

There was living in Bethlehem of Judea at this time a man by the name of Elimelech, with his two sons and his good wife Naomi. They were a simple farm family, without the slightest notion that they were to find an illustrious place in the history of the world. Certainly Naomi did not dream that her name would stand forever among women, an example to uncountable generations.

Naomi was simply a gentle housewife, busy at the hundred chores of a farm woman and keeping her sons and that other grown child, her husband, well fed, their garments mended, their beds soft and comfortable. For their comfort and happiness Naomi lived most of her waking time. When Elimelech said that he thought the family would have to move, that they must run away from the drought and the locusts, leaving their birth land, Naomi made no protest; she asked where they would settle.

"We will try Moab," announced Elimelech. Neither Naomi nor her sons lifted an eyebrow, although they all knew that Israelites avoided that part of the world. An old feud still flourished between the tribes and the Moabites, reaching back through centuries to the time of Joshua and Moses. Nevertheless, the young men and their mother helped Elimelech to pack, and turning to the high road, they left the green hills and the tall trees of Bethlehem and, with Naomi on a donkey, the others on foot, made the long descent through desert and mountains to the region immediately east of the Dead Sea. Here, in one of the numerous cities of east Jordan, Naomi made her new home.

In those days it was a green and fertile plateau of well-drained uplands, where the Moabites had been able to maintain themselves as a separate people for more than a thousand years. The boundaries were never more than sixty miles long and thirty miles wide, yet in the flourishing days when Elimelech brought his family there the population was well over half a million, and nearly everybody was making a good living, practicing advanced arts and crafts. The fields were feeding grounds for sheep and goats, grazing contentedly in rich pastures, so that the Moabites needed very little from the outside world, living off their own land and liking their isolation.

Yet the Moabites made the little Bethlehem family welcome, sold them land, helped them to prosper and, when the time came, arranged betrothals for Naomi's sons with two of their prettiest maidens, one of whom was called Orpah and the other Ruth.

For ten years they all lived together, and there was no feeling of homesickness upon the outlanders. But when, one after another, the loved ones of Naomi died, first the husband, next one son, and again the other, and in the household of Elimelech there were three widows in their grief, Naomi began to feel frightened and alone.

, The course of the widow was clear. She must not be a burden on these two women, still attractive and vigorous. They would find new husbands; as for herself, she felt a deep nostalgia for Bethlehem. Some of her old friends and relatives must still be living there. The famine was long since gone; she would find a way to support herself in her old age. Her daughters-in-law, those fresh-looking young widows, were not of the blood of the children of Israel, not bound by the laws of Moses to be forever kind and loving to a dowager mother-in-law.

"The Lord deal kindly with you," she said to the young widows, "as you have dealt with our dead and with me. I leave you, but the Lord grant that you each find happiness and peace in the house of a husband."

The young women answered: "Surely we will return with you to Bethlehem."

But Naomi gently shook her head. She had no more sons to offer them; let them look each for a Moabite husband.

Orpah tearfully kissed Naomi good-by and went her way but Ruth, her lovely face lighted up with devotion, eyes shining as if she saw some private vision, held aging Naomi tightly in her arms and whispered:

> *"Entreat me not to leave thee*
> *Or to return from following after thee:*
> *For whither thou goest*
> *I will go;*
> *And where thou lodgest*
> *I will lodge:*
> *Thy people shall be my people*
> *And thy God my God:*
> *When thou diest I will die;*
> *And there will I be buried.*
> *The Lord do so to me and more also*
> *If aught but death part thee and me."*

They clung together, they turned their backs on Moab, and set out together for Bethlehem, about the time of the beginning of the barley harvest.

But very few in Bethlehem remembered the homesick Naomi. Ten years had changed her as if they had been thirty.

"Is this Naomi?" people would ask with incredulity, and the widow would reply:

"Call me Marah." Which name, as we know, meant bitterness. In bewilderment, finding herself home among strangers, and facing the need for the simplest necessities of life, Naomi seemed unable to decide what they should do. But Ruth, tender always, had a suggestion: let her follow after the reapers in the fields and pick up the waste they dropped behind them. Then they would have enough to grind into flour and make cakes that would keep them alive.

Naomi told Ruth the hazards of such a plan. She was a foreigner, and no foreigner was popular; least of all a Moabite. Nevertheless, if she was still resolved to glean what the reapers left on the ground, God attend her.

So it was, and God did attend her. Barefoot, in beggar's clothes, yet beautiful even in rags, Ruth set out for the barley fields and, keeping a good distance between them, followed the harvesters in the fields, picking up grains here and there.

Now, as it happened, Ruth had entered the farm owned by a certain Boaz, a "mighty man of wealth," who was actually a kinsman of Elimelech. Boaz was a jolly man of middle age with no eye to miss such a beauty as this ragged stranger on his land. So he called his hired workers and demanded:

"Whose damsel is this?"

Told that she was a Moabitess, the daughter-in-law of Naomi, Boaz asked to have the frightened girl brought before him.

And so begins a tender love story incomparably told in the Bible's Book of Ruth:

"And it happened that the owner of that field was Boaz, who was of the kindred of Elimelech. And behold he came out of Bethlehem, and said to the reapers: The Lord be with you. And they answered him: The Lord bless you. And Boaz said to the young man that was set over the reapers: Whose maid is this? And he answered him: This is the Moabitess who came with Naomi, from the land of Moab, and she desired leave to glean the ears of corn that remain, following the steps of the reapers: and she has been in the field from morning till now, and has not gone home for one moment.

"And Boaz said to Ruth: Hear me, daughter, do not go to glean in any other field, and do not depart from this place, but keep with my maids, and follow where they reap. For I have charged my young men not to molest you. And if you are thirsty go to the vessels, and drink of the waters whereof the servants drink.

"She fell on her face and, worshiping upon the ground, said to him: Whence comes this to me, that I should find grace before your eyes, and that you should vouchsafe to take notice of me, a woman of another country? And he answered her: All has been told me, that you have done to your mother-in-law after the death of your husband; and how you have left your parents, and the land wherein you were born, and are come to a people which you knew not heretofore. The Lord render unto you for your work, and may you receive a full reward of the Lord the God of Israel, to Whom you are come, and under Whose wings you are fled.

"And she said: I have found grace in your eyes, my lord, who have comforted me and have spoken to the heart of your handmaid, who am not like to one of your maids.

"And Boaz said to her: At mealtime come you hither, and eat of the bread, and dip your morsel in the vinegar. So she sat at the side of the reapers, and she helped to herself frumenty, and ate and was filled, and took the leavings. And she arose from thence, to glean the ears of corn as before. And Boaz commanded his servants, saying: If she would even reap with you, hinder her not. And let fall some of your handfuls of purpose, and leave them, that she may gather them without shame, and let no man rebuke her when she gathers them.

"She gleaned therefore in the field till evening. And beating out with a rod and threshing what she had gleaned, she found about the measure of an ephah of barley, that is three bushels, which she took up and returned into the city, and showed it to her mother-in-law. Moreover she brought out and gave her of the remains of her meat, wherewith she had been filled. And her mother-in-law said to her: Where have you gleaned today, and where have you wrought? Blessed be he that has had pity on you and she told her with whom she had wrought and she told the man's name, that he was called Boaz.

"And Naomi answered her: Blessed be he of the Lord, because the same kindness which he showed to the living, he has kept also to the dead. And again she said: The man is our kinsman.

"And Ruth said: He also charged me, that I should keep close to his reapers, till all the corn should be reaped.

"And her mother-in-law said to her: It is better for you, my daughter, to go out to reap with his maids, lest in another man's field someone may resist you.

"So she kept close to the maids of Boaz; and continued to glean with them, till all the barley and the wheat were laid up in the barns.

"After she was returned to her mother-in-law, Naomi said to her:

My daughter, I will seek rest for you, and will provide that it may be well with you. This Boaz with whose maids you were joined in the field is our near kinsman, and behold this night he winnows barley in the threshing floor. Wash yourself therefore and anoint you, and put on your best garments, and go down to the barnfloor; but let not the man see you, till he shall have done eating and drinking. And when he shall go to sleep, mark the place wherein he sleeps, and you shall go in, and lift up the clothes wherewith he covered towards his feet, and shall lay yourself down there, and he will tell you what you must do. She answered: Whatsoever you shall command, I will do.

"And she went down to the barnfloor, and did all that her mother-in-law had bid her. And when Boaz had eaten and drunk and was merry he went to sleep by the heap of sheaves, and she came softly and uncovering his feet laid herself down. And behold when it was now midnight the man was afraid, and troubled; and he saw a woman lying at his feet, and he said to her: Who are you? And she answered: I am Ruth, your handmaid; spread your coverlet over your servant, for you are a near kinsman. And he said: Blessed are you of the Lord, my daughter, and your latter kindness has surpassed the former, because you have not followed young men either poor or rich. Fear not therefore, but whatsoever you shall say to me I will do to you. For all the people that dwell within the gates of my city know that you are a virtuous woman. Neither do I deny myself to be near of kin but there is another nearer than I. Rest you this night, and when morning is come if he will take you by the right of kindred, all is well; but if he will not I will undoubtedly take you, as the Lord lives. Sleep till the morning.

"So she slept at his feet till the night was going off. And she arose before men could know one another and Boaz said: Beware lest any man know that you came hither, and again he said: Spread your mantle, wherewith you are covered and hold it with both hands. And when she spread it and held it, he measured six measures of barley, and laid it upon her. And she carried it and went into the city and came to her mother-in-law, who said to her: What have you done, daughter? And she told her all that the man had done to her. And she said: Behold he has given me six measures of barley for he said: I will not have you return empty to your mother-in-law.

"And Naomi said: Wait, my daughter, till we see what end the thing will have. For the man will not rest until he has accomplished what he has said.

"Then Boaz went up to the gate, and sat there. And when he had seen the kinsman going by, of whom he had spoken before, he said to him, calling him by his name: Turn aside for a little while, and sit down here. He turned aside, and sat down. And Boaz taking ten men of the ancients of the city said to them: Sit you down here. They sat down and he spoke to the kinsman: Naomi who is returned from the country of Moab, will sell a parcel of land that belonged to our brother Elimelech. I would have you to understand this, and would tell you before all that sit here, and before the ancients of my people. If you will take possession of it by the right of kindred, buy it and possess it; but if it please you not, tell me so, that I may know what I have to do. For there is no near kinsman besides you, who are first, and I, who am second. But he answered: I will buy the field. And Boaz said to him: When you shall buy the field at the woman's hand, you must take also Ruth the Moabitess, who was the wife of the deceased, to raise up the name of your kinsman in his inheritance.

"He answered: I yield up my right of next akin, for I must not cut off the posterity of my own family. Do you make use of my privilege, which I profess I do willingly forego.

"Now this in former times was the manner in Israel between kinsmen, that if at any time one yielded his right to another, that the grant might be sure, the man put off his shoe, and gave it to his neighbor; this was a testimony of cession of right in Israel.

"So Boaz said to his kinsman: Put off your shoe. And immediately he took it off from his foot. And he said to the ancients and to all the people: You are witness this day, that I have bought all that was Elimelech's and Chilion's and Mahlon's of the hand of Naomi and have taken to wife Ruth the Moabitess, the wife of Mahlon, to raise up the name of the deceased in his inheritance lest his name be cut off from among his family and his brethren and his people. You, I say, are witnesses of this thing. Then all the people that were in the gate and the ancients answered: We are witnesses: The Lord make this woman who comes into your house, like Rachel, and Leah, who built up the house of Israel: that she may be an example of virtue in Ephratah, and may have a famous name in Bethlehem. And that your house may be as the house of Perez, whom Tamar bore unto Judah, of the seed which the Lord shall give you of this young woman.

"Boaz therefore took Ruth and married her and went in unto her, and the Lord gave her to conceive and to bear a son. And the women said to Naomi: Blessed be the Lord, who has not suffered your family

to want a successor, that his name should be preserved in Israel. And
you should have one to comfort your soul, and cherish your old age.
For he is born of your daughter-in-law, who loves you, and is much
better to you, than if you had seven sons.

"And Naomi taking the child, laid it in her bosom, and she carried
it, and was a nurse unto it.

"And women, her neighbors, congratulating with her and saying:
There is a son born to Naomi."

These women actually chose the name for the child; he was called
Obed, and was to grow up to be the father of Jesse, who would be the
father of David, the great king.

And that David, glorious king of Israel, would be born in Bethlehem, ancestor of the human mother and foster father of Jesus Christ,
a thousand years to come.

In that fact is the answer to an enigma.

When we read the Bible we may ask ourselves why this beautiful
Book of Ruth is so prominent; why so much space and importance are
given to the record of this one rather simple family. But the answer is
clear. By marrying Boaz, Ruth, the Gentile, became a progenitor of
the human aspect of Christ, who, according to the prophets, would be
sprung from the seed of David.

Thus the marriage day of Ruth and Boaz brought nearer the realization of a great idea—the idea that God is not the God of one family
or of one race or one nation only, but the Father of all mankind.

Meanwhile the Lord God, not long after the wedding feast of Ruth
and Boaz, spoke again to a mortal—to a boy in Israel whose name was
Samuel.

Chapter 19   THE VOICE IN THE NIGHT

T H E moonlight and the chill wind flowed together through the shut-
terless window in the room behind the kitchen. Stretched on a mattress, a quilt covering his huddled body, a boy lay slumbering. The
world of Israel lay sleeping all around him in the chill wind and the
moonlight, as the Voice that had been heard in Eden began to
speak again:

"Samuel!"

The boy fretted in his broken dreams and nestled closer under the woolen covering but the Voice persisted:

"Samuel!"

The boy opened his eyes, sat up, then leaped from under the cover, the stone floor chilling his bare feet. Running down the long, unlighted corridor, he stood at the door of the bedchamber from which came the smug snoring of Eli, priest and judge.

"Eli," faltered the youth. "You called me?"

But the blear-eyed old dignitary, annoyed at being roused, swore that he had not called his serving boy; let him go back to bed and stop walking in his sleep.

Fifteen-year-old Samuel lay on his mattress, wide-eyed and stirred uneasily by the certainty that he had heard a Voice, majestic and yet kind and rich with music in its tones, and that the Voice had spoken his name. As if it were an evocation, the memory of the mysterious summons called up a troop of old thoughts in the excited young mind, and he remembered that from the beginning there had been a mystery about his life; from his birth and even before.

His mother had told him how he had come into the world; Hannah, his mother, whose troubled marriage had made her feel kin to Sarah, the beloved of Abraham, and to Rebekkah, the sterile bride of Isaac. For Hannah was not the sole mistress of her household; her husband, Elkanah, had two wives, as was his privilege in those times. The other wife was called Peninnah, and while Hannah was barren, Peninnah had borne children to her husband and gave herself airs about it.

Yet—like Abraham and Isaac before him—Elkanah, who lived with his two wives at Ramah on Mount Ephraim in the hill country, loved his barren wife more than the fertile one. Hannah was the joy of his eye, and at public festivals he showed his preference, especially when, once a year, the people would climb the hillsides of Shiloh to make religious sacrifices. All the best of everything Elkanah gave to Hannah, while his other wife gave her scorpion glances and venomous words when the man of the family was not near enough to hear.

Yet years had to pass before Elkanah, the husband, discerned how the grief of Hannah was completely ruining her life. When he tried to console her she rushed away, hiding near to a deserted altar in the place of worship and offering up a distracted prayer.

If she were to be blessed with a son, she promised Heaven, then the boy child would be consecrated to the service of God. This was her petition, her vow, her bargain offered at the place of sacrifice, her head weaving from side to side, the tears spilling down her face—and there the high priest found her when he came softly across the open courtyard. Even then his sight was failing and, no doubt, his judgment with his vision, for the best he could say to the grieving woman was an accusation:

"You have taken too much wine."

"Nay," she protested, "I am a woman of sorrowful spirit."

So fusty old Eli made a decent apology and looked heavenward with her, asking God to grant her prayers. When Hannah left the altar her soul was filled with hope.

When the family returned from Shiloh to their house Elkanah saw that Hannah's face was bright. It was as if her troubles were really gone for good. A youthful attractiveness returned to her eyes, to the very way she walked. The husband's love for her was greater than ever; they knew a second honeymoon.

Before the next yearly visit to Shiloh a man-child was born to Hannah and she gave him the name of Samuel, which meant "Name of God"—the same Samuel who now, fifteen years later, lies sleepless in the moonlit room behind the kitchen, remembering the Voice:

"Samuel!"

The boy was startled out of his reverie of recollection. Surely he had heard the Voice this time! Or was it again a phantasm of the night?

Once more he stood outside old Eli's door and tried to rouse him, but no! Eli only coughed and scolded and sent him scurrying back to bed.

But it was still a restless bed, and his head was besieged with restless memories. From earliest days Samuel had lived in the house with Eli; he had never known boyhood days at home with his brothers and sisters, although a long parade of them had since been born to Hannah. She had kept her vow to the letter; no sooner was her firstborn weaned than she carried him into the place of worship and gave him bodily into the hands of Eli, who remembered his false accusation and saw now the fruit of their joint prayer.

Before leaving her first son in the keeping of the priest, Hannah offered up a new prayer, and a curious feeling came to her, as if an invisible mantle of prophecy was upon her. She began to speak like a seeress, while Eli listened in bewilderment; she was predicting how God would rescue Israel from all enemies. Hannah's magnificat sprang from her vision in which she foresaw the coming kingdom:

"The adversaries of the Lord shall be broken to pieces; out of heaven shall He thunder upon them: the Lord shall judge the ends of the earth; and He shall give strength unto his King——"

But things did not start off well. From the time that he could look about him and judge what was going on, the boy Samuel knew that this altar to the one true God was befouled with hypocrisy and betrayal. And Eli, the priest, refused to take notice or do anything about it. Most of the wickedness was committed by his own sons, and to that outrageous situation Eli stubbornly shut his eyes. And this, in spite of the fact that his sons—Hophni and Phineas—were priests like himself, serving with him in the Temple, sacrificing at the ancient altars, yet secretly adoring and serving evil itself as personified in the heathen Belial. Those sons of Eli worshiped that false god in upsidedown rites in God's own Temple, while good men were sound asleep in their beds. By a mouthful of pretexts, they squeezed money from the people, meanwhile seducing the women who came to them for spiritual advice. They were bad characters, those two sons of Eli. But he was blind to what they were up to, or acted as if he were, until one night a messenger of God, winged and full of light, came before him at his devotions and warned him. Then he did reprove Hophni and Phineas, but they counted on his doting love for them, on his infirm purpose, and they went ahead as usual.

Now the wide-awake Samuel, remembering all these dark matters, and the sound of the Voice he had twice heard this night, cupped his ear and for the third time and unmistakably heard the calling of his name:

"Samuel!"

Impressed at last—for Samuel had the hardihood to wake up Eli a third time—the priest declared it must be the Voice of the Lord; if he heard it again Samuel must give answer.

And soon he heard it clearer than ever:

"Samuel! Samuel!"

And the lad replied, just as Eli had instructed:

"Speak, for Your servant hears."

There and then the Voice gave Samuel a startling message. The house of Eli, the priestly judge, was going to be destroyed, because of its iniquity; the sons had persisted in their vileness, and their father had failed to punish them. When the Voice ended, Samuel fell back, eyes staring at the ceiling.

How could he tell Eli such news?

"It is the Lord Who has spoken," groaned the high priest next morning, having heard the lad's stumbling and embarrassed recital.

He was overwhelmed with the realization that the judgment was just. "Let His will be done."

Yet nothing tragic happened immediately. Years passed uneventfully, with Eli, unharmed, drawing near the century mark, and his sons unpunished still. But Samuel was maturing in manhood and there was a light in his eyes, assurance in his voice, wisdom in his words. From Dan up the coast, to Beersheba in the south, and through the length and breadth of Israel, Samuel was already the talk of the people: already regarded as a prophet of the Lord; they knew Eli and his sons for what they were and they knew that Samuel was beyond corruption.

In those intervening years trouble in plenty was preparing. Always the Philistines had stored aggression in their souls, regardless of treaties. Now they were getting ready to cook up and provoke a full sweeping war; spies brought word that already they were assembling troops. Israel would have to fight.

On a ridge at the place called Aphek the children of Israel struggled against the armed warriors of the Mediterranean coastal plain and the battle was like that of a pygmy against a giant. Defeat overwhelmed them; they fled in a rout.

Then, as usual, and only as a desperate measure, the elders of Israel thought of turning again to God, quite forgetting that they had not cleansed the altar of Eli and his sons, long before.

"Let us bring the ark of the covenant of the Lord from Shiloh that it may save us," they cried.

So the ark was removed from the high sanctuary and borne down to the scene of the renewed battle, the two hypocritical sons of Eli marching with it. Seeing the ark, the people sent up a great shout, so loud that it actually frightened the Philistines.

"What does this signify?" the enemy wondered, and spies told them of the mysterious reliance the Jews placed on the ark. The Philistine strategists were concerned:

"Woe unto us! Never has this thing happened before! O Philistines, you must not be made servants of the Hebrews, as they have been to you! Fight more fiercely still!"

So the ark of the covenant, raised in hypocritical hands, only inspired the enemy with redoubled fury. The irony of this was lost on the worsted infidel Israelites, as they fled before Philistine blows that massacred thirty thousand soldiers. Even the sacred ark itself had been captured by the enemy. And those conniving guardians of the ark, those greedy and lustful and unrepentant sons of Eli, were left dead on the field.

At Shiloh, his clothes rent in despair, and earth thrown upon his head, the aged Eli sat waiting by the side of the road, anxious for news of the battle, of the ark, and of his sons, when an exhausted messenger gave him the truth. With a gasp of horror the old priest toppled backward from his seat, breaking his neck. He was ninety-eight years old. He had judged Israel forty years. It was better for him that he died there and then; being utterly desolate in his own family, he did not live to see the desolation of all Israel.

Now only Samuel was left to guide the people. But could such an inexperienced leader recapture the ark from the Philistines? He was not a man of battle, but of prayer and contemplation.

Yet he knew, and the people knew, that the ark of the covenant was the symbol of all that was highest and best in the tribes. Unless it could be retaken from the Philistines the hope of the twelve nations would perish. Was this not why the Voice had called him from his boyhood dreams?

The life of Israel as a unified nation could never be achieved against so many jealousies and rivalries, unless a new leader arose, some consecrated, unpurchasable man filled with a holy spirit. Unless such a leader came soon the Philistine tyrants, who had combined their strength, would take over all the hard-won territory of the Promised Land.

Where was to be found such an amalgamator of a people forever at odds among themselves, their own quarrels inviting foreign domination? The answer had already been given in the calling of Samuel.

Chapter 20 SAMUEL AND SAUL

THE new leader of Israel had no doubt that troublesome years stretched before him. But he was priest and judge, far more than he was prophet; he could not foresee the ending of the rule by judges and the beginning of a dynasty of kings. Indeed, Samuel, who was anti-royal, an enemy of thrones, would have to stifle his almost ungovernable feelings about monarchs and scepters and crowns, would have to obey the Voice that had called to him in the dark and now would lead him into the light.

All that Samuel knew was that he had been entrusted with a divine message about Israel's future; that he must try to get his scattered and fugitive people together again, to call them down from the green forests and the valley caves and the sands of the desert, the runaways, and encourage them again to renew themselves as Israel, a nation, at the ancient altars.

So Samuel led the way back to Ramah; the place of worship on the peak at Shiloh was lost to the enemy, and the sacred ark of the covenant was in their hands. Remaining at the altar of Ramah, he kept praying for guidance. For seven desolate months he burned the incense of sacrifice and at night he would lie wakeful and listening for the Voice to speak again.

The silence itself seemed to speak of God's indifference, and Samuel did not guess that among the Philistines, the victorious heathen, his prayer as a priest of Israel was already being answered. But Samuel's faith was strong; he kept on praying and trusting, submitting all to the will of God.

Unheard-of things had been happening in Philistia, and more particularly at Ashdod, three miles from the sea and almost midway between Joppa and Gaza. One of the five famous cities of the Philistines, it had been glorious with its white towers and yellow battlements in the days of Joshua, but now it was more famous still, because it had become chief shrine of the pagans, the temple of the false god Dagon, worshiped throughout all southwestern Palestine. A name to chill any pious Israelite—Dagon; silver fish-god and golden grain-god, lord of the heathen nets and harvest fields, an old Canaanitish idol to which bloody sacrifice must be made when the rains dried up and earth's increase failed. Dagon, worshiped by Philistines and Assyrians and Babylonians, cruel and false Dagon had now become the guardian of the holiest of all holy things, the ark of God's covenant with man.

Guardian, yes; so said the heathen priests. But let the brazen image itself be guarded. The panic began as rumors flew about what was happening in the temple of Dagon, ever since the captured ark, treasure of the Hebrews, blessed oblong chest of acacia wood, containing deep within its boxlike cavity the two tables of stone—this priceless symbol, flaunted at a false and alien altar, was setting up strange disturbances.

No one in Philistia could laugh off what began and what continued when the priests with triumphant smirkings brought home the cherished box of the Jews and settled it down before the image of Dagon. The idol was immediately affected. In the presence of the ark it could not remain upright before the symbol of the covenant, which had led the way for the children of Israel through the wilderness, and at the crossing of the Jordan, and in the march around the walls of Jericho; the sculptured Dagon kept falling down; it could not remain upright, but like a doll with a weight of lead in its head, it kept tumbling over like Jericho itself; it fell upon its face again and again. When the idolators would raise its heavy weight to an upright position it would squat on its brazen haunches only as long as they kept their eyes on it; let them blink or look away and over it toppled. Finally one day it crashed once too often and smashed itself to pieces.

At the same time two new plagues swept through the back streets and the public squares of the gay city of Ashdod: an overrunning of mice in every man's closet and pockets, and a plague of boils rising painfully on the hips and breasts and backsides of the citizens; purple and tumid growths, full of yelllow matter that broke through and ran down the good skin, causing a vile smell, and bringing an agony of pain, an abyss of weakness, so that men and women were falling dead everywhere.

To Philistines this booty called the ark was a curse! The pale priests of Dagon had to take action at once. Calling a corps of husky servants, they ordered them to raise the golden ark and carry it, by staves thrust through the golden rings, out of the temple, out of Ashdod.

First they took it to the city of Gath, and then to Ekron, where lived one of their greatest warriors, a giant called Goliath. But the plague followed the ark, and the residents of Gath began to swell and die of the pursuing pestilence. The craven priests hesitated no longer; the thing for them to do was to let go of the ark altogether, to eject it across the borders of Philistia and shove it once more and forever into the hands of the Israelites. So they loaded the ark in a car with wooden wheels, pulled by two cows, and turned them loose with the wonderful burden, to go with it where they would.

And that was when Samuel—suddenly illuminated with knowledge before he had learned of these excitements by natural means—turned to the people and shouted the good news.

Even then the wandering cows without a driver were dragging the sacred chest across the empty fields, in a straight line, turning neither to right nor left, directly toward the town of Beth-Shemesh, stopping before a man called Joshua. And when the golden box was once more in the hands of Samuel and his priests they all realized that the Philistines had been anxious indeed to get rid of it, with good will on all sides, for they had packed with the ark itself a bundle of symbolic golden trinkets which their artificers had worked overtime to finish—five golden mice, all gifts from the enemy, and five golden boils, each glittering boil and each metal mouse for one of the five great Philistine cities. Surely their gifts and the return of the ark must mean the sunrise of peace.

In a great procession Samuel led the people to the top of the hill of Kiryath-Jearim where the ark was placed in the house of an old priest to be watched over by his son Eleazar, whom Samuel consecrated for the task.

But in the very midst of such triumph, something was wrong. They had the ark back; outwardly, at least, they were worshiping the one true God again, but there was a hundred little signs that they were still unreconciled to the God of Israel. They must do something. The people began to assemble at Mispah for a ceremony of public repentance and expiation, the crowds growing larger every day, as they entreated Samuel to intercede; nothing was so important to them now as to make peace with God.

Thus they trapped themselves into more trouble, for the spies of the Philistines saw them coming together and rushed back across the border to report that the Israelites were massing troops to begin a new war. Of this mistake, of course, the Israelites knew nothing. They were still imploring Samuel to help them when far below, on the plains, they beheld the flashing armor, the red cloaks, the green and purple banners of invading armies rushing toward them for the first battle of a "preventive war."

"Save us! Save us!" shrieked the frightened penitents, and Samuel, baring his palms to the sky, besought the forgiving intervention of God. And though these people had turned their backs to the altars, and had sinned as their fathers and forebears and ancestors had sinned, yet now the very heavens came to their rescue. Hasty black clouds swarmed in from all directions, lightning crackled, striking the glittering spears of the Philistine lancers, and burning their horses under them, so that troops of cavalry stampeded and companies of footmen broke in confusion and fled helter-skelter across the plains, through the downpour, homeward in a frenzy. Behind them charged the Israelites, flailing them with any weapon they could seize until the plains were emptied of their foes.

Before his shrine of Ebenezer, memorial to divine deliverance, a few miles north of Jerusalem between Mizpah and Shen, Samuel gathered his people again for prayer; let all men present and to come remember that the God of Israel had hearkened and will ever hearken to the prayers of the despairing.

And many captured cities were delivered in the days that followed from the hold of the Philistines.

This triumph of Samuel, man of peace so miraculously victorious in war, solidified his hold over the imagination of the people. They believed in him and trusted him and they prospered under his leadership. But even in the peaceful years of obedience, of worshiping the one true Deity, and tending their woolly white flocks, their brown herds and green fields, they were—fortunately so—not too blindly trustful and content. Their elders, especially, kept a canny eye on Samuel and the conduct of the Temple. They felt sure that their leader had a heart and a spirit beyond suspicion and reproach, but the day did come when they had to go to him and remonstrate—a new experience for Samuel, a lesson in humility and the bitter recognition that what we condemn in another's back yard we may one morning find in our own.

Wrathfully, in his young days, Samuel had blamed the old priest Eli for tolerating the wickedness, the faithless idolatry, of those Belial-loving sons of his. But now the elders came to Samuel himself to tell tales about his own sons.

Those young men—Joel and Abiah were their names—were not by one small virtue any nobler in character than the scoundrel upstarts of Eli. For Joel and Abiah were priests and judges, too, and they were under their father's supervision, and they, too, were rascals, taking bribes from worshipers and perverting justice.

Samuel was getting old. He knew it that bright morning, as he stood in his white robe and black phylacteries and sandaled feet, and faced the elders while they disgorged their story. Now he knew how Eli had felt, long ago. The elders saw Samuel growing older before their very eyes but stifled their pity. There must be action while there was still time. Heaven forbid that this old man should be taken away, for then Joel and Abiah would lawfully assume his authority and seek to be chief magistrates in Israel. They told Samuel so, to his face.

What, then, did they propose?

Their answer staggered the trembling Samuel. Of all things conceivable, they wanted a king. They wanted to do away with their system of judges and get themselves a new ruler, with scepter, crown, and throne. The Philistines had kings and they flourished. So did many other nations. Why not Israel?

Not why not, but why. Samuel insisted on knowing. The reasons of the elders were simple. In the heady independence of the tribes and their crisscross rivalries the Israelites were impossible to unite. That left each separate tribe weak and defenseless against enemies. A king would be the ruler of all and could unite all the tribes into one powerful nation.

Samuel's shaking hand squeezed his long white beard. But had they paused and considered? To invest any mortal man with such authority would be again to turn their backs on the altar; the king would take over the authority belonging to God. Not that authority of itself was a usurpation of God's power—but Samuel knew human nature. In one impassioned outbreak he warned them what a king would do to free people:

"This will be the manner of the king that shall reign over you: he will take your sons, and appoint them for himself, for his chariots, and to be his horsemen; and some shall run before his chariots.

"And he will appoint him captains over thousands, and captains over fifties; and will set them to ear his ground, and to reap his harvest, and to make his instruments of war, and instruments of his chariots.

"And he will take your daughters to be confectioners, and to be cooks, and to be bakers.

"And he will take your fields, and your vineyards, and your olive yards, even the best of them, and give them to his servants.

"And he will take your menservants, and your maidservants and your goodliest young men, and your asses, and put them to his work.

"He will take the tenth of your sheep: and you shall be his servants. And you shall cry out in that day because of your king which you shall have chosen you."

But Samuel's passionate remonstrance moved neither earth nor heaven. The elders persisted in their demands. And when Samuel went off to himself, to pray for advice from on high, the Voice bade him do what his people urged, even against his judgment—a situation forever plaguing executives, its wisdom hard to swallow.

"Hearken unto their voice"—Samuel heard the message distinctly—"and make them a king."

"So be it, then," Samuel, with long face and unkindling eye, told the people. "I will seek the Lord's choice in a king for the nation."

Who would be the first king of Israel? How and where was he to be looked for? That was Samuel's problem. The answer came in the darkest watch of night, and faithful Samuel was told just what to do.

There lived at that time in the town of Gibeah, midway between Ramah and Jerusalem, one of the handsomest of men. He was called Saul, and he was the son of Kish, a millionaire Benjamite. No man, rich or poor, in all that region of Judah boasted a more attractive son and heir than Saul; braver or more patriotic. For Saul was tall and straight as a tree, lithe and muscular as a leopard, a champion at running and wrestling and hurling the long spear, and now, in the prime of his life, his name was a legend over the countryside. He was able in thinking and doing, in learning and remembering; energetic, and smiling, warm-handed, and breathing out personal magnetism.

But those few who knew Saul intimately said that his faults, which more than a few knew about, were as remarkable as his talents. Often he would hide away from his family and friends, drawing curtains on himself, body and soul, while he slouched at ease on soft pillows and stared moodily into space; a pale, disordered victim of melancholia. These attacks were infrequent, but when they came, family and friends left him alone until he got over them; there had been times when he rolled on the floor in paroxysms that were like epilepsy. And at other times he looked at men as if evil spirits peered out of his eyes. Even his best friends were afraid of Saul at such times, avoiding him as men avoid the manic-depressive and the schizophrene.

One day, soon after Samuel had received his divine instruction on how to find the king, Saul was walking through the hill country with a servant. For two days he had been searching for some lost jackasses, never dreaming that he was to find a throne instead.

"If I do not return home soon," he exclaimed, "my father will think me lost with the asses."

The servant, having a frugal ambition to recover the lost property, made a suggestion. Before turning back why not seek supernatural help? Supernatural? Aye, master—help from a seer whose occult power was renowned through this region; he had heard of the wizard a dozen times from as many caravan drivers.

Saul was always beguiled by wonder and a mystery. But he had lost the money he had brought with him and he was wordly enough to believe that every wonder-worker must have his fee.

"I have a small piece of silver," said the servant.

Of some maidens passing by they inquired about the seer. The

maidens simpered and giggled and gave Saul sidewise glances, seeing
that he was "a choice young man and goodly," and told him just how
to find Samuel, on the top of a nearby hill, where the old man was
getting ready for sacrifice and evening worship. Turning from the altar
and looking over his right shoulder, the priest's dimmed eyes beheld a
stalwart vision against the clouds and Samuel knew that in this
stranger he had found his king.

To Saul the next twenty-four hours were like a dream. The strange
old priest treated him with princely hospitality and plagued him with
baffling remarks.

"As for your asses, lost three days ago, they are found," he announced with a casual air. He led his guest to a table not far from the
place of the high altar of the sacrifice and bedded him comfortably
overnight.

"On whom is all the desire of Israel?" asked old Samuel with a
prophet's voice. "Is it not on you and your father's house?"

But he would explain nothing to the puzzled Saul. To bed, to sleep,
for they must rise early. Before the dawn, when other folks were still
asleep, Samuel led Saul and his servant through the deserted streets,
moving quickly on some inexplicable errand. Finally, in the open
country again, the servant was sent on ahead, so that Samuel and Saul
could talk together unheard.

In the gray pinkness of the morning—one version of the Samuel
story calls it "the spring of the day"—the old man drew from his
pouch a vial filled with a fragrant oil, which had been blessed at the
high altar at Mizpah, and with solemn deliberation withdrew the
stopper from the neck of the flask.

"Bow your head, my son," cried Samuel. Raising his eyes toward
the sky, he poured the oil on Saul's head. The younger man's eyes
brightened with wonder and the old priest, returning his gaze
demanded:

"Is it not because the Lord has anointed you to be captain over His
inheritance?"

Now Saul had as much ego as any man then living. He considered
himself to be one of the handsomest, bravest, most interesting persons
ever born. But to be king? His shrewd incredulous black eyes and
whimsically pursed lips seemed to say: "Old man, you have kept me
under something like a spell, ever since I came upon you, last night.
But now I think your mind is wandering."

Samuel waggled a gnarled old finger admonishingly. Let the

annointed Saul listen now to certain precise predictions, and when they were verified he would believe, beyond all doubt.

First he was to start on his homeward journey to Gibeah but when he reached the sepulcher of Rachel he would meet two men who would assure him that his father's missing donkeys had been found.

Second, at Mount Tabor, three other men would meet him and give him two loaves of bread.

Finally, a little farther on, he would notice a group of unknown men descending the steep path of a hill, to the music of psaltery, pipe, and harp, and a small bow-shaped drum called a taborine. These strangers would be prophets. Saul was instructed to join them unhesitatingly, to prophesy with them, because the Spirit of the Lord would come upon him and he would be like another man, losing himself with the prophets in an ecstasy, an entrancement; vision would come to him, voices would speak to him, knowledge and wisdom flow into him.

"And we shall meet again in Gilgal," murmured Samuel as they parted at sunrise. Saul was to go down to Gilgal, between Bethel and Samaria, and wait there seven days. Then Samuel would come to him and show him what to do.

Saul doubted these predictions, but with a stealthy hope that there might be some truth in the old man after all. And step by step by step, the forecasts were confirmed. There was a man at Rachel's tomb, holding between his fingers the harness reins of the donkeys, lost and now found. There were three men at the lowest slope of Mount Tabor who gave him two loaves of newly baked, sweet-smelling bread. And there were prophets on the hilltop with their musical instruments, and Saul, joining them, was welcomed. And a dreamlike state did come over him, as his voice, of unfamiliar timbre now, began to name the things that were to come. Men who knew Saul, who had known him since infancy, looked up to the mystical assembly and recognized him in that strange company and their question is an ironic saying to this day:

"What has come over the tall son of Kish? Is Saul also to be numbered among the prophets?"

For their irony and skepticism Samuel cared nothing. He knew what he had to do and he was resolved to get busy about doing it.

Calling the people together once more at Mizpah, old Samuel stood before them. He had meant to have Saul stand with him but at the last moment the candidate for the kingdom would not show himself; the exhibitionist became shy, the show-off covered himself.

But Samuel was sure Saul had not gone far. He plunged into his speech, reminding them, not without an edge to his voice, that it was their own idea, their decision, to get themselves a king. And how the Lord, who was the King of kings and had always led them to victory whenever they deserved it, which was seldom, had nevertheless given them, through himself, Samuel, His servant, permission to do as they wished in the matter. Now the solemn hour was arrived.

Coming through the crowd he saw the searchers he had sent, returning with him they had gone to seek—a tall man, with sword and spear, taller and stronger than any other man there, among the assembled tribesmen of Israel; the handsomest, mightiest man among them, head and shoulders above the multitude.

"See you him whom the Lord has chosen," Samuel shouted. "There is none like him among all the people."

And for the first time in the history of the world there rose the cry that is both prayer and oath—"God save the king!"

Thus began the reign of the first monarch of the Israelites, when the proud and talented Saul was only thirty years old, a thousand years before Christ.

All these happenings, these deeply significant new beginnings, Samuel wrote down in a book which he placed among the records of the people. His trust in the guidance of the Voice had been absolute; he had done everything he had been commanded to do, and the genuineness of the Voice's origin was dramatically verified, as Saul began to show the kind of man he was when danger came.

On the way back to Gibeah the story reached him of a new danger beginning with the vulnerable people of the town of Jabesh. An army was ready to fall upon them, hosts of savage Ammonites encamped on the hills around Jabesh-Gilead. Long before, the Ammonites had settled east of the Jordan; they were degenerate nomads who countenanced the union of father and daughter, and who years before had been bloodily worsted in a battle by Jephthah, in a struggle for Gilead. Now they were ready to pounce once more; and Saul soon learned that his own leaderless people living near the frontier had no wish to fight; they wanted to appease the Ammonites and have peace, and that is what they did. Not until it was too late did they realize what appeasement would mean; gloating over their supine weakness, the invading generals demanded one eye—lids, lashes, eyeball complete—from every Israelite as the price of peace.

Then it was that the elders of Jabesh turned to Saul and then it was that all Israel learned that they had, indeed, a king. Saul's response was instantaneous, positive, and dramatic. He sent helpers for two oxen driven before him, shambling and lackadaisical, from the field. Kill the oxen. Cut them to ribbons and to little bits! Now, messengers; hundreds of messengers. Let them take these bleeding pieces of ox flesh in their hands and go running from farmer to farmer in all this frightened, poltroon neighborhood. Would the peasants relish being one-eyed slaves for the rest of their lives? All their oxen would be slain by their new king, just as these token oxen had been sliced to bits, if they did not have the courage to follow their new leader forth to victory against the Ammonites.

And victory it was. Saul had put them into three companies: "and they came into the midst of the host in the morning watch, and slew the Ammonites until the heat of the day."

Rejoicing in this extraordinary proof, Samuel called the people to Gilgal to renew the kingdom there; orated to them about his protégé, haranguing them in his joy but warning them that not Saul, but God, the one true God, Whose instrument Saul was, had given them their triumph:

"Now, behold, the king walks before you; and I am old and gray-headed, and my sons are with you. I have walked before you from my childhood unto this day. Behold, here I am; witness against me before the Lord, and before His anointed: whose ox have I taken? Or whose ass have I taken? Or whom have I defrauded? Whom have I oppressed? Or of whose hand have I received any bribe to blind mine eyes therewith?

"Serve the Lord with all your heart, and turn you not aside. . . . Only fear the Lord and serve Him in truth. But if you do wickedness you shall be consumed, both you and your king."

He could not prevent himself from again upbraiding them for adding to their sins in asking for a king. Let them remember that it was not the word of a warlike leader but the still, small Voice that came down from Eden that would keep them from harm. Thunder and rain deafened and drenched them at his mere appeal to that Voice; the people cowered before such a demonstration; they feared God, and that was the goal of Samuel's performance that day.

"As for me," he told them, "God forbid that I should sin against the Lord in ceasing to pray for you; but I will teach you the good and the right way."

Which he did with unshaken zeal, and for two years more under the new order of kingship there was peace and prosperity for the Israelites.

But Saul was a farseeing man. He felt that the prosperity of his people was bound to incur the envy of his neighbors; a new conflict was certain to come. In time of peace Saul prepared for war; he organized a well-trained army that would cause any jealous nation to think twice before attacking. In these military preparations he formed three thousand of his ablest soldiers into a kind of elite guard, all capable of becoming officers and training new recruits in an emergency. One thousand of these special troops he put under the command of one of the choicest spirits of the kingdom—Jonathan, his son.

Like his father, young Jonathan was eager, impetuous, heady, and new to power. Having soldiers under him, drilling day after day, efficient and obedient, Jonathan's pride in them grew until he began to wish he could see them fight in a real battle. Before long he could think of nothing else; one night the compulsion swept away his judgment and he gave fighting orders; he led his men against the Philistine garrison at Geba. And that was an unprovoked act of aggression. So Saul had to take over.

The Philistines were themselves well prepared. Thirty thousand chariots, drawn by battle-tested war horses, soon came rumbling to answer mobilization trumpets and flags; and six thousand mounted riders, and uncounted footmen with shields and spears.

From the tents of the Israelites, on the rocky wedge-shaped promontory of Jerusalem, Saul could look across to the hill north of the deep and narrow pass which leads from Bethel on to the tableland of Ephraim, down to Jericho, and see the hosts of the enemy. The king-general, himself not much more than a novice in battle, was nevertheless confident. Not for a moment did he fear those Philistine spears and javelins glittering across the valley in the morning sun. Saul had considered everything in his calculations; he had been chosen by God, through Samuel, to bring about victories. That was his destiny. Omnipotent power was on his side. This conviction gave him a very confident air.

It also made him impatient. There were the Philistines, girding for battle; here was his own army, eager for the fray, primed for action.

Delay was dangerous when matters had come to such a pitch. Yet Saul knew he should not venture forth without a prayer, a blessing on his troops, a sacrifice for victory at the altar.

Where then was that old snow-beard priest who had drawn him from comfortable obscurity and put him in this dangerous kingly position? Where was Samuel? Saul waited seven days for him; he had held back his blow, even while the growing spectacle of Philistine strength had begun to frighten his own army, and some despairing families were already running away from the terrifying accumulation of military striking power across the Bethel pass. Overcome with dread, men were evacuating the town to hide in thickets, in dripping caves, and behind granite boulders in the desert; others even swam the tumbling brown currents of the Jordan, climbing out on the opposite shores to seek security in Gad and Gilead. Time was escaping like water from a leaky gourd.

Saul, a heady fellow always, decided to wait for Samuel no longer. He saw nothing wrong in that. The king went to the altar himself. He made his burnt offering as if he, too, were a priest, consecrated to such sacerdotal duties. If it occurred to him that his act was presumptuous he was not deterred, for Saul was born to overstep authority.

The outraged Samuel discovered him at his sacrilege. In horror he told the king that he might have established a dynasty of kings over Israel, but now his kingdom could not endure for long.

"The Lord has sought him a man after His own heart, and the Lord has commanded him to be captain over His people, because you have not kept that which the Lord commanded you."

Another king? The dynasty to be changed, to be snapped off, before it had ever a chance to sprout? Proud Saul looked with sulky disbelief at his feeble sponsor, this faithful old priest who trembled, whose shaking fingers twiddled the long beard. Let be, then, what would be! Let the future shape itself and see how much Saul cared whether Israel got a new king or not. So, leaving the old prophet vexed, he stalked out, abandoning his plans to attack the enemy, taking his son Jonathan and six hundred men of war with him, and made camp in Gibeah. And while glooming Saul lay sulking and prostrate under the pomegranate trees, doing nothing but stare blankly up at the stars, raiders from the Philistine camp swooped down and seized the stores of the Israelites, carrying off whatever material they wanted.

When old men act childishly, young men get their chance. Too impatient to wait on a mood of his father, Jonathan called his armor-bearer to follow him on a secret sortie of his own. Together the two men, with no other help whatever, attacked a Philistine garrison between Michmash and Gibeah. In the darkness of night twenty of the enemy fell before their furious onslaught. Sudden dismay and confusion scattered the reason of the Philistines. They fled in a night panic; soon the whole countryside knew that the Philistines were retreating.

Now the mood of King Saul changed instantly. Seeing his opportunity, he made an oath that also became a military order, commanding that his Israelite followers, on pain of treasonable death, taste no morsel of food until the Lord gave them victory. For Saul had been thinking things over and this was the way he thought up to propitiate God and atone for his own offense at the high altar—not by any humbling deed of his own, but by making his own soldiers to go without food, fighting a war to the death while famishing.

With this solemn injunction, Saul led his forces to triumph all the way from Michmash to Aijalon. It was a glorious victory.

But naturally the fasting had left the soldiers hungry as wolves in the desert. In their distress they transgressed the dietary laws of the tribes, eating forbidden blood with meat, acts that had to be ceremoniously purified. Their misdeeds had been discovered by King Saul when he had heard, after the din of battle died, the bleating of a sheep and the lowing of kine. Like a detective, he investigated and discovered a general disobedience of his vow—and the fact that Prince Jonathan seemed to be the worst offender. The young man had eaten honey during the heat of battle—a spectacular flouting of the sacred oath of his father.

"Tell me what you have done," commanded Saul of his son.

The fact was that Saul, like many an angry father before him, would not listen. Perhaps he wanted to act toward his son as he feared God was acting toward him. In any case he did not realize that, marching in the van of the battle which he himself had started, Jonathan had not heard of the king's order to fast. In his ignorance, yes, he had eaten a little honey: the young man tried to explain but even so was ready to submit to the full penalty for his unwitting crime.

"You shall surely die, Jonathan," cried the skeptical King Saul, and there was no mercy in his voice or in his eyes.

Jonathan bowed his head, but hundreds of Israelites near by, hearing the sentence, were outraged.

"God forbid," they cried. "As the Lord lives, not one hair of his head shall fall to the ground, for he has wrought this great salvation to Israel."

There was nothing left for the angry king to do but to accept the mandate. But his whole being seethed with fighting rage, which was turned to patriotic account. Saul worsted his enemies on every side. They sprang up from Moab, from Ammon and Edom, and he conquered them and the kings of Zobah. And even though Samuel had warned him of the brevity of his kingdom, the old judge proudly watched his success, achieved while still under a cloud of divine displeasure, and said:

"Remember how the Amalekites beleagured the children of Israel on the way from Egypt, and brought them discomfort and the curse of the just Moses upon them? Now is it your duty to smite the Amalekites from the face of the earth, one and all, leaving no trace of man or possession."

In this advice Samuel felt that he spoke for God and the word He had inspired in His servant Moses. And Saul, flushed with his train of conquests, was soon besieging the walled and gated city of Amalek, and presently its inhabitants were at his mercy. Here, however, once again the rebellious self-will of Saul rose up. He had been told to exterminate the Amalekites. Yet he took Agag, their king, a live prisoner. Moreover, remembering old troubles, he permitted booty for his men: sheep, oxen, fatlings, and lambs. These deviations set at naught the tribal law of *herem*, the utter destruction of an enemy, which was regarded as an offering to God for the grace of victory, taking no personal benefit from it.

Until then there had sprouted a small, wild hope in Samuel's soul that God might change His mind, relenting toward Israel's brilliant, hard-fighting commander. But now, with this flouting of orders and of deep tribal concepts, all hope was lost. Pleading for Saul was in vain, intercession useless; Samuel knew that his next job was to find Saul's successor. And that was a sad assignment. Old Samuel had a real affection for his headstrong king. With no relish for his task, he went before Saul and denounced his latest defiance of God. How would he answer for this disrespect?

Saul admitted that he was personally responsible for keeping Agag alive, although bound with cords; and for saving enemy livestock; he had wanted to please the people. Anyway, the animals would have been used in offering sacrifices, perhaps.

"Behold," said Samuel, "to obey the Voice of the Lord is better than sacrifice, and to hearken better than the fat of rams. For rebellion is as the sin of witchcraft, and stubbornness is as iniquity and idolatry. Because you have rejected the word of the Lord, He has rejected you as king."

"I have sinned," agreed Saul, breaking down, "because I feared the people. I pray you to pardon my sin and permit me to worship the Lord God."

In a torrent of pleading the king seized the robe of the priest, pulling so violently against Samuel's swift departure that a piece of cloth was ripped off the judge's robe and left in his hand. And Samuel cried out:

"The Lord has rent the kingdom of Israel from you this day, and has given it to a neighbor of yours, who is better than you."

But Saul, sobbing bitterly, begged Samuel not to abandon him. The old priest was touched, and for himself forgave the humbled Saul. But the prophet-priest demanded at the same time the presence of Agag, king of the Amalekites. "And Agag came unto him delicately," fawning and saying: "Surely the bitterness of death is past?"

"As your sword has made women childless, so shall your mother be childless among women," roared Samuel, old eyes flashing with a young man's ire. Now he would show Saul what obedience meant; grasping a sword ready to hand, he hewed the unlucky Agag to pieces: head off, arms off, legs off, the torso disemboweled. Shocked at the ferocity suddenly inflaming every vein in the old man's body, Saul watched the butchering, a fighter with his breath taken away. So this was the vengeance of God, when it got into a man!

Snowy beard matted with a king's blood, Samuel dropped his sword. Then with a shock Saul saw that the old man, in his red-spotted robes, was leaving, and his ambitious mind instantly divined his errand; after this lesson printed in crimson, the priestly judge was going out to find a new king, one who knew how to obey as well as command.

"And Samuel came no more to see Saul until the day of his death."

There was much that the Voice from Eden had now given Samuel to do and the old man was perfectly aware of the fact that at every step he took his life was in danger. Saul suspected, and in spite of their natural liking for each other, the son of Kish would have no scruple in arranging for his assassination. Even so, Samuel still loved Saul and asked God to forgive him.

"How long," the divine Voice demanded to know, "will you mourn for Saul, seeing I have rejected him from reigning over Israel? Fill your horn with oil and go. I will send you to Jesse, the Bethlehemite, for I have provided me a king among his sons."

That was one of the earliest references to the great ancestor in mortal lineage of Christ the King when God sent his servant Samuel to Jesse.

But for that very earthly and human servant the hazard of such a mission was frightening.

"How can I go?" he countered. "If Saul hear it, he will kill me."

"Take a heifer with you and say I am come to sacrifice."

And so, with a young cow tied to a cord, Samuel, the aging judge and priest, set out for Bethlehem. By the time he reached his destination he had worked himself up, weary though he was, to a pitch of excitement, so that the elders of the tribe of Judah met him with misgiving on their faces, because of his vague, wild manner. They knew the great Samuel by reputation and they venerated his name. But here before them was a quivering old fellow with a haggard air, a robe splotched with bloodstains, and a quavering voice, a wanderer smitten with euphoria who might have lost his mind.

"Come you peaceably?" they inquired cautiously.

"Yes, my children," said Samuel. "Sanctification is my mission to you, and to Jesse and his sons."

Why especially to Jesse and his sons? They wondered at that curious remark too.

But Samuel would tell them nothing specific. His business was with the family of Jesse. When they were alone Samuel asked Jesse to parade his sons, one by one, before him that he might see and hear them in quiet judgment. By why? Any father would want to know. But the old man obstinately shook his head, revealing nothing. Jesse, however, was a man of prayer and this request called for prayerful consideration; of that he was certain. Meanwhile the prophet stood mute, his feeble eyes toward the sky, as if he saw into an illimitable distance. Jesse decided to obey him.

One by one his stalwart sons came marching past, while the eyes of Samuel strained to pick the likeliest and his heart listened for the prompting of the Voice. Eliab came, tallest, fairest, seemingly the most attractive of Jesse's strong brood.

"Eliab!" cried Samuel. "He must be the one I am to choose."

And then he heard the Voice:

"Look not on his countenance, nor on the height of his stature, because I have refused him; for the Lord sees not as man sees; for man looks on the outward appearance, but the Lord looks on the heart."

Which was a principle of divine action the world still has a hard time in grasping.

Samuel knew now that it was not Eliab. And if not he, then surely none of the other seven sons of Jesse. Were they all that Jesse had? There was one more, the youngest. But he was not like these other seven fine young men; the youngest was a queer fellow, by his own father's account of him; one who made up songs and poems, and played airs on tubes that he fashioned from reeds, and sweet strings fastened over a block of hollowed wood; he was a sheeptender and Samuel would surely not want him.

"Bring him," said Samuel patiently.

Word was carried out to the hillside where this teen-age son of Jesse was watching his flocks. There was a dreamy manner about the young man as he was led in from the fields, the green stain of grasses on his bare feet, the grace of youth and something else greater than mere youngness in his movements, his carriage, and the misty contemplation of his eyes. Here, thought Samuel, are strength and beauty and wisdom, dwelling with youth.

The priest smiled at the young candidate and welcomed the answering smile on the fair and ruddy face. The masses of the youth's curly red hair were shining like copper. Samuel's far gaze sharpened as he heard the Voice return to his ear:

"Arise, anoint him: for this is he."

Samuel beckoned the youth still closer and in a whisper asked a question.

"My name," the boy replied, "is David."

Without a word the priest-judge Samuel brought forth his vial and uncorked it, and as he had done once before, he poured the oil on the head of the shepherd boy.

This ceremony of anointment, the preparing of David to be king after Saul, was at first a secret, but it marked the beginning of unparalleled glory for Israel, and by the same sign it was the beginning of the end for tired Samuel.

Not that death was ready for him as yet. There were still years before him, and at least two crises, in which he was to be helpful. But the greatness of his work was behind him now.

Samuel's career was to have a powerful influence on the growing

Jewish legend. For his whole life was full of significance—not only the Voice, as he had heard It in the dark of the night when he was a child, but all the dramatic scenes in which he played so large a part thereafter: his rule over Israel when the ark of the covenant was captured and then returned by the Philistines and the marvelous way in which the enemies were destroyed; his resistance to the whole idea of kingship; yet his obedience to the divine command, his anointing of the first king—and now his final great deed, in anointing young David to displace the mighty Saul.

Where was ever a man who listened more intently to the inner Voice? Where was anyone else who, in spite of pride and self-love, obeyed the Voice no matter how deep his humiliation in reversing himself? Samuel is an example of particular meaning for thickheaded people of any day and country, in office and out, who need the humility and devotion of the Temple boy who became a kingmaker.

And David, his second choice, was to give renown to his chooser. For the spirit of the Lord came upon David, His chosen vessel, once the oil was poured on his head. After Moses, he was to become the chief figure of the Old Testament. From that anointing day forward, Israel would rise almost to the position of a major power among the nations.

But not without turmoil. There was trouble ahead. Already the spirit of the Lord had departed from Saul and an evil demon troubled his soul.

Chapter 21 THE SHEPHERD BOY AND THE GIANT

THE old judge and the young shepherd had much to talk about before Samuel returned to Ramah.

In many ways the inspired Samuel was baffled by this ardent mystical lad from grassy hillsides whom he had chosen under guidance to follow Saul. Anyone might believe that Saul would make a monarch because of his height and strength, his flashing eyes, his expertness in the skills of manhood.

But David was a wistful lad. Like Joseph of old, there was nothing about him to suggest a governor, a military leader, a man to command men. His very curls were against such a notion and so were the long, supple fingers of his hand, plucking the lyre. Of all things despised by men of action, David, the shepherd lad, was a poet. Even Samuel could not take the full measure of the youth he had been led to; perhaps like others he wondered at God as he looked at this stripling.

Not then, any more than they do now, did kingmakers search among poets for political material. This poor boy had, indeed, the glance and carriage of one born to the purple, a prince in lowliness. But when Samuel inquired about him among the neighbors they shook their heads and told him, with shilly-shally smiles, of how the boy loved, more than anything else—women or money or comfort or reputation in the games—to make up verses. He would also make up the music in which to sing his compositions. There were two or three tenderhearted men who praised the songs of the shepherd boy; they said that the music of those verses when strummed on the lyre would lift up all hearts.

And soon Samuel learned for himself that David had a natural skill in the contrivance of both words and music. He could reach out and seize, as from the skies, a melody, an agreeable and rhythmic succession of sweet tones, and that melody would perfectly fit the words of the verses he had fashioned. And then the cadence of his fine baritone voice, the modulation of his tones, was that of an inspired singer who, without instruction but with natural passion, draws out of his throat the very soul of the music.

One could not blame Samuel, even though he could hear occasionally the Voice of God, if he failed to see with his tired eyes that here in this youth was an unheard-of contradiction of the heroic and the damnable. Yet so it was.

In the lad from the bleating flocks of Bethlehem there glowed in very truth the visions of one of the greatest poets that ever lived, before or since. He would never lose his precocious skill to seize the dreams and visions and put them into the glorious preservative of Hebrew words and music. But here also was truly a warrior of terrible competence, one of kingly mind, born to rule. And here a very great transgressor as well; a gifted man but a sinner. David!

None of this worldly potency was evident in the young singer and shepherd as yet. Samuel counseled David in what was wise to keep secret, and how to bide his time, patient as his own sheep, until the Lord had made known what was next to be done. Let him lift his soul to God on the hillside, let him always keep in mind how uncomplainingly Abraham tended his flocks in Midian until he heard the Voice. Let him not expose his hopes to mockery; people would despise them as vain imaginings. Better to tell only the sheep his secret heart; they could not betray him.

David obeyed Samuel. He told no one that he had been anointed by a holy man, to prepare him for the throne. But the very fact that he had been secretly consecrated so excited his mind that he could think of almost nothing else. His thoughts dwelled on the patriarchs and heroes of Israel—Abraham, Isaac, Jacob, Joseph, Moses, Joshua. David loved to recall their noble deeds; and he piped on his flageolet fashioned from cane, to enliven the loneliness, as many a shepherd has done, before and since, and he also strummed his lyre, to whose strains he composed songs of praise: psalms they were called then, and still are.

Among the white rocks and green fields on the hillsides of Bethlehem, David watched the seasons come and go with their beautiful contrasts of flower, tree, and sky; he was filled with wonder at the ways of birds and animals, and the sun, the moon, and stars.

In those innocent young days everything spoke to David of its Maker, and he found these words for his awe:

O Lord our Lord, how excellent is thy name in all the earth! Who has set thy glory above the heavens.

Out of the mouths of babes and sucklings hast thou ordained strength because of thine enemies, that thou mightest still the enemy and the avenger.

When I consider thy heavens, the work of thy fingers, the moon and the stars, which thou hast ordained;

What is man, that thou art mindful of him? and the son of man, that thou takest thought of him?

For thou hast made him a little lower than the angels, and hast crowned him with glory and honor.

Thou madest him to have dominion over the works of thy hands; thou hast put all things under his feet:

All sheep and oxen, yea, and the beasts of the field;

The fowl of the air, and the fish of the sea, and whatsoever passeth through the paths of the seas.

O Lord our Lord, how excellent is thy name in all the earth!

Another psalm of these sheepfold days was destined to serve as everlasting comfort and hope to mankind, when confronted by evils and death, beyond any other words ever written. Conceiving himself as a sheep in the fold of the loving God, the worshiping poet sang:

The Lord is my shepherd; I shall not want.

He maketh me to lie down in the green pastures: he leadeth me beside the still waters.

He restoreth my soul: he leadeth me in the paths of righteousness for his name's sake.

Yea, though I walk through the valley of the shadow of death, I will fear no evil: for thou art with me; thy rod and thy staff comfort me.

Thou preparest a table before me in the presence of mine enemies.

Thou anointest my head with oil; my cup runneth over.

Surely goodness and mercy shall follow me all the days of my life: and I will dwell in the house of the Lord for ever.

David saw a universe of beauty and might, the work of God, the kind Maker of Eden and of Adam and his wife; One Who took a personal and solicitous interest in the welfare of people on the earth, in the midst of His universal artistic and creative works of wonder:

The heavens declare the glory of God; and the firmament showeth his handywork.

Day unto day uttereth speech, and night unto night showeth knowledge.

There is no speech nor language, their voice is not heard. . . .

The law of the Lord is perfect, converting the soul: the testimony of the Lord is sure, making wise the simple.

The statutes of the Lord are right, rejoicing the heart: the commandment of the Lord is pure, enlightening the eyes.

The fear of the Lord is clean, enduring for ever: the judgments of the Lord are true and righteous altogether.

More to be desired are they than gold, yea, than much fine gold: sweeter also than honey and the honeycomb.

Moreover by them is thy servant warned: and in keeping of them there is great reward.

Who can understand his errors? cleanse thou me from secret faults.

Keep back thy servant also from presumptuous sins; let them not have dominion over me: then shall I be upright, and I shall be innocent from great transgression.

Let the words of my mouth, and the meditation of my heart, be acceptable in thy sight, O Lord, my strength and my strength and my redeemer.

Throughout a lifetime of joys and griefs David would always seek consolation in composing these songs of his soul. Boy that he still was, he drew such inspiration from the invisible world that his words are a lamp to the feet, illumination for the spirit of today's men and women, and will be so tomorrow.

Yet there he lay with his sheep on the hilltop of Bethlehem, a lad almost unnoticed, one among thousands, but one who hid in his heart old Samuel's secret. And how his heart leaped up the day that a messenger came, seeking him out, an emissary with an immediate summons from the king.

Saul had sent for David!

Those who cannot conceive of a pattern in the will of God may think it only a coincidence, the way in which David was brought so close to the all-powerful Saul. It happened that Saul had again fallen into one of his black moods, and his melancholy was interfering with and delaying government business. For his gloomy silence was blighting not only his high spirits but any wish to work. Counselors said to him:

"Let us find a cunning player on the harp to banish this evil spirit that wraps you in its gloom."

Thus, thousands of years ago, wise men knew of the therapeutic power of music. It was the sagacious son of David who one day was to tell the world: "There is no new thing under the sun."

"Provide me such a man," assented Saul, and his counselors spoke of David, gifted shepherd boy of Bethlehem, a lad pleasing in person and valiant. So word was sent to Jesse, calling for his youngest son, who should not be wasting his musical talents on unappreciative sheep.

As he made ready for the journey David's mind was tormented with questions. Had the farseeing Samuel recommended him? he wondered. Was King Saul very ill? Could he, David, combat his illness with music: what would happen if he failed? Was this, perhaps, his first step in the mystical direction set by Samuel?

At the first sight of the young minstrel coming through the embroidered curtains of his throne room, impulsive Saul was pleased, and when, soon, David's fingers plucked the strings of his lyre, his songs began to soothe the king's haunted soul. In that first session of sweet music a black spell vanished from Saul's heart. There was such euphony, such sweet agreeableness of sound, as Saul had never dreamed could be. In pleasure and relief, his veins tingling from having listened, Saul decided that David was a necessity to him and must live near his royal house and constantly attend him.

Because David was sturdy and fearless in look and manner, Saul made him his armor-bearer, a remarkable honor. Some courtiers smiled superciliously at the appointment; a poor shepherd raised, because he could pluck the strings of a lyre, to being their equal, appointed bearer of spear and shield and all the panoply of fighting gear. David heard the bitter gossip, and while he said nothing, being born to discretion, he promised himself to prove his worth; the day would come when he would show his qualities, not as a herder of sheep but as a warrior. He did not have long to wait.

Living among the Philistines in those days was that most formidable giant, Goliath. The Israelites had long been in terror of his raids, but now he was making himself the vanguard of an invading Philistine army; roaring he came across the valley of Esdraelon, vowing that his country would stake the fate of the nation on one single-handed combat. Dared the Israelites offer a champion to face Goliath?

Old Accounts assure us that Goliath was ten feet tall. He wore brass armor and a coat of mail—"and the weight of the coat was five thousand shekels of brass; his spear's head weighed six hundred shekels of iron. And the staff of his spear was like a weaver's beam. The weight and length of his spear would stagger a strong man merely to lift, let alone hurl. His shield was the longest ever seen or heard of and his sword a fearsome blade."

"Choose you a man to meet me," Goliath shouted. "If he kills me, we will be your servants. But if I kill him, then Israel shall serve us. Have you a man to send?"

Even Saul, brave as any king, was dismayed, for he knew there was no man in his ranks or realm even a tenth the equal to Goliath, mighty son of Belial, whose height was six cubits and a span.

Then there stood at the foot of the throne the boy singer from Bethlehem. His ruddy face was paler now, but in his soft, dream-filled eyes there was a dauntless light.

For forty days, he explained, he had been going to and fro, attending to Saul, but also visiting his family keeping an eye on how his flocks were being tended. While visiting his brothers, who were now soldiers in Saul's army, he had learned of the giant's defiance.

"Let no man's heart faint because of Goliath," said David earnestly. "Your servant will go and fight with this Philistine."

Saul's eyes flashed with admiration at the courage and heart of such a stripling! But the king shook his head.

"You are not able to go against this Philistine, to fight with him, for you are but a youth and he is a man of war from his youth."

Passionately David spoke, as only a poet can speak under powerful feeling, entreating Saul to send him against Goliath—he was sure his skill would be a match for brute physical strength; nay, he had proved it twice before: he had killed a wild boar and a lion in struggles to the death. With only his crook and his muscular skill he had grappled with and killed both boar and lion.

Why did Saul permit the boy David to go out against the giant? Perhaps to shame his people, from whom had come no other volunteer. Perhaps already he was tired of his psalming musician. Perhaps because men often are driven obscurely to kill the thing they love.

The king showed David every mark of royal favor when he gave permission. It was Saul himself who armed David with his own helmet, his coat of mail, his sword. But David, who did not seem to fear Goliath, quaked before all this armor, fashioned for so much larger a man. He put it on but it was too much for him; he could not walk without staggering; even the sword was too heavy for him.

"I cannot go against Goliath with these," he said to the king.

For the outfit of armor he substituted a wooden staff, five smooth stones taken from a brook and dropped in his shepherd's bag, and, finally, a boy's sling, a pocketed thong to be whirled around the head, as he often had used one to drive wolves and foxes from his flocks. That was all.

"Go—and the Lord be with you," was the regal farewell.

When Goliath, the ten-foot giant, came swaggering across an open field, clanking and gleaming in his armor, he beheld a figure moving toward him up the deserted green vale of Elah, and squinted his vast eyes as if he could not believe them. Then he grinned down and winked at his amazed shield-bearer, as if to say: "Now for some sport with this child."

On came the shepherd boy, as if strolling without much purpose.

Finally he halted, taking a stand at a short distance from the looming hulk of Goliath in his brazen armor.

"Am I a dog that you come at me with staves?" yelled Goliath, with a curse for the club in David's hand. "I will give your pretty flesh to the fowls of the air and the beasts of the field—in dainty bits."

And David called back:

"You come at me with your sword and spear and shield but I come to you in the name of the Lord of Hosts, the God of the armies of Israel, Whom you have defied. This day will the Lord deliver you into my hand . . . And all the assembly shall know that the Lord saves not with sword and spear; for the battle is the Lord's and He will give you into our hands."

Goliath's answer was a stentorian roar, but David did not quail; nor did he take a backward step as Goliath started lumbering forward, ready to cut in half the crazy, impudent upstart with one swoop of his sword.

In David's mind was a profound belief in protection, in inspiration, in luck—in victory; somehow he was going to grapple with Goliath; to seize him, take hold of him, and lay him low—all at a distance. And in his heart rose his own poem in reassurance:

"Though a host should encamp against me, my heart shall not fear; though war should rise against me, in this will I be confident."

David advanced a step or two, swiftly estimating distance and wind. From his shoulder bag he seized one of the five brook stones, put it in his slingshot, took aim, and whirled it round his head. Straight as an arrow, the missile struck the bare forehead, where it sank to its depth.

Like an ox smitten by an ax, Goliath tumbled to the ground. The noise of the crash was like a cracking open of the earth. The giant's shield-bearers fell back, gaping, retreating as if before invincible magic. Losing not a moment, David ran to the unconscious giant, whose lips were already bubbling with blood froth, and seizing the enemy's sword, he hacked off the Philistine's head. Panting, he held aloft the dripping face against the brightening sky.

Eyes of men were not made to believe a sight like this. The Philistine soldiers turned and ran, and the watching children of Israel, who had dreaded an overwhelming assault, following David's expected failure, were now fired by David's deed and pursued the fleeing foe, slaying demoralized hosts.

It was Abner, captain of the army, who led the shepherd boy before the king. Down a maze of corridors they made their way toward the king's largest chamber, passing through sumptuous apartments on the way, all furnished in barbaric splendor. But David, exhausted, nearly naked, carried the leaking head of the giant, the blood spotting the palace marbles.

Saul received the shepherd boy for what he was now, the hero of the hour. He coaxed him to explain how one little stone, no bigger than an unripe fig had brought down the terrible Goliath.

Standing among the courtiers, and watching while David stammered answers to the king's questions, was Jonathan, Saul's favorite son. The fair young prince was like someone under a spell as he listened to the giant-killer's modest narrative. Especially he noted David's natural felicity of phrases, the accent of true poetry. How was it he had not been afraid? And this was David's answer:

"The angel of the Lord encampeth round about them that fear him, and delivereth them."

Here was a rare one, this David. So Jonathan thought as he broke the regal etiquette and rushed forward to embrace David as if they were brothers.

Closer far than brothers they were soon to be. The luster of their friendship will last as long as men are capable of liking each other. All that great men have had to say about friendship, from Cicero to Emerson, falls a little short of this supreme historic example of the love of two men. This Jonathan, the king's favorite son, loved David as his own soul.

At first Saul, too, was consumed with admiration. When Jonathan asked what reward he had in mind for the amazing young son of Jesse, the king decided to make the new hero a general, to set him over the men of war in Israel, boy though he still was. Genius, the king knew, was never to be measured by time, and as time went on this judgment, though it may have been swayed by emotion, proved excellent, for David bred fear in the Philistines whenever they heard his name, and with his troops he smote them repeatedly with crippling blows.

Could any young man stand, unspoiled, the praise and flattery being poured out on the new commander? David even feared for himself; he realized that flattery went to his head and in those innocent days he wanted only the favor of the Lord. But hero-worship could not be downed. Once, when David was returning with King Saul from a victorious battle, the women of some of the cities came out to greet them with taborets and dances. But their smiles and waving hands were not for King Saul; they were all for the ruddy-faced, goodly formed David, and over and over they sang a refrain:

> *"Saul has slain his thousands,*
> *And David his ten thousands."*

Who could blame if proud and sensitive Saul was irked? What did the moaning, swooning women desire: did they want the kingdom turned over to this glamorous boy? Already there were whispers of such treasonable notion; everybody knew that supremacy as a warrior generally carried with it the leadership of a nation.

Once again Saul began to brood, in an unspeakable chaos of thoughts. All night long he sulked over public ingratitude and fickleness; hour by hour his resentment grew. By morning he was in a villainous mood, and even before breakfast he commanded his general, who had once been his harpist, to come to the throne room and soothe his cankered mind. Obediently David appeared with his harp, as of old. But secretly Saul was determined to resist the spell of the music. So, although David strove hard to exorcise the evil spirit, the melancholy could not be dispelled from the king's mind. Frowning and muttering, Saul remained on his throne and glared at the harpist, as if daring him. Cantankerously from time to time he interrupted the musician, insisting that the harp was out of tune, or that David's fingers were plucking false chords—hoping to provoke the youth into an outburst of anger, so that he could justly punish him.

But David held his peace. Maddened at last, when he could not unsettle the serenity of his musician, kingly nerves on edge, Saul, like a manic-depressive, suddenly sprang to his feet and, seizing his javelin, hurled it at David, aiming to transfix him to the wall. Only by inches did the huge spear miss its murderous mark, and David ran from the throne room.

The boy general from Bethlehem told no one of the episode. He realized why he was in danger and, like a true poet, sought the way of escape by guidance from within. Meanwhile he acted toward Saul as if nothing violent had happened between them: an attitude that only increased the king's brooding madness. The fact that the spear had missed, bothered Saul, the marksman. Because David seemed to have a charmed life, protected by Heaven, he was now really someone to fear; better get rid of the fellow at once.

So David was sent away from court. He was ordered into active army service, captain over a thousand men. What Saul really hoped for was misfortune in war to stay the course of David's luck and success; a death wound in battle, for example. But no! After every armed clash the Bethlehemite emerged safely and the people loved him more and more. So Saul had to take a craftier tack.

Presently, to everybody's surprise, the king offered to the popular hero his eldest daughter, Merab, in marriage. And again to everybody's surprise—and to none more than Saul's—David declined the honor.

"Who am I that I should be son-in-law to the king?" he asked.

But it was hard to oppose a willful master like Saul. He wanted a daughter of his to be David's bedfellow, so that she could bring reports to her father of all the plots he was sure David would be up to. The situation grew more and more embarrassing; having said no to Merab, David was next invited to take her young sister Michal, who in desperation he finally agreed to marry, well realizing that his beauteous bride would be a spy at his pillow. But David also knew there would be no treason for her to report.

That being so, Saul again and again dispatched David on military adventures in which any less lucky man, or one less blessed, would certainly have perished. But always David returned victorious, and more and more the people acclaimed his name.

How could Saul get rid of such a menace? In his hate-clouded mind he turned to his son, Prince Jonathan.

Would Jonathan, his son, undertake to murder David, his dearest friend?

There was incogitable ignorance of soul in such a suggestion. Saul was incapable of knowing or understanding the character either of his son, Jonathan, or of his protégé, David. In his folly he put it to Jonathan—did he not see that David was ambitious to rule, to supplant the house of Saul? Aghast, Jonathan fled from his father, resolved only to warn David of his danger. It was a difficult duty for Jonathan because he also loved his father greatly, but he did not hesitate. Next day he went back into the throne room and tried to persuade the king to drop his evil designs. David, he argued, had done nothing but good to the kingdom.

"Will you sin against innocent blood, my father?" Jonathan demanded.

This plea seemed to have an effect. Saul sent for David and frankly offered to revive their friendship. But who could believe it would last? One morning, in a new fit of melancholy, he asked David once more to play for him. And again he hurled the javelin, again in vain!

There seemed no safety anywhere except in flight. What kind of life was it for a man when every shadow at a corner might be a hired assassin? The desire for the violent death of David was like a lust in Saul's mind; he conferred in secret with some of the lowest of criminals, paying well and promising more, and at their hands David would have indeed perished but for his wife. Michal, that daughter of Saul, had come so to love her husband that she warned him in their bed, tied sheets together, and let him down through a back window, and then used a dummy shaped like her husband to lie beside her in the moonshine.

Meanwhile David hid himself at Ramah. Still in hopes that he could be reconciled with the king, and shaken at last by a sense of unremitting peril, David met Jonathan in a field at midnight.

"What have I done? What is my iniquity?" he cried despairingly. "There is but a step between me and death."

"I will do whatever your soul desires of me," declared Jonathan.

"Tomorrow is the new moon, and I should not fail to sit with the king at meat," said David. "But I would rather go and hide myself in a certain field I know for the three days of feasting, and appear to have gone to Bethlehem for the yearly celebration."

Jonathan disliked deception and was troubled.

"Deal kindly with your servant, for have we not sworn one to another?" entreated David. "Slay me yourself if I have sinned, but do not force me to be with the king."

Jonathan said it was farthest from his wish to stir up more trouble. With heaven as witness, he and David made a solemn pledge of eternal friendship between their houses. As if one vow were not enough, the two young men swore it a second time. Their love that day was utterly unselfish and true, a deep union of the spirit.

Jonathan went off to see what he could do.

The vacant chair of David at the feast of the new moon was instantly noted by Saul. But the king bided his time. On the first day he said nothing; on the second he scowled and demanded:

"Wherefore does not the son of Jesse come to meat, neither yesterday nor today?"

Jonathan's smile was all placating as he explained: "Earnestly he asked leave of me to go to Bethlehem, where his family holds sacrifice."

Asked leave! Of whom? You! So Jonathan had taken it on himself to give permission! Saul heaped fierce, insulting words upon his son; a shameless tirade in which the king lost every shred of dignity and self-control:

"For as long as the son of Jesse lives upon the ground you shall not be established, nor your kingdom. Wherefore now send and bring him to me, for he shall surely die."

Ashen of face, but steadfast for his friend, Jonathan defied his father:

"Why shall he be slain? What has he done to deserve it?"

Maddened at this stammering son who went against him, Saul rose and lifted his arm deliberately. Once more he hurled his javelin, flying at his own flesh and blood. But Saul's marksmanship had not improved. He stood there cursing, calling down maledictions on Jonathan as the young man ran from the dining hall. Saul did not dare to detain him, nor dare to order hands laid on him; for everyone present, all the court, the bearded elders and generals at the feast, knew that Jonathan had not deserved such treatment.

By night and by stealth Jonathan hastened to David. Under the stars they clung together, wondering what next. Certainly David must get as far away as possible. Henceforth he would be a hunted man with all the royal hounds on his heels. Should he flee to mountains or desert?

And Jonathan said to David:

"Go in peace, forasmuch as we have sworn both of us, in the name of the Lord, saying, The Lord be between you and me, and between my seed and your seed for ever."

So parted the closest friends; in all his troubles the heart of David was thankful to God for Jonathan. Cut off from all that he held dear and desirable, the poet returned to his music, as he made his way alone on dark roads. In one new psalm he voices his indomitable faith:

Thou shalt not be afraid for the terror by night, nor for the arrow that flieth by day, nor for the pestilence that walketh in darkness, not for the destruction that wasteth at noonday.

A thousand shall fall at thy side, and ten thousand at thy right hand; but it shall not come nigh thee. . . .

Because thou hast made the Lord thy habitation there shall no evil befall thee, not affliction come nigh thy dwelling.

For He will give His angels charge concerning thee, to keep thee in all thy ways.

More than any other man who had lived since Adam, the runaway

David felt a sense of the divine fatherhood, blessing him, comforting and protecting him. The thought of that invisible and Almighty Father, always near, always dependable, always interested in him and hoping for his love, came to him like a vision. His soul, one of the first of mortals to recognize the beauty and universal happiness of that conception, was filled up with song and the music of it is deathless:

Thou knowest my downsitting and mine uprising, Thou understandest my thought afar off.

Thou compassest my path and my lying down, and art acquainted with all my ways.

There is not a word in my tongue, but Thou knowest it. Thou hast beset me behind and before, and laid Thine hand upon me.

Such knowledge is too wonderful for me; it is high, I cannot attain unto it.

Whither shall I go from Thy spirit? Or whither shall I flee from Thy presence?

If I ascend up into heaven, Thou art there; if I make my bed in the grave, behold, Thou art there.

If I take the wings of the morning, and dwell in the uttermost parts of the sea, even there shall Thy hand lead me, and Thy right hand shall hold me.

If I say, Surely the darkness shall cover me, even the night shall be light about me.

Yea, the darkness hideth not from Thee, but the night shineth as the day; the darkness and the light are both alike to Thee. . . .

I will praise Thee, for I am fearfully and wonderfully made. Marvelous are Thy works, and that my soul knoweth right well. . . .

Search me, O God, and know my heart; try me, and know my thoughts; . . . and lead me in the way everlasting.

From such a friendly Father help would always come, even against the might of Saul and his cohorts.

I will love thee, O Lord, my strength. The Lord is my rock and my fortress and my deliverer; my God, my strength, in whom I will trust; my buckler, and the horn of my salvation, and my high tower. . . . He delivered me from my strong enemy, and from them which hate me: for they were too strong for me. . . . The

Lord rewarded me according to my righteousness. . . . Yea, Thou
liftest me above those that rise up against me: Thou hast delivered me from the violent man.

But from that "violent man" David had yet much to suffer.

Chapter 22 THE WITCH OF ENDOR AND THE DEATH OF SAUL

SUPPORTED by his trust in divine protection, David lived through
many a hazard on that fugitive journey, hastening through the nights
toward a distant asylum. Once, having aroused the suspicions of a
petty Philistine ruler, he had to pretend madness. But escaping all
perils, and even managing to get back from the priests of Nob the
sword of Goliath, David reached the goal of his flight, which was the
Cave of Adullam, a great limestone hollow in Judean hills, about
twelve miles southwest of Bethlehem. There he settled down.

And soon, one by one and by twos and threes, David drew to his
side other men who were outcasts like himself, for one reason or another, from the wrath of Saul or who were discontented with the royal
tyranny and sought an unrestricted life. Among those who gathered
around him were his brothers and "all his father's house." Before long
there were about four hundred volunteers under David's leadership,
some of them stalwarts, afterward to be famous as his "mighty men"
—and all of them with revolution in their hearts.

Only David's parents were sent elsewhere; to protect them from revenge on the part of Saul, David found them a safe retreat with the
king of Moab. After all, Ruth, David's great-grandmother, had been a
Moabite.

These were years of a precarious freebooter life for David and his
miscellaneous band of followers. They had brought their families
along, to be supported in the wilds, and food was never an easy problem; it had to be plundered constantly, at great risk of capture. Always
looming in the mind was the image of the enemy. The king had not
forgotten David; the place soldiers kept up a vigilant search for the
outlaw, which was why David and his followers had to be forever on
the jump, to dart and dodge from place to place, from the forest of

Hareth all the way to Keilah, from Ziph to Maon, to Engedi, back again to Maon. It was often touch and go.

Raid and plunder to live as he must, David was wisely careful never to prey on the Judeans, who were his own people, and one day he would need them. He even defended them against other marauders, and shared his spoils with the elders of Judah. This was good politics against the future, and the enraged, exasperated Saul recognized the wisdom of the gesture.

Defied and made mock of by such audacity, Saul at last determined to crush this slippery upstart finally, forever, and at whatever cost. The measure of his bitterness was made clear when he had the whole company of priests slain in cold blood, because they had relinquished Goliath's sword to David and had given the fugitive hospitality, including "shew bread" consecrated to God.

But David's following increased with Saul's anger, reaching six hundred, well hidden in the wildernesses. And where Saul's hatred failed to find them Jonathan's love succeeded. One day there was an ardent greeting between the friends.

"Fear not," said Jonathan. "My father will not find you." So unselfish his love was for David that he added: "One day you shall be the king, and I shall rule with you."

David's idealism and noble nature were shortly to be shown at Engedi, where he and his men lay hidden in a cave. Lost in the shadows themselves, they saw King Saul, alone, unguarded and weary from a march, enter to rest a little in the coolness of the shadow. So close was the unwitting king that David cut a piece from his garment without detection.

"Now let us kill him," whispered his followers urgently.

"The Lord forbid," answered David. "I will not stretch forth my hand against the Lord's anointed."

Although his tough followers feared that their captain was going soft, they dared not disobey him. Yet to them it did seem a crazy notion—to spare an enemy who, as everyone knew, thirsted uproariously for your own blood.

When Saul was gone out of the cave some distance, David called after him, telling him in an even-tempered voice what he had just done in mercy to His Majesty.

"The Lord therefore judge between me and you, and see, and plead my cause, and deliver me out of your hand."

"Is this my son David?" cried Saul, thunderstruck. Turning back, he faced David in the cave and wept tears of shame and mortification.

In that moment of light he had an inspired understanding of his life's failure.

"Good for evil have you shown me," he cried. "The Lord reward you. Now do I know that you will rule in Israel. Swear therefore that you will not cut off my seed after me, nor destroy my name out of my father's house."

Strange indeed was this emotionally complex meeting between pursuer and the pursued, the cruel and the kind. Without hesitation David gave the king the oath of reassurance he begged for. But David would not parley further with Saul, knowing perfectly well that no matter what they agreed upon his enemy would soon change his mind again and his animosity would rise. He rejoined his own men; the meeting was over and Saul went his way.

It was not long afterward that David met a remarkable woman. She was called Abigail, and she was the wife of a wealthy citizen named Nabal. Often David had protected Nabal's livestock from desert raiders, but now, when the whole kingdom was mourning the recent death of old Samuel, David needed food. Would Nabal help them? No, Nabal would not. Why not?

He would not be squeezed, he said; and he said it with lofty disdain. David had to restrain his men from cutting down this superstitious man of wealth, for they were all fighters, they were all hungry.

What an unexpected sight for David to see, an hour or so later—Abigail, the wife of Nabal, leading a loaded ass up the hillside, burdened with baskets of fruit, dried meals and bread, and skins of good wine.

Straight in the height and beauty of her womanhood, Abigail stood before David, seeing him with divining eyes, beholding clearly what many others had missed. She saw David as one marked for a great destiny, hailing his future ascendancy, of which she was already convinced. And she hoped David would forgive her foolish husband Nabal.

Ten days later Nabal, the rich curmudgeon, fell dead. Enraged when his wife confessed to him her deed of generosity, he dropped from a stroke. Having wined and dined, and hated too deeply, he lay dead at her feet.

David waited until Nabal was buried and then sent messengers to ask the widow to be his wife. He was lonely, since Saul had already taken Michal, his wife, forcibly away and given her to another man. With a heart full of willingness beautiful Abigail accepted.

Not long afterward, the Bible also reports, David took another wife, called Ahinoam, so now he had two, in place of the lost Michal. But that was the custom of his time; only very slowly did man turn again to his pristine, monogamistic ideal.

Saul's spies were reporting all of these matters, and especially how David had been molding his band of stalwarts into a most effective fighting unit, a promise of what one day he would do with Israel's army under his own command. Two born warriors were David's chief men in the tiny army of six hundred—Joab and his brother Abishai.

No wonder Saul was disconcerted at these reports. The memory of his foeman's magnanimity in the cave had long faded from his mind, as David had anticipated. He could forget easily and his growing hatred brought on more fits of dark brooding, with no one now to pluck the harp for him. He was preparing to renew his man hunt when a group of Ziphites came to him and saved him the trouble, betraying the latest hiding place of David in the hills of Hochilah.

The old warfare flamed up again that very night.

Soon the spies of David reported that King Saul was marching against them with a troop of three thousand men, their camp pitched near by. Sizing up the encampment from the highest hill, David asked:

"Who will go down with me to Saul?"

"I will," spoke up Abishai the captain, always ready for adventure.

Together, on an almost hopeless errand but determined to try to avoid bloodshed, David and his aide set off at nightfall. It was full dark when they reached the outposts of Saul's troops. Stealthily picking their way, they evaded the sentries and discovered Saul fast asleep. David's second chance to get rid of his mortal enemy lay at his feet.

"Let me kill him," pleaded Abishai. "Now he is in our power."

"Destroy him not," ordered David fiercely. "His day to die shall come."

Inspired to a different course, David, with Abishai watching, knelt quietly and took away Saul's spear and a cruse of water from his side. And no one waked in the camp as they retreated, carrying their trophies with them. Reports of these personal belongings David sent back at noon of the next day as unquestionable evidence that the outlaw had spared the life of the king. Once more the volatile Saul was overcome with remorse and asked for a parley.

"I have sinned," admitted the contrite Saul. "Return, my son David: for I will no more do you harm."

"Send one of your young men for the king's spear," called out David. But he would not rejoin Saul; he knew him too well.

"Then blessed be you, my son David," said Saul, making no further overture. "You shall do great things, and prevail."

And again they parted; the war was called off.

The old freebooting existence was resumed, a time of ups and downs, of misunderstanding among his followers, even—so that for a few mad minutes his own men were ready to stone David to death. The skirmishes with the Philistines and the ever-treacherous Amalekites kept the outlaws endlessly in one struggle or another. Saul seemed no nearer a tranquil kingdom, David no nearer a throne, when one day word came of two singular developments.

One was a new plan of Philistia to mount a new, vast, resistless assault against the children of Israel and forever obliterate them.

The other was that Saul, terrified at the mighty armies collecting against him at Aphek, over against Jezreel, was going to commit one of the foulest sins in the Mosaic law: he was seeking help from black magic, from preternatural powers. He was a king without a prophet, having neither oracle nor dream. So the king, in desperation, disguising himself, was going to seek the help of a spirit medium, a witch as she was known. His aides were shocked at his determination. It was Saul himself who had banished all soothsayers from the kingdom. But surely, the king insisted, one must have remained to bootleg necromancy? Yes, there was one left, they told him. So now, riding incognito and in darkness across the valley of Jezreel, with blood creeping and nerves pricking, King Saul came to the witch in the cave of Endor.

"Bring me up him whom I shall name unto you," said Saul in a low voice.

The woman's wizened face was red in the firelight; the bold and gleaming eyes looked at the visitor distrustfully. Had he forgotten that the official penalty for conjuring up familiar spirits was death?

But Saul savagely ordered her to forget her fears. She was the witch of Endor; all Israel knew that ghouls haunted the damp reaches of her cave and preyed on the corpses in the surrounding hills. Through that cheerless doorway, where the skins of wild animals were hanging to keep out the winds, great lords and ladies had come to her. This was no time to bring up the laws. What if her hellish traffic had been forbidden by Moses? Anxiety in the visitor's mind had become unbearable. Diablerie or not, he wanted advice from the beyond.

The spirit medium of Endor cleared her throat with a guttural sound; the air in her cave was dank and cold. When she spoke her beldam voice was like a croak.

"Name the spirit," she said.

"Samuel," was Saul's reply, and his voice shook in his soul's emergency.

Haggard eyelids drooped in the fiery glow; gnarled brown hands came together behind the back as if there were some ritual in reverse of prayer; the shriveled body swayed from side to side as she sat on her haunches and muttered indistinguishable words. When at last she was still it seemed as if the quiet would never end. Saul's impatient eyes turned from the dimmish gloom of the roof to shadowy corners and murky, distorted corridors; in spite of his bravery, he felt an uneasy chill. What was going to happen here in this, the outermost of a chain of caverns, whose farther reaches no one had ever penetrated? Would he, indeed, see his old friend in this charnel place with this infernal old woman, rigid and unconscious, waiting in front of a dying fire for God knew what? The very air had a restless taint.

Then a gasp came from Saul. He had seen something moving in the shadows to the right of the cataleptic hag. At first it was a vagueness and a vapor, barely to be seen in its first faint, coiling shimmer. But its radiance grew brighter, its form more tangible; it took the shape and outline of a man, an old man with a white cataract of beard, a gleaming bald head, and luminous dark eyes. Who that had ever known him in life could mistake him now? This was the ghost of Samuel. When he spoke, it was in the same crisp, firm tones that in life had been the voice of Samuel.

"Saul, why have you disquieted me?"

"Make known to me what I shall do!" implored the unhappy king.

"Wherefore do you ask of me? Seeing that God is departed from you and is become your adversary?" The very tone of the specter was a rebuke. "The Lord will deliver Israel with you into the hand of the Philistines. And tomorrow shall you and your sons be with me."

Saul's very bones trembled. He fell to the ground, chilled and faint as the vision of Samuel paled and dimmed and faded away into invisibility and nothingness.

The witch of Endor did what she could for her visitor. She reached for a pot in the midst of her fire and poured out the hellbroth into a clay bowl and circled it under the royal nose, until the fumes of the magic stew fired the nostils of the unconscious customer. With luckless grace he scrambled to his feet, a man again, and a king, except for his face, all quivering lips and craven eyes.

Before another sunset the predictions Saul had sought in the witch's cave were overwhelmingly fulfilled. Throughout the day the battle was fought on Mount Gilboa. Saul—never a coward in battle—stalked tall and visible, rousing his men, himself a target for the Philistine archers. But the arrows seemed to dodge the king; he remained alive to see three of his sons slain by the enemy, and one of his dead sons was Jonathan.

In that tragedy was cracked and broken the last wish of Saul to go on living; a sense of inescapable fate convicted him within his own mind. With one despairing cry he called his armor-bearer.

"Draw your sword and thrust me through with it," he commanded. The man protested, yet knew he must obey. What was there left for Saul but death? Would he wait to be taken alive? The Philistines knew well how to have sport with their prisoners. With a king, what might they not do?

Even so, the armor-bearer quailed until the enraged Saul, roaring blasphemies, seized the sword himself and fell upon it. The armor-bearer did the same, and the king and servant died together.

Tomorrow, the Philistines would hang the bodies of King Saul and his three princes, including Jonathan, on the city wall of Beth-Shan. And the armor of the dead king would be put on exhibition in the heathen temple of Ashtaroth.

What was wrong with Israel? So far had the people wandered from divine guidance under the reign of Saul that they could ask themselves that question like men waking from a dream. Why had they been so helpless in those last battles? True, they had been deprived of smiths and metalworkers for years by arrogant neighbors. But when had such weakness mattered to Israel in the past? Was there no one now that was close to the old ideals? No one who in weakness and meekness before God could receive divine strength? There was one such indeed, though the people, drearily removing the four royal bodies from public gaze, burying the bones under a cyprus tree, and fasting in seven days' grief, had yet to remember him.

There was a shepherd boy from Bethlehem who had laid low the ogre, Goliath; there was David.

Chapter 23 THE LAMENT OF DAVID

W H E N David, returning to Ziklag, learned that Saul and Jonathan were dead, he tore his clothing to shreds, wept long and pitifully, and all his followers joined in his mourning. His stricken soul poured forth a lamentation over the royal dead, over his enemy, the king, and his dearest friend, the prince, a memorial in an unforgettable psalm:

The beauty of Israel is slain upon thy high places: how are the mighty fallen!

Tell it not in Gath, publish it not in the streets of Ashkelon; lest the daughters of the Philistines rejoice, lest the daughters of the uncircumcised triumph.

Ye mountains of Gilboa, let there be no dew, neither let there be rain, upon you, nor fields of offerings: for there the shield of the mighty is vilely cast away, the shield of Saul, as if he had not been anointed with oil.

From the blood of the slain, from the fat of the mighty, the bow of Jonathan turned not back, and the sword of Saul returned not empty.

Saul and Jonathan were lovely and pleasant in their lives, and in their death they were not divided: they were swifter than eagles, they were stronger than lions.

Ye daughters of Israel, weep over Saul, who clothed you in scarlet, with other delights; who put on ornaments of gold upon your apparel.

How are the mighty fallen in the midst of battle! O Jonathan, thou wast slain in thine high places.

I am distressed for thee, my brother Jonathan: very pleasant hast thou been unto me: thy love to me was wonderful, passing the love of women.

How are the might fallen, and the weapons of war perished!

And now David sought the advice of the Lord God as to where he would go and what he must do.

"Unto Hebron," was the direction the Voice brought into his mind. Hebron was a city once conquered by Joshua in the heart of Judah. There David and his men were made welcome, for the people remembered how David had shared old spoils of battle with the Judeans. They hailed him as a conqueror and the people shouted that he should be made king, and no one else.

There can hardly have been any illusion in David's mind that Israel would unite in offering him the crown. For years he had lived as a hunted man, an outlaw and rebel, depending for his very life on the reports of spies and friends. As well as any man alive he knew the politics, the feuds, the warring ambitions of tribal leaders. But he also saw that to be accepted first as king by Judea would be a very great advantage; with that scepter he might soon sway a unified people.

But not without bloodshed. From the moment he was acclaimed monarch in a public ceremony he knew that armies would be raised against him. Yet all the while the nearness of a glorious future warmed his veins as if in supernatural preassurance. He resolved to bring that glorious dream to reality, by peaceful means if possible, but, at whatever cost, he would make the tribes one people and over them he would rule, guiding them to world leadership.

David's first move was a deft stroke of diplomacy. He sent out messengers, carrying a scroll of thanks to the citizens of Jabesh-Gilead for the honorable burial they had given Saul and his sons. In his message he told them that he was king now, and meant to be their friend.

But trouble was already in sight. Abner, captain of the late King Saul's armies, knew what David was up to, as if he had read his mind. Quickly he proclaimed a new king over all Israel—a son of Saul, whose resounding name was Ish-Bosheth. A new capital and center of government would be set up across the Jordan, so declared Captain Abner.

And so began civil war, blood feuds among the Israelites, a long-drawn-out conflict between the house of Saul and the house of David.

Curiously, the old enemies, the Philistines, remained onlookers. They might have taken advantage of the civil dissensions going on apace in Israel, but they preferred to watch and wait, shrewd enough to calculate that a foreign attack would unite the Israelites once more.

For more than seven and a half years the Philistines watched the Israelites trying to destroy each other. In the military performance of David they also saw masterpiece upon masterpiece of strategy and valor. There were times when David must have thought the conflict would not be finished in his lifetime but the day did come when Captain Abner fell out with Saul's son, the pretender. That same day he came to David and offered him the whole of Israel.

David could be king, in fact, and indisputably, at last.

There never lived a more ambitious king, nor one more self-confident. In war David had never lost heart; in victory he was magnificent, an ambitious king installed on a tiny throne. Here was the golden opportunity he had been yearning for through many years. But more mature now, more politically wise, David announced that he would accept Abner's proposal only if Michal, his former wife, were returned to him. Thus he made himself once again the legal son-in-law of King Saul, legitimate ruler of Israel and not an adventurer coveting a kingdom.

The night of the day that Abner made his proposal he was murdered in his tent. The blood feud would not be abolished by treaty, not even if great armies surrendered. A whole series of revenge killings followed—it was Joab who had murdered Abner, but eventually Joab was slain, and so the blood ran until all the sons of Saul were dead except one—a lame prince with the mouth-filling name of Mephibosheth, whose nurse got him away to safety. And with the flight of limping Mephibosheth the civil war came to its end.

The genius of David as administrator, a governor with imagination and a deep love of masses of people, could now come to flower. Peace gave him his real opportunities. King of Israel at thirty-eight, the poet-monarch wanted to improve everything. No longer would Hebron or any other second-rate town be good enough for the city of Israel's master. Jerusalem and nothing less would do for his capital, and he made it so, after a few smashing blows at the protesting Jebusites.

And while many and various public-welfare projects were under way, the handsome young ruler did not forget himself or his glory. He wanted a fine palace built for the king to dwell in; something that would fill the eyes of foreign ambassadors with respect. Let the Chaldeans and the Egyptians behold what the Israelite people could achieve.

Up in the northern city of Tyre there ruled at this time Hiram, who was despot over a kingdom where artisans prevailed over farmers and shepherds. Hiram was willing to send David skilled workmen—carpenters, stonecutters, masons, and bricklayers, architects and decorators—to erect a habitation fit for a giant-slaying shepherd boy turned now into a king.

It was a glittering house of white marble and cedar, the palace of King David. In it were a hundred rooms just for his wives, of which he had many, and even more children. No such grandeur had ever before been seen in Israel; the upstart nation was becoming very powerful.

No wonder the Philistines worried. They plotted another preventive war, striking secretly and swiftly; it was a shock to David when they took his birthplace, Bethlehem, across the chasm from Jerusalem.

It was more than a shock to the king; it was an incalculable affront to the poet and mystic, parts of his character just as real as the military strategist and the inspired leader of men. His own forces were outside the walls of his home town, but the enemy was within Bethlehem, strong and defiant. It was in that crucial moment that the poet, the mystic, in King David decided capriciously that he was thirsty—and that no water from the wells of earth could quench his parched throat except a draught from the well inside the front gate of Bethlehem.

Because he wished it, three soldiers volunteered. With incredible daring and obedience they slipped through the enemy lines and fetched him back a jug of the home water. Then, having got what he had asked for, David was overcome by conscience at having sent faithful men into such unnecessary danger. He poured the Bethlehem water on the ground, an offering to Almighty God.

"Is this not the blood of the men who went in jeopardy of their lives?" he demanded. He asked forgiveness for such folly and prayed for guidance in the battle. Not a move would he make until he felt he had received a divine message. And when the wind rose and shook the mulberry trees he declared that breeze was a heavenly signal for battle. In that belief David smashed the armed might of the Philistines.

In celebration of his sweep of triumph, the ark of the covenant was brought from the house of Abinadab to the new capital, Jerusalem. The victory was being observed with delirious shouts and songs and dancing; King David gave himself up to public ecstasy, whirling madly and leaping at the head of a joyous procession, all dancing before the Lord. The holy ark of so many vicissitudes and wanderings was placed in the Tabernacle prepared for it, and to complete the festivities, food and wine were distributed freely to all.

But in the midst of all this rejoicing Saul's daughter Michal, the wife David had lost and recovered, glared at the festive king with dark contemptuous eyes. David, she said shrewishly, was losing all dignity in mixing and dancing as one of the common crowd; he was acting like a buffoon. And her charge stung the king.

"I will play before the Lord," David replied in chill rebuttal. He was an early and royal democrat. "And I will be more base in my own sight in His honor; and the people will understand."

From that hour Michal and David were as strangers, and she bore no children of his. The youngest of Saul's daughters had much to learn about her husband. She had been attracted to him before he had ever noticed her; she had plainly told her father that David was the man she wanted—feminine forwardness unusual in those days. But Michal wanted David as she would like to have him, not as he was. She saw him as another incarnation of her father. But David was not only a warrior and a strategist every bit as able as Saul; not only a governor with a great capacity for administration; in addition to these extrovert qualities David was creative. Nor was he a dilettante or pretender to the arts; he was one of the great poets of the ages. When his choristers joined with him in the singing of the psalms they were close to the highest peak of expression their people were ever to reach.

None of this penetrated behind the impatient mask of Michal's dusky and earthy beauty. She could not comfort David; if he was the first man to say his wife did not understand him, he did not exaggerate.

Even while he was restoring tranquillity to the land, organizing a close-knit nation, and governing it well, King David was dreaming his greatest dream.

In his busiest day the idea hung like a star in his mind, and at night it was the moon of his dreams. He believed, with the passion of a poet as well as the vision of a prophet, that the destiny of Israel was incalculable, now that he had led the people back to earnest, fervent worship of the one true God. He felt this return to the Lord God would be permanent, with no more backslidings, because one of his most charming qualities was his ebullient optimism in practical affairs. To celebrate this, the greatness of the one true God, David was dreaming of a Temple for Jerusalem.

In his poet's eyes it would be a fairer building than ever man had made before, a building of marble, cut from the quarries in the hills, and of cedar from forests in Lebanon, the mountain country of Hiram, king of Tyre; marble and cedar and gold, together in a Temple conceived and made to be beautiful within or without, wherever a man stood and looked. The Temple that David would build to the glory of God would be a psalm of frozen music and one of the wonders of the world.

By the light of torches in the night David in his palace would often study the drawings of his architects, calculate the costs with his builders. He was eager to start, hungry for the ring of hammer, the smell of fresh wood, the sight of the earth opening for the foundations. He was baffled at the inexplicable delays that plagued all his efforts. He ruled with despotic sway, an absolute monarch whose every command was obeyed by every citizen, all fearful of him and loyal to him. But nature and fate seemed to work against him, as he tried to get the building of the Temple under way.

And then one day there came to his palace an old man in a travel-stained blue robe; a bald-headed old fellow with stiff, brief beard who asked for an audience with the king. That was the first meeting of David with Nathan, whose name meant "God Gives" and whom the people called a prophet. There was some invisible guarantee of authority in all that Nathan said or did, and it was a good day for David when the old man walked in.

Before long David was to learn to look to Nathan for guidance in the administration of the spiritual side of his government. No man was ever a more fearless counselor than Nathan. He started right out by informing the king that he might as well dismiss all his Temple dreams; he would die and never see it a reality. Why? God had always dwelt with His people in a tent; build no house of cedar for Him now. But Nathan's shrug as he gave this evasive answer did not deceive David. Before he let the old man leave the throne room David had the truth. Who was David to build a Temple to the Lord?

He whose hands were stained with the blood of many battles; he who was such a mixture of ferocity and gentleness, who could dream such beautiful patterns and do such atrocious deeds; the almost inconceivable measure of good and bad that was mixed in him—who was he to build a Temple to the Lord?

Did Nathan, the prophet, foresee that blood would give this poet David thirst for more blood? That the brutality of his experiences would make his soul haughty, his passions overwhelming, so that soon he would stain his soul with private crimes? Even so, Nathan had a word of comfort for his frustrated majesty. It was a good dream, to build so wondrous a Temple. If David could not build it, yet it would be, in time, erected and by David's own flesh and blood. This was the promise: a son of David would build the Temple.

What more could the king say now? He accepted the verdict against him with true grace. If his son, and not himself, was to build the Temple, David, nevertheless, would help to get ready for that enormous undertaking. Among his preparations was the training of a thousand singers, by two hundred and eighty-eight masters of music.

And among the music they would sing were the new psalms that King David, the poet and musician, was composing.

For the further brightening of the earnest, though disappointed king, Nathan imparted the rest of the wonderful message he brought, in which it was promised to David that his kingdom would endure. For God had said:

"I will be his Father and he shall by My son. If he commit iniquity, I will chasten him with the rod of men. But My mercy shall not depart away from him, as I took it from Saul, whom I put away before you."

At this divine assurance David was profoundly moved. He thanked Him for all His mercies and loving-kindness. In deepest humility the king meant that day to do all that was right and just.

But like other men, before and since, David could not anticipate the strength of coming temptation. His own weakness he failed to estimate accurately. He plunged into new wars, feeling his battles to be every one justified. And it must be said that his enemies were many, they were persistent and intolerable; not only ubiquitous Philistines, but many other tribes, the Moabites, the Ammonites, the Edomites, and the clever Arameans of the Damascus regions. But he routed them all in shambles of defeat.

Soon Syria, a rich prize, came under his conquering dominion. Within a few years, by constant conquest, King David had made an empire that commanded universal respect and admiration. And Jerusalem, the golden "City of David," became a religious and political and social center, crowning in its wedgelike height and impregnability the land of milk and honey.

Perhaps it was then that David thought he could relax. He did not now have to attend to everything himself. His seasoned troops were managed by his General Joab, a tactician, a disciplinarian, a man to be feared. Joab would maintain and enforce the rule of David.

The king had also chosen high priests whom he trusted. Zadok and Ahimelech were appointed as chief priests of the sanctuary, thus consolidating the old conservatives together in a harmony of shared authority.

And now the land of Israel was prosperous and powerful. All the promises to Abraham, Isaac, and Jacob were coming true. David surrounded himself and his people with wealth, splendor, and garish luxury, and everyone was prosperous, while Israel forgot its long hardships and poverty. This was indeed living on the fat of the land.

But success would demand its price, and soon.

Chapter 24 DAVID AND ABSALOM

"Is THERE yet any left of the house of Saul, that I may show him kindness for Jonathan's sake?" asked King David.

He was still brooding over the violent death of Ish-Bosheth, the pretender, for no wrong that he had done except that he was used as a puppet for Abner; after all, Saul's son had been of truly royal blood.

Ziba, once a servant in the house of Saul, answered the king's question. One night he came to David and told of one sole survivor still left of the family of Saul; he was Mephibosheth, lamed brother of Jonathan. Immediately the cripple was sent for, and tenderly received at Jerusalem; David, the unforgetting friend of his father Jonathan, bestowed on the handicapped youth all his paternal inheritance, Saul's lands which had been seized by the state. David even made a place for the limping lad at the palace table. And Ziba, who had brought the facts to David, was assigned with his sons to be servants for Mephibosheth.

It was all heart-warming, and next the king looked for other opportunities for mercy and benignity. But when he tried to repay Hanun, son of the king of Ammon, whose father had also done David kindness in the past, there was trouble, more warfare, more extermination.

But David tarried in Jerusalem. He was in a strange mood, as if bored in the midst of the glory he had dreamed of for so long; as if wondering how he could get a new excitement from life in the jaded days of present. In this mood, one twilight David arose from off his bed, where he had lain in a kind of jejune listlessness. Walking on his roof in the cool of eventide, his eye was caught by a most beautiful woman in the bath of a nearby house. She was washing herself industriously, unaware that anyone was near.

Instantly David was enamored, infatuated with excitement such as he had not known for years. At once he sent servants to learn her identity.

The word that was brought back was that the strange beauty was called Bathsheba, faithful wife of Uriah, a Hittite. By David's orders, and in spite of wifely status, messengers kidnaped Bathsheba and carried her to the royal chambers. Then and here began a rapturous love affair, of king and soldier's wife. Soon Bathsheba was with child by David.

In this awkward plight, David ordered that her husband be released from the army, brought home from the field. By being at home, he could offset public suspicions of adultery, if he could be induced to accept his situation calmly.

But Uriah was not to be made a cuckold, even by his king. The husband refused to cloak the misdeed of his wife and her royal lover; in spite of David's commands, and later despite much plying of Uriah with wine, he absolutely refused again to consort with Bathsheba. Uriah was an obstinate and righteous citizen. As David saw it there was nothing else to be done except to get rid of the fellow.

So Joab was ordered to see to it that Uriah was put "in the forefront of battle."

This wicked order was obeyed. In the front line Uriah was soon cut down. No sooner was his death made sure of than David's guilty conscience caused him to send a placating word to Joab:

"Let not this thing displease you, for the sword devours one as well as another."

In the prescribed fashion Bathsheba mourned her husband's loss for a certain season. But when its period of observance was over she became David's wife, if not his queen. The hasty marriage aroused a typhoon of gossip in Israel. The people knew that a child was to be born to Bathsheba; but as no one protested openly, David seemed to have had his lustful will and paid no price.

Did not such a sensitive spirit as the poet David feel an awareness of God's displeasure? God had once proclaimed that David was a man after His own heart. Then, if that were so, he must never feel too safe in God's love; he was guilty of a presumption of God's mercy, always a dangerous blunder. In his headiness David perceived no incongruity between his flagrantly wicked deeds and God's affection.

It was not surprising that soon after the murder-stained marriage in the palace ragged old Nathan came forth from his cave and stood before the throne. And David, with a pang of conscience, remembered that Nathan was a spokesman for God.

Nathan began by giving him an account of a certain rich man with many flocks and herds, who, when feasting a friend, took a poor man's one ewe lamb for meat instead of butchering one of his own large number.

"That man shall surely die," declared David indignantly. "And he shall restore the lamb fourfold, because he did this thing and because he had no pity."

"You are the man," cried Nathan in a terrible voice. He made unmistakably clear the parable he had spoken: "You have despised the commandment of the Lord, to do evil in His sight."

And step by step Nathan sternly rehearsed the heinous offenses against Uriah, seduction and then murder, and he declared:

"Thus says the Lord, Behold, I will raise up evil against you out of your own house."

David began to weep.

"I have sinned against the Lord," he confessed, contrite and afraid. He feared that death was already breathing over his shoulder. But no! Nathan told him that it was not yet time for the Lord to permit him to die, but death would take the child born of Bathsheba. From the days of Moses, as David knew, the sins of the fathers were visited on the children. Now he was inconsolable. As predicted, his son died, and David poured out the anguish of his conscience in one of his greatest psalms:

> Have mercy upon me, O God, according to Thy lovingkindness: according unto the multitude of Thy tender mercies blot out my transgressions.
>
> Wash me thoroughly from mine iniquity and cleanse me from my sin.
>
> For I acknowledge my transgressions: and my sin is ever before me.
>
> Against Thee, Thee only, I have sinned, and done this evil in Thy sight: that Thou mightest be justified when Thou speakest, and be clear when Thou judgest.
>
> Behold, I was shapen in iniquity; and in sin did my mother conceive me.
>
> Behold, Thou desirest truth in the inward parts: and in the hidden part Thou shalt make me to know wisdom.
>
> Purge me with hyssop, and I shall be clean: wash me, and I shall be whiter than snow.
>
> Make me to hear joy and gladness; that the bones which Thou hast broken may rejoice.
>
> Hide Thy face from my sins, and blot out all mine iniquities.
>
> Create in me a clean heart, O God; and renew a right spirit within me.

Cast me not away from Thy presence; and take not Thy holy spirit from me.

Restore unto me the joy of Thy salvation; and uphold me with Thy free spirit.

Then will I teach transgressors Thy ways, and sinners shall be converted unto Thee.

Deliver me from bloodguiltiness, O God, Thou God of my salvation: and my tongue shall sing aloud of Thy righteousness.

O Lord, open Thou my lips; and my mouth shall shew forth Thy praise.

For Thou desirest not sacrifice; else would I give it: Thou delightest not in burnt offering.

The sacrifices of God are a broken spirit: and a broken and contrite heart, O God, Thou wilt not despise.

And David was comforted when another son was born to Bathsheba.

The new baby was called Solomon.

Two of the already grown sons of David—Absalom and Amnon—were prominent in the large family of the king, who had so many wives and concubines. All of the princes and princesses grew up in the new-rich luxury of the young kingdom, and that prodigality was no unmixed blessing. Ease and idleness had spoiled Amnon so overwhelmingly that in his teens he had actually seduced his half sister Tamar, when, pretending illness, he asked her to wait on him in his bedchamber. Then, as has often happened, once he had surfeited his lust, Amnon began to hate Tamar, could not bear the sight of his sister any longer, although she remained silent and did not denounce him, even by a glance.

Nevertheless, gossips told David what happened. And what did he do, in his regal wrath? Nothing. Like Eli, like Samuel, he took no action against his guilty son; like them, he had been a too indulgent father, and perhaps blamed himself the more. But that other son—headstrong, handsome, impetuous Absalom, who was Tamar's full-blooded brother—he nursed revenge for her in his heart until the first opportunity presented itself. Then, in the very height of the merriment at a wine party, Amnon was slain by Absalom's orders, while all the other sons of the king fled in fear from the scene of the murder, thinking their turn was next.

Absalom himself fled all the way to Geshur, where his mother's people were. There he remained an exile from court for three years, until his crime of fratricide had begun to fade from the public mind. But the thoughts of David about the crime were still a tormenting mixture, a conflict in which he often mourned alone for his murdered son, yet feeling also a perverse longing to see Absalom again; like all men, David had a mixture of loyalties that warred, one with another.

None knew better than Joab, the general, how David missed Absalom, his son. Hard as the old fighter was in battle, he sympathized with King David's troubled heart, and while others gossiped, Joab took action. Engaging a wise woman of Tekoah, he had her come to the palace courtroom and act the part of a mourning petitioner before David. Weeping, she told of her two sons who had hated each other, one killing the other. Now, she wailed, she was sorely beset in resisting the pressure of her family to have the fratricide punished with death, leaving her sonless.

"Protect my boy for me, O King," she implored.

"There shall not one hair of his head fall to the ground," cried David impulsively.

Cunningly, the widow reminded the king that he had a banished son of his own, one to whom he ought to be kind, and not merely guarantee kind treatment for humble subjects. David saw through her guile and he knew Joab as its instigator. Nevertheless, he was eased. He cross-examined the woman with the skill of a modern district attorney until she had to confess the ruse. Upon which, deeply touched at such a device to smooth his cares, David sent for Joab and granted him permission to go to Geshur and invite Absalom to come back to Jerusalem.

"But let him not see my face," said the father, still withholding full forgiveness. As months began to lengthen into years he continued to withhold it, and Absalom was so irked that after two years of cooling his heels, he began to plot mischief. In sheer, sullen resentment at Joab, that good-natured go-between, Absalom conspired to have his barley field burnt up. And when the fields were black ruins he impudently told Joab the cause.

Yet Joab went straight to the king, not to denounce Absalom but to plead the young ruffian's cause. Small wonder that David relented. He sent for his son and kissed him.

But Absalom, who believed he could charm himself out of any situation, was still far from satisfied. He had been taken back into the palace life, but only as one member of a very large family. He had been given no preference. Actually he now wanted to be nothing less than king.

He was already planning to replace his father as soon as possible, plotting to overthrow the reign.

First Absalom set himself to the task of winning the favor of the populace by beguiling all hearts with boyish manners and by helping people in trouble, with his influence. Next, in confidential meetings, he slyly assumed prerogatives of a ruler. Subversiveness was spreading in the air. He curried favor and support from the southen tribes; he divided loyalties one way and another until at last David was forced to listen to his spies and to realize that his own son's bedevilment was becoming a serious threat. Trying to attach first-rate men to himself, Absalom had won over even Ahithophel, the king's closest counselor.

And daily the conspiracy was growing stronger; David confirmed the fact that more and more people flocked to the secret banner of Absalom. He had stolen the hearts of the people of Israel; with the power of the masses behind him, he was a real threat to the throne.

It looked as if the great founder of the kingdom might be overthrown by his own son.

Chapter 25   SON AGAINST FATHER

EVEN NOW David did not want to believe the true depths and duplicity of Absalom's treason. He wanted to think of his favorite son as the victim and tool of clever enemies of the throne; and that the whole maladroit conspiracy would tumble into wreckage at the first sign of discovery. But such were not the facts.

Absalom was the very heart and soul of the revolution. In his easy smiling way he had already made himself familiar with the politics of the great world, already saw himself in his father's place. He had studied the kingcraft practiced by other monarchs and the diplomacy of their emissaries; he was full of self-confidence, sure he knew how to keep his place in an unfriendly world; an ambitious and conscienceless young prince, with no illusions whatever.

Around Absalom were gathered men equally determined and without scruple; their plans were well made, their support powerful in the rank and file; they were ready at any time for an armed uprising against David, and Absalom was quite eager to start.

In the lofty gloom of his bedchamber King David sprawled, and plucked at the strings of his lyre and sang sadly:

"Mine enemies speak evil of me. All that hate me whisper against me. Yea, mine own familiar friend, in whom I trusted, who did eat of my bread, hath lifted his heel against me."

Then, standing up with a deep sigh of pained acceptance of the facts, David gave his orders:

"Arise, and let us flee!"

Only ten women of his household were left to look after the beautiful palace. Already graying with the years, the royal refugee had now to run away, and he planned to seek refuge across the Jordan, where there was still support for him and untainted friendliness.

The countryside that morning was shaken with all the bright energies of spring; the wild primroses were coloring the fields, the cowslips startling in meadows green, but the farmers and herders who lived along the route wept openly as David and his loyal entourage passed by on their way toward the river. Faithful Zadok, the priest, and his Levites came close behind, carrying the ark into exile, but David ordered them to take it back immediately to Jerusalem. He was refusing to deceive himself. There was something degrading in this running away from his own son, his favorite, too, among so many—how could he be sure that God was with him in this blood feud? No, he would not presume on God's mercy and assistance; he would fight it out, by guile now, by military power later, and make no claim that he was being led by divine guidance.

Barefoot, and with head covered like a penitent pilgrim, David toiled up the Mount of Olives, on whose lower slope one day Jesus was to know the agony of Gethsemane. Weeping and wailing, his followers marched in sorrowful procession. It was to all of them as if the sun would no longer rise, with David off his throne and new recruits being reported joining the rebel banners.

On the hilltop Hushai, a tall, muscled Archite, greeted the weary king and announced that he desired to share David's fate whatever it might be, faithful to his last drop of blood. This well-meant bombast David received with thanks. There was, indeed, work for his adherents to do, and one task for which Hushai was well equipped. Had he heard of Ahithophel? That was a rhetorical question. Who had not heard of David's most intimate counselor, long accounted the wisest sage in Israel, and the grandfather of beautiful Bathsheba? Well, look at him now, this favored courtier of the great common sense, exalted to be adviser to the king; now he was counseling the treacherous

Absalom, a co-conspirator with him. The name of Ahithophel meant "Brother in Foolishness" and he was living up to it.

What David needed most was a trustworthy agent, a counter-espionage agent in Absalom's circle, who could hear the advice of the rebel's counselors and send it on by swift messenger to David. That was David's immediate proposal to Hushai: that he go back to Jerusalem and be a spy. The king and his new subject clasped hands on their bargain.

Hushai would watch artful Ahithophel, and would send young Ahimaaz and Jonathan, his own sons, as messengers. Hushai knew he was risking his life on this mission but he felt that he was shrewd enough in the ways of men to match wits with Ahithophel, who from all accounts held Absalom in the hollow of his hand.

So Hushai departed on his mission, just as Ziba, the servant of Saul's lame grandson, Mephibosheth, appeared with saddled asses and a store of fine food against long travel.

"These are for the king's household," Ziba said obsequiously.

"But where is the lame son of your master, Saul?" asked David brusquely. He was puzzled at the man's air and speech, which seemed to conceal some hidden purpose.

"Mephibosheth is in Jerusalem," admitted Ziba. "He expects that the house of Israel will restore to him the kingdom of his father."

So! There was not only Absalom but another claimant to the throne of Israel. The aging David winced at the sound of the words. He had tried so persistently to be a friend to this lame prince.

"All that pertained to Mephibosheth is now yours," decreed the king to Ziba, who prostrated himself in gratitude. Oh, that he might deserve this boon—and live to collect it!

The house of Saul haunted David this day, for still another whose name was Shimei came up to the exiled monarch as he walked across a field and cursed him spitefully, rejoicing in the uprising of Absalom against a tyrant. At a safe distance Shimei even cast stones at the followers of the king as they passed.

His soldiers would have cut off the head of the reviler without more ado, had David not stopped them.

"Let him curse," decided the king. "Behold, my son, which came forth of my bowels, seeks my life: how much more now may this Benjaminite do it? Let him curse."

Absalom, in Jerusalem, had met Hushai, the priest and secret agent, and had taken a liking to him. Of course Absalom knew that Hushai had been valuable to his father; but he saw nothing wrong in that—the fellow might now be valuable to the son.

So in Jerusalem before very long it soon became a contest of counsel between Ahithophel and Hushai. Of course the latter was secretly in behalf of David, who needed to gain time to organize defense. But Ahithophel was urging immediate pursuit over Jordan to strike a finishing blow at David while he was still weak. Such a course sounded like inspired good sense to Absalom and to the elders present, but only until Hushai, who was also listening, apparently with deep seriousness, advised against the plan. It was brilliant but far too premature, he argued; more preparations were required even at this weak moment, because David's men were fanatics; everyone knew their prowess under provocation.

"Gather all Israel behind you, and then go to battle in person," the priest-spy advised. He convinced Absalom, and the elders, too, that he was wise and right in his advice. He had won a breathing space for David.

The news of the respite was brought to David by the sons of the priests. But by ill luck their mission was discovered and Absalom sent men to capture the messengers. With a good start, and running like deer, the priests' sons had time to win the co-operation of a man who hid them in a well in his courtyard. And after they had gone down the well a friendly woman, whose name is lost to history, spread a covering of cloth over the hole and sprinkled ground corn on it, to conceal its real use. Safe in the well, the messengers crouched unseen, until the pursuers were gone. Then the pair sped on their way over Jordan and delivered Hushai's words of direction and assurance.

Meanwhile Ahithophel, full of chagrin because Absalom had listened to someone else, went out and hanged himself.

Following the advice of Hushai, David went to Mahanaim, that ancient and important city where once, perhaps a thousand years before, Jacob as he was returning from Mesopotamia fell in with the unknown angels of God. There the fugitive David was welcomed and succored, especially by one Barzillai, a Gileadite, who was heart and soul for the harassed king, and there he resolved to establish his headquarters. But soon Absalom got tired of waiting; he and his men passed over Jordan at last, with Amasa, his captain, pitting his strength and strategy against the soldiers of David's general, Joab.

David wanted to take an active part in the battle but his people would not hear of it.

"You are worth ten thousand of us," they cried, and would not see his life endangered. So David, bowing to their democratic will, had to stand by the gateside as the battalions went marching through. But he called to Joab one parting injunction:

"Deal gently with the young man—even with Absalom."

The battle began early in the wood of Ephraim. Before nightfall the slaughter in the rebel army was decimating; the sword of David's hosts unquenchable in blood, and the thick woods swallowed up uncounted dead of the revolutionists.

Completely defeated, Absalom, the upstart, mounted his mule and sought to escape southward, by a narrow, secret way through the woods. If he had gone carefully he might have made his escape, but Absalom was born to recklessness, to heedlessness, to haste. He whipped his donkey, resolved to put a chasm of space between him and his pursuers.

Thus it was that as he rushed on in the fading glow of late afternoon his extraordinarily long hair caught fast in the boughs of an oak, the branches and the thorn briars tearing the flesh of his face. From the bough Absalom dangled helplessly, until soldiers of David saw the hapless prisoner and, knowing it was the king's son, reported to Joab, the general.

"Why did you not smite him to the ground?" roared Joab, ready to burst in his absolute abhorrence of a traitor, king's son or not. "I would have given you ten shekels of silver and a girdle."

"Not for a thousand shekels would I have done it," said his informant. "For we all heard the king charge you to deal gently with him—"

The man's fears meant nothing to Joab, whose code consisted only of courage and fidelity. Taking three darts in his hand, Joab hurried off to where Absalom hung by the hair in his agony. The dispatch was quick and merciful; the old campaigner thrust the darts through the rebellious heart. Then ten of Joab's young aides joined him and slashed at the limp body of the lost pretender. Finished with their bloody work, they cast the body of the dead prince in a pit in the wood, heaping stones upon the spot, and even as the leader of the rebellion was being buried the horns were blowing in victorious signal.

"Cease combat!"

Victory at last. The sound of it reached the ears of David waiting, old and careworn, at the tower gate. The watchman warned David of the approach of a runner—of two runners. Hope and fear tore at the king's heart.

"All is well!" shouted the first courier, sweat pouring from him.

"Is the young man Absalom safe?" asked David.

Ahimaaz could not say, for he did not know; he turned aside from the look in the king's eyes. But the second messenger rushed up with the truth, and told the tale bluntly and without preliminary. For to the hard practical mind of that soldier Absalom was no more than any other enemy of his lord and king.

But to David, Absalom still remained, in his ignominious death, the darling of his heart and soul. The king-father's grief in the midst of military triumph was overwhelming. All in an instant he seemed to forget the treachery, the stark fact that his favorite would have killed his father if he could, would have taken his throne, worn his crown, and reigned by his father's murder. All bitterness drained out of David's heart. Weeping, he stood at the window of his private room and raised a broken voice to God:

"O my son Absalom, my son, my son Absalom! Would God I had died for you, O Absalom, my son, my son!"

No one could console him and after many weeks the prolonged mourning began to create resentful talk in the palace. An unending threnody of sorrow was all the life the court knew.

David was not king any more but a metrist of lamentation; as poet he remained endlessly indoors and fashioned psalms of woe:

"Absalom, my son!"

His despondency was like a disease that had crept over him and paralyzed his faculties. He turned his disheartened eyes to the clouds and stared as if wondering how he had lost his way to God.

At last Joab, the son of David's sister and general-in-chief of his armies, was moved to protest. Had the king, in his egocentric sorrow, forgotten what his devoted people had done, what risks of limb and life they had run to save him and his kingdom? Did he, then, love his enemies more than his friends? Let him answer; was the life of Absalom so precious that it outweighed all the love and service of his followers?

"Speak well to your servants, the people," warned the forthright Joab, "or worse evil will befall you than any hitherto in your life."

And that settled it. Even in his sorrow David was a mixture of passion and practicality, and he knew when to yield to one or the other. Removing the garments of his grief, the king pulled open the crimson curtains of his chamber and looked out at the world. He made a speech, a stirring appeal to the elders and people. And in response he heard the cries of frightened subjects from far and near:

"Return, O king, and all your servants!"

So David started back toward the Jordan and his beloved city of Jerusalem.

But trouble was starting again, even before they got back to the capital. There was, first and foremost, the murder of Amasa, his nephew. Some advisers had urged David to kill the hardy soldier the moment the revolution was ended. But David yearned for a general reconciliation; he wanted a unified kingdom, full of peace, and everybody forgiving everybody else and living agreeably together. To bring about the happy state, he made large concessions, as in the case of Amasa. David knew all of which Joab, his general, reminded him about the man's treachery. Amasa had deserted to go along with Absalom. But David, in his kingly desire to quiet all bad feeling and to show mercy to his defeated enemies, went to the extreme length of welcoming Amasa's return to the fold. More, David made that partner in revolution, a general of the armies.

Now Joab reported that a new revolt was afoot and Amasa had to be dispatched. At his death, the revolution had almost run its course. Abel, the only leader left to the rebels, was betrayed by his own people; a woman's treachery sent his bleeding head soaring over the wall of the last town to be besieged—and all resistance ceased.

Now David resolved to reign again as a monarch unequaled in the history of Israel. Before he crossed over the river many persons who had stood with his enemies in his long struggle gathered around him, wanting to be counted as lifelong friends. Among his former foemen were Shimei, who once had cursed him and stoned his men; Ziba, wily servant of Mephibosheth; and Mephibosheth himself; the crippled son of Jonathan.

When the once scornful Shimei bowed before the king, Abishai, General Joab's elder brother, held up his sword, drawn and ready to slay the betrayer—but David shook his graying locks; let the scoundrel go free. Even when Mephibosheth stammered aloud how Ziba had deceived him, as well as David, the king waved the treachery aside and sent them away unharmed. Not once during that wonderful day did David lose his temper, not even when one of his dearest wishes was balked. His heart was set upon taking back to Jerusalem with him Barzillai, whose loyalty had never faltered; the king wanted him to live in the palace at Jerusalem. But Barzillai was stubborn in his feebleness.

"I am fourscore," he pleaded. "Let me turn back that I may die in my own city and be buried with my father and mother."

The king kissed the grand old man and blessed him. For in the alembic of that experience, of flight, exile, revolution, and war with his most beloved son, the soul of the headstrong king had been tested, purified, and transformed.

In troubled days that were to come, and many peaceful years afterward, David was to write and compose some of the greatest of his psalms. He had come to know that God will speak to man, if man will listen:

Be still, and know that I am God!

As far as the east is from the west, so far hath He removed our transgressions from us.

Like as a father pitieth his children, so the Lord pitieth them that fear Him.

For He knoweth our frame; He remembereth that we are dust.

As for man, his days are as grass; as a flower of the field, so he flourisheth.

For the wind passeth over it, and it is gone; and the place thereof shall know it no more.

But the mercy of the Lord is from everlasting to everlasting upon them that fear Him, and His righteousness unto children's children.

David had three years of peace, during which he directed his country wisely and efficiently, healing the wounds of civil war. On the borders there were always skirmishes with the Philistines, and David meditated marching north to quell those persistent enemies. But the people protested, they loved their king too much ever again to let him take the field.

Yet even in the maturity of his wisdom David remained an impetuous man, with blood in his eye. After three years of restoration in the kingdom famine scorched the land, and everybody was hungry. David declared he knew why they were plagued with the parched fields: it was because he had been too merciful. Long ago he should have extirpated the last remnants of the ambitious family of Saul. Now he took up the purge with a frenzy of seeking out and sending spies and concentrating on the one bloodthirsty task. There were seven remaining relatives of Saul and all were caught, summarily condemned as potential pretenders, breeders of dissension and revolt, subversive characters all—and all were hanged on a hilltop outside of Jerusalem; all except one.

And that, too, was a characteristic act of the aging but unchanging David. With blood in one eye he glowed with mercy in the other. Famine or danger or whatever the future might bring, one of Saul's sons had to be spared the noose.

And the one who was allowed to live, of course, was that waspish lame prince, Mephibosheth, a mean fellow whom no one could trust.

In those times, regardless of famine and border fighting, David felt grandly secure. He reigned as a king and a judge of his people, Joab was commander-in-chief of the armies; Adoram, a faithful warrior, was put over the taxgathering; and Ira, another veteran, as the king's right-hand man.

David's confidence in the safety of people and kingdom found expression in a new psalm:

> The Lord is my rock, and my fortress, and my deliverer;
> The God of my rock; in Him will I trust;
> He is my shield, and the horn of my salvation, my high tower, and my refuge, my Saviour; Thou savest me from violence.
> I will call on the Lord, Who is worthy to be praised; so shall I be saved from mine enemies.
> When the waves of death compassed me, the flood of the ungodly men made me afraid;
> The sorrows of the grave compassed me about; the snares of death prevented me;
> In my distress I called upon the Lord, and cried to my God: and He did hear my voice out of His temple, and my cry did enter His ears.

Chapter 26 THE DEATH OF DAVID

THE glory of Israel's kingdom had never before been so bright as in those last days when David became old in years, and, as the ancient records tell, in all his veins and organs "he gat no heat," and a young girl was brought to lift his temperature. There has been much misunderstanding of this episode, but St. Jerome has set it forth in magnificent light, when he says, in his *Letters*:

Who is this Sunamite, wife and virgin, so ardent as to give heat to the cold king, so holy as not to provoke to lust, him whom she warmed? Solomon expounds on this when he says possess Wisdom . . . Don't desire Her and She will seize upon you. Love Her, and She will serve you.

Thus, in the Sunamite girl he sees a type of spiritual wisdom.

Stricken in years, the king began to live in the past, recalling again and again the exploits of his young days. Despite all hazards and obstacles, he had built a happy and prosperous nation. He loved to think of his "mighty men," old campaigners who had followed him through so many encounters, often down into the very throat of death. He enjoyed talking with grizzled comrades; a man had no brighter boast than to say he had fought with David. Like all veterans, they were yarn spinners—telling stories of how once one of those "mighty men" raised his spear against eight hundred and slew them all; how three others once broke through enemy lines merely to get their chief a drink of water from Bethlehem's well; how another went down into a pit on a snowy day and fought a lion to the death. Brave old days!

And while David warmed his heart with dreams of past glories and was gaining the reputation of being senile, new treason was being brewed against him.

As before, the leader of revolt was one of his sons; this time, Adonijah, born of Haggith. Considering himself heir, Adonijah could not wait for his father to shut his dimming eyes forever, so he organized his own palace revolution. He even convinced the pliant Joab, and the priest Abither, that they must conspire with him, traitors all together now; otherwise, without backing, how would the son who would be king win over to his side such an influential counselor as Nathan, the prophet, or any of David's mighty men that were left alive?

The ambitious son completely forgot—if he had ever known—that a prophet has his own way of getting at the truth. In his father he saw only a doddering old man who sat quaking upon his throne; the once handsome warrior king was so wasted in flesh, so much a bag of skin and bones, that he seemed too emaciated to be alive.

To counteract the shameless intrigue, Nathan, old and weak as he was also, went secretly to Bathsheba. In the eyes of most of David's loyal friends her son Solomon was the legitimate heir to the throne. His right was not only technical; young Solomon gave every evidence of being a kingly soul, born to rule. With the palace conspiracy ready to eliminate Solomon and put Adonijah on the throne, action was needed. So Nathan tried to recall certain old matters to the mind of Solomon's mother. Once, long ago, had not David sworn to Bathsheba, when they were both much younger, that her son and no one else should succeed him, should receive the scepter when it fell from David's fingers?

Surely, he had! Bathsheba could never forget such a promise. But did the old king still remember it?

That night Bathsheba and Nathan, the prophet, went to David together. Did he remember about Solomon—that he wanted the son of Bathsheba to rule? David smiled. Senile though he seemed, he remembered.

"Assuredly, Solomon, your son, shall reign after me," he declared to Bathsheba as she smoothed his forehead. "And he shall sit upon my throne in my stead; even so will I certainly do this day."

David issued orders that Zadok and Nathan, as priests of the Temple, were to anoint Solomon as his chosen successor in Israel, and that the trumpets be blown to proclaim the fact. Waste not a moment!

Thus before the conspirators were even aware that something was happening the great news was published and the people rejoiced with music and shouts:

"God save King Solomon! God save King Solomon!"

Voices cried that phrase all over the land. It quickly reached the ears of Adonijah and his subversive companions, holding a secret council out in the country. Surprise and consternation overcame them, and they hastily separated, each to his place. And in a panic, fearing the rage of his brother Solomon, Adonijah caught hold of the horns of the altar and cried like a child, beseeching God to protect him—that he be not slain for his sin.

Solomon's first public act was, on the sworn promise of honest and loyal behavior thereafter, to spare his brother's life. Mercy became the new sovereign in this first act near the throne.

On his deathbed David gave final charge to Solomon that he might always walk in the ways of the Lord God and thus deserve the divine promise of an enduring dynasty.

"I go the way of all earth," whispered the expiring son of Jesse, who had welded together and made strong the nation that Abraham, Isaac, and Jacob had founded. "Be you strong therefore, and show yourself a man."

Solomon drank in his father's words; magnanimity and retribution were mingled in the fading thoughts of the great king, his last words a farewell psalm:

> The Spirit of the Lord spake by me, and His word was in my tongue.
>
> The God of Israel said, the Rock of Israel spake to me, He that ruleth over men must be just, ruling in the fear of God.
>
> And He shall be as the light of the morning when the sun riseth, even a morning without clouds; as the tender grass spring out of the earth by clear shining after rain.
>
> Although my house be not so with God; yet He hath made with me an everlasting covenant, ordered in all things, and sure: for this is all my salvation, and all my desire, although He make it not to grow.
>
> But the sons of Belial shall be all of them as thorns thrust away, because they cannot be taken with hands:
>
> But the man that shall touch them must be fenced with iron and the staff of a spear; and they shall be utterly burned with fire in the same place.

So died David, one of the greatest of Israelites, one of the great men of history; the shepherd boy who had fought with the giant Goliath; the fugitive whose inspiring friendship with Jonathan taught all posterity gentleness and tenderness and goodness of heart; the pitiful king who was betrayed by his sons and most bitterly of all by beloved Absalom.

David was the poet of the psalms, and his songs were to become the hymnbook of the Temple yet to be built. The musician who could play on the psalter and the lyre was also the warrior who led his troops to victory and the statesman who could and did take a crude confederation of jealous tribes and mold them into a national state.

It was from David's time that Jerusalem because a metropolis and to this day poets call it the City of David. It was he who, moving the capital from Herbron, made Jerusalem the beloved center of the Jews.

After he was gone things were not to be so well for the people, but David's memory was an inspiration even in darkest times. Small wonder, then, that the Messianic hope centered in the house of David of which one day has to be born Joseph, the carpenter of Nazareth, and Mary, whose child would be born in Bethlehem.

BOOK SIX

The Glory of Israel

Chapter 27 SOLOMON

AND NOW there came to reign over Israel the son of David and of Bathsheba, the wisest of wise men, king among kings, and sire of prosperity for his people, a light for the ages to come—Solomon in all his glory.

The kingdom had been ushered in with Saul, but it was David who founded the dynasty, and Solomon, conceived in great wickedness, who was to bring to fulfillment the divine promises of the past. The greatness of God's chosen people had been forecast to Abraham and his son and grandson. Now at last the mysterious Voice was to be fully justified in this amazing era ushered in by the spectacular ceremonies with which Solomon was crowned.

For four centuries of Jewish history the Jewish people were still to be ruled by their kings. From the death of David to the destruction, in 586 B.C., of the Temple, built by Solomon as a symbol of a united and worshipful people, they would be playing a part on the stage of world affairs. But who in those four hundred years ahead would be the equal of Solomon?

He domineered over every soul in his kingdom; no one was safe from his arrogant interference; yet there was no one who did not sincerely and enthusiastically support him. Solomon was an executive and the citizens welcomed the experience for he was a good executive, a man of wisdom and therefore of principle.

His name in Hebrew meant "Peaceful," but the prophet Nathan, so we are told in the Second Book of Samuel, called him Jedidiah, which means "Beloved of God."

Solomon was strong and handsome as an athlete of today and studious as an honor man; a remarkable mixture of sportsman and student, scholar and hero. His black, luminous eyes could look tenderly on a woman and on his people, but they could blaze, too, with unquenchable light and heat, once his authority was contested. Mother Bathsheba had raised him for a prince's part in the world and his teachers had schooled him for government. But never had he been under a woman's thumb or a pedagogue's ferule; he was one of the most independent-minded men that ever was born.

And he needed all his forthrightness, his audacity, and his immense self-confidence the moment the old father-king was gone. The new ruler faced no love feast in Israel; the peace and prosperity that he was to establish in the kingdom were not a part of Solomon's inheritance; his legacy was a divided people. To set his house in order, to consolidate his position, were acute problems at the very outset. Joab, Abither, and Shimei, all power-hungry, would need a firm hand. And Adonijah, the pardoned plotter, immediately began a new intrigue, meant to challenge the new royal authority. Would Solomon be a real king or a shadow?

The answer came swiftly from the throne, and Adonijah, stealer of concubines, was put to death. Joab met the same fate, Abither, the high priest, was ousted from the altar and banished, and finally Shimei, always full of hate, disobeyed his guards and was killed by his commander. With these three summarily disposed of, Solomon could breath easier; Israel knew that he intended to rule.

But from the beginning the young king also showed political sagacity. Taking advantage of his lawful right to have as many wives as he chose, without ecclesiastical limit or the frown of public opinion, King Solomon made up his mind to have more wives than any other man, before him or after, and the record for marrying still remains his, unchallenged. This vast and ever-growing harem was peopled with his brides, not because Solomon was the slave of lust, or afflicted with any peculiar quirk that made a new woman every night the necessity of his passion. Solomon acquired his wives as part of his politics.

He was marrying himself into political and economic alliances, defensive and offensive, cultivating intimate relationships with nearby kings so that they and he should be grandfathers of the same grandchildren. His labors were to fertilize their daughters so that Israel would be blood relatives to many potential aggressors, thus cozened into being friends.

He began first with an Egyptian princess and for two good reasons: Egypt was on his borders, a people terrible in war and overwhelmingly armed. That was reason enough, but also Solomon loved the dazzling splendor of the Egyptian way of doing things; the Sphinx and the pyramids awed him, and so did the huge monoliths ranging in the long lines of temple corridors at Luxor and Memphis and Thebes. He loved the rainbow riot of Egyptian colors, their gilded chariots, their golden beds, their jeweled canopies, their oil lamps of hollowed alabaster. He love the rigid propriety of their deportment, the sumptuousness of their robes, silk and brocade, and velvet and painted linens, the fragrance of their perfumes, the delicacy of their cooking, their amorous complexities and resourcefulness.

All such things Solomon coveted for the glittering palace that David had built and that was now his own dwelling place. Solomon dreamed of glories even greater than these of Egypt; his heart yearned for power and fame and he had an almost barbaric ambition for splendor and show. These traits were joined in his marriage with an Egyptian princess, who through the years was to prove his favorite wife among all those he accumulated.

By the Egyptian alliance Solomon made friendly ties with a powerful neighbor. Why not continue the policy with other nations? One by one Solomon began taking their desirable, aristocratic daughters into his palace; the mariages were, of course, spectacular affairs of state—and soon the state began visibly to prosper under these tactics.

Meanwhile Solomon placed twelve dependable officers as deputy rulers over Israel to carry out his orders to the letter. It was one deputy's job merely to provide the vast quantities of food and clothing and other creature comforts for the inhabitants of the Jerusalem court. For his personal use, Solomon had fourteen hundred chariots, twelve thousand horsemen, and forty thousand stalls for the horses, some of which are to be seen today not far from the Aksa mosque in the old Temple area of Jerusalem. The deputy had to provide what was called "cities" as parking areas for chariots and quarters for horsemen.

Amidst Solomon's early flourishes of extravagance the threats of civil war died down. There came a blessed interval of peace and prosperity, when every man from Dan to Beersheba dwelt safely under his own vine and fig tree. It is known to historians as the period of the long peace, and that golden interlude was essential for one of the outstanding great missions of Solomon. For it was in this spell of tranquillity that the priests, the orators, and the poets had time to collect the literature of the race and save it from destruction. Much of the Old Testament was now put together, still nearly a thousand years before the coming of Christ, and in the four hundred and eightieth year since the children of Israel had escaped from Egypt.

Good fortune smiling on him, Solomon journeyed to the ancient high place of Gibeon to sacrifice and show his gratitude to God. Asleep within the shadow of the historic high altar, Solomon had his first supernatural experience.

God spoke to Solomon; not the Voice as it had addressed Abraham or Isaac, but in a vision of a dream. In the dream the same Voice spoke that all before him had heard. Solomon now listened in his vision to the great Voice of the one true God, speaking so kindly a word, with such unexpected favor and benignity that even in his slumber the son of David was awe-stricken. For the Voice was not commanding Solomon but inviting him:

"Ask what I shall give you!"

To which the dreaming Solomon, recovering himself, and in all humility, made an answer, of all possible answers, most pleasing to the Lord God:

"You have shown unto Your servant, my father, great mercy, according as he walked before You in truth, in righteousness, and in uprightness of heart with You: and You have kept for him this great kindness, that You have given him a son to sit on his throne, as it is this day. Now, O Lord, my God, You have made Your servant king instead of my father; and I am but a little child; I know not how to go out or come in. Your servant is in the midst of the people, a great people that cannot be numbered for multitude. Give, therefore, Your servant an understanding heart to judge Your people, that I may discern between good and bad; for who is able to judge so great a people?"

To which God replied:

"Because you have asked this thing, and have not asked for yourself long life, neither riches for yourself, nor the life of your enemies, but understanding to discern judgment, behold, I have done according to your words: lo, I have given you a wise and understanding heart; so that there was none like you before you, neither after you shall any arise unto you.

"I have also given you that which you have not asked, both riches and honor; so that there shall not be any among the kings like unto you all your days. And if you will walk in My ways, to keep My statutes and My commandments, as your father David did, then I will lengthen thy days."

And Solomon awoke; and behold, it was a dream.

Almost immediately after Solomon returned to Jerusalem he was confronted with a test of all his understanding and mercy, a most spectacular challenge of royal good sense, the testing of wisdom, gift of his oracular dream. The fame of the kingly dilemma was a sensational topic of conversation throughout the land, and people continue to tell it to this day.

Hardly had Solomon begun to hear the troubles of litigants who appeared before his throne when he found himself face to face with a heart-rending enigma. Two women stood in front of him, the red-haired to the right, the dark-haired opposite, and between them on the floor a straw basket, in which a tiny baby played with rosy toes. Each woman swore the child was hers. Each accused the other of monstrous falsehood. They were so passionately emphatic that it was difficult to disbelieve one or the other.

"Bring me a sword," commanded Solomon.

The armor-bearer, a slight lad not unlike the young David who once filled the office for Saul, fetched a long blade with two sharp edges and a great golden guard and handle, with golden chain jangling. King Solomon looked craftily from one woman to the other, composedly meeting their glittering eyes, for both were seething in fury. The king lifted the sword, so that the point was directed on an oblique line to the farther corner of the painted and gilded roof, the shimmering blade just above the middle of the baby's basket.

And then Solomon gave his jugment:

"Divide the living child in two, and give half to one, and half to the other."

Instantly a scream echoed through the vast audience chamber. The dark-haired woman was crying:"No! No! Never! Give the child to her beside me, and in no wise slay it."

In the very same breath the red-haired vixen was saying:

"Let the child be neither mine nor thine, but divide it!"

An instant later she could have bitten her tongue to strangle her own words but it was too late. Solomon, stroking his brief brown beard, dark eyes gleaming, had craftily listened right and left, and he had heard both of them.

For thousands of years afterward this moment would be recounted, how by the ruse of Solomon the true mother was revealed; she would not see her child killed, even though to keep it alive she must let it go to another woman.

Shrewdness and wisdom had long been rare in Israel, but now it flowered, and this one tale served to dramatize it in gossip that traveled widely. Tales of Solomon's judgment were recounted everywhere. This king, of which the nation was now so proud, became famous at home and abroad for the fair justice of his judgments. From many distant lands distinguished visitors came to Jerusalem, some of them even state rulers, all curious to hear his words of wisdom and witness the glory with which Solomon was more and more surrounding himself.

Things were going well with Israel. Too practical-minded to depend only on friendship engendered by a thousand marriages, Solomon kept his soldiers under arms; he built fortifications that ringed in his borders, while meantime encouraging every kind of international trade.

The great king also had a pact with Hiram by which the Israelitish merchant fleet sailed abroad with the protection of the Tyrenian navy, and every third year the ships came into home ports overladen with gold and silver, ivory, apes and peacocks, jewels and sandalwood.

Solomon used the money taken in by tariff levies on imports to beautify the capital, "Jerusalem, the Golden." The glory of Jerusalem was Solomon's deep delight; he was always thinking up plans for its improvement, and before long there revived in his own heart the forbidden dream of his father. David had longed to build a Temple of fitting magnificence for the housing of the ark of the covenant and the worship of the Lord God. But the divine will had refused to accept a Temple from such an architect; now Solomon decided to make that vast and noble dream a reality as the very center and core of his beloved Jerusalem.

The Temple, Solomon was resolved, would stun the civilized world not by mere size but with its beauty and magnificence. And since Hiram, king of Tyre, had fashioned such a gorgeous palace for the house of David, Solomon invited Hiram to Jerusalem once more, now to talk about the Temple.

Tyre was in Phoenicia, on the Mediterranean coast, and its people were traders of the seven seas, and celebrated also for their many crafts, especially their skill in architecture and interior decoration. The seafaring Phoenicians had voyaged to every shore and in their wide travels had seen the building marvels of all countries. The stores of gold and ivory, metals and precious stones in Tyre were incalculable and in their domain grew the forests of Lebanon to be drawn upon for the finest of cedars.

Hiram must have been inspired, for the Temple exceeded all expectations.

No one can be wholly sure today just what the finished building looked like—indeed, there are legends that its sanctum sanctorum was never finished—but there is a wonderful model to be seen in Harvard's Semitic Museum.

With the ardor of a creative artist, Solomon had sat with Hiram, poring over sketches drawn on lambskins, dreaming up new wonders. The world should be spellbound by this, the chief pearl of his capital. With the eye of statesman and artist and poet, Solomon saw Jerusalem not for just what it was but for what he meant to make it; a meeting place of East and West, high on its wedgelike rocky height, a guardian of the watershed between the desert and the sea. The mighty kings that had preyed upon his people had thought contemptuously that Jerusalem was a little highland village, but he would force it to become the "bride of kings and the mother of prophets."

North of the eastern hill he would build his glorious house to God on the site that David had chosen, on the great rock that had been the threshing floor of an ancient Jebusite. Of cedars of Lebanon and Jerusalem marble he would build; entrance, pylons, courts, and a *naos* giving entrance to the Holy of Holies, where forever would be housed, and forever guared, the sacred ark of the convenant.

King Hiram caught the passion of his fellow monarch's ecstasy. He boasted happily of his many skilled artisans and artificers, skilled craftsmen in wood and metal and stone, and all that he had would be brought to Jerusalem to work on the wonderful Temple.

There would be work enough for all the experts Hiram could send, Solomon declared. A large parcel of the land on Mount Moriah, the great Jebusite rock, would be set aside as the Temple Area, and that is the name by which Jerusalem calls it to this day. This area would be enclosed by a wall made of three layers of stone, on which a layer of cedar planks would be laid in the form of a gable. The floor of the court would be paved, and one would enter from the city itself through various gates: the Upper Gate, the King's Gate, Benjamin's, and others.

The Temple structure itself would be in the form of a rectangle, about one hundred and four feet long by about thirty feet wide and a height equal to its width. It would face the east. Inside the Temple there would be three parts: the porch, the sanctuary, and the Holy of Holies, the latter a perfect cube. The walls would be massive, the roof flat, supported by pillars within, especially two particular pillars, Jachin and Boaz. The walls would be wainscoted with cedar wood; the doors of solid olive wood; the decorations would be carvings overlaid with gold and jewels, of cherubim, palm trees, and open flowers.

And there would be "other chambers round about," and in the outer, general court a brazen altar for burnt offerings, highly ornamented and furnished with lavers and shovels and basins, and a series of ten tables for the shewbread of the ritual of worship.

Between the sanctuary and the Holy of Holies there would be a door in which would hang the veil of the Temple, a curtain hiding from view the ark, overshadowed by two gigantic figures of guardian cherubim with outstretched wings.

And within the ark would repose the two stone tables of the law.

So the two kings ardently planned a Temple that, while tiny in the eyes of an Egyptian, would be the most impressive monumental structure ever to be set up by the Israelites, and one of the loveliest ever made by man's hands.

Soon the great undertaking was started. Two hundred thousand men of Israel and Phoenicia were set to work in the forests, and in the labor of transportation, road building, and excavation. The muscles of man and beast were called on in endless strain, sweating in the torrid winds from off the desert. Other workmen burrowed underground to lift chisel and ax in dark caverns, in vast echoing caves of marble under a hill near Jerusalem. Here the rough ashlars were shaped into squared blocks of marble and then carried to the high flat plateau where the Temple was to rise. That was why it was said, as if it were a litany, that no sound of hammer and ax was heard in quarrying the stones.

Of Mount Moriah, the Temple was to be the beautiful crown, with other noble structures, walls, and landscaping leading up to it— palaces, gardens, pools, rare trees, and flowers. It was to be a spot worthy of heaven.

More than seven years the Temple was building; it was not finished until about 970 B.C. Into it went hewn stones of great size for foundation and retaining walls, and choicest woods of cedar and olive. Meanwhile artists were at work on the details—exquisite and elaborate hand carvings for every nook and cranny of roof, pillars, and walls, and a lavish overlay of gold wherever the eye rested, from floor to ceiling, from altar to cherubims over the mercy seat. The cherub, one of the most ancient images and symbols, consisted of a combination of lion, ox, man, and eagle, and in the beginning served to symbolize things secret and mysterious, sacred and unapproachable. Later it came to represent the sustainer of the glory of God and guardian of the mysteries of the law.

When all at last was finished, and the final piece of golden fretwork fastened in place, the last monolithic pilaster set squarely in the wall, and when the two kings had surveyed their handiwork and pronounced it good, the scaffolding was torn down, the tattered coverings torn away, and all Israel and with her the world came out to see the wonder.

And that was what they saw it to be, at first glance—a wonderful gem among the buildings of earth.

This House was God's, and Israel, with the princes of the tribes, and the heads of the families of Israel, gathered together with King Solomon that they might carry the ark of the covenant out of the City of David into its new resting place.

Chapter 28 THE SONG OF SOLOMON

S O L O M O N was a man of God but he also had an eye to himself and his own glory.

By his lights he was as worshipful a man as ever lived, but he also considered that he was a very great king indeed, and it did not seem to him now that the palace of King David, his father, really measured up to the dignity of a monarch such as himself; not after he had commanded world admiration for the Temple of Jerusalem. He wanted a new palace for himself and he wanted King Hiram to build it for him.

The amiable Hiram saw to it that Solomon's nearby palace, so lightly and so beautifully built, over against the wall from the Temple, and other companionable buildings in the general design were no less impressive and dazzling. All were finished after a labor of thirteen years, during which period, if the truth must be told, many serfs—"state slaves"—Hebrews as well as other nationals, were put into the labor gangs.

Actually Solomon's own palace was more grandiose in size, style, and ornament than the Temple itself, but there was no disharmony. His own assembly hall, known as "the house of the forest of Lebanon," was one hundred and fifty feet long, seventy-five feet wide, and about forty-five feet high, and of massive cedar boles.

Entire supervision of design and erection of Temple and palace had been left to the skill of the Phoenicians, at an annual payment of 220,000 bushels of wheat and 1800 gallons of finest olive oil. And the twelve appointed deputies under Solomon managed between them to raise that heavy sum, as well as keeping well supplied the huge royal household—by now seven hundred wives and three hundred concubines, all of whom had to eat three times a day, to say nothing of the armies of servants.

In these intricate works Solomon proved himself a brilliant organizer and executive. For financial support, outside the revenues of his realm, he built up an extensive trade, developed a merchant fleet on the Red Sea, levied high tariffs on merchandise passing through his domain, and bought and sold horses and chariots on a big scale, developing this business with Egypt and other adjacent countries. His income was said to be 666 gold talents a year, or about $20,000,000, which in the values of that day was vast.

Thus under Solomon the Israelites had rapidly become a cosmopolitan people for the first time in their history. They were already feeling their new position when the time came for them, humbly and fitting, to dedicate the Temple. And while the Temple itself was to pass away after four centuries, the words of the dedication have become immortal.

On the day of the ceremony the elders, the heads of the tribes, and the chief fathers in Israel, arrayed in gorgeous ritualistic robes of purple and silver, were assembled on Mount Zion. Led by priests carrying the ark of the covenant, they marched in solemn chanting processional to the glittering marble sanctuary on Mount Moriah, amid the smoke of many sacrifices on the way and the shouts of hundreds of thousands of spectators.

When the ark was placed under the golden spread of the cherubim wings, and the two tables of stone which Moses had received at Sinai became the heart and core of the new Temple, a cloud of silvery fog filled the inner Temple and the people cried that this must be the glory of the Lord—a fog so tangible and dense that the priests could not see their way about the altar until the cloud had passed away.

With awe and joy Solomon watched this phenomenon. Rising in shining robes, he watched the passing away of the silvery cloud and then addressed the worshipers:

"The Lord said that He would dwell in the thick darkness. I have surely built You a house to dwell in, a settled place for You to abide for ever.

"Lord God of Israel, there is no God like You, in heaven above or on earth beneath, Who keeps covenant and mercy with Your servants that walk before You with all their heart:

"Who have kept with Your servant David my father that You promised him, saying, There shall not fail you a man in My sight to sit on the throne of Israel; so that your children take heed to their way, that they walk before Me as you have walked before Me.

"And now, O God of Israel, let Your word, I pray you, be verified, which You spoke unto Your servant, David my father.

"*But will God indeed dwell on the earth? Behold, the heaven of heavens cannot contain You; how much less this house I have builded?*"

Arising from his knees, the fervent king blessed his people again, while sacrifices such as were never known before were offered up—of 22,000 oxen and 120,000 sheep, in one vast slaughter and burning, the ceremonials so multiplied and pressing that a place in the middle of the court before the Temple had to be hollowed for the burnt offerings.

For seven days Israel feasted to music and when, at the week's end, weary but uplifted in spirit, the people dispersed, everyone departing to his own abode, they knew that no one would ever forget those seven days of ecstasy; they were to be told about from generation to generation.

And like a fathering climax, rich in hope, God came again to Solomon. After the dedication and festivities were over, the Voice, in Its second visit to the builder-king, declared:

"I have heard your prayer and your supplication that you have made before Me: I have hallowed this house, which you have built, to put My name there for ever; and Mine eyes and Mine heart shall be there perpetually."

But even while making that covenant, the Lord did not fail to warn Solomon. He must guard himself, this Temple builder, against any breaking of His laws and commandments. As in Eden and in a thousand subsequent derelictions, punishment would follow violation; evil upon him and his house. Turn from the Lord God to other gods, and Israel would, as of old, suffer for its folly.

Solomon was right: there is, as he said, no new thing under the sun, no new wickedness or infidelity to think up. Behind him are a thousand years and more of experimentation with evil, since the garden and the fruit of the tree, and man's first disobedience. God the Father has had His line of heroes since the gates of Eden closed, and he, wise

Solomon, was standing in that line from Adam to David and on—and a long way yet to go before redemption reaches the earth. Now Solomon was being schooled by the Voice, the whisper from heaven that heroes hear; their old sins were clear before Solomon's memory: greed and lust and hatred and love of power and cruelty and blasphemy and the worship of false gods—nothing new, Solomon, and the penance certain, the punishment sure, now as well as then. Be careful, Solomon, the wise; you are with your people at the uttermost peak of glory. Where will you lead them now?

There is no question that on the day he heard the Voice, twice speaking to him, and with the smell of burnt flesh and incense filling his nostrils, Solomon was resolved to walk in the way that he should go. He had asked for wisdom and God had given it to him; surely he could live in that wisdom, by it and for it. The nations everywhere had heard of his talents, not only of his songs, their harmony and melody and the beauty of their lyrics, but also of his wise sayings, his epigrams, his proverbs. A collection of three thousand of them was gathered together, and a complete scroll of those sayings was regarded as a public treasure. It became so that any wise remark, even though it was hundreds of years old, was attributed to Solomon; the folk wisdom of his own people and of other races and nations, all were added to the hoard of proverbs, with Solomon getting the credit for them. So his three thousand gems, gathered into an anthology and a part of the Holy Bible, were really not all Solomon's. Generally the compilation which we know as the Book of Proverbs is a collection of terse, instructive, practical sayings; most of the apothegms and proverbs are as true for today as for Solomon's own far yesterday.

These proverbs are good medicine for everyday life. They expound the right rules by which men can get along together in moral integrity and good manners. But spirituality, the vision of the dreamer, the aspirations in which man surpasses himself and draws a little closer to God—these qualities are often absent from Solomon's writings as they were almost invariably present in the psalms of his father. Some of the famous proverbs, from the three thousand, follow:

> See you a man diligent in his business? He shall stand before kings; he shall not stand before mean men.
> He that loves pureness of heart, for the grace of his lips the king shall be his friend.

Rejoice not when your enemy falls, and let not your heart be glad when he stumbles.

Fret not yourself because of evil men, neither be you envious at the wicked.

For there shall be no reward to the evil men, neither be you envious at the wicked. For there shall be no reward to the evil men; the candle of the wicked shall be put out.

Let another man praise you, and not your own mouth; a stranger, and not your own lips.

Wrath is cruel, and anger is outrageous; but who is able to stand before envy?

Who can find a virtuous woman? Her price is far above rubies.

The heart of her husband doth safely trust in her, so that he shall have no need of spoil.

She will do him good and not evil all the days of her life.

She seeks wool, and flax, and works willingly with her hands.

She is like the merchant's ships: she brings her food from afar.

She rises while it is yet night, and gives meat to her household, and a portion to her maidens.

She considers a field, and buys it; with the fruit of her hands she plants a vineyard.

She girds her loins with strength, and strengthens her arm.

She perceives that her merchandise is good; her candle goes not out by night.

She lays her hands to the spindle, and her hands hold the distaff.

She stretches out her hands to the poor; yea, she reaches forth her hands to the needy.

She is not afraid of the snow for her household; for all her household are clothed with scarlet.

She makes herself coverings of tapestry; her clothing is silk and purple.

Her husband is known in the gates, when he sits among the elders of the land.

She makes fine linen, and sells it; and delivers girdles unto the merchant.

Strength and honor are her clothing and she shall rejoice in time to come.

She opens her mouth with wisdom, and in her tongue is the law of kindness.

She looks well to the ways of her household, and eats not the bread of idleness.

Her children arise up and call her blessed; her husband also, and he praises her.

Many daughters have done virtuously, but you excell them all.

Favor is deceitful, and beauty is vain; but a woman that fears the Lord shall be praised.

Give her of the fruit of her hands, and let her own works praise her in the gates.

Another book in the Bible that is attributed to King Solomon is called the Canticle of Canticles, or the Song of Solomon, and it is one of the most beautiful and passionate of poems. There are those who believe the book of the Song of Songs was really an anthology of rapturous ditties used at marriage festivals in or near Jerusalem. But they are unquestionably the word of God; of God to man.

In spite of the erudition of the scholars, and the apparent internal evidence that the Song of Songs was written in post-exilic times (evidence not as conclusive as pedants maintain), men believe that Solomon was the author, and that in his Song of Songs he came closest to an understanding of man in his relationship to his Creator. This is much more likely to be the true meaning of the Song of Songs; we find it included in the books of the Bible because it is the Church's declaration that this is so. It would be a mistake to accept the conclusion that, historically, the Song of Songs, the one love poem in the Old Testament, preserves for us the poems used in the old Hebrew marriage rites, when bride and groom and their gathered friends had parts to sing or recite, glorifying love and mating. The peasants of Syria today still practice similar forms and customs. It would also be a mistake to follow the theories of folklorists, who find a derivation for this paean of love in the ancient Near East's traditional annual ceremony of the marriage of the pagan god and goddess of earth's fertility.

The true meaning of the love poem is a part of God's great plan of creation. In the profoundest religious sense this Canticle of Canticles has been interpreted by the Jews as an allegory of the love between God and Israel, and by Christians as typifying the love between Christ and His Church. Prophets like Hosea had fathered the thought of Israel as God's bride, and in the New Testament the Church was likewise regarded as the bride of Christ, for whom He died.

Many of the great words of the Canticle of Canticles ring down the years:

". . . a cluster of camphire
In the vineyards . . ."

". . . the voice of the turtle . . ."
"The little foxes . . ."
". . . our vines have tender grapes."
"Every man hath his sword upon his thigh
Because of fear in the night. . . ."

Let him kiss me with the kiss of his mouth: for thy breasts are better than wine,

Smelling sweet of the best ointments. Thy name is as oil poured out: therefore young maidens have loved thee.

Draw me: we will run after thee to the odour of thy ointments. The king hath brought me into his storerooms: we will be glad and rejoice in thee, remembering thy breasts more than wine: the righteous love thee.

I am black but beautiful, O ye daughters of Jerusalem, as the tents of Cedar, as the curtains of Solomon.

Do not consider me that I am brown, because the sun hath altered my colour: the sons of my mother have fought against me, they have made me the keeper in the vineyards: my vineyard I have not kept.

Shew me, O thou whom my soul loveth, where thou feedest, where thou liest in the midday, lest I begin to wander after the flocks of thy companions.

If thou know not thyself, O fairest among women, go forth, and follow after the steps of the flocks, and feed thy kids beside the tents of the shepherds.

To my company of horsemen, in Pharaoh's chariots, have I likened thee, O my love.

Thy cheeks are beautiful as the turtledove's, thy neck as jewels.

We will make thee chains of gold, inlaid with silver.

While the king was at his repose, my spikenard sent forth the odour thereof.

A bundle of myrrh is my beloved to me, he shall abide between my breasts.

A cluster of cypress my love is to me, in the vineyards of Engaddi.

Behold thou art fair, O my love, behold thou art fair, thy eyes are as those of doves.

Behold thou art fair, my beloved, and comely. Our bed is flourishing.

The beams of our houses are of cedar, our rafters of cypress trees.

I am the flower of the field, and the lily of the valleys.

As the lily among thorns, so is my love among the daughters.

As the apple tree among the trees of the woods, so is my beloved among the sons. I sat down under his shadow, whom I desired: and his fruit was sweet to my palate.

He brought me into the cellar of wine, he set in order charity in me.

Stay me up with flowers, compass me about with apples: because I languish with love.

His left hand is under my head, and his right hand shall embrace me.

I adjure you, O ye daughters of Jerusalem, by the roes, and the harts of the fields, that you stir not up, nor make the beloved to awake, till she please.

The voice of my beloved, behold he cometh leaping upon the mountains skipping over the hills.

My beloved is like a roe, or a young hart. Behold he standeth behind our wall, looking through the windows, looking through the lattices.

Behold my beloved speaketh to me: Arise, make haste, my love, my dove, my beautiful one and come.

For winter is now past, the rain is over and gone.

The flowers have appeared in our land, the time of pruning is come: the voice of the turtle is heard in our land:

The fig tree hath put forth her green figs: the vines in flower yield their sweet smell. Arise, my love, my beautiful one, and come:

My dove in the clefts of the rock, in the hollow places of the wall shew me thy face, let thy voice sound in my ears: for thy voice is sweet, and thy face comely.

Catch us the little foxes that destroy the vines: for our vineyard hath flourished.

My beloved to me, and I to him who feedeth among the lilies,

Till the day break, and the shadows retire. Return: be like, my beloved, to a roe, or to a young hart upon the mountains of Bether.

Behold, thou art fair, my love; behold, thou art fair; thou hast doves' eyes within thy locks: thy hair is as a flock of goats, that appear from mount Gilead.

Thy teeth are like a flock of sheep that are even shorn, which came up from the washing; whereof every one bear twins, and none is barren among them.

Thy lips are like a thread of scarlet, and thy speech is comely: thy temples are like a piece of a pomegranate within thy locks.

Thy neck is like the tower of David builded for an armoury, whereon there hang a thousand bucklers, all shields of mighty men.

Thy two breasts are like two young roes that are twins, which feed among the lilies.

Until the day break, and the shadows flee away, I will get me to the mountain of myrrh, and to the hill of frankincense.

Thou art all fair, my love; there is no spot in thee.

Come with me from Lebanon, my spouse, with me from Lebanon: look from the top of Amana, from the top of Shenir and Hermon, from the lions' dens, from the mountains of the leopards.

Thou hast ravished my heart, my sister, my spouse; thou hast ravished my heart with one of thine eyes, with one chain of thy neck.

How fair is thy love, my sister, my spouse! how much better is thy love than wine! and the smell of thine ointments than all spices!

Thy lips, O my spouse, drop as the honeycomb: honey and milk are under thy tongue; and the smell of thy garments is like the smell of Lebanon.

A garden inclosed is my sister, my spouse; a spring shut up, a fountain sealed.

Thy plants are an orchard of pomegranates, with pleasant fruits; camphire, with spikenard,

Spikenard and saffron; calamus and cinnamon, with all trees of frankincense; myrrh and aloes, with all the chief spices:

A fountain of gardens, a well of living waters, and streams from Lebanon.

Awake, O north wind; and come, thou south; blow upon my garden, that the spices thereof may flow out. Let my beloved come into his garden, and eat his pleasant fruits.

Solomon resolved to heed the sonorous Voice that spoke in his heart, and to walk the straight way leading his people. He literally kept the vows he made that day; kept them by his limited lights.

Three times a year he sacrificed burnt offerings; and three times a year upon the Temple altar he burned incense. But for all his knowledge, for all his three thousand proverbs and the marvelous harmony and melody of his musical compositions, rich in wisdom as he was, Solomon did not have a complete and rounded idea of virtue, which is the imitation of God and the effort to learn His will and to do it. The forms of sacrifice, the convenient ritual, these outward symbols Solomon, the learned king, could understand and follow by rote. Yet the same king to whom wisdom had come as a personal gift, this magnificent Solomon was still obtuse on the simplest matters of personal behavior

His moral offenses were many. He was unceasingly lax in the direction of his much-mixed family. He looked the other way when his foreign wives and concubines continued to worship their native gods. He even considered himself broad-minded when he failed to forbid the establishment of special altars for their heathen worship. The effect of such tolerance was insidious; Solomon set a dangerous example for his subjects.

The king's extravagance was another deep-rooted fault, and an international scandal; before long he had incurred a burden of debt that in time was to become unbearable. To Hiram, king of Tyre, he had to cede twenty thriving towns of Galilee to settle the bills accumulated in the building of the Temple and the new palace.

Naturally the loss of twenty towns was not relished in Israel. Nor did Hiram himself like the final balancing of accounts; he felt that Solomon had outwitted him. While such trouble and disputes saddened Solomon, he had the ability to throw off a mood when it was not to his fancy. Today he might exclaim, "Vanity, vanity, all is vanity," but tomorrow he would order a new set of robes, all glowing with gold thread.

Tales of the royal extravagances were picked up by travelers and camel drivers and boatmen and carried around the known world, growing and being further exaggerated at every camp and resting place. By the time they had reached the lady known to history as the Queen of Sheba they were bloated into fabulous, incredible tales.

The dark queen's curiosity about such pomp was stirred to an intense pitch, and she began to consider leaving her kingdom, which was in southwestern Arabia, some fifteen hundred miles away from Israel, and traveling to the capital to see for herself. No wonder she was curious. The queen's own country of Sheba was more fruitful than most of desert Arabia, its exports being plentiful in incense, balsam, myrrh, spices, precious stones, and gold. The chief city of Sheba was considered impregnable in defense and gleamed with white marble palaces and rainbow gardens. It had a system of dykes and canals for irrigation, and the fertility of the land was praised by all travelers.

From this setting of wealth and grandeur, which she believed unsurpassed on earth, the queen, with a diadem of Ethiopia gleaming on her forehead, journeyed forth with a long train of camels bearing spicery, gems, and gold. No caravan like it had ever before been seen. In the queen's mind was more than curiosity; she was nurturing political schemes, seeking an alliance. Her gifts were calculated to outshine the rumored magnificence of King Solomon, which, she felt sure, was exaggerated. Also the clever queen came laden with something else— with riddles, hard questions to test Solomon's reputed wisdom. As it had been in Samson's time, so it was now—the great intellectual exercise of the Israelites and other peoples of the Middle East was riddle solving.

Thus armed and arrayed, Sheba came in great state to Jerusalem, and the town gave her a roaring welcome. The whole land was agog at the barbaric magnificence of her retinue, her bangles of star sapphires, her jewels and raiment, and she was astounded at the glory of Solomon's court, the costumes, the properties, the whole lavish show.

But soon, in a room of the inner palace, King Solomon and the dusky queen faced each other, friendly, away from all pageantry, ready for a riddling contest. Old legends, not in the Bible, tell us the story of some of the problems with which she confronted the wisest of men.

Among other tests the queen produced for him there was one that involved a sealed casket containing an unperforated pearl, a diamond pierced in minute labyrinthine paths, and a goblet of crystal. Unopened, the contents of the casket were to be described by Solomon, which he did easily with some unknown mastery. After that the queen challenged Solomon to perforate the pearl without injury, thread the diamond in its intricacy, and fill the goblet with water that must not have fallen from the clouds or bubbled out of the ground.

Still, according to the old legends (not to be found in the Bible), a demon and a raven helped the king pierce the pearl, as desired; a worm served him in threading the complex channels of the diamond; the goblet was filled with water by forcing a slave to run long enough to produce a flow of sweat that overflowed the glass.

For a man of Solomon's superlative wisdom, all of these tricks and stunts seemed as child's play, but to the queen they seemed of surpris-

ing force and power, and his answers to other riddles convinced her of
his towering mental eminence.

So overwhelmed by Solomon's knowledge and his grandeur was the
Queen of Sheba that she declared "the half was not told me."
Solomon's throne of beaten gold and carven ivory, with its twelve
great stone lions at either side of the six steps leading up to it,
stunned the royal visitor's oriental mind. So did the three hundred
golden shields on the walls of "the house of the forest of Lebanon."
The number of royal stables added to her wonderment.

And soon, as was the custom between host and guest, gifts were ex-
changed. The queen gave to Solomon camel-loads of golden talents,
and a great store of precious stones and rare spices. In return the generous king of Israel, by fiat, by positive and authoritative command,
"gave unto the Queen of Sheba all her desire" before she left to return to her own kingdom in Arabia—and that must have been, indeed, a great deal.

She departed, leaving Solomon sad and lonely in spite of all his
many wives. He was at the height of his fame; the queen's visit was
his grand climacteric. The years ahead were to bring troubles. They
were even then brewing under the outward panoply of the king's
power and his riches.

Foremost of the cankers were the foreign women of his harem—
Moabites, Ammonites, Edomites, Hittites, and Sidonians—who would
not forsake their heathen gods, and as the king got on in age these
women set to work, more and more, to weaken his own faith in the
one true God. Worse, they began to win a general respect for the false
gods of other lands—Ashtoreth, Chemosh, and Moloch.

Was it never to be different with these children of the one true
God, even under this wisest of leaders? Time and time again that
same Jehovah, having made the whole race, having given them a second chance, again and again, a thousand times again, saw them fall
away and worship strange, false gods. He gave them wise leaders and
they would not follow them. Their tribes were invariably scattered, as
often as the Lord God brought them together again; scattered by their
own tribal hates and lusts and greeds. As once upon a time they
fought a common enemy, now they tried to extirpate one another.

Yet in their hearts the truth had not altogether died. In their
darkest hours they had repeatedly come back to the concept of the
one true God, and they would once more. With the passing of the

centuries they were coming to have a new conception of His identity; not the Yahweh of old, which they had endowed in their mind with their own limitations, but now, with a larger vision, they had already begun to see Him as the Father Who loved His children. For this one fact of growth He would forgive them much.

But now, in Solomon's old age, they were falling again into idolatry and the Lord God of Israel said:

"I will surely rend the kingdom from you and will give it to your servant."

But even by the Voice of God Solomon in all his glory and approaching senility would not be warned. So, by the will of Heaven, adversaries were raised to go against the kingdom, especially the Edomites, Hadad, Rezon, and Jeroboam, the son of Nebat. The last was a strong political figure. Jeroboam sympathized with the tax-ridden Israelites, who were impoverished because they had to pay for the lifelong magnificence of their ruler. Jeroboam was a young man who thirsted for reform and easement of the burden borne by the people.

Hotly rebellious, he secretly tried to organize resistance to the aging king. He won support, but somehow the story became known, and Jeroboam had to flee for safety to Egypt. But Solomon made no effort to extradite the plotter and bring him home to justice. Let the firebrand burn itself out in the distant desert.

But would it burn out? Before he shook the dust of Israel from his feet Jeroboam met a prophet in the street, a seer called Ahijah, who rent his own garment into twelve pieces, saying:

"Take ten of these pieces, for the Lord has said, Behold, I will rend the kingdom out of the hand of Solomon, and will give ten tribes to you."

Knowing his life was sought by Solomon, the rebel remained in exile. Under the protection of Shishak, the Pharaoh of Egypt, Jeroboam remained away until the death of Solomon.

The end came after a reign of forty years, during which Solomon had risen to be a world figure; he had built the wonderful Temple, making worship beautiful, and had become the father of a noble Hebrew wisdom literature, represented by the Books of the Proverbs and Ecclesiastes, an ethical fountainhead. He was the greatest Hebrew lyricist, with some five thousand songs to his credit.

Feeble in mind as well as body, Solomon came to the end of his reign—a sad ending for such a great man. In the beginning his rule was full of peace and the pursuit not only of great projects but of wisdom. The foreign alliances which Solomon contracted, his shrewd treaties with Egypt and Phoenicia, his friendship with Hiram, king of Tyre, had kept safe in their kennel the dogs of war during the large part of the tenth century before Christ. But as he grew older a change had come over the wisest of men. He grew more and more despotic. He was to blame for the alienation of the north from the south which was to lead to the rebellion, and ultimately the separation, the uprising led by Jeroboam. Strange that a man could have spoken so wisely and then behaved with such foolishness and stubbornness in his old age.

We do not know how Solomon died. We do know that his passing came at a perilous time and that when Prince Rehoboam, son of Solomon, took the throne of Israel, to rule in the succession, the whole kingdom was in danger.

Chapter 29 THE TRIAL ON MOUNT CARMEL

ANOTHER hundred years had to pass before there arose among the vacillating children of the chosen tribes a man to whom the mysterious Voice would speak. And in that century—between the time that Solomon slept with his fathers, emtombed in the City of David, and the appearance of a vagrant new prophet with a flaming destiny—the kingdom of the Jews fell apart. For the strong monarchs had passed away, and witling sons who tried to take the throne and rule made a sorry mess of things.

It began when Solomon's son Rehoboam of the black curls and pale, graceful hands claimed the succession. Crowds of Israelites, waiting for him at Shechem, were willing to crown him king there and hoping only that he would be wise and kind and lessen their miseries, which were many, thanks to the extravagances of his gorgeous father.

But Rehoboam was young for his years. His thoughts were of gold and purple robes, jeweled-tipped boots, rainbow plumes, scepter and crown and power, and a court redolent with alluring ladies. He had no concept of a monarch's responsibilities to his people, nor his need for mercy and understanding and compassion. He was not even suspicious that politics might rise to plague him at his coronation.

As black-curled Rehoboam, in gleaming finery, stood on a hill, with the floods of people restless in great tides in the broad valley at his feet, he heard no shouts, hosannas, or psalms of welcome. Instead, mutterings were coming from ten thousand throats, stopping only when a ragged spokesman trudged up to face the king.

The people, the stranger said, wanted certain wrongs made right before the new reign became official. The taxes were too high. His spendthrift father had laid a yoke on their necks to pay for his squandering. Now they must have relief; the burden was unbearable; nobody had enough to eat any more.

"Better promise to help them," the elders whispered to Rehoboam. "They speak only the truth."

"Let them know that you are king," cried the young man's hot-headed cronies, not one of whom had the slightest experience in government. "Show them that you cannot be browbeaten. Be master from the start."

With delicate hands Rehoboam shoved both groups aside, as if he were a wise and kingly fellow and would make up his own mind. He took three whole days to meditate, and then, in warlike armor more magnificent than before, he stood on the hilltop, surrounded by spearmen, and bareheaded, eyes flashing with rage, he berated the whole multitude:

"My father made your yoke heavy, and I will add to your yoke: my father also chastised you with whips, but I will chastise you with scorpions."

A scream of wrath came from the throngs at these despotic words. To the forefront there suddenly sprang a lithe young figure who might have been the young tyrant's twin; for both had black curls and flashing eyes—but this was Jeroboam, son of Nebat, a mighty man of valor, and long an enemy of the government, a rebel for years. What was he doing here among these people? Rehoboam knew that this revolutionist had fled to Egypt for fear he would be killed as a pretender to the crown. But here he was back in Shechem, and with a howling mob of thousands of Israelites backing him up, and crying:

"What portion have we in David? Neither have we inheritance in the son of Jesse: to your tents, O Israel: now see to your own house, David."

In that crazy moment the kingdom, so long in being welded together was split in two with civil war.

The tribes of Judah and Benjamin in the south voted for Rehoboam to rule over them, with Jerusalem as their capital. But in the north the ten other tribes—like the dream of the prophet with the ten pieces of the prophet's gown—chose Jeroboam for their sovereign. That bitter rupture between the north and south was beyond all healing; the land was rent asunder, into two separate kingdoms, weak and tempting to fierce and predatory neighbors beyond their borders.

It ruined the chances of greatness gained with such effort and cost by David and Solomon.

Troubled years lay before the broken pieces of the kingdom.

In that futile, debased, and suffering time, while one petty king followed another on two inconspicuous thrones, the people fell far away from their old faith and lived like hungry serfs, working, eating, and sleeping with bad dreams.

The beautiful Temple of Jerusalem was in the kingdom of the south with the tribes of Benjamin and Judah, and the ten northern tribes were barred from its courts and sanctuaries, its gildings and its Holy of Holies, where still the neglected ark reposed, sole reliquary of the old bond between these ceatures and the one true God. Something had to be done about that, for the Temple still ruled the imagination of all the people, north and south.

So Jeroboam, of the northern half, after rearing two fortress strongholds for his soldiers, built two new sanctuaries, meager structures, neither beautiful nor consoling, one at Bethel, another at Dan. With almost defiant stupidity he substituted for the ark a golden calf for each, to glitter in the places of honor. They were to represent the good God of Israel—crude, blowzy images of the four-footed young of the cow for His people to bow down before and invoke the sacred presence.

The young man knew the Ten Commandments; he knew that graven images were forbidden. But he also wanted to be popular; and he remembered that idols had been for centuries a weakness of Israel. Now Jeroboam catered to that weakness, pandered to it, and furthermore, in his apostasy, he ordained priests from the lowest of his people for his new sanctuaries, men not of the tribe of Levites. That brash action went against the injunction of the Lord as once spoken to Moses. But he had also a deeper political reason—he did not want his people to yearn for Solomon's Temple; they might want to rejoin the southern kingdom someday. So he issued an edict: "It is too much for you to go up to Jerusalem; behold your gods, O Israel, which brought thee up out of the land of Egypt!"

Behold your gods—two golden calves!

Bad as things were in the north, they were even worse in the south. In the very midst of the Temple and its sacred ark, idolatry was also practiced.

The people were demoralized and hence without power or will to resist their foes. The Egyptians, under the Pharaoh Shishak, demanded the hundred golden shields of Solomon, with threats of extirpation, and got them, but it was a bargain made in secret. King Rehoboam did not dare confess this blackmail price; he had the shields duplicated in brass to hoodwink the people. War followed war, in a long monstrous series of aggressions and bloodlettings. The Hebrews could not fight the Arameans, the Assyrians, the Babylonians, whose troops came swooping down upon them in robbing forays.

The dolorous years rolled on. Now and then a good king would take charge, but none ever strong enough to stem the tide of degradation or bring peace in the sporadic wars between the upper and lower halves of Israel. There were treachery and assassination and usurpation. Nadab was slain by Baasha. Zimri, surrounded and trapped, burned down the palace of the north over his own head, perishing in the flames. Many and various, these reigns above and below the dividing line: Jehoshaphat and Elash and Omri, the captain of the guards.

But the struggle of good against evil in these little and yet immensely significant factions did not become strong and vital again until old King Omri, imitating King Solomon's matrimonial alliances, betrothed his son Ahab to a flamboyantly attractive young Zidonian princess, a hellcat whose name was Jezebel.

It was when Ahab and Jezebel became king and queen of the north that the old belief in the God of Abraham, Isaac, and Jacob seemed to be ready for final obliteration from the hearts of the Israelites.

For Ahab and Jezebel were aggressively, optimistically, fanatically anti-Jehovah. It was not that Ahab was a man of deep convictions, but the Syrian infidel who was his wife was a fanatic about her own faith. She worshiped the idol Baal and took a sensual joy in the orgies that went with his worship.

Almost the very first act of the new king, Ahab, was to order a present for his wife, which was a building to be called "The House of Baal," in which he set up an idol to his favorite sub-deity, the evil Melkart, favorite of the Zidonian people from which she came. It mattered nothing to Jezebel that for a thousand years the Israelites had known the one true God. She thrust aside the protests of the old people with contemptuous, perfumed fingers. She was bent on making Melkart, of the House of Baal, the god of everyone under her sway. From her country she imported four hundred and fifty prophets of Melkart together with four hundred others serving "the Asherah," a minor deity.

Protesting believers in the one true God were slain out of hand. A hundred of them sought refuge in a cave where Obadiah, the steward of Ahab, who was faithful to the Lord God, saved them from starvation with bread and water. Meanwhile, at Jezebel's command, the old altars were thrown down.

Through all his wife's doings, Ahab showed such an indifference that many suspected he had himself become a convert to Melkart, but there was no direct proof and no one dared ask him. It looked as if Jezebel and Melkart were to be triumphant in Israel, but in the very boil of the queen's persecution a strange and arresting figure suddenly appeared one humid, showery afternoon.

Spies had brought word to Ahab that a singular old man was marching down the soggy roads—a wild fellow in the rain, white hair wet and streaming down to the small of his sunburned back; the wind shaking the snowy cascade of beard that flowed to his creaking knees. Yet through the mire the traveler marched with bare feet. His enormous gnarled hands, which were like Abraham's, were clasped as if he prayed even while he ran, but his enormous eyes were open and glistening with joy as if he fully understood what he saw and heard as he watched the sky, never looking at the ground although he had run many miles, all the way.

"Who are you?" the sentries demanded to know.

He was Elijah the Tishbite, and he had run a hundred miles and more, all the way from Samaria, and he wanted audience with the king.

The sentries made him wait while they consulted the minister of His Majesty. Meanwhile the hangers-on in the courtyard circled round the hairy old stranger, wondering what sort of fellow he was. They could not know that they were in the presence of one of the great seers of history, this Elijah, who is also known to the Christian world as Elias. No one, then or now, could know much about him. His whole youth was lost in obscurity. From somewhere east of the river Jordan he suddenly appears, here in the palace gateway, soon to stand before King Ahab with a daring and accusing prophecy.

Here was a man with a mission, a zealot with one increasing purpose, which was to destroy the worship of pagan gods and to renew in the people a sense of adoration and justice and freedom. That day in the palace courtyard Elijah was on fire with a frightening enthusiasm. No man ever had more to contend with and, as we shall see, no one ever more completely succeeded in spite of all obstacles.

The sentries returned and marched him into the throne room, where Ahab on his gilded chair took one look and then leered at Jezebel. Here should be sport for a warm afternoon. But this tattered prophet from Gilead gave the king no time; without politeness or palaver he announced in a clear, orotund voice:

"As the Lord God of Israel lives, before whom I stand, there shall not be dew nor rain these years, but according to my word."

Crackpots were always appearing in Israel with their predictions of woe, and Ahab looked a little disappointed. He had hoped for something more original. But one of the minsters, cocking his left ear, raised a warning finger. The drumming sound on the rooftop had suddenly stopped; the minister ran to the door and pulled back the green and yellow draperies. The sun was shining and it rained no more. But who would take that clearing up as a serious omen?

Elijah was shoved out into the muddy road and told to go, and never to show himself in these royal parts again. The king thought no more about him that night, but when day followed day, weeks, months, and still no rainfall, when drought and famine made haggard the land and every face above it, the fields like ashes, then Ahab remembered Elijah. That ragged visitant had said that he could bring rain or withhold it, as would be pleasing to the one true God of Israel.

Urgent messengers were sent to look everywhere for that hairy, despised old man called Elijah; a long, heartbreaking search. Elijah the Tishbite, holy man from Gilead, could not be found because he had done what holy men seem often bound to do, and unholy men never—that is, go off to themselves and, in silence and solitude, remember and reflect and pray and listen.

Elijah had chosen the place of his retreat under the guidance of that powerful and compassionate Voice which after a hundred years of bloodshed and failure was speaking again in Israel. To a bank of the brook Cherith, a torrent valley, or wadi as Near Easterners say today, the hairy man came, finding an unvisited region where nothing grew, off the route of travelers. Here he would commune, as seers and prophets had done before, and wait for divine guidance. Already

Elijah was convinced that there was stirring work to be done and that he, for what reason he never knew, had been chosen to do it.

Thus Elijah was to found a long line of major prophets—seers of the Jews, who proclaimed that the spirit of worship was more important than its forms. Because they were regarded as men of God, speaking under inspiration, they dared to say things that would have gotten an ordinary man into trouble. But now a whole people were in deep trouble: an idol was winning out over the one true God; it was a time when no man could call another friend, in a land where lechery and nympholepsy and thievery and murder had been exalted as virtues.

Anyone who cared about Elijah might well have asked: "What will the poor old man eat in such a barren retreat? Nothing grows on the banks of Cherith and there are no fish in its waters. How can Elijah feed himself?"

For answer, the skies over the desolate landscape were, twice a day, darkened by a swarm of broad-winged black birds. Morning and evening the ravens came, with tidbits of meat and morsels of vegetables to drop into the old mystic's enormous hands. Until the brook Cherith ran dry in the continuing drought—and that took months— Elijah ate all his meals from the gleaming beaks of his friends the ravens—all eight kinds of them as found in Palestine. But when at last there was no more water flowing between the banks, and the bed of rock and mud lay dry and open to the eye like a cadaver in a surgery, the ravens croaked harsh farewell and flew away for good and all.

And again Elijah heard the Voice with Its precise instructions, speaking to him in the middle of the day and in the glare of a windless noon. "Go to Zarephath, Elijah; to Zarephath, which is in Zidon, where Queen Jezebel comes from. There you will meet another kind of woman and you are to dwell in her house, Elijah, and the lady will keep you alive."

The hairy old hermit, coming out of his wilderness to blink unhappily at a crowded world, tramped all the miles to his goal. Staff in hand, weary from his long journey, he arrived at the gates of the city of Zarephath and along the outside wall he found a woman gathering stray sticks for a fire. The eyes of the prophet picked her out, this widow whose name now no one remembers, and he asked her for food and water, as was the right of any wayfarer. Her reply, pious before the invisible but ever-present God, filled the old man with satisfaction, even though it sounded like a refusal:

"As the Lord your God lives, I have not a cake but a handful of meal in a barrel and a little oil in a cruse; and behold, I am gathering two sticks that I may go in and dress it for me and my son that we may eat it and die."

And she smiled, as if the immediate prospect of death can be a welcome and relieving fact. But Elijah shook his tired old head and spoke with gentle authority, undisturbed by her statement that she did not have enough to keep herself and her son alive. He reassured her with a miraculous promise. Elijah ordered her first to make for him a cake. Afterward she must cook a meal for her son and herself. "For thus says the Lord God of Israel," he assured her, "the barrel of meal shall not waste, neither shall the cruse of oil fail, until the day that the Lord sends rain upon the earth." And all this happened just as the visitor predicted.

But later, when her son fell sick and died, the widow whirled on Elijah, cursing him as a wizard who had used necromantic power to bring death to her only child.

"Give me your son," said Elijah, and, grunting, lifted the body of the boy in his withered arms. As if divinely strengthened, he carried the corpse to the loft where he had been living in the widow's house. Alone with the dead, the prophet Elijah cried unto the Lord to restore the life taken so young. There was no hesitation or doubt in the old man's voice, no question in his large, farseeing eyes. Closer and closer he hugged the young dead boy as if he would warm the lifeless chest against his own. . . .

When the widow heard the old man calling to her, hours later, she scrambled up the stairs and in the doorway beheld her living son. Elijah had called him back from the grave, the first of the few who have been called back from the dead.

"Now by this I know you are a man of God," she sobbed.

For three years the meal in the barrel sufficed, and the oil in the cruse. Then, in the third year of drought, the Voice spoke to Elijah:

"Go, show yourself to Ahab; and I will send rain upon the earth."

Not a day had passed in those three years that Ahab's men had not been seeking, far and wide, for the man who had told the king there would be rain or not, as he asked. Now suddenly the hairy old man reappears; with famine's hands at Samaria's throat, there rises against the horizon a wild and shaggy silhouette, the shadow of the missing prophet. First to see him was that haggard and hungry steward of the king, Obadiah, who was looking haplessly around the countryside for grass to feed his horses and mules, and there was no grass. Without a word Obadiah turned and fled back to the palace and told Ahab the lost was found, the man whose warning had turned the countryside to a pile of cinders. The king did not wait for Elijah; he followed his minister down the dusty roads, purple robes flapping at his heels. At last the frightened but still haughty young ruler stood face to face with the walking prophet, dripping with the sweat of his travels.

"Are you he who troubles Israel?" asked the king.

"Not I, but you," answered Elijah.

The king looked astonished. He, who loved his people, to be blamed for the famine? Come, old man, what do you mean?

"You have forsaken the Lord and followed Baal," said Elijah.

The king blinked incredulously. This little business of worshiping— surely it was not important! For political reasons he made it a policy not to interfere with the followers of Jehovah on one hand, or Baal-Melkart on the other. Was not the prophet, with power to bring rain or drought, making far too much of a small matter? After all, the king put it persuasively, was not one religion as good as another?

Elijah's answer to that persisting error was wholly practical—realistic, indeed, and pragmatic. There could be but one true God—why not find out which was which, and be rid of the brummagem substitute, cheap and bogus as it must be?

And Elijah proposed to the king that the Baal prophets, all eight hundred and fifty of them, including the four hundred installed that were around Queen Jezebel's quarters and ate at her table, meet him on Mount Carmel in a public contest, a duel of prayer, to prove which was the true God, theirs or his—Baal or the God of Abraham, Isaac, of Jacob and Moses and Joshua, of David and Solomon. A fair challenge, Ahab agreed. His word was law, so the Baal prophets and the children of Israel were soon gathered on the green-wooded headland above the Mediterranean. Elijah stood facing the throng and put his case:

"How long limp you between two opinions? If the Lord be God, follow him, but if Baal, then follow him."

No answer came from the people.

Then Elijah outlined the test.

"I, even I only, remain a prophet of the Lord; but Baal's prophets are four hundred and fifty men. Let them therefore give us two bullocks; and let them choose one bullock for themselves, and cut it in pieces and lay it on wood and put no fire under; and I will dress the other bullock and lay it on wood and put no fire under. And call you on the name of your gods and I will call on the name of the Lord; and the God that answers by fire, let him be God."

To these terms the excited people screamed their agreement.

The priests of Baal did not relish this extraordinary contest, but they knew there was no escape. In the parched and waterless time the king would try anything that might lead to rain, even the mad duel which Elijah was proposing. For surely, who could make fire, could make rain.

The two bullocks lay dead on the piles of firewood, and Elijah smilingly insisted that Baal's priests make the first try. Their leader began with a long speech, bragging about what they were going to do, and so delaying matters as long as possible.

Then began a weird rite imploring a god that in their hearts they did not believe in to do something they were certain was impossible. Forward they crept, chanting heathen litanies, while their acolytes whirled fragrant torches overhead and older attendants clashed brazen cymbals. A whole morning the devotees of Baal prayed and chanted. But all in vain.

Angrily they stamped on their improvised altar.

"Cry aloud!" mocked Elijah. "For your god may be on a journey, or peradventure he sleeps and must be awakened."

The priests milled around, cutting their own arms and legs with knives in their frenzy. They were persistent, those infidels. Hour followed hour but they did not pause in their clapping of hands and the incantation of magical words, uttered in solemn but ever faster rhythms. Evening came, and still no answer from Baal.

Then, in the gloaming, Elijah took twelve stones and built a special altar for his bullock with a trench under it. He put the wood under it, and then staggered them all by commanding a new and audacious detail; twelve barrels of water must be thrown upon it all, and that was done until the trench was overflowing. One disdainful glance Elijah bestowed on the regiment of heathen priests. Pagans! Unbelievers! his eyes seemed to say; his glance was volcanic, heaping the air with reproaches. Then Elijah lifted up his eyes and hands and prayed:

"Lord God of Abraham, Isaac, and Israel, let it be known this day that You are God in Israel, and that I am Your servant, and that I have these things at Your word. Hear me, O Lord, hear me, that this people may know that You are the Lord God, and that You have turned their heart back again."

The result was instantaneous and terrifying. Whole sheets of fire fell from the skies, consuming not only the wood and the bullock but the stones and the very dust, the fiery red-orange tongues licking up every drop of the water.

"The Lord, He is the God!" roared the people, again and again, and again, shaking fists at the dumfounded priests of Baal.

"Take the prophets of Baal; and let not one of them escape," Elijah roared back to them. The eight hundred and fifty died there at the brook Kishon, and not until then did Elijah confront the king:

"Get you up, eat and drink; for this is a sound of abundance of rain."

Without waiting for a reply, the prophet withdrew to a cave on the top of Mount Carmel, where he lowered his face between his knees in silent prayer.

"Look to the sea," he called to his servant without changing his position. The man looked and saw nothing. Seven times Elijah told him to look down on the Mediterranean, and on the seventh the servant reported a little cloud, "no bigger than a man's hand." But that was enough. Soon the sky was black with clouds, the winds were blowing a gale, and a torrential rain poured upon the parched earth.

And Ahab went home to Jezebel.

Chapter 30 WHAT DO YOU HERE, ELIJAH?

THE word came back to Elijah that on the very next day his life was to be taken—and the murderous message came straight from Jezebel. Why she warned him the prophet could only guess; either she wanted him to suffer like a mouse who sees a hungry cat coming after him, or she wanted him to leave the kingdom and save her the need of having him killed, for his rising popularity might make her pause before ordering his throat cut.

Whatever the motive that brought warning from the court at Jezreel, Elijah acted. He fled to Beersheba, in the south, and in the wilderness back from the sea he sat down under a withered juniper tree and let melancholy roll over his soul.

What had he accomplished in trying to obey the Voice of the Lord God? Nothing, so it seemed to the despondent Elijah; the bleakness of his spirit was like a hot, dry, desert wind, a *khamsin*, blowing through mind and heart. In utter depths of hopelessness he fell asleep.

Did he dream now—or was it supernatural vision that possessed him, this feeling of being touched by a ministering angel of grace, of cool fingers on his humid eyelids, and a whisper at his dusty ears? He roused himself, awake and looking around, and then he gasped. How could his vision have been merely a dream when, there before him, were goblets and gourds and platters, bread and wine?

"Eat well," some ministering angel of grace seemed to murmur to the old mystic; there was a long journey still for him to make and his legs would need strength and fuel.

Many days and nights Elijah traveled through the gray, hot sands of the wilderness until at last he saw before him a mountain he could not mistake. Dark and desolate it loomed above the plain, Horeb, which was Sinai, the Mount of the Tablets of the Law. At sight of that historic height, Elijah knew that this was his destination—it was as if the ministering angel of grace took his hand and led him to a grim, forbidding fissure in the mountainside, entrance to a deep resounding cave—and Elijah, walking barefoot on its smooth cool floor, losing his moist face in its ever-deepening shadows, heard the Voice once more:

"What do you here, Elijah?"

Bitterly the old prophet replied, reporting the apostasy in Israel. He alone was left to fight the evil, and even his life was now being sought for the truth he told. The Voice was silent until the sorry tale was ended; then Elijah was told to leave the cave, climb the mountain, and stand upon the topmost peak.

"And, behold, the Lord passed by, and a great and strong wind rent the mountains, and broke in pieces the rocks before the Lord; but the Lord was not the wind. And after the wind an earthquake; but the Lord was not the earthquake. And after the earthquake a fire; but the Lord was not in the fire. And after the fire a still small voice:

"And it was so, when Elijah heard it, that he wrapped his face in his mantle, and went out, and stood in the entering in of the cave. . . .

"What do you here, Elijah?"

Again the prophet told how downcast he was over all Israel. In a cryptic answer the Voice bade him start off on another long, long journey toward the region of the city of Damascus. There he was to anoint a man named Hazael to be king of Syria, and likewise to anoint another man, Jehu, the son of Nimshi, to be king over Israel. And for a third ceremony, Elijah was to find a young man called Elisha, the son of Shaphat, and anoint the youth as his own successor in prophecy.

"Him that escapes the sword of Hazael shall Jehu slay," said the Voice, "and him that escapes from the sword of Jehu still Elisha slay."

It was an extraordinary visitation at the mouth of the cave. The Lord told Elijah that there were seven thousand faithful souls in Israel who had never bowed the knee to Baal, nor kissed his image; seven thousand Israelites who could be a leaven of righteousness in restoring the whole nation to faith in the one true God.

It was clear now what Elijah must do. He had hoped to hide for the rest of his days in the cool hermitage of his Sinai cave; an eremite meditating in damp solitude and a dim light even at noon; a recluse whose work in the frightening world outside was over and done. But not so!

Elijah had not gone far on his new journey out of the wilderness before he passed a great hillside farm and saw a good-looking young plowman in a broad brown field turning over the soil. Elijah halts at the side of the road and watches for a long time, as the young plowman goes and comes back, behind his bladed stick pulled by a mule. The busy young man salutes the stranger but does not recognize him.

The old man takes off his ancient mantle. He stops the plowboy with a gesture and carries his cloak, age to youth, and wraps it around the young man's shoulders. What meaning—to receive the mantle of a prophet!

Look, Mother! See, I wear this old man's robe. Good-by, Mother. See, Father, I have the mantle of Elijah the Tishbite. Good-by, Father. I must go.

And go he did. Elijah had obeyed God, and now Elisha, too, obeyed the call without questioning. After a feast of farewell for the neighbors with the boiled meat of two oxen, Elisha forsook his native place to follow Elijah. The two men started off to anoint two new kings.

All these events were happening in an uneasy time. King Ahab and his Jezebel were never free from fear, for everywhere around their frontiers were unfriendly neighbors. Their leader, Ben-Hadad, king of Syria, had thirty-two rulers of smaller kingdoms ready to follow him in any cause and he had recently been making impudent and impossible demands—the surrender of Israelite women and treasure, on the threat of leaving, of the northern kingdom and its people, naught but a handful of dust.

In a brief war that had been fought, King Ahab found that the Lord seemed to be on his side. Some nameless, wayside mystic had sworn that it would prove so. While Ben-Hadad and his fellow kings were drinking themselves into sottishness in the vine-grown Syrian land, the Israelites took them by surprise. Eventually the enemy leader put on sackcloth and draped ropes on his head in token of sorrow and submission. Ahab, always willing to appease, proclaimed an amnesty and now, relishing peace with great relief, Ahab and Ben-Hadad called each other brother.

Who could frighten Ahab now? The victory of the king's armies had been due to God's help and purpose for the Israelite people, but King Ahab took the credit to himself. A very heady Ahab now sat on the throne, and when another anonymous mystic of the streets foretold his death because of his easy attitude toward Israel's enemies, Ahab brushed aside the warning. He was Ahab, the king who won the war; he could say what he liked and do what he pleased.

But not altogether. There were still a few laws in Israel which even a military hero must respect, and presently that necessity made trouble.

Ahab was coveting another man's vineyard, an estate on land of remarkable favor, its grapes full of juice and succulence, which Ahab coveted to make a garden of that plot and there grow flowers for Jezebel, the gorgeously colored, brief-lived blossoms of that thirsty land—roses of Sharon, hyacinths, tulips, anemones, and the sword lilies, as well as stranger blossoms from other lands. These he would plant and seed to brighten the eyes and widen the nostrils of Jezebel, who made a great show of having the exotic tastes proper to a queen. But something stood in the way of making and growing Jezebel's garden. The land belonged to a stubborn citizen who loved his vineyard and did not care to part with it. The ground belonged to Naboth, the Jezreelite, and he declined to sell his inheritance from his forefathers. By the laws of Israel, his right to it was inviolate; not even the king could gainsay that. So Ahab retired into his palace and sulked like a child.

"Why is your spirit so sad?" inquired the ever-watchful Jezebel, and when her husband explained she laughed.

"Who governs Israel?" she wanted to know. "Be merry. I will give you that vineyard of Naboth's, never fear."

That same day the doting Jezebel wrote letters to pious old elders and nobles, still firm in the true faith of Israel, complaining that their neighbor, Naboth, had blasphemed both God and king. A strange complaint from one who worshiped Melkart. Next Jezebel suborned two false witnesses to swear to her own lies. Such accusations were most serious, because the penalty was death; and although Naboth was entirely innocent of any wrong, he was dragged outside the city walls and stoned.

Then Jezebel smiled at her husband.

"Now, arise. Take possession of the vineyard! For Naboth is no longer alive."

Glad in his greed, Ahab strode through the palace gate to possess the vineyard he had coveted. What a strong-minded queen his Jezebel was! But suddenly his gloating thoughts stopped; that same unbearable old man, that ragged prophet, was barring his way.

"Have you found me, O mine enemy?" gasped Ahab. It was indeed Elijah, stalking through Naboth's vineyard, directly toward him.

"In the place where the dogs licked the blood of Naboth shall dogs lick your blood! Even thine," cried Elijah, repeating the word of the Lord, as the Voice had just given it to him. "And the dogs shall eat Jezebel by the wall of Jezreel."

Ahab tore his kingly clothes, put on sackcloth, and fasted in deepest fear. As was his wont, having delivered the divine message, Elijah disappeared.

Like so many leaders of the Israelites before him, Ahab did not mend his ways even though he had been thoroughly frightened; he could not bring himself to drive the evil out of his soul. Although he had an easy treaty with Syria and it had lasted three years, peace taught him nothing. Ahab longed to possess, not merely a vineyard next, but the city of Ramoth-Gilead, east of the Jordan, a valuable trade post and a defense bastion, never relinquished by the wily Syrians. By his own self-serving logic Ahab convinced himself that the harbor city should be his, and before long he determined to get it at all costs.

And suprisingly it was to the two separated tribes that he turned for allies: to the long-hostile Benjamin and Judah in the south—the lost other part of Solomon's kingdom, unhealed scar of civil war. With smiling effrontery King Ahab asked King Jehoshaphat of Judah to join him in his greedy purpose to steal the maritime city of a neighbor nation.

Here Ahab met another kind of king.

Jehoshaphat was a pious man, unaggressive, a deep believer in the Lord God. Even though his weaker kingdom had much to fear from Ahab in the north, Jehoshaphat suggested that first the Lord God be consulted about going against Ramoth. And Ahab, always all things to all men, assented.

So it was that some four hundred prophets of the upper kingdom were convoked into a general session at Ahab's palace. What servants of the Lord they were, too—a subservient lot of self-styled prophets who grinned from ear to ear when Ahab smiled. They encouraged the king's campaign just as he wanted them to do, and they predicted his certain triumph.

But Jehoshaphat was not so naïve as to be convinced by these timeservers. At his request another prophet, Micaiah, was brought forward to have his say, much to Ahab's disgust. For, as he told his brother king, this gloomy Micaiah seemed never to see anything but evil ahead.

Seated on thrones, the kings of Israel and Judah had listened for hours to all the ingratiating palaver of four hundred prophets who, as one man, prophesied the triumph of Ahab in battle. Now Micaiah arose and told his vision:

"I saw all Israel scattered upon the hills, as sheep that have not a shepherd. Behold, the Lord has put a lying spirit in the mouth of all these thy prophets, and the Lord has spoken evil concerning thee."

Desperate forecast! Ahab stamped his royal foot and screamed in a tantrum. Though expecting pessimism from Micaiah, he had never dreamed of such dire effrontery as this. As for the four hundred prophets, they hissed the man who would set their united word at naught.

"Take Micaiah! Put him in prison! Keep him on bread and water until I return the victor," cried Ahab, glowering.

"If you return in peace, the Lord has not spoken by me," replied Micaiah, standing his ground.

No more delay now; it was decided at once to attack the coveted city of Ramoth. Hearing of the plans from his own spies, the Syrian king gave curious orders. The Syrian bowmen and hunters must keep Ahab as their chief objective; he did not fear the Israelite people but he knew Ahab to be the enemy of Syrians and his own people as well. Ahab did not know that he had been singled out, but he was always a careful fellow and so, on the day of battle, remembering Micaiah's warning which he had seemed to despise, he nevertheless disguised himself in common clothes. Not so King Jehoshaphat. That man of God went forth to battle in his royal robes, and once Jehoshaphat was almost mistaken for Ahab by the Syrian bowmen and missed capture by a hair.

As it turned out, "a certain man drew a bow at a venture"; he let loose his arrow at an inconspicuous figure, as the troops met, and his target proved to be Ahab, pierced through, blood flowing all over his chariot. He died at evening.

So ended the battle of Ramoth in Gilead. The dying king was brought back to Samaria, where he was buried. His chariot was washed in the pool and the dogs licked up his blood, just as Elijah had foretold in the vineyard of Naboth.

And there was still an unfulfilled prophecy about the widow Jezebel.

That wronghearted female, capable of anything, now took all the reins into her own hands. So they had lost the battle! What of that? She refused to see in the defeat the exposure of the false prophets and the vindication of Micaiah's word. She sneered when she heard about how stricken King Jehoshaphat was, because of what he conceived to be God's displeasure.

King Jehoshaphat returned to Judah, where Jehu, the son of Hanani the seer, met him with reproach for his weakness, his lack of spiritual courage in giving assistance to the ungodly. But the king returned no answer. Deep thoughts deepened within him as he continued his quiet way. For the rest of his life he spent most of his time penitently endeavoring to stamp out the worship of false gods, and because of his repentance the land of Judah prospered under him, even though, in high places, the worship of Baal still persisted and people burned incense to the idols.

Come what may, the widowed Queen Jezebel had made up her mind to be the ruling power in Israel. Her young son Ahaziah took the throne. For two years the young king walked exactly as Mother told him to, listening to Jezebel and serving her Baal.

One day in Samaria, King Ahaziah was idly looking through the lattice in an upper story of the palace and suddenly, overcome with dizziness, toppled out of his chamber window. Taken up badly injured and put in his bed, he said to his messenger:

"Go, inquire of Beelzebub, the god of Ekron, whether I shall recover from this hurt."

And the god of the young man's people heard what he said.

Anyone who studied the history of these tribes would know that wickedness would thrive for only a little while and then God would take notice. So, now, an angel of the Lord appeared once more to Elijah the Tishbite, saying:

"Arise! And meet the messengers of the sick king." The prophet was fully instructed as to what he must say. So, to the emissaries of Ahaziah, when finally the hairy old hermit met them, he duly delivered the messsage: because Ahaziah had sent messengers to Baal instead of the Lord God, "he shall not leave his bed but surely die."

These messengers, servants of the old faith of Israel who believed the prophet's word, hurried back to the badly injured king. But Ahaziah was furious. Why had they not done as he directed? He had told them to ask of Beelzebub. He didn't care what some stranger had to say. He wanted to know why they had failed to go on to Ekron for knowledge. And what manner of man had he been that intercepted them?

"He was a hairy man, girt with a girdle of leather about his loins," they replied.

"It is Elijah!" exclaimed the sick king, falling back in dismay. At once he sent a captain and his fifty men to fetch the impudent prophet. The searchers spied the old man on a hilltop and the sight of him made them quake, for they had heard tales of what the prophet of the Lord could do in high places. Their worst fears were realized immediately, for Elijah called down fire from heaven upon them, and they were consumed where they stood. Likewise, a second fifty, sent to capture the prophet, were burned alive. But a third fifty, set to the same task, were spared the fire, and Elijah came with them of his free will to the bedside of Ahaziah.

A deathly fear glowed faintly in the eyes of the young king, mutely asking the great question. Before Elijah had repeated his word the prophecy was out, the prediction fulfilled, the king was dead.

Poor little puppet kingling, his youth had been graceful and he had made many friends, who now were overcome by his death. Not so his mother; not Jezebel. The old queen acted with promptness, as usual, and picked another son, Jehoram, to succeed to the throne, since Ahaziah had left no child of his own to inherit the crown. With her new puppet Jehoram in power, Jezebel still held full sway.

It was time for Elijah to leave the court again. Joining his young disciple Elisha, he led the way from Gilgal. But as they trudged along from town to town Elijah would urge his young companion to linger behind; people could hear his message, while the older man plodded on. Always Elisha refused to remain; he was obstinate at Bethel and stubborn at Jericho where they rested.

Elisha also well knew what lay in the near future; already he had received within his own consciousness, and spiritually, a message that his leader, his ideal of manhood, was about to be taken from him. Elijah's days were numbered and Elisha felt impelled to stay close by his side.

Perhaps that was why Elijah performed the miracle of the Jordan.

When they came to the bank of the river old Elijah folded his mantle and smote the water, and the turbulent stream parted, as in the days of old, and the two of them could walk on dry land to the other side. There Elijah laid his hand on Elisha's shoulder and said:

"Ask what I shall do for you before I be taken away from you."

"I pray you that a double portion of your spirit be upon me," said the tremulous Elisha.

"A hard thing," sighed Elijah. "But if you see me when I am taken from you, it shall be so unto you; but if not, it shall not be so."

"If you see me—"

What could that possibly mean? How could the young man actually see a soul taking wing from the earth? How could anyone see death?

The question was answered soon enough:

"And it came to pass, as they still went on, and talked, that, behold, there appeared a chariot of fire, and horses of fire, and parted them both asunder; and Elijah went up by a whirlwind into heaven. Elisha saw it, and he cried, My father, my father, the chariot of Israel and the horsemen thereof. And he saw him no more; and he took hold of his own clothes, and rent them in two pieces."

The end of Elijah had been a fitting completion of a strange life—a career whose beginnings no one knows, but which blazed forth in sudden light, full of melodrama, at a time when he was needed. For Elijah raised from the dead the son of a poor widow; he fought what is perhaps the strangest duel in history, a duel of stones and fire and water, and triumphed over the priests of Baal; he heard the still small Voice on Mount Horeb, and when he was hungry he was fed by the ravens. Fitting climax, indeed, was his departure from this earth—riding in a chariot of fire and wrapped in a whirlwind.

Ever since that fiery day and all down through history his fame has grown. When John the Baptist preached by the river Jordan the Judeans asked if he were the reincarnation of Elijah, whose return to earth had been prophesied. Jesus Himself was asked the same question. The splendor of Elijah's fame has been hymned in the Mendelssohn oratorio which bears his name. Man of fire and passion, he consecrated body, mind, and soul to the God of his fathers. The world is always waiting for another Elijah, whose name meant "The Lord Is God."

His successor, Elisha, was another kind of person.

Chapter 31 THE STRANGE CAREER OF ELISHA

WHEN Elijah rode up and off in his chariot of flame he left behind him not only his protégé but also his mortal enemy, that bloodthirsty heathen woman, Queen Jezebel.

The new prophet realized that he had inherited a bitter feud. He knew, too, that the old Tishbite, Elijah, had opposed the infernal cunning of that royal female demon with the powers of grace that God, the one and the true, had furnished him with. In these struggles that he must now carry on, would Elisha be able to summon up equally miraculous powers?

Standing by the riverbank, with the glitter of the flying chariot just vanished in the distant heaven, the new prophet decided to seek the answer to his doubts, in this same place. Elijah's mantle was lying on the ground where it had fallen. The young man lifted it with both hands, raised it over his head, and with a swift smiting motion, slammed the garment against the foaming surface of the Jordan, crying as he did so the deepmost doubt and challenge of his soul:

"Where is the Lord God of Elijah?"

And with ready answer the new prophet of Israel saw that he was truly one of that long line, running back to the days of Moses, who had beheld the miraculous works of God exhibited in the waters of this same river Jordan. Even as Elisha watched, as if it were a miniature Red Sea, and as if the God of the exodus from Egypt remembered, the narrower torrents of the Jordan were dammed up and parted, north and south, the coming and the going currents held back as if by Jehovah's very hands, and rocks and stones revealed the silt in the bed of the river that had lain hidden by the waters since time began.

Thus, as Elijah ended his career in a miracle of fire, Elisha began his with a miracle of water.

Watching all this from afar was a company of some fifty men, a special group who were sons of lesser prophets of those days. Seeing the waters part, they acclaimed their new leader:

"The spirit of Elijah does rest on Elisha."

Having begun his ministry on the wondrous stroke of a parted stream, Elisha then headed into the political huggermugger of his day and for long years afterward he wielded increasing supernatural force until his extraordinary deeds were talked about wherever ships sailed and camels marched.

At the very start of his career he healed the brackish waters and barren ground around Jericho by the sprinkling of a cruse of salt and a prayer that all be purified. Walking toward Bethel on another afternoon, he was tormented by a pack of wild and vicious children, whose parents had not taught their young the old religion, but the practice instead of the murderous, abominable, and orgiastic perversions of Baal, the god of Queen Jezebel. The crowd of children swarmed around the prophet, who, raising his staff, called on the Lord for deliverance. Mankind has ever since recoiled from the dismal memory of that afternoon in early summer when two shebears, erect on hind feet and roaring to the winds, came lumbering forward and tore asunder forty and two. That shocking report spread everywhere and Elisha was named with dread.

Yet he was the friend of people, not a spiritual bully, imposing his own will by the grace of God. One day a widow came weeping to the door of his hut, crushed with grief because she could not pay a debt, and the creditor was on his way to seize her two sons and sell them into slavery.

"What have you in the house?" asked Elisha.

"Not anything except a pot of oil."

"Go borrow vessels from all your neighbors. Borrow not a few. And when you are in the house, you shall shut the door upon you and upon your sons and shall pour out into all those vessels. . . . Go sell your oil and pay your debt."

Then there was the amazing case of the Shunammite woman, a great lady of broad estates who still worshiped the one true God. When she learned that Elisha was serving Jehovah as a prophet, tramping the countryside, reiterating the Ten Commandments, retelling the past from the Garden of Eden to the days of oppression in Egypt, Moses, the wilderness, Joshua, David, and Solomon, she took an interest in the ragged stranger and made him welcome in her house. She gave him a room just for himself, with Gehazi—a servant Elisha had picked up along the road—sleeping outside the curtained door. And there seemed no way by which Elisha could repay her kindness; the rich lady of Shunem wanted nothing.

"What is to be done for her?" Elisha asked Gehazi. The servant looked sideward and downward, with a wily smile. The lady had no child—and her husband was an old man. Rebekkah! Sarah! Rachel! And now, after nearly a thousand years, Elisha promised the Shunammite woman, against all likelihood, that she, too, would conceive.

"You man of God! Do not lie to your handmaid," she protested, her voice like an echo from the long past of Israel and a whisper of a future still far away.

But, as people were saying to each other everywhere in those days, Elisha's prophecies were never proved false. The lady of Shunem did indeed bear a son, strong and energetic, and as the years passed he grew to be a fine and comely lad, first heir to the gardens and broad lands of his mother. He was no princely idler; he was learning everything about the management of the estate, and like many a son of a wise owner, was learning his trade from the start. Then one day at harvest time, as he worked with the reapers in the fields of golden grain, his head began to ache and he fell in a faint. Carried to his mother's arms, he died.

This terrible fact was accepted by his mother with a serenity that shocked all the mourners. A woman of action who was governed by faith, she did not hesitate in what she knew must be done. She lifted the dead body of her son and, seeing her inflexible gaze, no friend or servant ventured near her, as she carried her burden not to the rooms of state in her magnificent house but to that bare back room upstairs where now and then the wandering prophet had been lodged. She laid the dead boy on the bed of Elisha and ordered that no one come near it. Then, saddling her favorite donkey, she went riding away alone.

It happened at that time that Elisha had gone into a retreat, meditating and praying in his dark cave that once had known Elijah's prayer and solitude, that dark old hollow in the rocks that travelers visit to this day on the height of Mount Carmel. Taking a walk, Elisha observed, far down the steep and winding road, a woman in familiar robes, tortuously coming up on the back of a donkey.

"Behold the Shunammite!" he exclaimed to Gehazi. "Run and ask her if all is well."

The servant Gehazi was, like many another helper to great men, an officious fellow. He tried to show his own importance by sending the grieving woman away; his master was here for prayer and solitude, renewing his spiritual forces, and should not be disturbed by anyone. But Elisha shoved him aside and tenderly received her.

"Take my staff," said Elisha to Gehazi. "Go with her and lay the staff on the face of her child." The servant hurried on ahead, as the grieving mother returned homeward with the prophet.

But soon Elisha knew, as by some mystical telepathy, that the attempt had failed. The rod of the prophet, laid on the cold face, brought no flutter to the eyelids, no stir of breath or returning life.

Reaching the house, Elisha asked to be left alone with the corpse. He lay down on the bed, prone on the lifeless boy, the warmth of his own body touching the icy figure, while he seized the rigid jaws and forced them open and breathed down the empty throat.

And surely there was never a stranger sound than suddenly exploded in the prophet's bedroom. The dead young man sneezed violently. Seven times and loudly he sneezed. The sound of it was heard by the mother, waiting and praying, outside the curtained doorway. And the young man opened his eyes.

Elisha called her into the room, his own voice shaken with joy as he said:

"Take up your son."

Many other astonishing things were told of Elisha. He fed a hundred hungry men with not enough food for a fifth of that number, and had bread left over: once more a prefiguring of miracles to come with the dawn of a new era when Jesus of Nazareth would feed four thousand with seven loaves and a few little fishes.

But the story of Elisha's mighty wonders that has most stirred the imagination of people is the tale of his encounter with a military officer, Naaman, captain of the host of the Syrian army. Naaman was a forthright, honest soldier, a realistic and somewhat impatient man, decent in all his dealings but cursed with the horrible disease of leprosy. All the famed physicians of that day had tried to cure him of the loathsome affliction—sores and a slow eating away of the body—and all had failed.

As it happened, there lived in the house of the leprous officer a captive little Israelite girl who served as maid to Naaman's wife. One day this young slave spoke to her mistress about a prophet in Israel who could cure sick people, no matter what the disease. His name, she said, was Elisha.

When word of this claim was brought to the king of Syria he immediately wrote a letter and sent it with gifts of gold and silver and
raiment to the king of Israel, beseeching him that his favorite soldier,
Captain Naaman, be cured.

But on reading the communication, the king of Israel rent his
clothes.

"Am I God to kill and make alive?" the baffled and frightened king
cried in despair. He was suspicious that this proposal might be a trick
to provoke or incite a war. But somehow Elisha heard of the message
and sent word to the troubled king:

"Let the man come to me and he shall know there is a prophet in
Israel."

Not long afterward Naaman stood at the door of Elisha's upstairs
room.

"Go and wash in the Jordan seven times," was all the prophet
would say to him.

Go and wash in the Jordan! The captain of the Syrian host swore
disdainfully. What silly hoax was this? In high dudgeon he stamped
downstairs and started off for home. But his servants reasoned with
him along the road, about the simple ways of prophets, and finally
persuaded him at least to try the directions, no matter how meaning-
less he thought them. So they turned off their course and went to the
banks of the Jordan and Naaman bathed, as he had been told.

In that same hour his flesh became as clear and healthy as that of a
little child. The leprosy disappeared completely.

Naturally, then, the contrite captain wanted to thank the prophet,
but Elisha waved him away. He did not welcome gratitude. His
delight was in the law of the Lord and in that law he meditated, day
and night. No man with healing power from God wants pay for his
use of it.

"Go in peace," said Elisha.

But the servants of God's servants are not always as scrupulous as
their masters, though living intimately with sanctity. Gehazi for example; Gehazi, the servant of Elisha, ran after the grateful Syrian, already started on his way home, and, lying in his own teeth, declared
that his master had been suddenly visited by two needy young men.
Therefore he would appreciate the gift of a talent of silver and two
changes of raiment, not for himself, of course, but for those needy
guests. Unsuspecting, Naaman was delighted to bestow not one but
two talents of silver, as well as the garments.

"But he went in, and stood before his master, and Elisha said unto him, Whence come you, Gehazi?

"And he said, Your servant went no whither.

"And he said unto him, Went not mine heart with you when the man turned again from his chariot to meet you? Is it a time to receive money, and to receive garments, and olive yards, and vineyards, and sheep, and oxen, and menservants, and maidservants?

"Is it time to receive money and gifts?" repeated Elisha.

The prophet was infuriated at his servant's lying and thievery. He had witnessed all the skullduggery with farseeing eyes.

"The leprosy therefore of Naaman shall cleave to you, and unto your seed for ever," he said solemnly.

And blighted Gehazi turned as white as snow.

In the Louvre Museum at Paris there is on exhibition a startling original piece of evidence which testifies to these times in Israel's history. The exhibit is called the Moabite stone, and casts of it are shown in the Oriental Institute of the University of Chicago and in the British Museum. The actual stone has been preserved in spite of a hard and foolish bargain driven by the Arabs who found it.

The avaricious Bedouins put a fire under the stone and, pouring cold water on it, broke it in pieces, which were distributed through the tribe so that it could·be sold piecemeal at rising prices. Most of the fragments were recovered and put together by the help of imperfect squeezes taken before the monument was broken.

The language in which the stone is written is of particular interest, showing what were the forms of the Phoenician letters used on the eastern side of the Jordan in the time of King Ahab. The forms employed in Israel and Judah on the western side could not have differed much; and thus we come face to face in these venerable characters with the precise mode of writing employed by the earlier prophets of the Old Testament, a contemporary record chiseled in stone. There on the Moabite stone is set forth an amazing tale, also to be found as Holy Writ in the Second Book of Kings: the history of another and most famous miracle of Elisha. That wonder was performed when the prophet provided water for the Israelite army, perishing of thirst; on stone and in the Bible one reads of the puzzling ditches that the prophet advised to be dug; and the hallucinations of "bloody water" in the deceived sight of the enemy.

It happened not long after the she-bears had attacked the children who plagued Elisha. Under the thumb of the Queen Mother Jezebel,

Jehoram reigned in the northern kingdom of Israel. Trouble started immediately. For years the subject people of Moab had been paying tribute money to Israel, but now that a new king, his strength untried, had been crowned, the Moabites decided it was time to rebel. As soon as spies brought this word to the inexperienced Jehoram he decided to look for outside help in the coming war. Like his father Ahab before him, Jehoram enlisted the aid—given most reluctantly and only because he was a friend—of Jehoshaphat, king of the southern kingdom of Judah. The ruler of Edom also joined in the alliance; the three kings merged their troops and marched.

But after seven days the soldiers found themselves trapped in a waterless plain, in danger of imminent battle, and with no springs, no gourds of water even, left to slake the thirst of fighting men. Then it was that Jehoshaphat—a weak but convinced worshiper of the one true God—could no longer hide his feelings. In a voice that trembled he cried:

"Is there not here a prophet of the Lord, that we may inquire of the Lord by him?"

Now Jehoram, like his mother Jezebel, cared nothing for the Lord and believed in Him not at all. But it was a dire plight they were in, and Jehoram welcomed the whispered suggestion of one of his aides—there was Elisha. How about him?

And so a stern-faced, unflattered Elisha came to stand before the king. He knew Jehoram; true, he had publicly put away the images of Baal, but in the privacy of his palace there was no perversion, no abomination of that false god that was not practiced in drunken, gleeful antics.

"What have I to do with you?" Elisha demanded. "Get you to the prophets of Ahab and Jezebel, your father and mother."

And then Elisha suddenly heard the Voice—perhaps for the first time he heard it—calling upon him to hearken. In an altered mood Elisha called for music. Minstrels and players were instantly summoned and sound of padded hammers on taut strings seemed to stir the strange man's sense of prophecy. In a trance, an ecstasy, Elisha gave the three kings assurance of victory over Moab. Then, when they thought the vision was over, he went on to advise them how to obtain water. They must dig ditches in certain places, and when they had obeyed him the ditches were suddenly overflowing with water, coming from nowhere and spreading in all the valley.

And next a strange turnover in events.

From a great distance the Moabites were watching, observing the curious activities behind the Israelite lines. And now these vigilant watchers were deceived by an optical illusion.

The slant of the afternoon sunlight on the newly spreading water gave the pools and streams the red look of blood. Foolishly concluding that the allied kings had fallen out and fought one another, and that the Israelites were now without leaders, the Moabites rushed forward pell-mell to gather spoil. Instead they found the Israelites ready for battle. So ghastly was their defeat that King Mesha of Moab, full of insane fear and frustration, sacrificed his own son and heir on the wall as a burnt offering to the God of Israel—all to no avail.

That miserable Mesha, king of Moab, broken in his defeat, carved his unhappy history on what is called today the Moabite stone, beginning:

"I, Mesha, son of Chemosh-melech, king of Moab, the Dibonite. My father reigned over Moab thirty years, and I reigned after my father. I made this monument to Chemosh at Korkah."

He was an obscure king and that was a tiny, obscure war that left no other traces in the story of mankind. But the finding of that stone, in 1868, at Dibon, confirms expressly this minor episode in the Old Testament. Year by year new attestation comes that the Bible is an authentic record.

It was not long after the defeat of Moab that Ben-Hadad, king of Syria, plotted war against Israel. This time Elisha seemed to read thoughts from afar and gave warning to his own king of what was afoot. Told of this apparent mind reading, Ben-Hadad raged and threatened and gave orders to have the prophet seized and brought before him. But the abductors, arriving near Elisha's lodging, suddenly found themselves groping in darkness, instantaneously struck blind. It was Elisha who took them by the hand and sent them homeward.

And then the Voice spoke to Elisha, in a mysterious summons to finish a commission that had been long ago entrusted to Elijah, and now was ripening for action—nothing less than the anointing of a new king for Israel.

Elisha called to his side a young friend, the son of a village mystic, and gave him a box of oil.

"Go to Ramoth-Gilead," Elisha said. "Look for Jehu, son of Jehoshophat, son of Nimshi. And pour this oil on his head. And say, Thus says the Lord, I have anointed you king of Israel. Then tarry not."

Although this was a fantastic, even treasonable action, the messenger did just as he was bidden. Jehu, captain of the host and with a reputation as a fast and furious driver of chariots, was called upon by a young stranger. Told to kneel, he did so. The oil was rubbed into his bushy hair and he was told to smite the house of Ahab, root and branch, for that family had brought suffering, sin, and wanton murder to Israel through Jezebel, the Zidonian queen.

"Who was that mad fellow?" asked his men of Jehu when the messenger had run off without pause for further ceremony.

When Jehu informed them of what had taken place the men, deeply moved, took off their outer garments and piled them on the top of the stairs to make a throne for their captain. They blew trumpets and the shout went up: "Jehu is king!"

At once the newly proclaimed monarch set about his commission from God's prophet to wipe out the house of Ahab. First he raised troops and drove on to the plain of Esdraelon, at full chariot speed, with a detachment of cavalry galloping after him. There at Jezreel lay King Jehoram of Israel, wounded in a recent Syrian battle, and squatting by his side his nephew, King Ahaziah of the southern kingdom, Judah.

A sentry on the tower spied the cavalcade coming at a distance, and a horseman was sent out to meet them and ask: "Is it peace?" But the horseman did not return. Another rider was sent, with the same ominous result. Sick as he was, Jehoram clambered into his chariot, as did Ahaziah, and neither spoke of the fact that the meeting was at the vineyard of Naboth, a place once named in a prophecy of doom by Elijah.

There Jehu killed Jehoram with an arrow, and the terrified Ahaziah fled the place only to be slain in the open road that same day.

This bad news soon reached Jezebel; all of it, including the battle cry of Jehu's soldiers: "What peace, so long as Jezebel and her witchcrafts are so many?"

So Jezebel painted her cheeks, reddened her lips, and lined the arches of her eyebrows. She attired herself alluringly and sat in the window of her palace. Bold and defiant, she mocked at Jehu as he entered the gate. He commanded her own eunuchs to throw her out of the high window; her broken body was trodden under the feet of the horses where she fell, and her blood sprinkled the wall with crimson. Dogs came and ate her flesh, leaving only the skull and the feet and the palms of her hands.

313

Which horrible fate, people now remembered, was in precise fulfillment of the long-ago word of Elijah.

Everyone connected with the reigning house was slain by Jehu, including seventy sons of Ahab and forty-two relatives of Ahaziah, the late Jehoram's nephew.

"Ahab served Baal a little, but Jehu shall serve him much," declared the new king to the people.

This shocking announcement filled the followers of the Lord God with dismay. Why had Elisha called this man to be king if he would out-Ahab Ahab in the worship of a false heathen idol? They did not realize that Jehu's speech hid a secret meaning. They did not know that Jehu was a fanatic, with all the dangerous cruelty and cunning that goes with overzealousness. He ordered the priests of the house of Baal to proclaim a full assembly of all the false god's worshipers. They crowded into the temple, every one, and Jehu himself offered a special sacrifice. The festival was a notable one.

But secretly Jehu had stationed fourscore men around the Temple with instructions to murder the whole congregation when the signal was given. Just at the end of the burnt offering the soldiers of Jehu crashed into the throng of unsuspecting worshipers and left not one alive to tell the tale. The idols of Baal were broken to bits. It was a purge, so Jehu thought and hoped, a wholesale and bloody sweep of reform in Israel.

But as always in forced reforms, the golden calves of Bethel and Dan still remained potent in the heads of the sullen people. For his original desire to cleanse the land of wickedness, the Lord had promised Jehu that four of his generations would rule. But before his own reign of twenty-eight years had ended Israel stood face to face with an inescapable crisis. A great turning point had come in the long and jagged course of her career, a shadow falling down from the future upon the kingdom's troubled present—a shadow from the north. Far upland there was the growing and despotic emergence of Assyria, and its conquering monarch, Shalmaneser III, was looking around him. His eye had fallen on Israel and he contemplated its people, its resources, and its king.

It would be easy to gobble up that little kingdom in one little war. So Jehu was confronted with blackmail. Pay as tribute, or Assyrian troops will annihilate you.

There is a carving that has the vividness of a photograph, recording that ancient crisis: King Jehu kneeling abjectly before the all-conquering Shalmaneser, while Israelites come bearing tribute of gold and precious fabrics for the new master. All this is on the famous Black Obelisk, displayed in the British Museum, whereon Shalmaneser III has inscribed his boasts. For young Shalmaneser was master and Jehu was a captive king of Israel, and Elisha was soon to die. The darkest times of all the history of Israel were coming on swiftly.

And where was Elisha, amid the gathering darkness that began to overshadow the two kingdoms, Israel and Judah? The courts of the childish kings knew him no longer; in his dark cave, meditating on the crest of Carmel, in desert vigils and wilderness prayers, he spent his time, turning his back on a heedless world. It was a bloodthirsty spectacle from which the aging prophet fled, a stage of swiftly changing scenes of kings dying too soon and princes born too late, of strife, marauders, battles, victories, and retreats—but in all the stratagems, plots, schemings, and desperate essays no one turned to the one true God, as Elisha had urged them to do. So what more was left for him to say?

Jezebel's daughter, a sharp-eyed vixen called Athalia, saw her son ruling in the south, but when word came from Jerusalem that the king was dead she usurped the throne of Judah, sitting in state on the throne of David and Solomon. Her recipe for security was murdering all the seed royal, every living soul with a drop of David's blood in his veins; she slew them all but one.

That was Joash, the infant son of Ahaziah, who escaped the swords of her executioners; the priests hid him in Solomon's Temple, with Queen Athalia not dreaming of his existence. She believed that all possible pretenders to the Judean crown were now liquidated, and that she could rule in utter peace of mind, while paganism seemed to come to full power in the city of the Temple. Ruthlessly, Athalia had put a stop to the worship of the one true God; spending the taxpayers' money with squandering hands, she built another, rival temple in Jerusalem, a temple to Baal, her false god; she relentlessly persecuted those who worshiped in the old ways and drove them to the altar of her idol.

Nevertheless, the underground was busy; there has never been a persecution yet that could drive out the worship of God from the hearts of those that love Him. Let Athalia conjure up what torments she would; invent new agonies, revive all the tortures of rack and stretch and bloodletting, beds of fiery coals, eyes pierced with silver needles—still the soul of the persecuted loves his Lord and will not be estranged.

So by moonlight, while the court was sleeping, the bearded priests, without their sacerdotal robes, would teach the growing royal child of the high destiny to which he was born, for he was the legitimate heir to the throne of Judah. And one fine day, when the child was seven years old, the priests opened the Temple of Solomon early in the morning. They had figured out exactly what they must do to rally the people and they were inspired to believe that now was the time. Jehoiada, the high priest—although long before officially stripped of that office—was ready to restore the worship of God to Jerusalem.

Shrewdly taking advantage of a change of palace guards on this crucial Sabbath morning—and assisted by those same guards, who had come to loathe the queen—the high priest made a new king for Judah. Shyly the lad Joash stood beside the great pillar of the platform, as he was being anointed, then hailed as king, with trumpets and shouting. It was not long before the news of all this was brought to the ears of Athalia in her palace, and not even waiting to tidy her dress, she sped in her chariot to the crowded Temple on the hill.

At the sight of the queen the throng parted; the way opened up, and she beheld the boy Joash, her grandson, with the crown on his head. The jewels in the crown were glittering as if in defiance of her power, and all the people, she knew, had only a moment before been rejoicing with music and song.

"Treason! Treason!" she screamed, tearing her clothes in the traditional gesture.

But the crowd, silent at her entrance, was not cowed or swayed by her theatrical performance.

"Long live the king!" they called, and the sound of those words so provoked Athalia that she cursed the people she wished to rule.

"Take her away from the Temple and slay her outside its holy boundaries," commanded the high priest Jehoiada to his captains. "And if any follow her, deal with them likewise."

The worshipers of Baal mourned loudly at the passing of their queen. Her death meant a dim future for their cult in Judah.

Thus—while damnation seemed to be creeping upon the upper kingdom of Israel and its distracted ten tribes—reforms began to make the future seem brighter in Judah. The people of the south seemed happy and sincere in their return to Jehovah and the revival of worship brought on a busy time.

Jehoiada, the high priest, who had saved the house of David from extinction and oblivion, now made a fresh and formal covenant between the Lord and the boy king and his people, promising that Jehovah alone should be their God. He wiped out of existence the house of Baal, its chief priest Mattan, and all the idols. Once again the people could come freely to worship in the Temple that Solomon had built.

Large sums of money were collected for repairs to the Temple, for years of neglect had brought the glory of Jerusalem to a pitiful state, and it took years to restore it. And, fallen human nature being what it is, there were thefts during the long project. There were misappropriations of money, even by the priests of the temple, until Joash, when he grew to full manhood, called them to account. But finally the task was finished, to the pride of the workmen on wood and stone, more honest than the priests who put their hands in the till; again, in spite of the weakness of men, the Temple stood white and beautiful on the height.

Who could have believed then in the joy of rehabilitation that before long the Temple would be robbed, despoiled, and desecrated—by the king himself?

Yet it was so. For just as Elisha had foretold, Syria began to roam abroad like a hungry lion, and King Hazael descended on both Judah and Israel. He plundered and ravaged as far south as Gath in Philistia, and in the sweep and carnage of his invasions reduced the Hebrews in both kingdoms to vassalage. The king Joash was compelled to ransom Jerusalem from the Syrian conqueror—and the price was all the golden treasure still left to the Temple and royal palace, even relics that were hallowed and historic. In the bitterness of his humiliation the king sighed with gratitude when conspirators in his own household came to cut his throat.

Nor did his twenty-five-year-old son Amaziah help matters much when he was crowned. True, he won a military victory over Edom's army but the Edomites won a spiritual victory over Jerusalem—the revolution against Baal, the reformation of the government, and the repairing of the Temple came down to one ignoble compromise: victorious Amaziah, to placate the fallen foe, as a matter of conciliatory state policy, bowed down to the false gods of Edom. That was a deed

317

that would have horrified his father; the faith of Judah had once more descended to idolatry.

Meanwhile, up north in Israel the shadows of misrule and misworship continued to deepen. Hazael, the Syrian scourge, had forced King Jehoahaz, son of old Jehu, to reduce his army to impotence, with a limit of fifty horsemen, ten chariots, and ten thousand footmen. Of Israel it was said that Hazael "had made them like dust by threshing."

For the whole length of his reign Jehoahaz was ineffectual, and Jehoash, his son, when he came to be king, realized that the land was languishing for leadership. The new king had a wise and simple thought; there was one man of God still alive in the land—Elisha. Why not go to him?

Elisha had lived on through all the troubles and crises of these several kings, and now the prophet was hoary with years. Yet his mind was still keen and his heart still devoted to God, and he could still foresee the cycles of wisdom or folly that men would move in. Once he had wept publicly over what he foresaw that Hazael would do. But in that same sad vision he had seen the waning of his triumph.

When King Jehoash found Elisha he was on his deathbed—but the land of Syria still troubled his mind. Jehoash wept when he laid eyes on the feeble prophet. He repeated aloud the words that Elisha had spoken to Elijah that day he was caught up into heaven:

"O my father, my father—the chariot of Israel and the horsemen thereof."

And the Bible then records a singular story. Sitting up in bed, the dying prophet made a queer request. He bade Jehoash to get his bow and arrows and then open the window. All of which the king did.

"Shoot!" said Elisha, whose name meant "God Is Salvation." "It is the arrow of the Lord's deliverance from Syria. For you shall smite the Syrians till they are consumed."

Enigmatic words, but the king obeyed. An arrow whizzed from his bow out of the window. In a fierce fervor Elisha called for others to follow it. But the impatient archer-king stopped at three; they were enough. Elisha gave him a terrible look of disappointment and with his last breath cried:

"There should have been shot five or six arrows! Then would Syria had been consumed, where now you shall smite only three times!"

True to what the prophet had foretold on his deathbed, Syria fell from the dominance with the end of Hazael, whose son Ben-Hadad was beaten thrice by King Jehoash. Thus he recovered the cities which had been lost in war by his father, and he also attacked Jerusalem, dealing Judah, the sister kingdom, a staggering blow, looted it, and carried off hostages to guarantee good behavior thereafter. And so for a little while Judah in the south was subject to Israel in the north.

Chapter 32 THE SINGULAR TRAVELS OF JONAH

THE people that the Lord would favor, if they would only let Him, were prosperous again, and greedy eyes were on them. From beyond the frontiers they were being watched, but they were too lost in pleasure to feel their danger. The glow of excitement that brightened those days was like the flush of a lethal fever. Both the old Israel and the old Judah, once the united kingdom of David and Solomon, were getting ready to die.

But no one could make the separated tribesmen believe the portents. It was a gay and deceptive time when King Jehoash died, and his son Jeroboam II ascended the throne. By conquest and loot the new prosperity came; the new king won back to Israel the rich region of Transjordania, with Moab and Ammon subdued. Simply from the control of the resources of those uplands, business flourished as never before and Israelite wealth accumulated. Under the forty-one-year reign of Jeroboam the younger, fourth and last king of the line of Jehu, a "golden age" of Israel seemed to return—at least for certain privileged classes.

Flush with money, and indulging more and more in luxuries and lax living, new millionaires built fine town and country homes, decked with silken upholsteries and ivory-inlaid divans. Those who could afford it, and they were many, arrayed themselves in the finest of clothes—stuffs brought by caravan from all parts of the world. Jeweled headdresses became popular, and rings, bracelets, collars, and necklaces of precious stones, so that Isaiah, a prophet, was soon to be heard, deriding this coxcomb way of life:

Moreover the Lord saith, Because the daughters of Zion are haughty, and walk with stretched forth necks and wanton eyes, walking and mincing as they go, and making a tinkling with their feet:

319

Therefore the Lord will smite with a scab the crown of the head of the daughters of Zion, and the Lord will discover their secret parts.

In that day the Lord will take away the bravery of their tinkling ornaments about their feet and their cauls, and their round tires like the moon,

The chains and the bracelets, and the mufflers,

The bonnets, and the ornaments of the legs, and the headbands, and the tablets, and the earrings,

The rings, and nose jewels,

The changeable suits of apparel, and the mantles and the wimples, and the crisping pins,

The glasses, and the fine linen, and the hoods and the veils.

And it shall come to pass, that instead of sweet smell there shall be stink; and instead of a girdle a rent; and instead of well set hair baldness; and instead of a stomacher a girding of sackcloth; and burning instead of beauty.

Food was abundant, too, in those days—meats and every variety of grain, wines, and oil. Feasts and carousing filled the homes, until its tastes and vices Samaria resembled a little Babylon. The idle rich surfeited themselves with licentiousness and entertainment, while the masses were poor and without rights and could even be sold into slavery for small debts or lost legal disputes.

The old religion of the one true God remained ostentatiously the religion of the state, but actually the golden calves, permitted by the first Jeroboam, were still being worshiped at the sanctuaries of Bethel and Dan: the bloody reformation of Jehu, which had been supposed to stamp it out, was already forgotten. As if all this corruption and backsliding were not enough, some of the Israelite leaders began to give themselves international airs. Bloated with a belief in their own importance, incredible as it sounds, they began to dream of world empire.

After all, were they not the Lord's people? So they argued. In their conceit they wholly discounted not only their own neglect of that Lord but also the completely visible fact that nearby Assyria was already a menacing shadow to the peace of any other country, a shadow growing bigger and blacker as its own internal dissensions lessened. Much more realistic and less conceited enemies were already contemplating moves of conquest.

It was in these days that the prophet Jonah lived. Jonah was the son of Amittai, "the truthful one." Though Israel in this, its worst era of fleshpots and immorality, seemed to need someone to hold up the mirror of truth to its face, the only prophet of the moment was sent on another errand. The word of the Lord came to Jonah that he was to go to Nineveh, to the capital in Assyria, and there denounce its wickedness and call for repentance.

The very thought of such an undertaking terrified Jonah. He knew that Nineveh was a city of imposing grandeur and had 120,000 inhabitants, "who could not discern between their left and their right hand." Fourteen miles long was Nineveh, and forty-six miles all around its circumference, with a wall a hundred feet high and thick enough on the top for a race between three chariots running abreast.

The Voice that had been heard in Eden spoke to Jonah, with instructions. Jonah was to enlighten the ignorance of Nineveh, be a missionary to these far-off and despised heathen, which was something unheard of among the tribes of Israel. Typical of the insular Hebrew of his time, Jonah felt he must have misunderstood the meaning of the Voice. He simply could not bring himself to undertake the task. Boarding a Phoenician ship, riding at anchor off Joppa, Jonah set sail, not for any port near the Assyrians, but for the harbor of Tarshish.

Thus he disobeyed God and went in a contrary direction. But, after all, he reasoned, why should he imagine that Jehovah would bother with heathen? Why would He dispatch Jonah to save the Assyrians from perdition to which all outlanders well belonged, anyway? These were natural questions of a man of that time.

Hardly was the ship at sea before out of a clear sky a tremendous gale blew up. In the midst of the stormy uproar Jonah lay asleep, untroubled by conscience, he alone of those aboard unconscious of the danger. The billowing, surging sea was terrifying to behold; the crew were expecting the vessel to founder any moment.

"Let us cast lots," the sailors said, "that we may discover who causes this evil."

Jonah, rudely awakened, was forced into the lottery with the others and his number proved to be the guilty cast. As far as the frightened sailors were concerned it was Jonah who had brought the terrible storm upon them.

"Why have you done this?" the sailors asked him. "Why have you angered the Lord—and how?"

Jonah, suddenly remembering and stricken with guilt, confessed how he had, indeed, disobeyed the precise instructions of the Lord God.

"Then what shall we do to you that the sea may be calm?"

"Cast me forth," pleaded Jonah, now full of self-condemnation and wretchedness. But the seamen were opposed; they wanted no murder on their souls. Turning back to their sails and ropes, they tried to steer the ship toward harbor. But it was too late in those raging seas; their efforts hopeless. Then it was—with a prayer not to be held responsible for their desperate act—the crew tossed the praying, conscience-stricken passenger over the rail.

As Jonah plunged into the water it was as if magic prevailed. The tempest was stilled; as the body of Jonah disappeared beneath the water, so vanished the storm as if he had sucked it all under with him.

What had happened?

The adventure of Jonah is one of the most exciting tales ever told in the world in spite of the fact that many people refuse to believe that it ever could have happened. But the Scriptures do tell us that a great fish was lurking under the stormy waves and as Jonah splashed into the water he was promptly swallowed by the great fish, or leviathan of those waters, some colossal beast of the sea. In the roomy belly of the green behemoth he remained, terrified and shaken with every turn and dive, for three days and three nights. Sincerely contrite, and begging the mercy of the Lord for his stubborn disobedience, Jonah was finally vomited safely upon the shore.

Safe on the shore himself, Jonah still had his job to do.

"Arise, go unto Nineveh," came the Voice of the Lord again into the mind of Jonah.

Forthwith, the chastened prophet decided to obey. By ship and land he journeyed to the spectacular capital of Assyria, and there to street-corner crowds he hastily proclaimed the city's utter destruction. So convincing was the foreign prophet that the people believed him and many put on sackcloth and ashes, and fasted. Jonah felt like a man who had done his work too well. The Assyrians repented of their wicked ways; they eschewed all future plans of aggression and violence and in the king's chamber his counselors decided with him to forsake conquest and be satisfied thereafter with what they had.

This repentance was actually a deep disappointment to Jonah. He had been promised the demolition by Almighty God of the proudest city then on the earth. But the Voice, revisiting him in the night's silence, told him that because of the very genuine repentance of the Assyrians they should have mercy. The capital was not to be destroyed.

Jonah was in a tantrum at these face-losing tidings. He saw nothing of the irony of the situation—with the God of Abraham, Moses, and David forgiving a heathen crowd the moment they were sorry, while Israel, where the old laws were recited by rote every day and listened to by no one, was bowing down still to the calves of gold and all that those brazen idols stood for.

In this sardonic fact Jonah, although a prophet or a great missioner, seemed to see no meaning. Ingrained racial prejudice was in his heart, as well as jealousy that Jehovah would show love for these "outsiders." In his misery over God's own mercy, Jonah actually prayed to die. Beyond the city limits he squatted in grim ill-humor at the side of a booth he had erected for himself. And that was an appropriate time for Jonah to receive a sign from on high.

It chanced that a gourd grew high enough to cast a grateful shadow over his bare head, shielding it from the sun; the shade also soothed his fevered body. But during the night the Lord caused a worm to eat away the plant and sent a piercing east wind to blight it. By sunrise the plant had no more shade to give, while hot light and fierce wind joined in making Jonah feel faint. Railing because of the withered gourd, Jonah cried out again that, like it, he wished to die. And God heard him scolding at the heavenly injustice of the plant.

"Do you do well to be angry for the gourd?" inquired the Voice.

"I do well to be angry, even unto death," groaned Jonah, supremely sullen even in conversation with the Most High. But God, as always, was patient, as He pronounced Jonah's lesson:

"You have pity on the gourd, for which you have not labored, neither made it grow; which came up in a night and perished in a night: and should I not spare Nineveh the great city?"

Then Jonah realized that Jehovah was not merely God of the Hebrews but the one true God of all mankind, including the worst heathen. To him, this was a revolutionary, epoch-making thought that was one day to affect the world.

Does it not seem strange that God should have chosen Jonah for such extraordinarily important errands—this stiff-necked, grumpy, unco-operative Jonah, who brooded and thought dark thoughts and, in spite of his littleness, received the largest of visions, which is the one true God, the Father of all? It was said of Jonah that in spite of his failings he was a remarkable Messianic forerunner; the day would come when the Messiah Himself would mention Jonah.

Chapter 33 "I DESPISE YOUR FEAST DAYS"

B u t other inspired voices were also echoing the great Voice, at home as well as abroad.

There was now no Elisha left to counsel the frightened ruler of the people, but a new admonisher was heard, clamoring in the streets, denouncing the wickedness of all the tribes, and promising infinitely greater disasters to come in punishment for their falling away from faith. God's justice would soon overwhelm them, stormed the clarion tongue of this inspired man, the prophet called Amos, from among the shepherds of the hills of Tekoa, not far from Jerusalem.

Amos, the "peasant prophet," was not only a herdsman but a dresser of sycamores, a tree doctor, but God spoke through him during the declining years of the kingdom.

Bluntly and precisely he warned the people what was going to happen. They would be led captive out of their own land. And for these terrifying predictions he was chased away by the high priest, not an unusual phenomenon in history.

Yet in spite of ecclesiastical rebuke, Amos remains in a secure niche of mortal remembrance. Throughout the ups and downs of the Hebrews they had been warned, by one of God's favorites after another, against the tyranny of rulers and the backslidings of the people, but Amos was first of the whole line after Moses to write down and preserve what he had to say. We have his words, recorded in the book which bears his name in the Old Testament, a book fulminating against soulless rites and bleak rituals, when faith and love of God are left out. For more than twenty years he wrote and spoke, not only in his native southland but also in hostile cities of the northern kingdom, foretelling doom but not utter hopelessness—a brighter day beyond was also in his vision.

Standing in the temple at Bethel, Amos raised his voice in denunciation of a whole string of wicked cities. Naturally his listeners liked this kind of talk and they applauded. What excellent sense this visiting prophet had! But their clapping hands were stilled, their voices silent, when the old man's tongue turned next to their own abysmal shame:

> The God of hosts, the Lord saith: I hate, I despise your feast days : . . Though ye offer Me burnt offerings and your meat offerings, I will not accept them: neither will I regard the peace offerings of your fat beasts.

Take you away from me the noise of songs; for I will not hear the melody of thy viols.

But let judgment run down as waters, and righteousness as a mighty stream. . . .

Behold, I will raise up against you a nation, O house of Israel, says the Lord, the God of hosts; and they shall afflict you from the entering in of Hamath unto the river of the wilderness. . . .

And the high places of Isaac shall be desolate, and the sanctuaries of Israel shall be laid waste; and I will rise against the house of Jeroboam with the sword.

Much more the prophet Amos predicted. His castigation was directed at the rich and affluent, his sympathy and pity reserved for the oppressed poor. Justice, justice, justice—this lost treasure of the people was his main theme; he was the first prophet of social justice, and without it, as far as Amos was concerned, all sacrifices were vain.

The Bethel temple audience, many of them drunk and maudlin, gave Amos jeers and hoots. They were more amused than aroused, until he uttered a sentence against the king, Jeroboam II. Amaziah, priest of Bethel, sent a report to the king that a wild-eyed Judean had loosed treason in the midst of the sanctuary. And to the herdsman-prophet himself the priest said:

"O you seer! Go back to Judah whence you came! There eat your bread and do your talking. No more prophecy here, for this is the king's holy place, a royal house!"

And Amos answered: "I was no prophet, neither was I a prophet's son; but I was a herdsman, and a gatherer of sycamore fruit: and the Lord took me as I followed the flock, and said unto me, Go, prophesy unto my people Israel.

"Now therefore hear you the word of the Lord:

"You say, Prophesy not against Israel, and drop not your word against the house of Isaac. Therefore thus says the Lord: Your wife shall be a harlot in the city, and your sons and your daughters shall fall by the sword, and your land shall be divided by lines; and you shall die in a polluted land: and Israel shall surely go into captivity, forth of his land."

Having delivered his full terrible say, Amos went back to his Judean hills, there to write down his oracles. Meanwhile he troubled Israel no more with his presence, though he was to be remembered again when a succeeding prophet, Hosea, of Israel itself, one of the most farseeing of inspired men, echoed the unheeded warning of the Tekoan herdsman. With unfaltering clarity he predicted the decline and fall of Israel. But he also reiterated that the love of God would never fail.

The end of Israel was being foreshadowed and no one could say the people had not been warned.

Nevertheless, among other civic works, Jeroboam II was refortifying Samaria so that it might stand impregnable. It never seemed to occur to this king, nor to many of his predecessors, that military fortification and preparation alone is no security. Not once does he seem to have reflected that the secret lies in changing the heart, the mind, the attitude, the pattern of behavior—nor that loving God as a father and all men as brothers may be, as God has so often instructed, an indispensable approach to security.

Not so in the brain of Jeroboam II. He went right on with his defense program. A double wall was built around his capital. At the estimated weakest point of assault it was thirty-three feet wide. Put to the test later on, it proved so strong a defense that it was to take Assyria, with all its men and engines, three years to conquer Samaria. Small wonder, then, that the people of Israel were lulled into feeling safe, and when Hosea, their own native prophet, lifted his warning voice in forecast of coming doom, a repetition of what Amos had told them, they gave him a deaf ear also.

Unlike Amos, however, the new prophet preached not only the justice of Jehovah but His everlasting love that longed to enfold mankind. While Hosea rebuked his nation severely for its sins, its persistent moral and religious blindness, he grieved over it with a tender heart, more personal in feeling than any exhibited by Amos. Only natural, perhaps, for Amos was a Judean and had no close ties in Israel.

Hosea picked up the symbolism of Amos. He used himself as the figure of one married to an incorrigible prostitute, an imaginary woman called Gomer. Gomer could be thought of as the land of Israel, apostate, licentious, and deceiving. Aware of her faithlessness, he would forgive her repeatedly and restore her to his side. This tolerance went on and on. Yes, the Lord God was like that husband, and Israel was like Gomer, the unfaithful wife—Hosea thereby greatly shocked respectable people.

Jehovah married to a harlot nation, indeed! Hosea must be raving mad. Either that or a poet whose figures of speech must never be taken literally.

Unperturbed, Hosea went on to pour gourds of scorn on the golden-calf worship still to be seen in Israel, the choice of materialism instead of spirituality. Again and again he stressed his argument that knowledge of God was more desirable than all the burnt offerings ever made. To the lack of that knowledge, to the confusion of letter with spirit, were due all the present abominations of murder, thievery, false swearing, and drunkenness.

Retribution was inevitable. Hosea, too, foresaw the coming of a conqueror who would scatter Israel like chaff, for Jehovah now must act in His long-restrained vengeance:

"The days of visitation are come! The days of recompense are come! Israel shall know it!"

Yet, love, as preached by Hosea, endured all things, forgave endlessly, and never ceased to hope. So even in his direst predictions there was the ground-note of universal love for all people:

"And I will sow her unto Me in the earth; and I will have mercy upon her that had not obtained mercy; and I will say to them which were not My people, You are My people; and they shall say, You are my God."

Not as unmovably stern as Amos had been, Hosea was convinced that God would succeed in His purposes for the salvation of the whoredom of Israel at last—and always because of the great quality of His love, the hope He still held for the reality of His dream of creation.

Spiritual as he was in his vision, Hosea was not indifferent to mundane matters. Constantly he warned the nation against the folly of foreign alliances that were shortsighted and contrary to the will of God.

Through the reigns of four kings and including part of Jeroboam's Hosea spoke of God's wonderful love and the need for repentance. But his voice carried little weight. However, when written down for future generations to read, his warnings are like torches for the darkness. He spoke to his own time and got the ear of the ages.

Chapter 34 THE FALL OF THE NORTHERN KINGDOM

THE day came when the Assyrian came down like a wolf on the fold and all Israel, the ten tribes of the northern kingdom, fell to his power.

Not that it was an easy victory. Faced with the inevitable, the Samaritans and the Galileans fought patriotically. Until the final crisis their leaders had done their best to appease, paying blackmail. King Menahem, for example, in his day had bought off the threat of invasion by paying a thousand talents of silver—a fortune taken from the coffers of Israelite millionaires. But not appeasement and not resistance would help this chosen people, still straying from the ways of their Maker; King Jeroboam II died; King Zechariah was assassinated, and his killer slain a month later by that same Menahem.

The last effort to save the land was made by King Hoshea, who made a secret alliance with the king of Egypt.

That was the spark that set off the powder keg. The affronted overlord of Assyria at once began a siege of Samaria. For three years the extraordinary fortifications did keep the enemy at bay. Shalmaneser died before the assault ended, but Sargon II, King of Kings, continued stubbornly in his stead. And in the ninth year of Hoshea's reign, 721 B.C., the city was taken and the king made prisoner.

And now, as the prophet had for so long foretold, Israel was to be punished. The northern kingdom was smashed to bits; 27,290 of its best people, the brains of its society, were seized and transported to the distant regions of "Gozan, and in the cities of the Medes." Dispersed and distributed at the will of the conqueror, they had no longer any cohesion of race, as hitherto, or unification of thought or purpose. Settlers from Babylon, Elam, and Syria were given their land holdings in demolished Israel.

Never were the ten tribes—to be known ever after as the Lost Tribes—to come together as a nation again. The prophecies of Amos and Hosea were fulfilled:

"Therefore the Lord was very angry with Israel, and removed them out of His sight: there was none left but the tribe of Judah only."

Chapter 35   THE LITTLE ANGEL AND THE BURNING COAL

"THERE was no tribe left but Judah only—"

And men were already asking how long the little kingdom of the south could save itself from also being gobbled up by conquerors from the north. Through the fabulous crescent that curved from Babylon through Damascus, the conquerors had surged down, taking Israel. Surely Judah's turn would be next.

Yet the time of collapse was postponed for one hundred and fifty years. In that century and a half, bad king followed good king, wise men and fools sat on the southern throne, and in the endangered land the people and their leaders swayed and wavered, as of old, between the one true God and their idols.

So Amaziah, king of Judah, had his throat cut in a conspiracy, to be followed by the pious and wise Azariah, who was also called Uzziah, a believer in preparedness. He enlarged his armies and trained them diligently; on the towers and bulwarks of fortified Jerusalem he placed new weapons, invented by the best scientific brains he could assemble. These scientists and engineers built him contrivances that would shoot forth blazing arrows and others that would hurl down boulders on enemies outside the walls.

But Uzziah was not merely a military organizer; he was a statesman in love with his people. Under his wise husbandry policies, new vines were planted in the hills, more cattle bred on plain and green slope, and in the yellow desert places men dug and dug and dug until they at last found water.

Why then did Uzziah find, one day, a leprous spot on his forehead: why had the Lord smitten him?

Because, it was very clear, he had not put down idolatry in the hills and high places, while he, himself, had gone into the Temple to burn incense—a rite reserved for priests and no one else, not even a king.

The procession of royal failures that came after Uzziah was long and dismal. Jotham and then Ahaz, his son, who raised new brazen figures to heathen Baalim, and permitted and even practiced the most hideous abominations of the heathen in that valley of Hinnom over which there hangs to this day the dark memory of babies burned in sacrifice on the altars of evil. A wicked opportunist, this Ahaz, who tried to get help from the Assyrians for foes nearer at home. He offered treasure from the Temple and the palace and the Assyrians carted it away but gave him no help at all. He tried in every way to show his infidel enemies that he believed with them, shutting up the Temple doors, breaking up the holy vessels and bending the knee to the gods of Damascus. His death was a blessing to the kingdom.

Then Hezekiah came to the throne and Hezekiah was of a different sort altogether.

As soon as the crown was on his head Hezekiah called the priests and the Levites together and told them he was going to lead his people back to the worship of the Lord God, Jehovah. Open the doors!

Repair the battered Temple! Sanctify themselves! With the utmost speed the nation must rededicate itself to the service of the one true God.

The word went round the countryside: a message from Hezekiah, addressed to the people of Judah and Ephraim and Manasseh, yes, and even conquered Israel, calling on the people not carried away captive to return to Jehovah while there was still time.

"Be not stiff-necked as your fathers were," was King Hezekiah's message. "For if you turn again unto the Lord, your brethren and your children shall find compassion before them that lead them captive, so that they shall come again into this land, for the Lord, your God, is gracious and merciful and will not turn away His face from you if you return unto Him."

As a result of the king's exhortation, something akin to a religious revival swept the land. People flocked into the capital city from everywhere around and there was a seven days' feast; not since the time of King Solomon had the populace danced and sung with such joy: "Then the priests and the Levites arose and blessed the people; and their voice was heard and their prayer came up to His holy dwelling place, even unto heaven."

But now it was too late, even with such ecstasies of devotion, to turn aside the darkness clouding in the north. Fourteen years of statesmanship Hezekiah gave the throne, a reign of true kingliness, only and finally to confront a diabolical problem.

The king of Assyria was restless and prowling once more. His name was Sennacherib, and parents frightened their babies by saying: "Sennacherib will get you, if you don't go to sleep."

No ordinary enemy, this son of Sargon, one day to be murdered by his own sons. The monarch was to win naval and military victories to astound the world; he constructed canals and aqueducts, embanked the Tigris, and erected a magnificent palace at Nineveh, and he was now just becoming aware of his own powers, as he threw his might upon the southern kingdom. Into a very nimbus of fear the Assyrian came marching against the fenced cities along the northern frontier.

King Hezekiah resolved to stop at nothing to make peace. What is your price, Sennacherib? Name it and Hezekiah will pay. He will give you all the remnants of silver that are still left in Solomon's Temple. He will strip what little gold is left clinging to the ornamental doors. He will appease you, Sennacherib!

But the Assyrian officers told their king to stop his ears against the pleas of Hezekiah. Everywhere fright lay over the land of Judah—and no one knew what to do next.

It was then that King Hezekiah sent messengers to call on one of the greatest figures in the history of the world—the prophet Isaiah.

Let us look backward for a moment at the earlier days of Isaiah and at what had happened to him before he was called to counsel the king.

In the history of religious experience, of prophetic vision, of zeal for God, of the writing of great words, no name is more illustrious than Isaiah. The book which bears his name in the Bible contains sublime poetry. Always it is written in an exalted tone, that of a man who lived intimately with the Lord God, Whose major prophet he was. Isaiah sounded again the opportunity of the chosen people in a bewildered world; God had chosen them not out of mere fondness but for the supreme purpose of being His teacher to mankind, until the arrival of the Messiah.

This incomparable figure of prophecy was a Hebrew aristocrat who lived at the court of Jerusalem, a friend of royalty, a man of brains, and a reformer. In unsettled times he foresaw the dangerous future. Those days, roughly around 700 B.C., were crucial for Judah—with Israel already overrun, Samaria taken. He spoke out boldly for religious and political reform. In a very hurricane of magnificent phrases he opposed the schemes of Egypt to make the nation its cat's-paw in standing off Syria, yet for this course he was punished with great unpopularity and was called unpatriotic. But the wisdom of his ideas were ultimately to triumph in the reforms of King Hezekiah.

His words would most seize upon the imagination of the people. Those words forecast the fall of Jerusalem, in the time of Cyrus, when all the dire predictions of Isaiah had come to pass. Its chapters contain a wonderful prophecy of the coming of the Messiah.

The religious experience, what might well be called the conversion, of Isaiah, is a vivid episode in the Bible.

The prophet-statesman appeared on the Judean scene, to serve his country for more than forty years, saving them in desperate crises, as often from themselves as from enemies from without.

Living in the Tyropoean Valley, between two of whose hills Jerusalem is built, Isaiah was a young married man of wealthy connections. There was nothing devout or inspired about the young aristocrat until the day that his life was changed in Solomon's Temple. One moment he was there in the inner court, perfunctorily about some sacrifice; the next instant a trance had seized him. In the strange state in which he found himself, he seemed to be alone in the universe with his Maker, and in that majestic aloneness the earth was filled with the Lord God's blinding glory.

Isaiah was shaking with fear. But one of the little angels of the heavenly hierarchy, a seraph, flew down and touched his trembling lips with a burning coal, and the fiery heat of it did not hurt but healed him.

He heard the Voice from Eden, once again speaking in Judah:

"Whom shall I send, and who will go for Us?"

"Behold, me! Send me!" cried Isaiah in ecstasy.

"Go, tell this people," the Voice said.

Such was Isaiah's ordination. As he himself relates the facts:

"In the year that King Uzziah died, I saw the Lord sitting upon a throne, high and lifted up, and His train filled the Temple. Above it stood the seraphim: each one had six wings; with twain he covered his face, and with twain he covered his feet, and with twain he did fly. And one cried unto another, and said, Holy, holy, holy, is the Lord of Hosts: the whole earth is full of His glory.

"The posts of the door moved at the voice of him that cried, and the house was filled with smoke. Then said I, Woe is me! for I am a man of unclean lips, and I dwell in the midst of a people of unclean lips, for mine eyes have seen the King, the Lord of Hosts. Then flew one of the seraphim unto me, having a live coal in his hand, which he had taken with the tongs from off the altar, and he laid it on my mouth, and said, Lo, this has touched your lips; your iniquity is taken away, and your sin purged.

"Also I heard the Voice of the Lord, saying, Whom shall I send, and who will go for Us? Then said I, Here am I; send me. And He said, Go, and tell this people. You hear indeed, but understand not; you see indeed, but perceive not. Then said I, Lord, how long? And He answered, Until the cities be wasted without inhabitant, and the houses without man, and the land be utterly desolate, and the Lord have removed men far away, and there be a great forsaking in the midst of the land.

"The Lord spake also unto me again, saying, As this people refuses the waters of Shiloah that go softly, now, behold, the Lord brings up upon them the waters of the river, strong and many, even the king of Assyria, and all his glory; and He shall come up over all His channels, and go over all His banks; and He shall pass through Judah; He shall overflow and go over, He shall reach even to the neck; and the stretching out of His wings shall fill the breadth of your land, O Immanuel. Associate yourselves, O you people, and you shall be broken in pieces; and give ear, all you of far countries: gird yourselves, and you shall be broken. Take counsel together, and it shall come to nought; speak the word, and it shall not stand; for God is with us."

Such a man, convinced that he had been witness to divine revelation, could not be brought to compromise. Isaiah warned and defied one king after another. Himself a citizen of Jerusalem, Isaiah looked upon its persistent materialism, its pertinacious and ineradicable love of luxury, and its incurable lusting after strange gods, with the same aversion and anger as had been shown by those two preceding prophets, Amos and Hosea. Unceasingly Isaiah proclaimed the message— the holiness of Jehovah and the need to purify the morals of the nation. Imbued with an almost fanatic fire, he named his wife "the prophetess," and called his first son She'ar Yashub, meaning "A Remnant Shall Return," to remind the people of God's word, long ago, and of the power of a righteous leaven in the descendants of Abraham.

During the bad reign of Ahaz, Isaiah exerted himself to the utmost to influence the king toward good judgment, and always stood against appeasement, even of the unbearable Assyrian chief, Tiglath Pileser III, against subservience and loss of freedom. He orated "at the conduit of the upper pool," where he found Ahaz surrounded by his court counselors, plotting to eat the bread of the conquered. Quoting the Lord to the king, Isaiah cried:

"Take heed, and be quiet; fear not, neither be fainthearted for the two tails of these smoking firebrands . . . Thus says the Lord God, It shall not stand, neither shall it come to pass. . . . Ask you a sign of the Lord your God: ask it either in depth or in the height above."

But King Ahaz, young in judgment and influenced by doubting favorites, said:

"I will not ask, neither will I tempt the Lord."

Isaiah's confident challenge not being met, he spoke as if he saw the future with mystical clarity:

"Hear you now, O house of David: Is it a small thing for you to weary men, but will ye weary my God also?

"Therefore the Lord Himself shall give you a sign; Behold, a virgin shall conceive, and bear a Son, and shall call His name Immanuel."

This was the farthest reach of Isaiah's spiritual sight, a prophecy of the coming of Jesus.

But though Ahaz was plainly assured by God's prophet that he had nothing to fear, he went directly contrary to the inspired advice. He did pay tribute to Tiglath Pileser of Assyria. It was a fatal policy, to seek relief from national fear at the cost of self-respect, principle, and eventual subjugation.

Thus Isaiah was defeated by the human weakness for expediency. He had to content himself with a large sign which he set up in a public place, on which was written, "The Spoil Speeds, the Prey Hastes," and in sad memory he gave his second son that phrase for his name.

To his own generation, and all ages that came after, Isaiah brought a wealth of spiritual treasure. Some of his ancient sayings are in the very blood stream of modern phrasing:

"To what purpose is the multitude of your sacrifices unto Me? says the Lord. I am full of the burnt offerings of rams, and the fat of fed beasts; and I delight not in the blood of bullocks, or of lambs, or of goats. Bring no more vain oblations. . . .

"When you spread forth your hands I will hide My eyes from you; yes, when you make many prayers I will not hear; your hands are full of blood. Wash you, make you clean; put away the evil of your doings from before My eyes. Cease to do evil; learn to do well. Seek judgment, relieve the oppressed, judge the fatherless, plead for the widow."

Isaiah again predicted the coming of the Christ in these words:

"The people that walked in darkness have seen a great light. They that dwell in the land of the shadow of death, upon them has the light shined. . . . For unto us a Child is born, unto us a Son is given: and the government shall be upon His shoulder: and His name shall be called Wonderful, Counselor, The Mighty God, The Everlasting Father, The Prince of Peace."

And again:

"There shall come forth a rod out of the stem of Jesse, and a branch shall grow out of his roots, and the spirit of the Lord shall rest upon Him, the spirit of wisdom and understanding, the spirit of counsel and might, the spirit of knowledge and of the fear of the Lord; and shall make Him of quick understanding in the fear of the Lord.

"He shall not judge after the sight of His eyes, neither reprove after the hearing of His ears; but with righteousness shall He judge the poor, and reprove with equity for the meek of the earth. He shall smite the earth with the rod of his mouth, and with the breath of his lips shall he slay the wicked. Righteousness shall be the girdle of his loins, and faithfulness the girdle of his reins. The wolf shall dwell with the lamb, and the leopard shall lie down with the kid, and the calf and the young lion and the fatling together; and a little child shall lead them."

And it was Isaiah who predicted the day to come when men "shall beat their swords into ploughshares and their spears into pruning-hooks; nation shall not lift up sword against nation, neither shall they learn war any more."

And Isaiah also said:

"Come now, and let us reason together, says the Lord; though your sins be as scarlet they shall be as white as snow; though they be red like crimson, they shall be as wool. . . .

"Howl you, for the day of the Lord is at hand . . . I will punish the world for their evil, and the wicked for their iniquity; I will cause the arrogancy of the proud to cease, and lay low the haughtiness of the terrible.

"I will make a man more precious than fine gold.

"And Babylon, the glory of kingdoms, the beauty of the Chaldees, shall be as when God overthrew Sodom and Gomorrah. It shall never be inhabited, neither shall it be dwelt in from generation to generation; neither shall the Arabian pitch tent there; neither shall the shepherds make their fold there. . . .

"It shall come to pass that your choicest valleys shall be full of chariots, and the horsemen shall set themselves in array at the gate. You have seen the breaches of the city of David, that they are many; you have numbered the houses of Jerusalem, and the houses have you broken down to fortify the wall. In that day did the Lord God of Hosts call to weeping, and to mourning, and to girding with sackcloth; and, behold, joy and gladness, slaying oxen, and killing sheep, eating flesh, and drinking wine; let us eat and drink, for tomorrow we shall die. Behold, the Lord will carry you away with a mighty captivity. He will turn and toss you like a ball into a large country; there shall you die, and there the chariots of your glory shall be the shame of your Lord's house."

Chapter 36 THE ASSYRIAN COMES DOWN

ISAIAH did not thunder alone. Other admonishers were inspired, among them Micah, the Morasthite, native of a small town of Judah. Isaiah was an aristocrat, Micah was a peasant, with a knowing sympathy for farmers, constantly suffering eviction under warrants from greedy landlords. Micah's influence was very great, his general outlook broad and humane, and he was a pioneer in the dream of universal peace.

Some of his blasts of invective set a record for denunciation:

"Hear, I pray you, O heads of Jacob, and ye princes of the house of Israel; Is it not for you to know judgment? Who hate the good, and love the evil; who pluck off their skin from off them, and their flesh from off their bones; who also eat the flesh of my people, and flay their skin from off them; and they break their bones, and chop them in pieces, as for the pot, and as flesh within the cauldron! They shall cry unto the Lord, but He will not hear them: He will even hide His face from them at that time, as they have behaved themselves ill in their doings."

But Micah could be gentle, too, and winning with a soft and wonderful persuasion, as when he put his whole creed in a simple statement:

"What does Jehovah require of you—only to do justly, and to love mercy and to walk humbly with your God."

Whether Isaiah and Micah ever met is not recorded, but the peasant spokesman for God might easily have been the disciple of the aristocratic prophet who lived in the "Valley of Vision."

"How long? How long, O Lord?" Isaiah would cry, and Micah with him. But King Hezekiah did not take his prophets of doom too seriously. He thought he knew what he was doing, felt sure he could avoid playing mouse to the Assyrian cat; he would and could keep Judah free, by powerful foreign alliances.

But Isaiah, farseeing prophet, disapproved of these alliances, which actually suggested a conspiracy for war against Assyria. To show his disapproval of the intrigues stewing among several nations who had nothing in common except their fear and hatred, Isaiah, in obedience to the Lord, appeared one day at the door of his house and walked the streets of Jerusalem barefoot. He was portraying himself as a miserable captive, to illustrate personally how the loser of the imminent war would fare—the loser being Egypt, Ethiopia, and their smaller conspirators, including Judah. For three years Isaiah walked barefoot among the people, a living protest against unreliable and dangerous political alliances.

He was proved right when Sennacherib came down, capturing forty-six fortified cities.

Relics of those direful Assyrian victories are preserved for our late eyes to see. In the Oriental Institute of the University of Chicago there is a contemporary monument of the time of this conquering Sennacherib, a bas-relief on dark marble, showing the return of the soldiers, carrying the decapitated heads of their foes, and leading bound prisoners along with enslaved children and women in a march of triumph.

There is also the famous "prism of Sennacherib" to be seen in the British Museum; a clay hexagonal cylinder which gives this Assyrian king's own account of his campaign against Hezekiah, whom he scornfully describes as "a caged bird." While he verifies the Bible account, however, he leaves out the most important event—the miracle.

All signs pointed to the kingdom of Judah as the next target for the Assyrian, and King Hezekiah began to wonder if he might not better have a talk with Isaiah. To the astonishment of the king, the stalwart old agent of the Lord now advised the king to stand fast. By the power of the one true God, Isaiah insisted, the enemy would be blasted.

But as the armies of Sennacherib drew ever nearer, and his advance guards began throwing up towers and fortifications around the city, in obvious preparation for a siege, the king found it hard to share the holy man's confidence. In the turmoil of his thoughts he did one wise thing—he turned and implored help on his own account, beseeching the Lord concerning the king of Assyria, in the words of Isaiah: "He shall not come into this city, nor shoot an arrow there, nor come before it with a shield, nor cast a bank against it. . . . For I will defend this city, to save it, for Mine own sake, and for My servant David's sake."

These were astounding words, with destruction seeming to loom close, and the numbers of the Assyrian hosts as sands of the seashore. Any day, any hour now, the blow would fall. And then, in the very midst of King Hezekiah's doubts, it happened—a miracle unsurpassed in all the strange stories of Holy Writ.

During that time of breathless expectancy an angel of the Lord passed through the camp of the sleeping Assyrian troops and struck a blow that ended in one night the lives of 185,000 men.

Utterly demoralized, the rest of the army fled from the plague's invisible sword:

> The Assyrian came down like the wolf on the fold,
> And his cohorts were gleaming in purple and gold.

And the sheen of their spears was like stars on the sea,
Where the blue wave rolls nightly on deep Galilee.

Like the leaves of the forest when summer is green,
That host with their banners at sunset was seen;
Like the leaves of the forest when autumn has blown,
That host on the morrow lay withered and strown!

The people who had wandered so far from the Lord were closer than ever to the punishment of their infidelity—yet here, in the hour of their greatest danger, the power of God to help them was brilliantly displayed.

Never again was Sennacherib to strike against Jerusalem. While at worship in Nineveh, he was slain by his own sons. Awed and enormously relieved at what had happened to their seemingly invincible foe, the people of Judah hailed their prophet Isaiah. But the old seer was not misled. He knew his people. He knew their future. Isaiah saw his beloved Jerusalem saved only temporarily, he knew that retribution had only been postponed; suffering alone could purge the sins of Judah.

Not long after the massacre of the enemy armies King Hezekiah became ill, and his condition began to be rumored around. With guileful sympathy, Merodach-Baladan, the new ruler of Babylon, sent costly presents, and this action delighted the ailing king. Amid general amiability Hezekiah was coaxed to display to the Babylonian ambassadors all the accumulated treasures of Jerusalem. When the visitors had departed Isaiah questioned Hezekiah about them. From whence came they? Their purpose? The king showed the prophet how flattered he had been by the attention and praise of the men from Merodach-Baladan. But Isaiah's face was grave, his voice sorrowful:

"Behold, the days come, that all that is in your house, and that which your fathers have laid up in store unto this day, shall be carried into Babylon: nothing shall be left, says the Lord. And of your sons that shall issue from you, which you shall beget, shall they take away; and they shall be eunuchs in the palace of the king of Babylon."

In spite of his past experience with Isaiah, the ailing monarch did not want to believe this distressing forecast.

"Is it not good if peace and truth be in my days?" he protested, nor was he the last appeaser who believed he had bought "peace in our time."

Isaiah turned away with sad eyes. King and prophet parted, and nothing is heard of any more talk between them. Isaiah busied himself with his preaching, beginning now to tell the people that beyond their coming tribulation he foresaw the bright dawn of a new day of salvation, when the Messiah should come to serve and heal.

Thus he was reassuring the people when the well-intentioned King Hezekiah passed on.

The son who took his place on the throne, the Prince Manasseh, was the direct opposite of his father. Instinctively he seemed to relish everything that was vicious and evil. A born tyrant, he persecuted the prophets of Jehovah and rebuilt altars to heathen gods which his father had cast down. Even the precincts of the Temple which Solomon had dedicated to the Lord God were desecrated. And Manasseh shed innocent blood until "he had filled Jerusalem from one end to the other." Yet his reign was long; he was king from the age of twelve until he was sixty-four.

Legend argues that Isaiah was one of the wicked Manasseh's chief victims. According to those unverified, uninscribed traditions, the aged prophet, after more than forty years of holy service, wise statesmanship, and spiritual vision, was tied to a log of cedar and sawn in two. Such a horrible form of execution of the death sentence was certainly known to have been practiced, even as far back as the days of Saul and Samuel. And such is the strength of tradition in the East, one may well believe that being sawn in two was the fate of that invincible teller of truth called Isaiah.

It was Isaiah who gave substance and a sense of reality, of imminence, of impending arrival, to the Messianic hope. He said that the Son of God was coming to the world to redeem it from an impossible situation—"Surely, He has borne our griefs."

And in our own time there has been discovered a manuscript that immensely fortifies our faith in the accuracy and scrupulous fidelity of the old Bible texts. "The greatest Bible discovery of modern times," as it has been called, was a scroll of the Book of Isaiah found by a group of wandering Bedouins not far from the northwest end of the Dead Sea. This scroll, virtually identical with the Book of Isaiah as we have it in our Bibles today, has been scientifically proved to have been written down on the parchments before the time of the birth of Christ.

It was in 1947 that Arab goatherds found in a cave the sealed jars containing the scroll. Professor Carl H. Kraeling of Yale declared the newly found manuscripts triumphantly affirm the authenticity of the traditional texts. On this point an anonymous writer in the New York *Herald Tribune* made an interesting observation:

> It is fortunate that the old scribes and copyists were necessarily forced to employ tools and materials that stand up against time almost as well as their writings. The leather scrolls are still intact; the inscriptions legible enough to be read in photographs. An ancient custom decreed that disused or mutilated copies of the scriptures must be buried rather than destroyed; that is why such finds as that just made are still possible . . . undoubtedly there will be other enlightening discoveries made beneath the earth of Palestine.

It is as if we could reach out hands across the centuries and touch the major prophet, the inspired Isaiah.

Chapter 37   THE BOY KING

I T S E E M S an odd coincidence, too, that within a few years after the death of King Hezekiah—about the start of the sixth century before Christ—another manuscript was found in Judah that was to have a profound effect upon the people. This is how that discovery came about:

The affliction of the times, the apostasy, the infidelity, the turning back to God and then away from Him again, all were going on as usual. There were unspeakable abominations under Manasseh, and after Manasseh was gone his son, the young King Amon, was murdered and then there came to the throne a boy called Josiah.

Between Rehoboam, the long-ago and very first king of Judah, and Josiah, the boy king, there lay a period of more than three centuries. Now at the end of those three hundred and fifty years the kingdom of David had sunk to a new low level. Not only did the great soul and words of Isaiah fail to have any permanent effect on the population; even confronted with the terrifying lesson of Israel, the northern kingdom, wiped from the face of the earth for its persistent sins, Judah still clung to unregenerate ways.

Little Josiah was eight years old when he was placed on the throne once occupied by the majestic shepherd lad of Bethlehem. Of course he had to be guided by older heads and hands, but by the time he had turned sixteen the royal boy showed a zealous spirit for the restoration of Jehovah as the only true God. And there was no outside disapproval; instead, there was opportunity for religious leadership and reform in Judah now. For the Assyrians, who from without really dominated the politics of the kingdom, were indifferent about such matters, being themselves harassed by onrushing hordes of barbarian Scythians. Indeed, the great Assyrian Empire was trembling before a ferocity that seemed more than a match for its own; the Assyrians were getting at last a taste of their own bitter medicine.

In the eighteenth year of Josiah's rule, with no threat against peace on the horizon of Judah, the high priest Hilkiah was given orders by the young king. The Temple of Solomon must again be repaired. For what purpose? For the sole purpose of restoring undivided worship of the one true God.

Meanwhile King Josiah had also commanded a general abolition of idolatry. Everywhere within the borders of Judah images and altars of Baal were burned to rubble. Human sacrifices, a son or daughter to Moloch, a murderous practice which the late King Manasseh had encouraged, were forbidden, as were other unspeakable rites. The very dust of the places polluted by heathen worship was carried off and strewn deep in the valley of Kidron. And the golden bulls and calves set up long before King Jeroboam in Bethel and Dan were pulled down and melted.

Josiah was twenty-six years old when the repair work on Solomon's Temple was begun. Even from the poorest of his subjects there came voluntary contributions; yes, and also from the remnant of the ten tribes left up in Israel. The long-neglected sanctuary of Solomon's genius was to take on again some of its lost beauty and grandeur.

Still to come was the most thrilling event of all this period of belated reformation. One day Hilkiah, the high priest, found in a closed and forgotten chamber of the Temple a dusty manuscript, or scroll. It was a copy of early Scriptures assembled under the title of "The Law of Jehovah given to Moses." No one is quite sure today if all the Pentateuch was included in this scroll, or merely certain parts. In whole or in part, the sacred words lifted the hearts of the people—sacred words beyond all price. After so many years a reverent reading of the text brought home poignantly to the people their supreme offense of neglect and indifference to their heritage from the one true God.

A divine message had for so long been treated as so much trash!

Hilkiah commanded his scribe Shaphan at once to read the documents to the king. As its promises and curses were solemnly read to him, King Josiah was shaken with consternation. Clearly enough he saw that Judah by its centuries of waywardness had forfeited great promises of the past and had earned only curses. In his prolonged agitation, King Josiah even drew into consultation a prophetess, Huldah —but she could give him no comfort. Woe, woe, woe—such was all the burden of her soothsaying.

Nevertheless, it was decided to have the law read aloud again in the presence of the people. The covenant with Jehovah was renewed. Also the Feast of the Passover was to be reinstituted and kept religiously. Since Moses' day it had fallen from remembrance except when Joshua held the memorial feast. Now they would go back to the forgotten piety of long ago. King Josiah saw to it that all these things were done.

Yet, even so, the future seemed ever darker. Could centuries of backsliding, continuous breaking of God's laws, be overlooked, and with no retribution exacted? True, the Lord God had always been quick to forgive the sinner. But all indications were that He was wrathful at Judah "because of all the provocations that Manasseh had provoked Him withal." And Jehovah had said, so Isaiah had reported: "I will remove Judah also out of My sight, as I have removed Israel."

The virtue of Josiah was not enough to fend off punishment for his people, and new prophets arose to make that fact clear. There was Zephaniah, who pronounced doom upon all wicked nations, doom at the hands of the barbarous Scythians, people who had had no benefits and promises such as the enlightenment the Lord had given to the favored people. Behold, the Scythians in their terrible chariots of wheeled knives were coming closer to Jerusalem! Thus the prophet Zephaniah, in that ominous time, about 630 B.C., first began to call upon the people to "change their minds," to "repent."

And Nahum, another prophet, added his voice to Zephaniah's impassioned orations. Nahum drew a marrow-curdling picture of the approaching downfall of the highly civilized city of Nineveh. He foresaw it taken by the Babylonians, a prediction which actually came to pass in 612 B.C., while King Josiah still sat on the Judean throne. In a frenzy of joy and poetry Nahum hailed the end of Judah's century-long enemy on the Euphrates:

"Woe to the bloody city! It is all full of lies and robbery; the prey departs not; the noise of a whip, and the noise of the rattling of the wheels, and of the prancing horses, and of the jumping chariots. The horseman lifts up both the bright sword and the glittering spear; and there is a multitude of slain, and a great number of carcasses; and there is no end of their corpses; they stumble upon their corpses. Behold, I am against you, says the Lord of hosts . . . And I will cast abominable filth upon you, and make you vile, and will set you as a gazing stock. And it shall come to pass, that all they that look upon you shall flee from you and say, Nineveh is laid waste; who will bemoan her? whence shall I seek comforters for you? . . . There is no healing of your bruise; your wound is grievous; all that hear the bruit of you shall clap the hands over you; for upon whom has not your wickedness passed continually?"

Soon a prophet greater than either Zephaniah or Nahum was to come forth and stand by his people and Jerusalem in their worst despair and desolation. This was Jeremiah, the great one, who served selflessly and valiantly "in the days of Josiah, Jehoiakim, and up to the eleventh year of Zedekiah, unto the carrying of Jerusalem captive."

But Jeremiah's forty years of labor for the Lord came mainly after the days of Josiah. The king's earnest efforts met only with heartiest approval from the young prophet, though he was still only a fledgling priest of a village some three miles northeast of Jerusalem.

For most of his reign King Josiah ruled in peace, but finally he took up arms against the invading troops of Pharaoh Necho II of Egypt. These invaders were on their way northward to join forces with baited Assyria. When Josiah was killed in the famous Battle of Megiddo he was just thirty-nine years old.

Thus died the last king of Judah who merited the name of a good and true man. In his prophecies Jeremiah lamented for him, and "the hill of Megiddo" became a symbol in the public mind for the eclipse of the last gleam of the people's glory.

Chapter 38 THE FALL OF JERUSALEM

T H E last days of the southern kingdom were degraded almost beyond belief.

It was as if a whole nation, with the few exceptions, had gone insane. The people seemed to have no sense of reality about what was happening in the world. They could not grasp the fact that the Battle of Megiddo was for them a disastrous defeat. When the Egyptian Pharaoh, Necho II, pressed on north, without pausing to punish the Judeans, they acted as if they had won the war.

In their mistaken elation they proceeded to choose a new king to rule over them, as if Necho II would have nothing to say about the succession. They chose Prince Jehoahaz, a son of the slain Josiah, but no sooner was he crowned than Necho snared the kingling in a pit, and then led him off with a ring in his lips.

A king of Judah with a ring in his lips!

In place of the prisoner Necho put Jehoiakim, the brother of Jehoahaz, on condition that the Judean king bow head and knee to Egypt and pay, in yearly tribute, one hundred talents of silver and one talent of gold—equal to about a quarter of a million American dollars today. Under that burden all Jerusalem groaned. But worse was forthcoming, for the new King Jehoiakim, puffed up by his own importance, began maintaining a false grandeur with lavish extravagance. In an orgy of spending public money he built himself a gorgeous new palace, all with forced labor.

Thus, as so often before, the righteousness and fear of the Lord that King Josiah had restored went into the dust heap, as once more the people turned back to idolatry. Their practices became more obscene than ever. At this time the idol called Astarte, the so-called "Queen of Heaven," was worshiped, especially by women. In Solomon's Temple, Baal was worshiped as in the days before Josiah. Horrible to remember now, human sacrifice, in the frightful form of burning children alive as an offering to Moloch, was again revived in the valley of Hinnom. King Jehoiakim sanctioned this rampant apostasy, and both the Temple of Jehovah and the offices of government were undermined, rotted, and corrupted.

Yet strangely, in this saturnalia of paganism, the priests and the people still continued to believe in the inviolability of the sanctuary. While the Temple stood in Jerusalem they were certain in their faith that the city could never be taken by a foe.

It was because of this fallacy that Jeremiah was electrified into action.

Let it be said that although today his name is a synonym for denunciation and scolding on a cosmic scale, Jeremiah was at heart a mild soul. Because he was gentle, he could see clearly and report what he saw—and no wonder that his very soul exploded at such sights as his eyes beheld. Like most of the others, Jeremiah is known by various names; some call him Jeremias, and some just Jeremy—but all the names mean the same thing in Hebrew—"God Casts."

And like other men who insisted on seeing and speaking clearly, Jeremiah was detested by many of the very people he wanted to save. In addition he had against him the same kind of privileged caste which Jesus was to denounce, six hundred years later. In that early day Jeremiah saw that the letter of the law kills where its spirit quickens. He was not satisfied with mere forms and ceremonies; he preached the religion of the inner life. Nor had he been very hopeful when the young King Josiah announced that he was going to reform the life of the people; the prophet smiled doubtfully through his tangled beard.

From the outset it was clear to him that these reforms would be in the letter of the law, not in the hearts of the people, which was what really mattered. Already he had foreseen the invasions of the Scythians and again after the terrible defeat of Megiddo he began again his outbursts and prognostications. Unless they reformed, he told the Judeans, God would come upon them again in His wrath, and when Nebuchadnezzar did, indeed, march down, Jeremiah hailed him as God's appointed scourge, wreaking upon the people the vengeance of Heaven, readily deserved.

Naturally this confirmation made Jeremiah even more unpopular. The king cut his book to shreds, and later he was flogged, imprisoned, and narrowly escaped death.

Not these or other persecutions could hush the voice of Jeremiah. Still he preached that political revolution was worse than foolish and that the only revolution worth while must occur in the human heart. When Jerusalem fell Jeremiah would be taken into Egypt to be heard of no more.

We know him best from his hired scribe and companion, Baruch, who helped the prophet write his wonderful poems. Jeremiah also wrote the Book of Lamentations. His point of view is as important today as it was twenty-five hundred years ago.

One morning Jeremiah addressed the assembled people in the Temple court and riddled with scorn their belief in the protection of the house of God when, all the while, their lives were a living insult to the Most high. He quoted the Lord to them:

"I will do to the house which is called in My name, as I did to Shiloh."

Which words recalled the destruction of the sanctuary by the Philistines in Samuel's day.

To Jeremiah's audience this quotation was blasphemy, a crime punishable by death. Jeremiah's death was actually demanded; only the intervention of a powerful friend saved the prophet's neck that day.

But the religious leaders continued to scorn Jeremiah as a false prophet; they jeered at his prediction of a scourge of Scythians which had not come to pass. But before long this mockery by the priests was to change entirely, for soon it became unmistakably clear that mild Jeremiah had been picked out by God to be His chief spokesman during the years of the decline and downfall of Judah. The Voice had spoken to Jeremiah when he was twenty-four years old:

"Before you came forth out of the womb I sanctified you and I ordained you a prophet unto the nations."

"Ah, Lord God! behold, I cannot speak: for I am a child," protested the young man.

"Say not, I am a child," said the Lord, "for you shall go to all that I shall send you, and whatsoever I command you, you shall speak. Be not afraid of their faces: for I am with you to deliver you."

And it seemed to Jeremiah as if he could feel the Lord touch his mouth with His hand:

"Behold, I have put My words in your mouth. See, I have this day set you over the nations and over the kingdoms, to root out, and pull down, and to destroy, and to throw down, to build, and to plant."

Surely that was appointing Jeremiah His fully accredited representative on earth. Furthermore, Jehovah warned his servant not to marry—the families of Judah were to be consumed with sword and famine.

"Enter not into the house of mourning," said the Lord. "I will cause to cease out of this place in your eyes, and in your days, the voice of mirth, and of the voice of gladness, the voice of the bridegroom, and the voice of the bride."

Yet as events fell out, Jeremiah's first assertion about the future failed to come true. Not until much later would people realize that Jeremiah had not failed in his first prophecy; that instead he had foreseen with the greatest clarity. The Scythian barbarians had indeed been on their way to lay waste and pillage all Judah. But they had been bought off by Egyptian spies, appeased and sidetracked. This interception was a long time coming to light. Meanwhile priests and people were sure Jeremiah was a mere pretender and charlatan. Kings, princes, and military men were to oppose him with tongue and hand. Again and again he was imprisoned and put in stocks in a dungeon.

But changes were coming to pass.

Assyria, the terrible, was waning in power when Jeremiah began his ministry. Nineveh had already fallen to the Chaldeans, an aggressive

Semitic people of Babylon, and to their allies, the Medes, in 612 B.C. Seven years later Necho II, at the Battle of Carchemish, was thoroughly beaten by Nebuchadnezzar, the Babylonian monarch. Thus the Chaldean became the newest overlord of Judah.

But what did the change matter? Just an exchange of tyrants; that was the general opinion among the Hebrews. Only Jeremiah, reading the future, saw otherwise.

In Nebuchadnezzar the prophet recognized the agent of the Lord for the punishment and purification of Judah. At last he had arrived! So Jeremiah declared now on every occasion. Naturally such tirades and pronouncements of doom fomented fresh animosity against him. No one would believe him, and the baffled prophet sighed:

"Can the Ethiopian change his skin, or the leopard his spots, then may you also do good, that are accustomed to evil."

Nevertheless, Jeremiah continued doggedly to preach, trying to save people in spite of themselves. Even amid hopelessness he was holding out hope. If they would only repent, change their minds, and go back to the God of ever-loving-kindness. At a corner of the market place he mourned:

"The heart is deceitful above all things, and desperately wicked: who can know it?"

His frank and fearless talk, delivered at every opportunity, finally evoked the serious displeasure of King Jehoiakim. By royal command Jeremiah had to withdraw from public speaking. Privately, however, he dictated many sermons to his scribe and friend Baruch, and then, in open defiance of the king, he caused them to be read aloud on a feast day in 603 B.C. This defiance created a sensation. Certain princes who heard the full message were profoundly stirred. They declared it must be read to the king also, but as a precaution, they warned Jeremiah and Baruch to go into hiding. They knew their sovereign.

The sermons, true and wise, pointing out the pathways of righteousness and reform, angered King Jehoiakim to such extent that he seized a knife, cut up the scroll into small pieces, and flung them on a charcoal fire. And he ordered that the author be immediately arrested.

But Jeremiah and his scribe had fled to safety beyond the king's jurisdiction, remaining out of his reach until his death, which was not long deferred.

For King Jehoiakim next tried to betray Babylon, which had made him its puppet. Although publicly forswearing allegiance to the rival Egypt, he connived in secret with the Pharaoh. At the first whiff of this treachery Nebuchadnezzar took action. It was not direct; he withheld his might and simply aroused neighbor countries against Judah, until the kingdom soon was beset, again at war.

This disaster should have been a warning to King Jehoiakim but he remained false to Babylon. Then the dictator acted on his own behalf; watchful waiting over, Nebuchadnezzar took the field, laying siege to Jerusalem in 597 B.C. And sometime during his assault on the capital perched high on the wedge-shaped rock, the foolish puppet king of Judah died, though it was not known where or how. Tradition says variously that he was murdered and his body thrown into the streets of Jerusalem; or that he was enticed into the enemy camp on a pretense and slain. Jeremiah had predicted an evil end for him:

"Therefore thus says the Lord concerning Jehoiakim the son of Josiah king of Judah: They shall not lament for him, saying, Ah, my brother! or, Ah, sister! they shall not lament for him, saying, Ah, lord! or, Ah, his glory! He shall be buried with the burial of an ass, drawn and cast forth beyond the gates of Jerusalem."

The besieged city was temporarily saved from complete destruction by its timely surrender. This act was ordered at the word of Prince Jehoiachin, son of the vanished king, but the young man was not rewarded with the throne for his pains. At the royal nod of Nebuchadnezzar, another of Josiah's sons, Zedekiah, was made puppet king. But there was no mercy in this arrangement.

The captivity of the people of Judah at last was upon them. Misery followed upon misery. Prince Jehoiachin, with his mother, members of his court, the other princes, and about ten thousand of the leading citizens of Judah, were bound with cords and taken away from their homes, walking all the way to Babylonia. There Jehoiachin was to remain a prisoner for thirty-six years.

Unrecognized at this grim moment in their experience, there walked among these deported people a priest who was to become their spiritual mainstay. The Lord could be trusted to provide help and comfort, then, as always. He was a prophet of extraordinary visions and a preserve of religious forms of Hebrew worship. His name was Ezekiel, of whom there will be more to tell.

Meanwhile Jeremiah felt it was safe to return to desolate Jerusalem under Zedekiah and renew his ministry for God to the new vassal state, which was Judah. More opposition than ever awaited him in the conquered capital. His conviction, still strongly expressed, that Nebuchadnezzar was an instrument in the hand of the Lord for their deserved chastisement was bitter medicine; he became as unpopular as a plague. At last Zedekiah, unable to scowl him into silence, threw him down into an empty, noisome cistern and left him there to die.

But Jeremiah did not die. Rescued from a living death, he was pulled out of the cistern by a friend; he was next arrested and consigned to imprisonment. In his cell Jeremiah, tormented to the limit of his great endurance, cried:

"I am in derision daily, every one mocks me," and "Woe is me, my mother, that you have borne me, a man of strife and a man of contention to the whole earth. Cursed be the day wherein I was born: let not the day wherein my mother bare me be blessed."

But under all his personal despair there burned indestructible hope. Yes, truly, God would punish the people for sin, but He would also, and just as surely, care for His people again, if and when they were cleansed.

The Voice had said to him:

"And I will give them an heart to know Me, that I am the Lord: and they shall be My people, and I will be their God: for they shall return unto Me with their whole heart."

Jeremiah had also to ponder on what the Lord had said to him of two baskets of figs, one of good fruit, the other bad. The former represented the exiles in Babylon, the latter those Judeans who were left in Jerusalem under Zedekiah. So the prophet deduced that in God's sight the exiles, not the stay-at-homes, must be the seed and hope of the future. Therefore the exiles must be patient, sensible, and make the best of their lot until the appointed hour of liberation, a time known only to God. Jeremiah wrote a letter of advice to the Babylonian captives in which, speaking for the Voice, he said:

"Build houses and dwell in them and plant gardens and eat the fruit of them. Take wives and multiply and be not diminished; and seek the welfare of the land whither I have carried you into exile, and pray God for it; for in its prosperity rests your own prosperity."

As Jeremiah foresaw it, the exile would last over a period of seventy years. Meanwhile the situation looked desperate among the "bad figs" in the basket of Jerusalem. King Zedekiah, himself obsessed with a treacherous idea, fancied he saw a chance to rebel successfully against Babylon when the Egyptian Pharaoh, Psammetichus II, invaded Palestine. This aggression brought about a widespread revolt in the country, in 588 B.C., and King Zedekiah joined the uprising.

Now or never, he thought. And it was never.

Infuriated beyond all bounds, Nebuchadnezzar a second time besieged Jerusalem. For two brave stubborn years the city held out against him, but succumbed at last. When it surrendered, in 586 B.C., all but the dregs of the population were deported. Virtually the whole nation was now prisoner in Babylonian exile.

The Holy City was wrecked. The Temple of Solomon was burned to the ground, flaming symbol of the end of Judah. What treasures were left from various lootings were confiscated for the adornment of Babylon. Feckless King Zedekiah tried to escape, but he was caught and carried off in chains. Guards put out his eyes but just before they blinded him they forced him to watch while his sons were stoned to death.

After enduring for 427 years, David's kingly line was ended.

Into the rubbled waste that was now Jerusalem, as he and Hosea had both foreseen, Jeremiah was released from prison by the Chaldeans, conquerors from Babylon, who felt quite friendly to him. They offered the choice of leaving or remaining. Jeremiah decided to stay with the ruins. He would help bind up the city's wounds. To Jeremiah the true religion was everlasting, and he was sure that in God's own time His chosen people would be restored to grace.

And Jeremiah said to the Jews who were being marched away as captive slaves for Babylon:

"When you get there, you must read these words again, and remember what God says about that beautiful country. And when you have read this book, you shall bind a stone to it, and throw it into the river Euphrates, and say, Thus shall Babylon sink and shall not rise."

The Chaldeans made Gedaliah, a man of exemplary character, the governor of devastated Jerusalem. As if they were not in enough trouble already, the remaining Jews next learned that during the night the new governor had been assassinated. The Hebrew remnant of the population was terrified. What reprisals might not they expect from the Chaldeans, with such a provocation for vengeance?

"What shall we do?" they cried to Jeremiah in their extremity.

After prayerful meditation, communing with God, the prophet told them that the Lord wanted them to remain where they were, in spite of the fact that they, meanwhile, had set their hearts on seeking refuge in Egypt. But he was speaking against their wishful thinking, and they decided to disbelieve him. They denounced him as being prejudiced, with collaborationist leanings toward the Chaldeans. Threatening him bodily, they compelled him to flee to the land of the Nile, a region he had begged them to stay away from.

As in Jerusalem, so in Egypt, Jeremiah caused new anger and dismay to his compatriots. One day they beheld him carrying large stones to lay before the royal palace in Tahpanhes. Questioned, he told them they were to be a base for the throne of Nebuchadnezzar, who would also conquer Egypt. In this fashion he taught the refugees that their flight from stricken Jerusalem had not removed them from the long reach of their chastiser.

To show their disgust for the message of the prophet of God, the discomfited Hebrews in Egypt turned to worshiping idols—the idolatrous virus still in their blood—with Astarte their favorite. For this, Jeremiah predicted their extermination. Let Jeremiah rave! And that is the last we hear of the great prophet. Legend says that he was stoned to death by his own people in Egypt, who could endure no longer his prognostications and rebukes:

"Therefore hear ye the word of the Lord, all Judah that dwell in the land of Egypt. . . . Behold, I will watch over them for evil, and not for good: and all the men of Judah that are in the land of Egypt shall be consumed by the sword and by the famine, until there be an end of them."

And the future was to show how attentively the old man had been listening to the Voice of the Lord God—and how clearly he had looked into the future.

BOOK SEVEN

The Babylonian Captivity

Chapter 39   EZEKIEL AND THE WORDS OF ISAIAH

WHERE NOW were all the dreams of heaven for the great experiment with a chosen people? First Israel and now Judah had become broken nations and there seemed to be little waiting for them in the inglorious future: Where now the inspiration of Moses, the brilliance of David, the wise rule of Solomon?

There is only the final fall of the people and their dispersion.

Alexander will overpower them; the king of Egypt will steal them for slaves by the hundred thousand. Solomon's Temple in ruins, and much worse is to come upon the people who had the smile of God upon them and turned their backs against Him—as many still did, although captives in Babylon.

What was it like in Babylon?

For one hundred and fifty years the people of the ten lost tribes of Israel, the northern kingdom, had been prisoners in a foreign land. Now many from Judah, the southern kingdom, were also taken into exile, uprooted from a beloved land. This was the last, sad state of the children whose thousands of years flowed back to the garden of Adam and Eve. Yet it was not, at least at first, a reign of terror under which they were compelled to live.

In their daily lives they were not objectionably circumscribed in Babylon. The policy of the government toward captives, especially before the destruction of Jerusalem, was enlightened and even generous. In this attitude the Babylonians rejected the cruel practices of the Assyrians when they were in power. Living amidst the magnificence and affluence of Babylon, the Hebrew exiles pursued opportunities in business with little hindrance. They were allowed to retain their own religion, to assemble freely, and to speak their native tongue in public as well as in private.

The educated among them could not escape the realization that, although prisoners, they were in the cultural center of the known world, with schools and famous savants, and many advantages of progress.

And to live in Babylon itself was like a mystical dream, for it was a place of beauty as well as strength. Its glittering palaces and temples, its courts and open spaces and thousands upon thousands of ample dwellings, its coiling streets and many bazaars, all were surrounded by five miles of wall, one hundred feet high, with a hundred bronze gates and the famous hanging gardens with their blazing reds, yellows, and greens. Those city walls were eighty feet wide, broad enough for chariot races, a marvel of construction. The gardens were a sign of the fertility of the land, watered by innumerable canals and channels of irrigation. Crops of every conceivable kind were plenteous.

The walls of the great palace of Nebuchadnezzar were twenty-four-yards thick. But it was his hanging gardens that people talked about most; they were counted among the seven wonders of the world. The king had built them for his Median wife-queen to console her for the absence of her native mountains. Could Nebuchadnezzar have been looking at those "wonders" when he bragged: "Is not this the great Babylon that I have built?"

But that was before he was smitten by the wrath of Heaven and made to be like an animal eating grass for his pride.

In Nebuchadnezzar's capital the exiles were well treated but they were unhappy. They wanted, as they wanted nothing else in the world, to be taken back home. The glories of Babylon were to them as nothing at all. They thirsted for home, were famished for it, yet no clear realization seemed even yet to have overwhelmed them that their captivity was the result of their outrageous behavior to their Creator, their Father in heaven.

"They have sown the wind and they shall reap the whirlwind," Hosea had said, when he had pleaded with the people, having heard the Voice: "Come, let us return unto the Lord."

And Joel, who had told them that their young men should see visions and their old men should dream dreams, might well have added:

"Of what good are the dreams, what hope in the visions, if you have eyes and do not see, ears and do not listen?"

Amos had warned them that God would "turn your feasts into mourning and your songs into lamentations"—but now that it had happened, the meaning still escaped them—or most of them. The plaint of captive men and their wives and children, the lamentations of the homesick, are preserved for us, like living cries recorded, in the Book of Lamentations of the Bible.

From where would enlightenment and consolation come now? Who could halt the final crumbling of faith? Who but that obscure, goodhearted priest of the true and living God? One man among the first ten thousand persons, citizens of rank and ability who had been carried off to Babylon, Ezekiel, ardent admirer and follower of the prophet Jeremiah.

Ezekiel's, too, was a queer story.

Settling in Babylon, he had been in exile for five years before his call came "in the land of the Chaldeans by the river Chebar." On the green banks of that alien stream Ezekiel had beheld an awe-inspiring vision. He saw the throne of God in a dark storm cloud, flashing with lightnings, and he heard the sound of rushing waters. The throne was borne by four winged creatures, like men yet unlike them, for while the heads were, indeed, those of men, they were also the heads of a lion, an ox, and an eagle. An Assyrian cast of a protecting spirit image, with the body of a lion, wings of an eagle, horns of a bull, and the head of a man, quite like those described by Ezekiel, is on exhibition in the Harvard Semitic Museum.

Ezekiel's mystical throne had four glittering wheels, on the rims of which revolved a multitude of eyes. These four wheels, he learned, represented the four corners of the world, and the eyes were the stars of heaven.

It was the first of Ezekiel's many strange visions in which symbols expressed esoteric ideas for the prophet to interpret.

At sight of the heavenly throne, Ezekiel fell on his face, but the Voice of Jehovah commanded:

"Son of man, stand upon your feet, and I will speak with you."

Arising, the prophet listened attentively and was told that he must devote himself to the guidance and comforting of fellow countrymen in exile; he must offer consolation without fear or favor, declaring the truth no matter how sad or bitter. In the end it would be sweet as honey.

Ezekiel was then given a scroll which contained what he was to preach and what he must do thereafter.

For seven days the newly ordained prophet was in a state of stunned torpor as the result of his vision. But on the seventh he listened to the Voice again:

"Son of man, I make you a watchman in the house of the Lord."

Then Ezekiel girded his loins, for he knew that he was ready. First and foremost, he began to teach his fellow captives in exile the concept of individual responsibility to God, to society, and to man. Sin was not communal, as the majority had fancied; sin was individual.

Repentance and salvation must also be individual, Ezekiel explained. Every man must stand or fall by himself. With the Lord's word in his mouth, Ezekiel had the audacity to go far beyond the olden notion that "the fathers have eaten sour grapes, and the children's teeth are set on edge." Each person, he insisted, is rewarded or punished for his own deeds, not for those of another.

During a heartbreaking period of about twenty-three years Ezekiel was the real pastor of the exiled flock.

When Ezekiel began his ministry in Babylon, Jerusalem had not yet been destroyed, and Zedekiah was still a puppet king under the suzerainty of Nebuchadnezzar. And half of Ezekiel's prophecies were concerned with the coming downfall of the beloved city of Jerusalem —a prophecy which was terribly disheartening for his hearers, who were anxious for release and return just as Jeremiah had foreseen.

To all the captives, nevertheless, there was no place on earth like Mother Jerusalem, from which they were separated—"and for how long, O Lord? How long?"

At first, even when he felt the invisible mantle of prophecy fall upon him, Ezekiel could give them little comfort. Right up to the fall and ruin of the Holy City, Ezekiel was largely a prophet of doom, drawing his forecasts from weird, apocalyptic visions and interpreting them in dramatic monologues. But after the destruction of Jerusalem he became a prophet of restoration.

In this consoling role he reached a height of marvelous imagery in his vision of the Valley of Dry Bones, symbols of a people buried in exile. In it the Lord challenged:

"Son of man, can these bones live?"

And Ezekiel answered: "O Lord God, You know."

"Prophesy upon these bones, and say unto them, O you dry bones, hear the word of the Lord. Thus says the Lord God unto these bones: Behold, I will cause breath to enter into you, and you shall live. . . . So I prophesied as I was commanded; and as I prophesied, there was a noise, and behold a shaking, and the bones came together, bone to his bone. . . . Thus says the Lord, Come from the four winds, O breath, and breathe upon these slain, that they may live. So I prophesied as

He commanded me, and the breath came into them, and they lived, and stood upon their feet, an exceeding great army. Then He said unto me, Son of man, these bones are the whole house of Israel. . . . Therefore prophesy and say unto them, Thus says the Lord God: Behold, O my people, I will open your graves, and cause you to come up out of your graves, and bring you into the land of Israel."

Ezekiel also developed the idea of God as the Good Shepherd, Who would gather together His scattered flock and bring them home to happiness, if they would but repent and become worthy. And he taught: "We love God because He first loved us."

But the people, the exiles, so dense, so childlike, were more interested in the vision of a restored Jerusalem, its glorious Temple rising again from dust. In vivid detail Ezekiel told of a coming formalized order of priesthood, and the creation of a perfect theocracy, the dream of their forefathers of old. The harmony and welfare of the nation could come only when the political state was subject to ecclesiastic governance. Lifted into ecstatic trance, Ezekiel saw God Himself as the Shepherd of Israel, and under Him His servant David (another name for the Messiah) reigning in the new Jerusalem.

To this day his prophecies are a challenge to the skeptical mind, if only for the fact that his remarkable prediction concerning the downfall of Egypt is within the power of the most ordinary observer to confirm in its complete historical fulfillment.

Elders came to Ezekiel regularly for instructions and advice. The people listened reverently to his sermons, often acted out dramatically in the manner of Jeremiah. He did not spare their feelings or mitigate their faults, especially hammering at their hardness of heart and their willfulness.

Ultimately his sermons, carefully dated and preserved, became the seed of a religious revival. For Ezekial was the true forerunner of Ezra, who was to re-establish the worship of Israel in the Temple of Jerusalem when it was rebuilt. The old spirit of Deuteronomy was strong in Ezekial, and all its laws and forms were his natural creed.

When Ezekiel died we are not told. But some years after the delivery of his prophecies, about 570 B.C., things began to change.

The exiled heir to the throne of Judah, Jehoiachin, was released from his prison by Evil-Merodach, the Babylonian monarch then ruling. Only a few years ago testimony was dug up by archaeologists to confirm the story of King Jehoiachin's imprisonment. The records were found on unearthed cuneiform tablets—there were three hundred of them and more—reclaimed near the Ishtar Gate in the ruins of Babylon. This was a contemporary record of the thirty-seven years of the king's captivity.

Now Jehoiachin was an elderly man. As if in inexplicable apology for his long immurement in prison, the king of Babylon gave him a place of honor; "set his throne above the thrones of the kings that were with him in Babylon." And inexplicably, too, for the rest of his days Jehoiachin was pensioned royally.

With the death of Ezekiel, the people turned more and more to the great counsellors of the past, and especially to Isaiah.

That prophet's spiritual sight had seen far into the future that was now the present but he had not dwelt on punishment and retribution. Instead he was passionately sympathetic to the troubled people, so desperately wanting to be free.

"Comfort ye, comfort ye, my people," is his opening message.

He sees Palestine a land of desolated cities, Jerusalem in "heaps," the Temple gone. He sees Zion as a childless widow. The Hebrews are scattered in misery—nobodies. True, some of the exiles had become prosperous, but not many; the great majority suffered and struggled in poverty. These poor must be given cheer; they must glimpse a bright new hope, shining ahead. The seer's lofty thought and enthusiastic confidence in coming redemption were a fountain of solace for weary, disheartened people. He depicted their captive nation as one to be exalted in some indefinite future, above all other nations:

"Says the Lord:

"And kings shall be your nursing fathers, and queens your nursing mothers: they shall bow down to you with their faces toward the earth, and lick up the dust of your feet. . . .

"Speak you comfortably to Jerusalem, and cry unto her that her warfare is accomplished, that her iniquity is pardoned; for she has received of the Lord's hand double for all her sins. The voice of him that cries, in the wilderness: Prepare ye the way of the Lord, make straight in the desert a highway for our God.

"Every valley shall be exalted, and every mountain and hill shall be made low; the crooked shall be made straight, and the rough places plain; the glory of the Lord shall be revealed, and all flesh shall see it together, for the mouth of the Lord has spoken it.

"Behold My servant, whom I uphold; Mine elect, in whom My soul delights. I have put My spirit upon him; he shall bring forth judgment to the Gentiles. He shall not cry, nor lift up, nor cause his voice to be heard in the street. A bruised reed shall he not break, and the smoking flax shall he not quench: he shall bring forth judgment unto truth. He shall not fail or be discouraged till he have set judgment in earth; and the isles shall wait for his law.

"Now says the Lord, Fear not, for I have redeemed you; I have called you by your name; you are Mine. When you pass through the waters I will be with you; and through the rivers, they shall not overflow you: when you walk through the fire you shall not be burned, neither shall the flame kindle upon you. Fear not; for I am with you. You are My witnesses, that I am God. Yea, before the day was I am He; and there is none that can deliver out of My hand.

"I am the First and I am the Last; and beside Me there is no God.

"I will go before you and make the crooked places straight I will break in pieces the gates of brass and cut in sunder the bars of iron; and I will give you the treasures of darkness, and hidden riches of secret places. I form the light, and create darkness. I make peace, and create evil. I have made the earth, and created man upon it: I have stretched out the heavens and all their host have I commanded. I have raised him up in righteousness, and will direct all his ways. Look unto Me and be you saved, all the ends of the earth, for I am God. . . .

"How beautiful upon the mountains are the feet of him that brings good tidings, that publishes peace, that brings good tidings, that publishes salvation; that says unto Zion, Your God reigneth! Your watchmen shall lift up the voice; with the voice together shall they sing: for they shall see eye to eye when the Lord shall bring again Zion. . . ."

Repeating as in some of the preceding verses, Isaiah had also predicted and hailed the coming of the Messiah. In so doing, he originated and developed the revolutionary idea of the Suffering Servant— the innocent suffering for the guilty in vicarious atonement. The good were those who gave their lives for others, and who, through their sacrifice, helped redeem the sinful, unworthy though they were.

These views were new, startling, hard to grasp, beyond the comprehension of many. Isaiah's immortal crown of prophecy was his conception of a Messiah—not a dazzling, potent prince, but instead:

"He is despised and rejected of men; a man of sorrows, and acquainted with grief; and we hid as it were our faces from him; he was despised, and we esteemed him not. Surely he hath borne our griefs, and carried our sorrows: yet we did esteem him stricken, smitten of God, and afflicted. But he was wounded for our transgressions, he was bruised for our iniquities: the chastisement of our peace was upon him; and with his stripes we are healed. All we like sheep have gone astray; we have turned every one to his own way; and the Lord has laid on him the iniquity of us all . . . he has poured out his soul unto death: and he was numbered with the transgressors; and he bare the sin of many, and made intercession for the transgressors."

Nothing like this description had ever been said before of the hoped-for Messiah. Naturally there was little understanding in the ears of the multitude. But through a restored Israel, and the world's Redeemer yet to appear, this profound prophet foresaw the conversion of the whole earth to the one God, whom he quoted:

"I will also give you for a light to the Gentiles, that you may be My salvation unto the end of the earth."

Isaiah was one who saw to its fullest the transcendence of God and the unity of man.

Chapter 40 WHY MUST THE INNOCENT SUFFER?

N o w all the people would listen to the prophets, then or ever. Skeptics, cynics, and rebels who, believing in God, turned from Him —there were many such, forever asking hard questions: demanding to know why the one God, the true God, would permit the horrors of the later days—dispersal of two nations, oppression, the ruin of Jerusalem. True, the people had sinned. Some of their leaders had even coaxed them into the worst of misdeeds. But not all had followed their wicked advice. In the midst of fashionable disobedience, many had remained uncorrupted; had worshiped God in spite of great personal danger to themselves, in a kind of underground of the soul. Yet here they all were captives in the same undiscriminating punishment.

Why should the innocent suffer with the guilty?

The superb answer which the people found was contained in one of the strangest and strongest and most important stories in the Holy Bible, the Book of Job.

No one knows who wrote the book. No one can be sure if it is a history or a parable, but the intuition of humanity for centuries has affirmed that its message is true. The hero of this mighty saga of the soul of man lived in the patriarchal days and, if he was an actual personality, and not a symbolic figure, he may have been a friend of Abraham. Through thousands of years the tale of his fantastic experience has persisted, its meaning today bright, unchanged, as potent as ever. The form it takes in the Bible is dramatic, and that, too, is odd, because the ancient Jews had no theater, no drama, no place in their way of life for theatrical pretense of comedy and tragedy; such things belonged to other peoples. Yet Job is a drama that, with scarcely any tampering, could be mounted on the modern stage.

Someone, some inspired poet and prophet in the time of Ezra, took the ancient story of Job and recast it in the idiom of the times. The answer to the riddle of "Why must good people suffer?" was to serve all future ages as well as that dismal present; the purposes of the infinite God cannot be understood by the finite mind of man. But God's justice, mercy, and righteousness are unchangeable and ever-lasting.

Job, the hero in the tale of this anonymous philosopher-poet, was a man of Uz, an Arabian sheik of immense wealth, highest social position, and unimpeachable character. A large family of adoring children surrounded him. His goodness and charity were renowned; he was a perfect and upright man, who rendered all that was due to God in love, service, and obedience. As the man of Uz described himself:

"I delivered the poor that cried, and the fatherless, and him that had none to help him. The blessing of him that was ready to perish came upon me; and I caused the widow's heart to sing for joy. I put on righteousness, and it clothed me: my judgment was as a robe and diadem. I was eyes to the blind, and feet was I to the lame. I was a father to the poor: and the cause which I knew not I searched out. And I brake the jaws of the wicked, and plucked the spoil out of his teeth. Then I said, I shall die in my nest, and I shall multiply my days as the sand. . . . Unto me men gave ear, and waited, and kept silence at my counsel . . . I chose out their way, and sat chief, and dwelt as a king in the army, as one that comforts the mourners."

But going to and fro upon the earth, the Spirit of Evil, Old Satan, seeking the ruin of souls, enemy of mortals ever since Eden, marked this paragon among men and insolently challenged God as to the reason for Job's unexampled goodness.

"There is none like him," said the Lord, proud of His servant.

"Does Job fear God for nought?" sneered Satan. "Have You not made a hedge about him, and about his house, and about all that he has on every side? But put forth Your hand now, and touch all that he has and he will curse You to your face."

The Lord accepted the challenge. Let Satan himself test Job:

"Behold, he is in your hand, but save his life."

Satan, as usual, wasted no time. At once he began afflicting Job.

With one fell blow of fortune all of this perfect man's riches in flocks and herds were lost, some stolen by desert thieves, others blasted in a storm. Next seven sons and three daughters were killed in a tornado. Within one hour everything of earthly value to Job had vanished. Crushed, the good old man rent his mantle, but persisting in his trust in God, he cried:

"Naked came I out of my mother's womb, and naked shall I return thither: the Lord gave, and the Lord has taken away; blessed be the name of the Lord."

"Do you still retain your integrity?" gasped his stricken, earthbound wife. "Curse God and die."

"What?" cried Job. "Shall we receive good at the hand of God, and shall we not receive evil?"

Even as Job was standing steadfast in his woe, he suddenly found himself mysteriously covered from head to foot with boils and eruptions. In ashes he squatted, scraping his sores with a shard of broken pottery to relieve the intolerable itching. Nor did the lowest beggar refrain from spitting in his face.

What a state for the good servant of the Lord! Never before had a man fallen so swiftly from such heights of wealth, fame, wisdom, and honor to such dire poverty and misery. And he had done nothing to deserve this suffering.

Now came to Job three of his old cronies—Eliphaz, Bildad, and Zophar. Their sympathy was obnoxious. Apparently they came to comfort him in his affliction, but nevertheless they could not help feeling that surely he must have done something to deserve such a fate. That was their set opinion from the time they opened their mouths, which was late in their visit; first the three dismal visitors sat with Job in seven days of silence. Finally Job said:

"Let the day perish wherein I was born, and the night in which it was said, There is a man child conceived. . . . Why died I not from the womb?"

One after another, with rebuttals from Job, the three condolers prated about possible reasons for his grievous state, but all of the reasons could be resolved into one accusing word: Sin. Some secret sin of his had brought him to this pass. To them Job's clandestine guilt was becoming more clear, the more they chattered; it was retribution that had come upon him, he was being called to contrition and penitence. The Lord was always just, rewarding those who served Him and punishing those who broke His commandments.

Job answered them sarcastically: "No doubt but you are the people, and wisdom shall die with you!"

More and more defiantly, as they condemned him, he declared himself an upright man. But his three friends would not be convinced.

"Know that God exacts of you less than your iniquity deserves," said Zophar smugly.

"Is not your wickedness great?" demanded Eliphaz. "And your iniquities infinite?" Those oblique expostulations of his friends wounded Job more than all the downright blows of Satan. Passionately he maintained his innocence. True, he conceded, he may have sinned. All men do. But he did not deserve such loss of loved ones, ten in all; such losses of property, such boils. Why was God so very angry with him?

"He tears me in His wrath, Who hates me," he cried. "He gnashed upon me with His teeth."

Say what they would to Job, it seemed to the good man that God acted as if He were his enemy, and for what reason? That question Job hurled to high heaven; yet curiously, all the while and deep within his heart, Job believed that God would redeem and justify him.

"I know that my Redeemer lives," he insisted, "and that He shall stand at the latter day upon the earth. And though after my skin, worms destroy this body, yet in my flesh shall I see God: Whom I shall see for myself and my eyes shall behold, and not another . . ."

But all that his three visitors could think of was their own horror at Job's previous defiance. Had he not accused the Almighty of hatred and malignity? Their faces were stony. In his agony, longing for sympathy instead of lectures on right and wrong, Job begged of the smug Eliphaz, Bildad, and Zophar:

"Have pity on me, have pity upon me, O you, my friends; for the hand of God has touched me. Why do you persecute me as God?"

The three comforters were impervious, their opinion irrevocable: Job must be guilty. When the long-tormented Job reached the limit of his endurance he was in the deepest pit of despair, and challenged the universe:

"Oh, that one would hear me! Behold, my desire is that the Almighty would answer me!"

And then God answered poor Job out of the whirlwind:

"Who is this that darkens counsel by words without knowledge? Gird up now your loins like a man; for I will demand of you, and answer you Me. Where were you when I laid the foundations of the earth? Declare, if you have understanding. Who has laid the measures thereof, if you know? Or who has stretched the line upon it? Whereupon are the foundations thereof fastened? or who laid the corner stone thereof? When the morning stars sang together, and all the sons of God shouted for joy? . . .

"Can you bind the sweet influences of Pleiades, or loose the bands of Orion? Can you bring forth Mazzaroth in his season? or can you guide Arcturus with his sons? Know you the ordinances of heaven? Can you set the dominion thereof in the earth? Can you lift up your voice to the clouds, that abundance of water may cover you? Can you send lightnings, that they may go, and say unto you, Here we are? Who has put wisdom in the inward parts? or has given understanding to the heart?"

Abashed and abased, Job, amidst his losses and his boils replied to questions about these incomprehensible wonders beyond all mortal imagination:

"I know that You can do everything, and that no thought can be withholden from You . . . therefore have I uttered that I understood not . . . Wherefore I abhor myself, and repent in dust and ashes."

As a climax of this extraordinary colloquy between God and man, Job's three friends were rebuked by the Lord for their lack of understanding. Only Job's prayers for them would save them from punishment for their false counsel.

And the Lord made good all the losses of Job. Twice as much wealth as he had before his trial of faith came to him now; prosperity, esteem, and happiness were his in plenty. Seven new sons and three new daughters were born to him. Years later, Job died full of years and honors.

To the people of the one true God, the paradox of innocent suffering was becoming clearer—they began to understand that the godly may be afflicted so that they may be brought to self-knowledge and self-judgment.

There was much more that God had to say to Job. The words in Chapters 38, 39, 40, and 41, Book of Job, are incomparable in the literature of the world; never elsewhere has God come so impressively alive to man. Gilbert Chesterton said of Job:

"He turns rationalism against itself. . . . The Everlasting adopts an enormous and sardonic humility. He is quite willing to be prosecuted. He only asks for the right which every prosecuted person possesses; He asks to be allowed to cross-examine the witness for the prosecution. . . . He asks Job who he is. . . . The riddles of God are more satisfying than the solutions of man."

"Even more terrifying than God's splendor," says another, writing of Job, "is his sarcasm."

But the greatest lesson of Job comes from God Himself, when He warns all mankind that we cannot hope to understand the divine will, and for all mankind Job's answer can stand, full of trust in goodness and wisdom:

"Though he slay me, yet will I trust in Him. . . .

"If a man die, shall he live again?

"I know that my Redeemer lives!"

Chapter 41 THE HANDWRITING ON THE WALL

THE figure that dominated the fears of the Jewish captives was Nebuchadnezzar, the king of Babylon.

That mouth-filling name of the ruler of their world meant, in the language of Babylon, a man who would protect the boundaries, and Nebuchadnezzar lived up to his name. He was the second and the greatest of the new Babylonian dynasty in the fifth and sixth centuries before Jesus. He subdued the Egyptian threat and conquered the Jews. He had personally entered the city and himself ordered the burning of Solomon's Temple, the palace, and the great houses. He broke down the city walls and finally carried away most of the best specimens of the people, leaving "the poor of the land to be vine-pressers and husbandmen."

Though he had left Jerusalem in ruins, the king was nevertheless a mighty builder, and by his restoration of old palaces and his creation of new ones he made his own capital of Babylon with its hanging gardens and square white monuments the greatest city of the ancient world.

The whole strange tale of Nebuchadnezzar is told in the Bible's Book of the Prophet Daniel, even to the details of his madness.

A proud and ambitious tyrant was this Nebuchadnezzar II, builder of fortifications, bastions and battlements, heathen temples, palaces, canals, and fine streets, all of which puffed him up with pride:

"Is not this great Babylon, which I have built for the royal dwelling place, by the might of my power and for the glory of my majesty?"

He boasted of his capital's great population, the millions agglomerated in the maze of its streets, clustered densely everywhere beyond the palace and the gardens. And on every corner a taxgatherer squatting before the red and gilded abacus, making his reckoning with sliding ivory balls, taking toll on every private transaction, a percentage for the king.

He even began to rebuild the famous ziggurat, or Tower of Babel as we remember it, of which only the ground plan now remains. He also restored an abandoned temple for Marduk, or Bel, still chief god of Babylon, a structure which had stepbacks like modern skyscrapers. A clay cylinder of Nebuchadnezzar's reign with a cuneiform inscription about his restoration of temples and walls is to be seen in the Pennsylvania University Museum.

Seizing Jews and carrying them off into exile was a persistent practice of King Nebuchadnezzar. Relentlessly until his death in 562 B.C. he continued to transport some fifty thousand men with their families to Babylon, selecting, of course, the strongest and handsomest and most intelligent he could lay hands on. For the king was more than soldier and tyrant; he could appreciate brains and talent and beauty as well as brawn and he made no secret of his hope to enrich his kingdom with the finest of human materials.

Among those included in these selective mass migrations were at least four most extraordinary youths; and the greatest of the four was Daniel, of noble blood, although born in captivity. Daniel's name meant "God Is My Judge." His book in the Bible is one of the latest in time of composition. Daniel wrote in two tongues—the ancient Hebrew and the Aramaic, which was coming to be the popular language; it was the one later to be spoken by Jesus and His disciples and all the Israelites of that time.

Daniel is the great hero of his own book as he certainly was that of the captivity, and his three companions were Hananiah, Mishael, and Azariah. Part of the policy pursued by Nebuchadnezzar was that members of the most promising of the younger generation of Hebrews were picked and taught the language and literature of the Chaldeans. They must be indoctrinated, with the expectation that after a period of three years, as scholars and men of broadened view, they would be ready for preferment and executive office.

The four Hebrew youths had been chosen for this honor, and, as was customary, they were given Babylonian names; Daniel became

Belteshazzar, and the other three were called Shadrach, Meshach, and Abednego. Now, in name, at least, the four were Babylonians.

All went smoothly with them, according to the overlord's plan, until Daniel, who was destined to be a man of God, exceptionally gifted, handsome, and prepossessing, objected to eating food which a faithful Jew would have to consider unclean. Of course this food was of the choicest, it was furnished by the great king, and to refuse it was an insult. Furthermore the prince of the palace eunuchs declared that the food had been carefully selected and prepared by dieticians to build the body to its physical best. Healthy looks and strength were a requisite of the court.

Did Daniel wish to be weak and pale—he who was so fine-looking and so handsomely dressed?

There is an ancient description of how Babylonian gentlemen looked; Herodotus says:

"For clothing, they wear a linen tunic, reaching to the feet; over this the Babylonian puts on another tunic, of wool, and wraps himself in a white mantle; he wears the shoes of his country, which are like Boetian sandals. Their hair is worn long, and covered by caps; the whole body is perfumed. Every man has a seal and a carven staff, and on every staff is some image, such as that of an apple or a rose or a lily or an eagle: no one carries a staff without a device."

But Daniel, handsome in such a costume, nevertheless was firm about the virtues of a vegetable diet.

"Give us pulse to eat," he said, "and only water to drink, and look at us then in ten days."

Having been born with the gift of persuasion, the young Hebrew had his way, and the four young men visibly flourished on the simplest of meals. Healthy in body and mind, their well-being was obvious; they heard no more about changing their diet. When the education of the four youths was completed they stood before the king, and Nebuchadnezzar found them "ten times" more intelligent than others.

And soon Daniel began to find, rising mysteriously within himself, like Joseph of old, a genius for visions and the interpretation of dreams.

The king was impressed with this power of his to analyze dreams and before long it was called into important use. That was when the Babylonian king was haunted by a nightmare which, while it weighed on his waking hours, could still not be clearly remembered.

It was like an invisible sword over the monarch's head and after several days of anxiety Nebuchadnezzar felt he could no longer endure the constant feeling of frustration and dread. What *was* that dream?

He called upon his professional magicians and astrologers, his sooth-sayers and thaumaturgists and conjurers and wonder-workers, but all failed to help him recapture a memory of his phantasy. The arch-image of all the wizards declared that such a task was too difficult for even a chief sorcerer to perform. Nevertheless, he was commanded to try again and his underlings with him. The king gave them more time to consult their spirits and oracles, but promised that if they failed to bring him the true answer soon they were to be cut into pieces as mere pretenders to supernatural knowledge.

This edict from the throne could also affect the four young Hebrews, because they were looked upon as wonder-workers. However, Daniel boldly promised the authorities he would discover the dream of the king and tell him its import.

"But there is not a man on earth who can," was the skeptical reply, "for it is only known to the gods."

And Arioch, captain of the king's guard, friend of the astrologers and soothsayers, was all for killing the four young Hebrews, in case this Daniel might succeed where the wonder-workers had failed. But Daniel insisted on seeing the king face to face. In the throne room he asked Nebuchadnezzar II for a little time to solve his riddle. Permission granted, he returned to his three friends and they all fell to praying together for a revelation of the vanished dream. And suddenly the answer came.

Like a vision in the mind, the whole story of the dream was imparted in full to Daniel, and he happily blessed the Lord for the sudden illumination:

"I thank you, and praise You, O You God of my fathers, Who have given me wisdom and might, and have made known unto me now what we desired of You."

Divinely inspired, Daniel asked to be brought at once before the king. Back in the throne room, he told Nebuchadnezzar that none of his soothsayers could possibly have solved the enigma given them. Only the God of Judah and of Israel knew all secrets of the earth; nothing could be hidden from Him, and He had bestowed on Daniel what the king desired to know:

"O king, your thoughts came into your mind upon your bed, what should come to pass hereafter. And you saw a great image whose form was terrible. Its head was of fine gold, its breast and arms of silver, the belly and thighs of brass, legs of iron, and the feet part iron, part clay.

And there was a stone cut out without the labor of hands, and it smote first the feet and broke them to pieces, then it broke the rest to pieces, and it became like chaff of the summer threshing floors. And the wind carried them away. The stone that smote the image became a great mountain and filled the whole earth."

The king shouted aloud with relief. Yes, that was his dream; Nebuchadnezzar recognized all the details. But what did they mean? What did they portend?

Daniel, the re-evoker of a dream image, now became the interpreter. He explained that Nebuchadnezzar II was the head of gold on the image, representing the first world empire; that there was to be a second empire of the silver breast and arms; a third of brass belly and thighs; and a fourth of iron legs with feet of iron and clay.

Four empires, though Daniel did not, of course, name them, were to be known in history as Babylon, Persia, Greece, and Rome, in that order of succession. The mystic stone made without hands was, so Daniel told the king, a unity of Judah and Israel, and in filling the earth it symbolized the coming of a fifth empire—the Kingdom of Heaven, which would destroy all worldly kingdoms and rule the earth.

"God has made known to the king what shall come to pass hereafter," said Daniel, whose eyes pierced the far future. "The dream is certain, and the interpretation thereof sure."

So overcome with awe and reverence was Nebuchadnezzar that temporarily he laid aside his vast sense of superiority to all humankind. He actually prostrated himself before Daniel and ordered incense to be burned as an oblation.

"Of a truth it is that your God is the God of gods," conceded the heathen monarch. "And a Lord of kings, and a revealer of secrets."

Swift was the result of this momentous interview between the potentate and the prophet of exile. The Babylonian magicians and astrologers were in disgrace while Daniel was showered with gifts and made ruler over the province of Babylon as well as chief of wise men in the kingdom. He was given his own apartments in the palace and was recognized as the king's favorite.

But in his elevation Daniel did not forget his three friends. He found for them honored positions too. Everything in their lives seemed wonderful now, except that the behavior of the king began to alarm Daniel. Apparently the prophecies had, as the saying is, gone to his head.

Apparently, too, the image of his dream usurped his imagination. Incorrigibly vain as he was, Nebuchadnezzar now had made a golden statue of himself, ninety feet high, and set it up in the nearby plain of Dura. Next his subjects were commanded to be present at its dedication. None dared to be absent.

But no mention is made that Daniel attended.

"O people, nations, and languages," cried a herald of the king on this great occasion, "what time you hear the sound of the cornet, flute, harp, sackbut, psaltery, dulcimer, and all kinds of music, you fall down and worship the golden image set up. And whoso falls not down and worships shall be the same hour cast into the midst of a burning fiery furnace!"

Willingly the people obeyed; idolatry of a king was no novelty to the Babylonians. But when the ceremonies were over murmurs began to be heard against Daniel's friends. A complaint was lodged that those three Jews called Shadrach, Meshach, and Abednego had refused to fall down before the golden image of the king. Insult of insults!

Infuriated at these ingrates—who actually put religious principle above their own security—Nebuchadnezzar forgot his love for Daniel. In bitter dudgeon he commanded some of his army men to heat a royal furnace to seven times its ordinary firing. Then came further orders, to bind the Hebrew rebels, who insisted on putting their faith and trust in the power and protection of the one true God of their people.

Cast them into blazing coals! Burn up the fanatical fools!

Behold! The heat of the furnace was so terrible that it even set fire to the men who thrust the three culprits into its fiery mouth. But God was there in the midst of the red fury to help his faithful ones. Dressed though they were in flimsy inflammable garments, and helplessly bound, wrists and legs, Shadrach, Meshach, and Abednego stood in the fiery heat of the furnace and, like the bush and the fire before Moses, they were not consumed.

The watchers could not believe the incredible sight. These men stood erect and calm in the burning core of that furnace and yet not a hair was singed. At the cries of amazement from the guards, the king himself, purple robes lifted in both hands, came running to see.

The astounded Nebuchadnezzar shouted:

"Did we not cast three men bound into the fire?"

"True, O king," came the unanimous answer.

"Lo, I see four men loose, walking in the midst of the fire, and they have no hurt; and the fourth is like the Son of God."

Stunned, Nebuchadnezzar ordered the non-combustible men to be taken out of the furnace, which was done, and then all witnesses could see for themselves that not an inch of their skin had been scorched nor did they smell of smoke or fire.

"Blessed be the God of Shadrach, Meshach, and Abednego," cried the king, humbled again in his own sight and before men. "I make a decree: that every people, nation, and language, which speak anything amiss against their God shall be cut to pieces, and their houses shall be made a dunghill: because there is no other God that can deliver after this manner."

As usual, it was only for a little while that the proud and arrogant king enjoyed his humility. Only for a few days could he make obeisance to a Power supreme above the world. Soon he grew impressed by illusions contrived to flatter him by his old crew of court magicians and advisers. Really, he thought, he must be a favorite of his own gods, too, after all. Bloated with reassurance, the king laid his head on his pillow and, lo! Another plaguing dream.

In this second nightmare there was a tree that grew until it seemed to spread over the earth, a mighty tree which furnished food and shelter for all manner of life. Nothing else in the world was equal to that tree. Yet in a trice it was cut down, and a watcher from the skies descended and saw to it that the stump remained in the tender grass of the field, where the dews might wet and nourish it. And a voice proclaimed:

"Let his heart be changed from man's and let a beast's heart be given him: and let seven times pass over him."

What could they mean, these enigmatic, ominous-sounding words? The king roared for Daniel as soon as he was awake. And Daniel, although dismayed, had to tell the king of Babylon the truth.

Alas, he declared, the great Nebuchadnezzar would suffer a strange fate; he would become as a beast in the field, going on all fours and eating grass, until he learned, once and for all, that the Most High, the one true God, ruled in all the kingdoms of men. It was to be a last lesson in humility.

But the king only chuckled. Things like that simply did not happen to a king. He still thought the universe his own footstool.

Yet, impossible as it did seem, Daniel had rendered the exact meaning of the dream. Such a creeping transformation came over the king that, by his own attendants, Nebuchadnezzar was driven out of his palace. Turned into a beast, it was now his fate to eat grass; to become as an ox, "till his hairs were grown like eagles' feathers, and his nails like birds' claws."

The metamorphosed king crawled on all fours, helpless in the strange spell. When the predicted time had passed, his reason and proper shape returned. Then, he declared, he had learned his lesson. and he began glorifying the Ruler of heaven and earth.

The very doorstep of Nebuchadnezzar, over which he was shoved out into the meadows, is to be seen today in the British Museum, and on it are graven these words:

"For Nebo, the exalted Lord, who hath lengthened the days of my life, his temple anew have I built."

But now the hapless king put Nebo, the false god, out of his life. Until he died he confined his worship strictly to the God of the Hebrews.

But one man's moral lesson is not always enough for another's guidance, even in the same case. When Nebuchadnezzar died, there came to the throne the melodramatic villain of Daniel's great narrative, King Belshazzar.

Not so many years ago skeptical historians, criticizing the Holy Bible, declared that no such king had ever ruled in Babylon. Belshazzar appeared to them no more than a myth; the last king of Babylon, they asserted, was Nabonidus. Thus the contradiction between history and Scripture seemed complete. But no more. Inscriptions since deciphered have revealed that Belshazzar was eldest son and heir to Nabonidus, that he was regent in Babylon during his father's absence, and that he was killed the night the Persian army entered the inner city. This inscription, on a stone now in the British Museum, vividly confirmed the accuracy of the Book of Daniel. It also explained why Belshazzar, as a reward to Daniel, promised to make him "third ruler in the kingdom." Belshazzar himself was only second.

This Belshazzar was the personification of royal ostentation. He did not know it—but he was to be the last Chaldean king of Babylon.

The egomania of Belshazzar reached its pinnacle one night when he gave a sumptuous feast, attended by a thousand of his lords. For his heathen gratification and for general bedazzlement, Belshazzar had all the sacred golden vessels, long ago taken from the Temple of ruined Jerusalem, used in the gluttonous dining and wining. Sacred to

Jehovah, all these gleaming flagons, chargers, basins, goblets, trays, and dishes. Ho, then—who and where was this Jehovah? Let us see if for this profanation He will punish me, Belshazzar!

That was a great night in Babylon, the height of Balshazzar's pomp and power, yet also the nadir of his life, its lowest possible point. There sat the king in his golden robe, under his baldachin of rich, brocaded silks, hanging over his throne like a rainbow canopy, a thing costing thousands of shekels from lands far to the east. The air was heavy with perfumes of women and the spicery of cooks; the musicians were playing soft, enticing strains on their bandores, lutelike instruments, some shrill as fifes, others soft as winds in the woods, while singers sang jubilantly, exultantly glad of the might and power of the kingly host under the shimmering canopy.

Revelry and mockery were at a noisy peak when suddenly a breath of cold fear blew through the vast red-marbled banquet chamber. That fearful wind chilled them all; whispers rustled, mouth to mouth, like echoes of a gale. The face of the braggart king turned waxen in the candlelight, and his knees smote each other, for he was seeing a strange thing, and so were all his thousand frightened guests. It was on the wall.

Behind the long dais a spiritual hand had appeared in mid-air and with pointed forefinger was tracing unknown words against the marble. At the sight of that great bodiless hand all whispering ceased and the silence was like a paralysis until Belshazzar shattered the quiet with a scream.

Upright and swaying in his golden robes, ornaments rattling on his wrists as his hands tore at his black beard, he shrieked for his astrologers and soothsayers. They hurried forward, stared at the haunted wall, mumbled and shook their heads. They were helpless. The ghostly hand had written words they could not translate:

"Mene, Mene, Tekel, Upharsin."

As the hand vanished from sight confusion, a crazy noise of frightened voices, filled the festive scene. Steeped with wine, the nobles seemed ready to break into a fury of mob violence, trying to escape. Only the queen was quick-witted. In this awful hour she remembered the reputation of Daniel in the realm of the supernatural. By the queen's order, the Jewish prophet was bidden to appear.

With an air of simple dignity Daniel walked into the banquet hall.

"Make known to me the interpretation thereof," said Belshazzar, pointing to the handwriting on the wall. "And you shall be clothed

with scarlet, and have a chain of gold about your neck, and shall be
the third ruler in the kingdom."

Daniel rejected in advance any reward: no pay for God's work. But
he was ready to read the riddle of the words traced from fingers that
were not of flesh. He began by reminding Belshazzar of the punishment of Nebuchadnezzar for his overweening pride. Now this handwriting bespoke what was to happen to Belshazzar and for a like
offense: because of his act of sacrilege to the Lord God in misusing
the vessels of the Temple. Slowly, clearly, Daniel read aloud the mysterious message on the wall:

"Mene, Mene, Tekel, Upharsin."

What did the words mean? That you, O king, have been weighed
in the balance and have been found wanting. The kingdom shall fall
to your enemies, to the Medes and to the Persians.

This dreadful prediction might well have cost the courageous
prophet his life. But Belshazzar believed him and knew, therefore,
that he needed him. Even though Daniel desired no reward, the king
would have his way; at once a scarlet robe was draped on him, and a
chain of gold looped around his neck, and he was pronounced the
third ruler in Babylon, second only to king and regent, in keeping
with the royal promise.

That night, however, was not over. When the gay feast broke up in
gloom and silent horror the words on the wall were fulfilled in the
sudden end of Belshazzar. His death came with terrifying suddenness.
One moment the king stalks down the colonnade of purple marble,
his crown is on his head, his golden robes enwrap him, his jeweled
scepter asserting human power gleams in his lifted right hand. One
groan and he stands there no more; the scepter falls from his hand
and breaks on the tessellated pavement; the king lies near the shattered rod, a forlorn heap in golden cloth.

That same night Darius, the Median, marching through the city
gates with his conquering armies, proclaimed himself master of
Babylon.

New plots against Daniel began immediately among the astrologers
and the magicians. They worried more about him than about the new
masters of Babylon. At first they worked in deep secrecy, for they did
not know the kind of man Darius was, and were determined to be
careful. No one else was ever to know much about him, then or now
—he was not the same as Darius I, called the Great; nor Darius II
Nothus, which last word means illegitimate, he was the son of his

father's concubine. Nor was he Darius III, who was defeated by Alexander the Great. There is nothing to be found out about him, so far, from any other sources except the Bible's Book of Daniel, but there it is recorded that he came to the throne after that tragic feast of Belshazzar—and life thereupon began to change for the man who had read the handwriting on the wall.

In spite of all previous troubles, Belshazzar had been Daniel's protector. No longer was he the king's darling; Darius knew little about the outlander and seemed to care less. The magicians and the astrologers went to work. In spite of Daniel's intercession in the past—which had saved their necks from the executioner's sword—they plotted his downfall.

Knowing Daniel's habits of prayer, the court conjurers first managed to arrange for a new decree that, by the word of Darius, became a royal statute—no one should petition any god or man for a period of thirty days on penalty of being thrown into a den of lions maintained for criminals. It was clear enough why this was done. Daniel was a Jew, and meticulously kept up his religious observances. When they procured from Darius the new restraining order against worship they well knew that Daniel, as a Jew, would disobey. Thus they would be able to show the king that Daniel was a recalcitrant subject.

Daniel's crafty enemies had calculated well. No decree, nothing mortal, could ever stop Daniel from praying to God. Three times daily he opened his window wide, faced himself toward Jerusalem, and knelt in prayer. It was therefore a simple matter to catch him in the forbidden act. At the order of King Darius, the Mede, Daniel was ordered cast into the lions' den. And it was done.

But while the jealous rivals rejoiced at the sentence, King Darius passed a sleepless night. Many had spoken to him in high praise of the condemned man and the king's mind was troubled. Early in the morning he went to the sealed door of the den and called out:

"Daniel, O Daniel, servant of the living God! Is your God, whom you serve continually, able to deliver you from the lions?"

To his complete surprise, he heard the voice of the prophet:

"My God has sent His angel and has shut the lions' mouths, that they have not hurt me."

The royal conscience was infinitely relieved and impressed. Instantly Darius clapped his hands, ordered the God-favored prophet freed from the den of the lions, and commanded that the accusers, their wives and children themselves be given to the hungry lions, which, horrible to record, was done.

Darius, impressed to the point of conversion, then issued a new decree:

"That in every domain of my kingdom men tremble and fear before the God of Daniel: for He is the living God, and steadfast for ever, and His kingdom that which shall not be destroyed, and His dominion shall be even unto the end."

And "unto the end" became the chief vision of the many new and mystical visions which the prophet Daniel saw in apocalyptic trances.

The first vision was of four great beasts out of the sea—a lion with eagle wings, a bear with three ribs in its mouth, a leopard with four wings of a fowl on its back and four heads; but the fourth beast was the most terrible and strong, with iron teeth to devour, and with ten horns on its head.

As in the dream of Nebuchadnezzar, these phantasies symbolized the kingdoms of the world, which Daniel saw cast down into nothingness before the Ancient of Days, while he also saw the Son of Man coming in the clouds of heaven. The Ancient of Days is on His fiery throne, countless angelic hosts attend, and the Books of Judgment are opened. Everlasting dominion is given the Son of Man by the Ancient of Days.

In another vision Daniel beheld the time of the end of exile of the Israelites, as predicted by Jeremiah, who had counted it as seventy years. After fasting and prayer by Daniel, the Angel Gabriel disclosed the real meaning of Jeremiah's seventy years, which was actually seventy hebdomads of years, or 490 years all told. Then would Jerusalem be again the home of the scattered Hebrews, and heaven and earth be one.

Also among Daniel's wondrous visions, which often made him tremble with their vast sweep of time, even to eternity, was the "time of the end" and the "great tribulation such as never was since there was a nation," when "your people shall be delivered, every one that shall be found written in the Book. And many of them that sleep in the dust of the earth shall awake, some to everlasting life, and some to shame and everlasting contempt. And they that be wise shall shine as the brightness of the firmament; and they that turn many to righteousness as the stars for ever and ever."

Thus Daniel grasped the concept of heaven and hell; he foresaw the resurrection.

His words were held to be profoundly inspired by both Jesus Christ and by St. John on the island of Patmos, both quoting the far reaches of his vision.

Chapter 42 THE SINGULAR STORY OF TOBIAS

DURING the centuries of captivity the people chosen long ago by the one true God to be His teachers to the rest of mankind were able, in an extraordinary degree, to preserve their identity. In Persia and in Babylon, Jews were still Jews as they had continued to be Jews in the days of the Egyptian bondage, more than a thousand years before. Most of them remained faithful, clinging to each other, to the past, to the God of their fathers—an indestructible unity of faith, hope, and charity. Their solidarity in the midst of their longing and home-sickness has been preserved in the Lament of the Captives, Psalm 137:

> *By the rivers of Babylon,*
> *There we sat down, yea, we wept,*
> *When we remembered Zion.*
> *We hanged our harps*
> *Upon the willows in the midst thereof.*
> *For there they that carried us away captive*
> *Required of us a song,*
> *And they that wasted us*
> *Required of us mirth, saying,*
> *Sing us one of the songs of Zion.*
> *How shall we sing the Lord's song*
> *In a strange land?*
> *If I forget thee, O Jerusalem,*
> *Let my right hand forget her cunning.*
> *If I do not remember thee,*
> *Let my tongue cleave to the roof of my mouth,*
> *If I prefer not Jerusalem above my chief joy.*

Their faith was indestructible that God would not forsake them; that God should free them at last, as every winter must change to spring.

While Daniel was still a living counselor of his fellow captives and of the kings, Darius and Cyrus, the Persian, the people were singing such psalms and learning to pray with renewed fervor. Often and often, in those times, Daniel's restless head, tumbling his pillow, was full of dreams and starlit visions. He wrote them all down to spread the word among his people, and meanwhile, by wise words and by the example of a prophet's life, he began to make an impression on the clear, logical, and basically decent mind of Cyrus. Someday, Daniel felt certain—because he often heard and always trusted the Voice—the king, without shilly-shallying like the ancient Pharaoh, would let the people go, free to return to Jerusalem.

Meanwhile Daniel encouraged his people to remember their heritage. The scrolls were read aloud to listening groups every day, and the story of the world and their mission in it was graven on their minds. Adam and Abel, Abraham and Isaac, Jacob and Joseph, Moses and Joshua, David and Solomon all lived again in the listeners' imagination, with the Voice echoing in their conscience, pleading with them to seize the fallen light of ancient truth and carry it forward, in spite of tribulations.

The sorrows of the captive people were also sung forth from the poems of the Book of Lamentations in the Holy Bible. There are five such poems which set forth not only how the people felt but also their awareness of the heavenly reproaches which the people had brought upon themselves, through centuries of mockery and heresy, against the long-suffering patience of Jehovah.

Life among the exiles was an experience not only of grief but of work, of adjustment, of action, often in dangerous situations. The Jews who were faithful to their own altars in spite of threats and perils gained the respect and confidence of their oppressors. That triumph of faith was true of Tobias.

The story of Tobias, heroic servant of the Lord, is found in the Book of Tobias, which is included in Roman Catholic editions of the Holy Bible, known as the Douay version, but does not appear in the King James or other Protestant editions, except when included at times in an appendix, as a part of what is called the Apocrypha.

Taken captive in the downfall of Israel, Tobias managed to become the Assyrian king's friend and purveyor, even while remaining fully loyal to his faith and rites. He was particularly noted for his generosity with tithes and almsgiving.

But the sympathy of Tobias for his less fortunate and persecuted brethren, especially his secret burial of Jews slain by royal decree and left to rot in public disgrace, brought Tobias eventually to prison. He might have suffered death himself, but the king was persuaded to pardon him.

Still Tobias continued to help his afflicted race. At the Feast of Pentecost he sent his son—also named Tobias—to seek out a poor Jew to join him in holiday feasting. The young man returned, horrified at having found a strangled countryman lying dead like rubbish in the street. The elder Tobias rose from his comfortable couch and that same night, and with his own hands, buried the corpse. But this act of charity rendered him unclean for the holiday feast and this man of good deeds felt he had to spend the night outdoors.

While in deep slumber in the courtyard, hot dung from a swallows' nest fell upon Tobias' eyes and made him blind. It was like a symbol of other misfortunes, following fast. Kindly Tobias sank into poverty, with his wife Anna forced to support the family by weary hours of spinning. Nor did she bear the burden cheerfully; she constantly complained against her husband and his blindness until, with Job, he prayed to die.

At the same time, in far-off Ecbatana of Media, a young woman named Sara, unhappy daughter of Raguel and Edna, also was longing for the release of death. Haunted by a demon called Asmodaeus, who, in succession, had slain seven men who had married her, each one on the wedding night, Sara despaired of all happiness.

The prayers of old Tobias and the seven-times widow Sara were heard in heaven, and the Archangel Raphael was sent to look after the two woeful mortals, who had reached the limits of human endurance. But knowing nothing of the angels, blind and sorrowful Tobias, expecting the end of his days, called his son and enjoined him to be ever a righteous man. He bade him journey to the Median city of Rages, where for inheritance he was to collect ten talents of silver lent by his father long since to one Gabelus, a former close friend of their family.

For this trek through an unknown land the son needed a guide and it was the glorious Angel Raphael (in the guise of a mortal bearing the name of Azarias) who offered his services. The arrival of the stranger seemed providential to father and son, and young Tobias and "Azarias" set out, with a favorite dog romping ahead of them in anticipation. Only Anna wept, refusing to hope.

"Our son is lost to us," she cried to her husband.

Dusty and footsore, Tobias was glad when they reached the banks of the Tigris River, where he could bathe and relax in the refreshing waters. But no sooner had he plunged in than he was attacked by a monstrous fish. Undoubtedly he would have been killed except for the directions given him by "Azarias" in the battle with the ferocious Tigris creature. Victorious, Tobias was next told by his wise counselor

379

to cut out and preserve the heart, liver, and gall of the dead fish for later medicinal use. Wrapped in salt, these parts were carried along on the journey.

Reaching the city of Rages, the two travelers found the home of Raguel and Edna, where they were met with hospitality, and where Tobias proceeded to fall deeply in love with Sara and ask her hand in marriage.

Being a decent man, Sara's father was disturbed. The young lover from Nineveh was not to be discouraged by past events; he knew the facts; he had heard all about the seven previous fatalities and still wanted to marry Sara. Secretly Tobias had been assured by "Azarias" that the demon could be exorcised. Tobias must burn the liver of the Tigris fish on coals the night of the marriage; the noxious odor would drive Asmodaeus, the spawn of hell, from the wedding chamber.

"And," added the heavenly guide, "for three days do naught but pray with her."

Tobias literally obeyed. Leading Sara into the bridal room, he explained his plan to her as he dropped the salted fish liver on red-hot coals. Together they knelt in prayer, not knowing that even while they prayed old Father Raguel, expecting the usual result of this baneful love, the death of the eighth bridegroom, was busy already digging a grave under the midnight stars.

The powerful odor of the fish's head and liver did cause the demon Asmodaeus to fall in impotent defeat. Humiliated beyond measure, he sought refuge in Egypt, but Raphael, the angel of the Lord, pursued him there and bound him into helplessness in the desert sands.

Just as apprehensive as her grave-digging husband, Edna, the mother of Sara, sent servants to find out if tragedy had struck again. The report came back that the bride and groom were lying side by side and fast asleep. She and Raguel gave thanks to God, the earth was shoveled back into unneeded grave, and in overwhelming joy the parents planned wedding festivities for fourteen instead of seven days.

Before this festive time had passed "Azarias" had sped back to make all arrangements for the reimbursement of the ten talents of silver, and invited Gabelus, the friendly debtor, to return with him to the home of Raguel. There Gabelus showered his blessing on the bride and groom, who were also given half of Raguel's wealth as they set forth for Nineveh—a rich and joyous pair of young people.

Quite otherwise was the mood of Anna, the mother of Tobias. Every day, although certain she would never see her son again, she went to a hilltop to watch and to feed on doubt. Never would she forgive her husband for sending their only son away on such a fantastic errand. Poor blind Father Tobias was also beginning to feel guilt as well as grief.

But the sudden unbelievable sight of the returning wanderer changed Anna's black mood. Rushing from the hilltop, she told the glad tidings to her husband, who struggled to his feet to greet his son, hearing with an old man's joy the bells of the camel train. Before it ran Tobias' dog, barking his delight.

Even greater joy was in store. On instructions from the wonderful "Azarias," the galls of the Tigris fish were applied to the eyes of old Tobias, and lo, the white film over them dissolved. The good old man could again see the faces of those he loved.

But above all, such happiness posed a question: how to repay the inestimable services of "Azarias." Father and son agreed that to halve their wealth with him would be little enough, in conscience. Smilingly their great benefactor refused any award.

"For I am the Angel Raphael," he said. "One of the seven who stand before the Lord."

With these awesome words he vanished, and the family thus favored of heaven fell prostrate on their faces, praising God for His gracious kindness.

The elder Tobias lived to see his grandchildren's children, and died giving a prophecy of the destruction of Nineveh from which he warned his kindred to flee. In his vision he saw the restoration of Jerusalem, the Holy City, where Jews and Gentiles would dwell together in peace and brotherhood.

BOOK EIGHT
The Return

Chapter 43 FREEDOM AT LAST

I T W A S a merciful day for the captive Jews when Cyrus took the throne and became the friend of Daniel.

Hardly had the new king come to power before he issued a resounding public statement of what he considered his obligation to the prisoners from Jerusalem:

"All the kingdoms of the earth has the Lord God of heaven given me and He has charged me to build Him a house in Jerusalem which is in Judah. Who is there among you of all His people? The Lord his God be with him and let him go up."

Liberation! After 490 years, freedom at last! Is it any wonder that Isaiah so long before had called the Emperor Cyrus "the Lord's anointed"?

A truly great emperor, Cyrus. The world's tongue praised his comity with serf and freeman, his kindly consideration for others. It was he who was the real founder of the Persian Empire and a threat to all the European West. At the height of this power he subdued territory as far as what is now called Afghanistan. No independent country could be tolerated in the political plans of Cyrus and that was why he fell upon Babylon in its weakest time and under its weakest monarch. Cyrus put an end to the Chaldean dynasty, if it can really be called that. But with its downfall, authentic knowledge about Cyrus, the emperor, also came to an end. Only legends follow—a whole literature of them, tales of an intrepid and inspired military commander, a wise monarch, a good and sensible man.

Certainly, the Jewish exiles had cause to think him good and sensible. Where other kings had held them captive, Cyrus captivated them. For whatever reason of buffer politics he may have had, Cyrus re-established the kingdom of Judah; he set God's people free, and he did it in wholly friendly fashion.

On the famous Cyrus Cylinder, which has come down to us as a page of ancient history, the Persian monarch puts down to his own credit his record of how he restored their gods to the various peoples he brought under his dominion; it was his settled policy to permit them to follow their own religion unhindered, for that, in his view, was the chief factor in human contentment and happiness.

Isaiah had gone on to hail Cyrus actually as the Lord's shepherd who "shall perform all My pleasure: even saying to Jerusalem, You shall be built; and to the Temple, Your foundation shall be laid." It was easy for the Jews to agree that Cyrus was one anointed of the Lord, "Who raised up the righteous man from the East, called him to His foot, gave the nations before him, and made him rule over kings."

"I am Cyrus, king of the world, the great king, the mighty king, king of Babylon, king of Sumer and Akkad, king of the four quarters of the world."

Braggadocio, it would seem, could go no further, but it was true of the world as it was known in that day. Having taken Babylon, Cyrus let the great city stand unharmed. Meanwhile many of the exiles were getting ready to leave at once, but not all. Indeed, the majority behaved with great wariness. They thought they would wait and see, for it was no easy trek across the desert to Jerusalem. To families comfortably settled in the luxurious everyday life of Babylon, the Judean capital was known only as a place of ruins and rubble with poverty-pinched inhabitants. Besides, argued prosperous Jews, why deliberately leave the magnanimous protection and generous administration of a good king like Cyrus?

On his part, Cyrus urged the exiles to pull up stakes and pioneer in the reclamation of their wasted country. As an inspiration to the patriotic and an example to the materialistic, he appointed Sheshbazzar, prince of Judah, as the governor of Jerusalem, and turned over to him the sacred vessels of gold that Nebuchadnezzar had stolen from the Temple.

Cyrus perfectly understood that the Temple in Jerusalem was the very soul of the people, and with a statesman's vision he urged that it be rebuilt as quickly as possible, restored to its grandeur.

More than forty-two thousand of the exiled Hebrews joined in the homeward march to Jerusalem. They made the long journey under the leadership of Sheshbazzar, whose aides were Zerubbabel, of the house of David, and Jeshua, chief of the priests. In the host of pilgrims were two hundred singing men and women, and all the long way these choir people cheered the weary plodders with psalms of David.

But once arrived at Jerusalem, the exultant pilgrims were immediately plunged into despair.

Things were worse than they had expected. Even in the palliating glow of the sunset the city of Jerusalem was a discouraging sight: walls crumbling, arches broken, rubbish piled on rubbish—and the population shabby and ill fed.

This, that was once the golden Jerusalem!

Judah itself had shrunken to about twenty square miles—all that was left of the kingdom of David! And, sorrow crowning sorrow, the shattered Temple—the house of the one true God—forgotten by the earth, a bat's nest and a lair for wolves.

Nor were the pilgrims welcomed by the tattered dwellers in Jerusalem. At best the home folk were indifferent. Some were resentful of the prosperity, even wealth, carried back by the newcomers. Others, heathen folks who had also settled in Jerusalem, were hostile, neighbors of different racial strains who had come to despise the Jerusalemites as people deserted by their God. For years they had jeered: "Where is your vaunted, almighty Jehovah?"

The first answer to their contemptuous attitude was made when the émigrés from Babylon erected an altar to the Lord and instituted burnt offerings morning and evening. Also they observed the joyful Feast of Tabernacles, which drew some of their alienated brethren into participation.

Foremost in the minds of the Babylonian Jews was the restoration of the Temple, but settling themselves, with all of the domestic details involved, was their first task, and it took time. It was in the second spring that Zerubbabel, who had taken Sheshbazzar's place, began laying new foundations in areas left undermined and useless, and before long a plan for a Temple was taking shape. The base was for a smaller, scrubbier building than Solomon's but nevertheless a real Temple to the Living God. The faithful were overjoyed.

Hosannas and songs, shouting and laughter rang out above the clang and clatter of hammer and saws.

News of the undertaking was carried to far-off ears, and the people left behind in northern Israel also became excited. The Samaritans sent a delegation to Jerusalem to make an offer.

"Let us build with you; for we seek your God as you do."

Bluntly, the petition was turned down. To the faithful worshipers of Jehovah the inhabitants of Samaria were not worthy to join in; they had degenerated into idolatry, they partook of unclean food, as designated in Mosaic law; the sacred rituals had been tainted. Ultimately this disagreement was to lead to the Samaritan Schism and the erection of a Samaritan temple on Mount Gerizim.

In retaliation for the Jerusalem rebuff, the Samaritans and other excluded peoples of Palestine stirred up all kinds of opposition. Counselors were hired to interfere with their endeavors. Complaints against the Jerusalem builders were constantly lodged with Cyrus, and later with Artaxerxes, who succeeded to the Persian throne. Artaxerxes ordered all work stopped on the Temple and so matters stood for about fifteen years, or until the second year of the reign of a new Darius who took the throne.

But meanwhile, as always, prophets arose to oppose the intrigue and the sabotage. They seemed, these two men, Haggi and Zechariah, to have been born just to take up the cause of the neglected house of the Lord. They faced a discouraged populace, for many hopes beside those of the Temple had been frustrated. Heaven had not favored their crops, source of prosperity. Unemployment had sapped ambition. Misery and discontent prevailed. What was the use of anything?

With determination and eloquence Haggai roused the flagging will of Judah, and Zechariah, too, stirred the souls of his hearers from inertia. One of the prophets urged physical action, the other preached the bitter fruits of sin and the flowers of repentance and obedience unto the Lord God. Haggai was practical, Zechariah spiritual. Between them they managed to reinvigorate a people who had virtually given up all ideals and all hope.

Three weeks after Haggai started on his fervid campaign, work on the Temple was resumed in earnest.

When enthusiasm lagged on the job (it was largely a labor of love) Haggai would be on hand to pronounce and reiterate that, without the Temple completed and made fit for His dwelling place, they could not expect God to be with them. Did they want His smile or His frown?

After five months the voice of Haggai was no longer heard—whither he had gone we do not know—but Zechariah continued his preaching until the last stone was in place. What was the object of Zechariah's orations? They were intended, like those of Haggai, to stimulate the returned captives to rebuild the Temple and restore the regular worship of God, but even more important, to encourage faith and hope in the promise of a coming Messiah.

At last, in March of 516 B.C., which was in the sixth year of Darius, the Temple was once again a completed structure on the rocky, wedge-shaped height. When Darius gave the new structure his royal nod of approval it was dedicated with solemn joy. Wonderful to see, the Passover and the Feast of Unleavened Bread were once more being celebrated in the Presence of Jehovah in His sanctuary, as had been ordained by Moses.

But even with this concrete earnest of the people's faith, and the inspired promises of Haggai and Zechariah, there was no fulfillment of the hopes of betterment in their lot.

The crops were still meager, and spoiled by pests, and the economic depression did not lift. These hard times were taken to mean but one thing—Jehovah must be mysteriously, incomprehensibly, offended.

Even more puzzling, it was observed that the few in their midst who did prosper were far from righteous men.

What was the answer to this paradox?

Again there came a prophet to interpret the ways of God to men. This time it was Malachi ("My Messenger") who rebuked the people for their expectation of rich reward for their efforts. Because God had not acted immediately and exactly according to their material wishes, and what they considered their proper due, they were ready to abandon their religious duties. Their priests were no better than the crowds. Malachi was blunt:

"You have wearied the Lord with your words. Yet you say, Wherein have we wearied Him? When you say, Every one that does evil is good in the sight of the Lord, and He delighteth in them; or, Where is the God of Judgment? . . . Will a man rob God? You have robbed Me, says the Lord. But you say, Wherein have we robbed You? In tithes and offerings."

And so they had, in withholding sacrifices. They had been cynical of age-old truths and righteousness. Malachi was scornful; did they actually think that Jehovah needed them, was happy only when His chosen people behaved themselves? That was inflated nonsense, Malachi declared. Hearken! Jehovah demanded sincere worship, and would accept it even from the heathen! And Malachi repeated the declaration of the Lord on this revolutionary fact:

"From the rising of the sun even unto the going down of the same My name shall be great among the Gentiles."

No favoritism was to be found in Jehovah:

"For behold, the day comes that shall burn as an oven: and all the proud, yea, and all that do wickedly shall be a stubble; and the day that comes shall burn them up, says the Lord of Hosts, that it shall leave them neither root nor branch."

But the words of Malachi, "My Messenger," made little impression on the complaining people.

They justified themselves. They argued that they had done what was required of them in the building of the Temple, and had received no divine recognition. Malachi felt sorry for their inability to understand. He ceased his rebukes and tried to assure them of God's enduring love, that in the end all would be well.

Meanwhile uneventful years passed over moribund Judah until the time of Ezra. This priestly scribe from Babylon, hearing of the prevalent distress, decided to make the long journey to Judah and see what he could do. He wanted to rehabilitate the religion of the bewildered people. Despite Malachi's discouragement, they must be made to understand.

Gathering a following of some five thousand of his fellow Hebrews, who believed in him, Ezra set out for Jerusalem. With them they carried large sums of money collected from supporters, further golden vessels long stolen from the Temple, and above all a "Book of the Law" that would teach again the old statutes and ordinances to faint hearts and backsliders in the Holy City.

The journey took four months. Along the way fears and hazards were many. But the Book of Ezra tells us that "the hand of our God was upon us, and He delivered us from the hand of the enemy, and of such as lay in wait by the way."

It was a shining band of believers that was led by Ezra. New blood, new ideas, new wealth were being carried into Jerusalem with this caravan of good cheer. A real welcome was theirs, although some who greeted them as apostles of a new day were secretly uneasy and worried. They had a sense of guilt about the laxity in conduct and morals that Ezra, esteemed scribe, might discover. The apprehension spread when it became known that Ezra brought with him that "Book of the Law of Moses which Jehovah had commanded to Israel."

Soon, among the masses, curiosity was almost uncontrollable; Ezra was implored to publish the message.

With the population assembled to hear him in a large open field near the water gate, Ezra mounted a pulpit especially set up for the occasion. Before the immense concourse he opened the book with reverent hands. He blessed God. The great congregation bowed low, crying, "Amen, Amen," and uplifting their hands in token of obedience.

The reading took a long time. Every half hour Ezra was relieved by assisting Levites. His phrases were carefully spoken and they were interpreted at once so that all might understand the meaning. As the words sank into the hearts of the listeners and they realized how remiss they had been, many began to weep, but Ezra consoled them:

"Go your way. Eat the fat, and drink the sweet, and send portions unto them for whom nothing is prepared. For this day is holy unto our Lord: neither be you sorry; for the joy of the Lord is your strength."

Preaching gladness in life, Ezra won all to his side. Next day the Law of Holiness in the book was read to a select few; the Feast of Tabernacles was celebrated for seven days, and during those happy times other portions of the book were read aloud. But more serious hours were to come. In full assembly, the Book of the Laws was read again, and its priestly code made perfectly clear. Now sackcloth and ashes were the order of the day, and the people confessed their sins before God and men.

The climax came when a new covenant was written, sealed, and ratified by all present, and so Judah "entered into an oath, under penalty of a curse, to walk in God's law, which was given by Moses, the servant of God, and to observe and do all the commandments of the Lord our God, and His judgments and His statutes."

Theocracy was going to be a reality, with the priests supreme in the state, obeying the written word of God, given through Moses.

Chapter 44 THE STORY OF ESTHER

I T W A S during the time of the return to Jerusalem, and while there were still a great many exiles left in Persia, that there came into the world one of its great love stories, an incomparable narrative, rich in beauty of telling. It is also an early example of the long and bitter problem of racial animosity, a tale still repeated at the Feast of Purim: the starkly realistic and yet warm and lovely story of Esther.

This modest dark-eyed girl lived in the Persian capital, never dreaming that one day she would lift her eyes to the throne, or that an emperor might desire her to be his queen.

During those days five emperors—the great Cyrus, Cambyses, Darius, Xerxes, and Artaxerxes—had occupied the Persian throne.

Cyrus' rock-hewn tomb, which has been uncovered, bears the inscription:

"O, man, whosoever you are and whencesoever you come, for I know you will come, I am Cyrus, and I won for the Persians their empire. Do not, therefore, begrudge me the little earth which covers my body."

On the tomb of Darius was inscribed: "Says Darius, the king: By favor of Ahura Mazda I am of such sort that I am a friend to the right; I am not a friend to the wrong; it is not my desire that the weak man should have wrong done him by the mighty, nor is my desire that the mighty man should have wrong done to him by the weak."

Xerxes, who ruled in the time of Esther, was the son of Darius. Like his father before him, he was a worshiper of Ahura Mazda, Zoroastrian god of light, or goodness. He had another name by which the Holy Bible calls him: Ahasuerus. He was said to be the tallest and handsomest man in the empire, but capricious and cruel. One may see how Ahasuerus was dressed in a bas-relief from the portico of his palace courtyard at Persepolis, Iran, which is on display at the University of Chicago. His capital was Shushan, place of magnificent palaces and famous hanging gardens.

The drama of Esther began just before the king set out on a campaign against Greece. In anticipation of a victory, never to be won, Ahasuerus instituted grand festivities. For six months, in his role of "king of kings," he entertained illustrious visitors, ending up with a seven-day feast in the royal gardens, where the tables were a blaze of golden plates.

On the seventh day of feasting Ahasuerus, heady with wine and flattery, was seized with a toper's silly and graceless whim. He wanted to show off to his guests the physical perfections of his queen. But Vashti—and who can blame her?—declined to be put on exhibition. The king roared his displeasure. A woman had dared to cross the regal will? What did he care if she was a queen? She would not be such for long. For her disobedience to his will, the affronted Ahasuerus divorced Queen Vashti. She was lucky to escape with her life.

But when the king came home from war, a badly defeated man, his mind dwelt gloomily on the beauteous queen he had cast aside. There was, he knew, no hope of reunion; proud Vashti was gone forever. She had fled the country and no one knew where she was. So the king began to fret for another queen, one as fair as Vashti, and orders went out that all the beautiful virgins of the land should be brought together at the court. From the lovely, unviolated lot of them the king would choose his new queen.

Among those who read the royal notice was Mordecai, a Benjamite who lived near the palace. Old Mordecai had a beautiful niece, Hadassah, and he saw no reason why she should not be a candidate for the king's favor. After Uncle Mordecai had a private talk with an influential friend at the palace, Hadassah was enrolled in the competition under the changed name of Esther, which means "the star."

For twelve months young Esther was put through a prescribed course in the arts of beauty and deportment. So well did she study and practice her lessons that when the king finally saw her he was enraptured by her looks and manner. Esther won approval over all the other virgins and she took the place of Vashti in the heart of Ahasuerus. So infatuated was the king that he did not inquire deeply into the history of his new lady; Esther became queen of Persia and the king did not know he had married a Jewess.

Meanwhile Uncle Mordecai had also gained royal favor for himself by discovering and reporting a conspiracy against the king's life. But his sudden rise naturally raised a crop of enemies, especially a court favorite whose name was Haman. Between Mordecai and Haman, the Amalekite, deep trouble was brewing its roots in the traditional enmity of two races. Stiff-necked Mordecai, feeling himself in high favor, refused to pay the slightest homage to the Amalekite, even after the king had commanded all his palace servants to prostrate themselves before Haman.

Certainly Mordecai's attitude was provocative, but it was the only possible course, because no Jew could offer any act of obeisance to any Amalekite, without reproach of conscience.

But Haman naturally hated Mordecai and plotted to get even. Whenever he had a private audience with the king he began to pour poisonous thoughts into the ears of his master. Was there not a national danger in permitting a certain race of people in his domain to persist in the practice of their own customs and laws, in open defiance of His Majesty's government? For such disloyalty and intransigence Haman placidly suggested their extirpation. Of course the Jews did have considerable wealth, and that would all be forfeit to the crown. Ahasuerus was persuaded.

Letters bearing the royal seal and setting a date for the massacre of all Jews were sent to every province of the empire. No one, high or low, was to be spared: a pogrom of thousands.

Mordecai was one of the first to hear the whisper of the news. He rent his clothes and wailed aloud, so that one of the maids rushed to tell Queen Esther of her uncle's strange behavior. The old man cried to her to save their doomed people; she herself, he was certain, would be among the victims. And he warned her that perhaps she had been chosen for the throne in the design of God for this very emergency.

Queen though she was, Esther was trapped. It was the law—and the laws of the Medes and Persians could not be changed even by a king—that no one might approach the throne except by express command; the penalty of breaking the rule was death. Unless the king held out his scepter in sign of pardon, death for any suppliant who took the chance was inevitable.

Well, Niece, what will you do?

Esther did not hesitate. She told her despairing uncle to gather together all the Jews in Shushan. They must fast for three days, praying for her success with Ahasuerus. She and her maidens would also fast.

"And so I will go unto the king, which is not according to law," she said, "and if I perish, I perish."

It was a solemn moment when, unbidden, unannounced, Esther entered the throne room. There sat the stern, tall man, her husband, who had sent Vashti, his wife, into exile because she denied his drunken whim. But now he is not drunken; he is sober, severe, austere, and his thoughts in this hour of pomp and circumstance are on affairs of state. His wife at the door? What does the woman here? It would be weakness in a king to act softly to an intruder, even though she be his wife and lovely.

The silence was long. What would her lord and master do, now that he beheld her venturesome boldness? Would he reprove her for temerity? That reproach alone would mean death; the executioners would seize her.

The king held out the golden scepter toward his wife. It was his sign of indulgence, his invitation for her to approach without fear. "Speak!" was the word from the throne; let the dear wife ask what she would; half the kingdom was Esther's if she desired it.

Esther simply requested that her lord and his favorite Haman attend a little dinner, just for the three of them. Astonished at the simplicity of the request, Ahasuerus laughingly agreed. Women, he thought, were hard to understand. His curiosity was further whetted by an air of mystery in his wife when the three sat down together and ate that wholly delightful meal, especially when Esther proposed a second banquet to follow a few days later.

Certainly Haman was vastly enjoying these royal parties. He had no reason to suspect Esther; he was flattered to dine privately in the exclusive company of king and queen. The only drawback to his thrilling joy was that his enemy, Mordecai, was still alive and reviling him. But why should Mordecai trouble Haman? asked his wife and his friends. They told him just what to do:

"Let a gallows be made of fifty cubits high (about seventy-five feet) and tomorrow speak to the king that Mordecai may be hanged thereon."

Why, of course! So Haman had the gallows built and it reared beyond any possible requirement, the highest gallows ever. From it Uncle Mordecai was doomed to dangle like a dead crow against the sky.

That night the king happened to be sleepless. To entertain and divert himself, Ahasuerus asked to have the book of records read to him to refresh his mind on certain state affairs. But curiously, coincidentally, as if some higher power were arranging matters, out of the droning throat of the reader came the name of Mordecai, reminding the sleepless king of his service to the king in the conspiracy against his life. Mordecai had saved his sovereign from assassination and yet had never been properly rewarded. How could Ahasuerus have been so negligent? That ingratitude began to trouble his conscience.

Morning saw Haman, his gallows ready, seeking an audience with the king. He had a simple request to make. He desired to hang Mordecai of the proscribed race, hang him at once. But to Haman's consternation the king asked a riddling question.

"What shall be done unto the man whom the king delights to honor?" he demanded of Haman.

Flattering himself that he must be the man to be honored, Haman recommended splendid apparel, and why not let the man wear a temporary crown of honor, and be given the king's horse to ride on in a procession around the city? In all this vision Haman was seeing himself lifted in glory.

"Do even so to Mordecai the Jew that sits at the king's gate: let nothing fail of all that you have spoken," was the paralyzing rejoinder of Ahasuerus.

Paralyzing, because of all the facts. The expression "living in the gate" meant that a person had the authority of a judge or ruler. The ancient oriental city gates had wide arches with spacious recesses, and there leading citizens gathered for the transaction of business or the adminstration of justice. Much more, then, was in the king's mind for Mordecai.

The dazed Haman had to obey his monarch's order, and even worse was to follow. At the second banquet with Queen Esther she dramatically and suddenly begged her lord to spare her life. The king looked in amazement. Yes, lord—and the lives of all her unfortunate people.

Frowning and quite baffled, Ahasuerus wanted to know who had dared threaten her life. The king rose to his feet, already pale at the very thought.

"The enemy is there," said Esther, pointing to Haman. And to its bitterest detail she laid bare Haman's hatred and his plan of annihilation. Unable to speak, Ahasuerus strode out into the garden to find calm reflection, but the more he thought it over, the more his rage increased. When he stalked back it was only to command:

"Hang Haman on his gallows!"

Thus the world has a saying—President Woodrow Wilson once used it—to hang a man "as high as Haman."

As for courageous Esther, she obtained a decree from the king which gave her people the right to arm themselves and to punish those who had sought to slay them:

"Thus the Jews smote all their enemies with the stroke of the sword, and slaughter, and destruction, and did what they would to those that hated them."

Mordecai, too, was made important in the land. It was he who established the yearly Feast of Purim in commemoration of the reprieve of the Jews and their vengeance.

Esther was, in truth, the "star" of her people.

Chapter 45   THE BUILDING OF THE WALL

W H E N Ahasuerus died and Artaxerxes succeeded him, there was another Judean patriot who became popular at the Persian court. This patriot's name, also famous in the Bible story, was Nehemiah, who served as cupbearer to the king. Naturally Nehemiah was rich and influential; nevertheless, his mind dwelt constantly on his homeland, and when he heard tales from returned captives, reports of Jerusalem with its walls still in ruins, its population at bitter odds, he was so affected that he wept and prayed.

His melancholy was noticed by King Artaxerxes, who inquired the cause.

"The city, the place of my fathers' sepulchres, is a waste and its gates consumed with fire," Nehemiah explained.

"For what do you make request?"

Nehemiah said he would like permission to go himself to Judah that he might help rebuild the holy city. A capital without a wall was like a naked beggar, exposed to the scorn of men. Fond of his cupbearer, Artaxerxes granted his wish and more; he not only gave the letters of authority for a big building project but appointed Nehemiah sole governor of Jerusalem.

Escorted by an armed guard, Nehemiah reached Jerusalem in early summer. Without flourish he entered the city, and on the third night he made a private inspection of the ravaged walls, noting with the eye of a trained architect what repairs should be done; they would be extensive and costly.

Formulating a practical reconstruction plan, Nehemiah put his ideas before an assembly of priests, nobles, and leading citizens. Most of them were enthusiastic, ready to help, but from the broken, abandoned kingdom of Israel in the north there came criticism. Sanballat, governor of Samaria, and his henchmen ridiculed Nehemiah's scheme as visionary. Walls, indeed, for that hopeless, ruined mess which was Jerusalem! The notions of this Persian-tainted governor!

So once again, as so often before, there was trouble in Jerusalem.

Nevertheless, the priests, led by Eliashib, together with men from neighboring towns as far as Jericho, began to organize for the hard labor. With administrative skill Nehemiah drafted all the able-bodied Jews he could muster, and under his direction work began at once. But from the start spying and conspiracy were carried on by the Samaritans.

When the walls were about half finished an attack was actually planned against the workmen. Malice could go no further. Warned in time, Nehemiah armed his corps of helpers with swords, spears, shields, and bows, and they took turns at labor and at watch. From sunrise to starlight the massive stone-laying went on, the toilers not even pausing to change their clothes.

There were also, and as usual, internal troubles. Many of the inhabitants who could have enlisted in the service of Nehemiah were too ill fed and oppressed to be useful. Usury held them in chains of utter poverty. As governor, Nehemiah reproached the moneyed class for this oppression, and set an example, by taking no salary for his office and providing food for a hundred and fifty and more mouths at his own table daily. Some of the profiteers were sufficiently shamed to follow his example and relieve the widespread malnutrition.

But Nehemiah's foes watched every chance to thwart him. Attempts were made to lure him outside the city limits where he could be conveniently done away with. Failing this, there were efforts aimed at poisoning the mind of Artaxerxes against his ever wary and prudent cupbearer. But every obstruction failed, and finally the Jerusalem walls were solidly rebuilt—the job finished in the astonishingly short time of fifty-two days.

The dedication ceremonies were solemn; two processions marched in opposite directions around the walls and met at the Temple, chanting and singing all the way. Numerous sacrifices were offered up to the one true God and the joy of Jerusalem was told everywhere, by caravan travelers going east and west.

For twelve years thereafter Nehemiah was governor of Jerusalem, and divided his time between the Holy City and the court of Shushan, the Persian capital. During his administration he brought about many excellent reforms. The Sabbath, which through carelessness and laxity had become a market day, was once again devoted to the Lord.

At the close of his labors Nehemiah said:

"Thus I cleansed them of all strangers, and appointed the wards of the priests and Levites, every one in his business. . . . Remember me, O my God, for good."

It was a stabilizing time for the people, whose greatest lessons were still unlearned. But this was a period when they turned to old and new prophets, seeking comfort in the midst of action, uncertainty, and fear. One of the new prophets, Zechariah, advised them:

"Thus speaks the Lord of Hosts, saying, Execute true judgment, and show mercy and compassion every man to his brother; and oppress not the widow, nor the fatherless, the stranger, nor the poor; and let none of you imagine evil against his brother in your heart."

Also Zechariah made them a promise:

"The seed shall be prosperous; the vine shall give her fruit; the ground shall give her increase; the heavens shall give their dew; and I will cause the remnant of this people to possess all these things. And it shall come to pass that, as you were a curse among the heathen, O house of Judah and house of Israel, so will I save you, and you shall be a blessing. Fear not, but let your hands be strong."

And again, Zechariah:

"These are the things that you shall do: Speak you every man the truth to his neighbor; execute the judgment of truth and peace in your gates; let none of you imagine evil in your hearts against his neighbor; and love no false oath; for all these are things that I hate, says the Lord.

". . . and the Lord shall yet comfort Zion, and shall yet choose Jerusalem."

In these days there were mighty promises, like the prophecy of Micah:

". . . and they shall beat their swords into ploughshares, and their spears into pruning-hooks; nations shall not lift up a sword against nation, neither shall they learn war any more. But they shall sit every man under his vine and under his fig tree, and none shall make them afraid, for the mouth of the Lord of Hosts hath spoken it. For all people will walk every one in the name of his god, and we will walk in the name of the Lord for ever and ever."

And Malachi told them how the dream of peace would come to the earth:

"Behold, I will send My messenger, and he shall prepare the way before Me; and the Lord, Whom ye seek, shall suddenly come to His Temple, even the messenger of the covenant, Whom yet delight in. Behold, He shall come."

And now the life of the people as an organized nation was being resumed in good order. In the swift process of rebuilding the wall "the people had a mind to work" and that spirit continued in them. Their leaders set up their offices in Jerusalem and were busy in dutiful and astute administration. They convinced the people that there could be no true prosperity if everyone insisted on living in the capital, and so there was held a great meeting with a drawing of lots, one out of every ten drawing the short piece that entitled him and his immediate family to remain Jerusalemites. The other nine must leave, going to the hinterland towns and helping to build them up into flourishing communities.

All these things the people agreed to and performed happily. They sang their rejoicing as we can sing it today in Psalm 126:

> When the Lord turned again the captivity of Zion,
> We were like them that dream.
> Then was our mouth filled with laughter,
> And our tongue with singing:
> Then said they among the heathen,
> The Lord has done great things for them.
> The Lord has done great things for us;

Whereof we are glad.
Turn again our captivity, O Lord,
As the streams in the south.
They that sow in tears shall reap in joy.
He that goes forth and weeps, bearing precious seed,
Shall doubtless come again with rejoicing,
Bring his sheaves with him.

EPILOGUE

Between the Old Testament and the New

Chapter 46 THE UNWRITTEN YEARS

AND NOW the grand plan of the Father in heaven, the dream that had begun in Eden and which had been stretched out for so long and so disappointingly—and yet never without persisting gleams of hope —was approaching a curious interval, a lapse, an abyss, between two great periods, the time, unrecorded in the Bible, between the Old and the New Testaments.

The Old Testament story was coming to a finish—with renewed persecutions.

Persia had ceased to be a friend of the people of God. Good rulers had come and gone, but with the accession of Artaxerxes III, called "the bloody Ochus," another period of oppression and bondage began. A born tyrant, this third Artaxerxes reoccupied Jerusalem, and a whole generation of Jews were ground under his heel.

But even as the persecuted Jews had hailed the conqueror Cyrus as a deliverer, they now again saw hope, a reversal of fortune for themselves, in a new sweep of conquest. A new tyrant was loose in the world—the young Greek, Alexander the Great, already master of the eastern Mediterranean world, including Egypt, and turning greedy eyes on Persia. When mighty Persia, long master of Israel and Judah, went down to defeat at the Battle of Issus, all Palestine and Syria fell to Alexander.

As with his other conquered countries, Alexander's influences were immediately felt; the population must be at least slighty Hellenized. To all he offered a program of arts, science, and social life. Though in his twenties still, Alexander, brilliant pupil of Aristotle, had his own strange dream of an enforced brotherhood of man. Its foundation, of course, in his view was to be Greek culture. He died before the dream could come true or false; before his thirty-third birthday he was in his grave.

Alexander's empire, forged and welded by his special gifts, split eventually into three parts, because the inevitable lust for power took possession of his generals. Ptolemy I, one of the generals, obtained Egypt, and soon he took possession of Jerusalem and Judea, the Greek name for Judah, and treated it well enough. But trouble would soon be coming; Palestine had always been a political football in the game played by dominant powers, because of its strategic territory at the crossroads of East and West. So Syria was again casting greedy eyes on it, waiting only to pounce, and the opportunity came in 198 B.C.

Once again the Jews were confronted with an overlord, Seleucid Antiochus III, imposing ideas upon them, all in contempt for the ways of Abraham, Moses, and David. The Syrians had no use for Judaism —not for any part of it—and every possible effort was made to make the Hebrews become like their masters. But the Jews simply could not adopt the ideas of the Greeks which had swept the rest of the world: their love of beauty and intellect, with no real God. For this loyalty to their own creed they were again subject to persecution, which reached its bloodstained limits when the weird king Antiochus IV Epiphanes was on the throne.

This king was a Hellenist almost to the point of insanity. His one fixed idea was to stamp out Judaism, no matter at what cost. Studying the situation in Jerusalem, he saw there was discord in the ranks of the Temple priesthood. Corruption was already a tool to his hand there, and he made the most of it. The office of high priest had become a rich plum in revenue for self-seekers, and for years it had been sold to the highest bidder. Naturally, too, only sycophantic tools of the king were chosen.

Never had the priesthood been more debased; it was worse than in the days of Eli. They defiled their own sanctuary, "and neglecting the sacrifices they hastened to enjoy what was unlawfully provided in the palaestra, after the summons of the discus; making no account of the honors of their fathers and thinking the glories of the Greeks best of all."

Righteous Jews, in the vast majority, were shamed to their souls.

To complete the demoralization, the cynical Antiochus Epiphanes had the Temple desecrated by erecting there a statue of Zeus, the chief Greek god. The face of the idol, of course, bore the king's own features. Then he ordered pagan rites to be celebrated. A Greek altar was erected, and, on pain of death, the Jews were prohibited from observing any and all forms of their ancestral worship in their own Temple. No more sacrifices to the Lord God. Nor keeping of the Sabbath. Circumcision became a heinous crime. Possession of a copy of the law meant treason to the crown and a traitor's end. The eating of swine's flesh was made obligatory, and was to be used in burnt offerings.

Anathema! The situation was intolerable. Some weaklings despaired and capitulated, but the strong stored up resolution until their wrath burst forth unexpectedly in the little hill-country town of Modin, outside Jerusalem. Here, as elsewhere, a pagan altar had been set up, and officials of the Seleucid despot were present to see that his maniacal edict was enforced.

A cowering Hebrew was being forced to consent to heathen rites before a gathering of his fellow villagers when suddenly Mattathias, an aged Jewish priest, stepped forward and slew the turncoat where he stood, as well as the Syrian officer beside him.

In the general panic, Mattathias fled into remote hills, together with five stalwart sons and a small following of sympathizers. Nor was the old priest long content with mere hiding. He threw down heathen altars wherever he encountered them. He killed more renegades who served them. His righteous violence proved an inspiring call to action for those who would rather die than forsake their ancient faith.

How could a pygmy band of zealots make more than an ineffective gesture against a great empire like the Seleucid Syria, even with such devoted, magnificent madness?

But history is a kaleidoscope of many patterns and unpredictable turns. Enfeebled, perhaps, by his heroic activity at his age, and suffering exposure and hardship as an outlaw, Mattathias died not long after his flight. Dying, he appointed his eldest son Judas to take his place as rebel leader. In those early times there was still no stain on the name of Judas; indeed, this heroic son of a heroic priest was to cover the name with honor.

Fortunately for what seemed a forlorn cause, Judas had a talent for guerrilla warfare; he was a master of surprise tactics and sudden blows of such weight and consequence that he received the cognomen of "Maccabaeus"—the word for "Hammerer."

He was called Judas Maccabaeus, and "Sound an alarm!" became his tocsin throughout the land. His story is told in the Book of Macabees, included in the Douay version of the Bible.

Astonished Syrian forces, sent with scornful confidence to quell the poorly equipped amateur soldiers, were harrassed and harried by every device of strategy useful in mountain passes, especially in unexpected forays at all hours—early dawn or late night. Four Syrian armies, one after another, were routed by "the Hammerer," who then armed his men with the weapons of slain enemies. This Judas, Hasmonaean captain of the band, was indeed a dangerous foe.

And the Book of Daniel was causing trouble! Scrolls of that masterpiece were being secretly circulated among the Jewish population—a volume that proved a trumpet call to all believers in God.

At length, realizing the gravity of the impasse, the Syrians called back to their capital their armed forces from the hostile hills. Next they meant to plan an invincible campaign against these gadflies annoying His Majesty, Antiochus Epiphanes. The whole affair was becoming dangerously absurd.

But while the Antioch council of military bigwigs was in session, in 165 B.C., Judas Maccabaeus led his men in a surprise march on Jerusalem. He took possession of the profaned Temple. Fiercely the contaminating idols were smashed to rubbish (Zeus, in particular!) and all heathen appurtenances wrecked beyond recognition. A new altar was erected for proper sacrifices to the Lord.

So the Temple was cleaned of its filth and rededicated. It was all wonderful to the faithful; only a few years after the uprising in his little town of Modin, Judas had accomplished what had seemed impossible.

As always, Godliness in Israel had shown itself the source of the people's strength, great enough to overwhelm worldly might. Antiochus Epiphanes (the "little horn" of Daniel's long-ago prophetic vision) died shortly after the cleansing of the Temple. But the conflict went on between the Syrians and the Maccabaeans, until at last, tired of the chase and its prohibitive cost in lives and prestige, Lysius, the Syrian generalissimo, considered peace advisable. He made it a reality by granting the religious freedom for which Judas the Hasmonaean had fought with such unconquerable will and resourcefulness.

God was looking after those who loved and served Him. But Judas knew that he must continue to serve God vigilantly; he was not lulled into neglecting his guard. He suspected that perhaps the "peace" was only a truce. And Judas was right.

The successors to Antiochus Epiphanes sent several fresh armies into Palestine and finally with deadly result. At the Battle of Elasa, Judas Maccabaeus, champion of Hebrew liberty, was killed, his forces shattered. That tragedy happened one hundred and sixty years before Jesus was born.

Undespairing at the death of Judas the Hammerer, his brother Jonathan decided to carry on. With only a remnant of followers he returned to the guerrilla tactics of Judas. Fortune favored him too—the internal affairs of Syria were sapping governmental morale and purpose. As Maccabaean leader, Jonathan gained control of Jerusalem once more; a warrior worthy of his great brother, he captured the port of Joppa from the overlords and gained a few other towns. Together with another brother, Simon, he once more established political freedom for his people.

Thus, after nearly five hundred years of almost continuous subjugation, the Jews won religious and political freedom, thanks to the three fighting Maccabaeas brothers, all of whom, as a result, met with violent death.

Later, under successors in the Hasmonaean dynasty, the Jewish kingdom spread almost to the size of David's glorious empire.

It was during this period of long-fought-for-freedom that certain books appeared from time to time whose purpose was to encourage and maintain patriotism and faith. Written for the most part in Greek, these devout, inspirational scrolls were circulated among the leaders, the subject matter made common knowledge, and came to be cherished as sacred. Revered, these various books were included in the Old Testament compiled in Alexandria, and known as the Septuagint. But the Palestinian Jews refused to put them in their Canon of the Scripture.

However, when St. Jerome (c. A.D. 340–420) prepared his famous Vulgate edition of the Latin Bible he included these books with one exception, "The Prayer of Manasses." They have always been recognized as authoritative by the Roman Catholic Church. It is believed by some that St. Jerome also accepted the designation "apocrypha," or "hidden," for them, a term which implied esoteric truths for the initiated.

These books, which serve as a historic link between the Maccabaean revolt and triumph and the century before Christ, are Tobias, Judith, Wisdom of Solomon, Ecclesiasticus, Baruch, Maccabees I, II, and certain additions to the Book of Daniel, including the story of Susanna, Bel and the Dragon, and the Song of the Three Holy Children (Shadrach, Meshach, and Abednego of the fiery furnace); as well as a continuation of Esther, which imparts a religious tone to the heroic story.

If we look ahead to the Epistles in the New Testament, we see that St. Paul seemed to have some parts of the Wisdom of Solomon in mind when he wrote to the Colossians and to the Romans. St. John, too, in his Gospel reflects some of the Wisdom's teaching.

It was in this miserable time that the Messianic hope, the long-prophesied coming of God's Redeemer to the world, lived like a great light of hope in the thoughts of the people. They remembered the prophecies—there had been many—and some instinct seemd to stir warmingly within them, assuring them that all was soon to be fulfilled.

Throughout the books of the Bible, and their strange, eventful history, all the way from Genesis and the promise made by God to Adam, there were repeated reassurances that the Messiah would come to earth and make peace between man and God. Men applied to the promised Messiah many Biblical verses. There was first of all the passage where God promises a Redeemer to Adam (Genesis 3:15):

"And I will put enmity between thee and the woman, and between thy seed and her seed; it shall bruise thy head, and thou shalt bruise his heel."

He is to be of the stock of Sem (Genesis 9:26):

"And he said, Blessed be the Lord God of Shem; and Canaan shall be His servant."

Of Abraham (Genesis 22:18):

"And in thy seed shall all the nations of the earth be blessed; because thou hast obeyed My voice."

Of Isaac (Genesis 26:4):

"And I will make thy seed to multiply as the stars of heaven, and will give unto thy seed all these countries; and in thy seed shall all the nations of the earth be blessed."

Of Jacob (Genesis 28:14; Numbers 24:17):

"And thy seed shall be as the dust of the earth, and thou shalt spread abroad to the west, and to the east, and to the north, and to the south: and in thee and in thy seed shall all the families of the earth be blessed."

"I shall see him, but not now: I shall behold him but not nigh: there shall come a Star out of Jacob, and a Sceptre shall rise out of Israel, and shall smite the corners of Moab and destroy all the children of Sheth."

Of the tribe of Judah (Genesis 49:8–10):

"Judah, thou art he whom thy brethren shall praise: thy hand shall be in the neck of thine enemies, thy father's children shall bow down before thee.

"Judah is a lion's whelp: from the prey, my son, thou art gone up: he stooped down, he couched as a lion, and as an old lion; who shall rouse him up?

"The sceptre shall not depart from Judah, nor a lawgiver from between his feet, until Shiloh come; and unto him shall the gathering of the people be."

And of the family of David (Isaiah 9:7):

"Of the increase of his government and peace there shall be no end, upon the throne of David, and upon his kingdom, to order it, and to establish it with judgment and with justice from henceforth even for ever. The zeal of the Lord of hosts will perform this."

Moses declares that He will be a great Prophet (Deuteronomy 18:18):

"I will raise them up a Prophet from among their brethren, like unto thee, and will put My words in his mouth; and he shall speak unto them all that I shall command him."

Isaiah says that His coming will be preceded by a universal peace (Isaiah 2:4):

"And He shall judge among the nations, and shall rebuke many people: and they shall beat their swords into ploughshares, and their spears into pruninghooks: nation shall not lift up sword against nation, neither shall they learn war any more."

And Malachias writes of His precursor (Malachi 3:1):

"Behold I will send my messenger, and he shall prepare the way before me: and the Lord, whom ye seek, shall suddenly come to His temple, even the messenger of the covenant, whom ye delight in: behold, He shall come, saith the Lord of hosts."

He is to be born of a Virgin (Isaiah 7:14):

"Therefore the Lord himself shall give you a sign; Behold, a virgin shall conceive, and bear a son, and shall call His name Immanuel."

In the city of Bethlehem (Michah 5:2):

"But thou, Bethlehem Ephratah, though thou be little among the thousands of Judah, yet out of thee shall He come forth unto Me that is to be ruler in Israel; whose goings forth have been from of old, from everlasting.

Before the complete subjection of Israel, and the destruction of the second Temple (Genesis 49:10; Daniel 9:24–27):

"The sceptre shall not depart from Judah, nor a lawgiver from between his feet, until Shiloh come; and unto him shall the gathering of the people be.

"Seventy weeks are determined upon thy people and upon thy holy city, to finish the transgression, and to make an end of sins, and to make reconciliation for iniquity, and to bring in everlasting righteousness, and to seal up the vision and prophecy, and to anoint the most Holy.

"Know therefore and understand, that from the going forth of the commandment to restore and to build Jerusalem unto the Messiah the Prince shall be seven weeks, and threescore and two weeks: the street shall be built again, and the wall, even in troublous times.

"And after threescore and two weeks shall Messiah be cut off, but not for himself: and the people of the prince that shall come shall destroy the city and the sanctuary; and the end thereof shall be with a flood, and unto the end of the war desolations are determined.

"And he shall confirm the covenant with many for one week: and in the midst of the week he shall cause the sacrifice and the oblation to cease, and for the overspreading of abominations he shall make it desolate, even until the consummation, and that determined shall be poured upon the desolate."

The prophets continually style the Messiah the Lord (Psalms 2:2):

"The kings of the earth set themselves, and the rulers take counsel together, against the Lord, and against His anointed."

Jesus or the Saviour (Isaiah 2:5; Habakkuk 3:8):

"O house of Jacob, come ye, and let us walk in the light of the Lord."

"Was the Lord displeased against the rivers? was thine anger against the rivers? was thy wrath against the sea, that thou didst ride upon thine horses and thy chariots of salvation?"

The Mighty God (Isaiah 9:6):

"For unto us a child is born, unto us a son is given: and the government shall be upon His shoulder: and His name shall be called Wonderful, Counsellor, The mighty God, The everlasting Father, The Prince of Peace."

The Immanuel, or God with us (Isaiah 7:14):

"Therefore the Lord himself shall give you a sign; Behold, a virgin shall conceive and bear a son, and shall call his name Immanuel."

They tell of His poverty (Psalms 86:16):

"O turn unto me, and have mercy upon me; give thy strength unto thy servant, and save the son of thine handmaid."

His obedience and meekness (Psalms 39:9; 119:7):

"I was dumb, I opened not my mouth; because thou didst it."

"I will praise Thee with uprightness of heart, when I shall have learned Thy righteous judgments."

His public preaching (Isaiah 9:1, 2):

"Nevertheless the dimness shall not be such as was in her vexation, when at the first he lightly afflicted the land of Zebulun and the land of Naphtali, and afterward did more grievously afflict her by the way of the sea, beyond Jordan, in Galilee of the nations.

"The people that walked in darkness have seen a great light: they that dwell in the land of the shadow of death, upon them hath the light shined."

His miracles (Isaiah 35:5, 6):

"Then the eyes of the blind shall be opened, and the ears of the deaf shall be unstopped.

"Then shall the lame man leap as an hart, and the tongue of the dumb sing: for in the wilderness shall waters break out, and streams in the desert."

His founding of a universal eternal kingdom (Psalms 44:7, 8; Psalms 2:7, 8):

"But thou hast saved us from our enemies, and hast put them to shame that hated us.

"In God we boast all the day long, and praise Thy name for ever. Selah.

"I will declare the decree: the Lord hath said unto me, Thou art my Son; this day have I begotten thee.

"Ask of me, and I shall give thee the heathen for thine inheritance, and the uttermost parts of the earth for thy possession."

They tell us that Christ will be a rock of scandal, and the occasion of ruin for many (Isaiah 8:14):

"And he shall be for a sanctuary; but for a stone of stumbling and for a rock of offence to both the houses of Israel, for a gin and for a snare to the inhabitants of Jerusalem."

That He will be sold for thirty pieces of silver (Zechariah 11:12):

"And I said unto them, if ye think good, give me my price; and if not, forbear. So they weighed for my price thirty pieces of silver."

Led as a lamb to the slaughter (Isaiah 53:7):

"He was oppressed, and He was afflicted, yet He opened not His mouth: He is brought as a lamb to the slaughter, and as a sheep before her shearers is dumb, so He openeth not His mouth."

To be crucified (Zechariah 13:6):

"And one shall say unto Him, What are these wounds in Thine hands? Then He shall answer, Those with which I was wounded in the house of My friends."

While the people mock Him (Jeremiah 20:7; Psalms 21:8):

"O Lord, thou hast deceived Me, and I was deceived: thou art stronger than I, and hast prevailed: I am in derision daily, every one mocketh Me.

"Thine hand shall find out all thine enemies: thy right hand shall find out those that hate thee."

The soldiers cast lots for His garments (Psalms 21:19):

"They parted My garments amongst them: and upon My vesture they cast lots."

And offer Him vinegar to drink (Psalms 68:22):

"And they gave Me gall for My food, and in My thirst they gave Me vinegar to drink."

His sepulchre shall be glorious (Isaiah 11:10):

"The bricks are fallen down, but we will build with square stones: they have cut down the sycamores, but we will change them for cedars."

His body free from corruption (Psalms 15:10):

"Because thou wilt not leave my soul in hell; nor wilt thou give thy holy one to see corruption."

And He shall dwell at the right hand of God (Psalms 15:11):

"Thou hast made known to Me the ways of life, thou shalt fill Me with joy with Thy countenance: at Thy right hand are delights even to the end."

To pour forever His Spirit upon all flesh (Joel 2:28):

"And it shall come to pass after this, that I will pour out My spirit upon all flesh: and your sons and your daughters shall prophesy: your old men shall dream dreams, and your young men shall see visions."

Job identifies the Messiah with God (Job 19:25, 26):

"I know that my Redeemer liveth, and in the last day I shall rise out of the earth . . . and in my flesh I shall see my God."

But none of the Holy Books of Israel and Judah, disputed or not, could by their teachings overcome the rivalries and jealousies of men bidding for worldly power. As the Greek power declined, new aggressors came seeking world empire: the Romans.

When that new phase of history began the Jews were still free. Until then the Maccabaeans had won and preserved Hebrew liberty for a hundred years. Now Pompey, the Roman conqueror, had already put Syria in his pocket as a province of Rome and was at Damascus not far away, when he heard of contention between brothers for the throne of Jerusalem. In that quarrel the Romans were asked by one faction, the Hasmoneans, to intervene.

Pompey lost no time in laying siege to Jerusalem. After three months the city fell, in the year 63 B.C. Ruthlessly Pompey slew thousands in a purge of the city; he forever outraged the Jews by his roughshod entry into the Holy of Holies in the Temple, merely out of infidel curiosity.

Pompey had both Syria and Palestine in his chain of conquests and all the territory of the East, which had opposed Roman domination long and bitterly. It was the perihelion of fame for this most successful general. In all the turmoil of the next decades the helpless people were at the whim and mercy of contending Roman egomaniacs. One of them was Marc Antony. This soldier, who had divided powers with Octavian, found a supporter in Judea, an Idumean Arab by the name of Herod.

That fierce, impetuous, cruel freebooter was an able soldier and a wily fellow, a fighter and a diplomat when he needed to be. As go-between for Antony and Cleopatra, he made himself indispensable and wound up on the throne of Jerusalem, a puppet king of Rome.

The history of Herod was one of terror and violence and wrath. Having made the Judeans hate and curse him, he built them a Temple more magnificent than Solomon—and on the same hallowed height. But it did him no good. In his old age he lived in fear of death and so murdered wife, sons, friends, a man frightened by shadows. But a greater fear was to fall upon Herod—as he stood, all unknowing, when two dispensations were to meet—a past in which prosperity had been the hope of men and a future in which adversity would be counted as a blessing.

That was when he heard a report from his watchers in the town—a tale of three kingly strangers from afar, wise men, sages, savants, coming in caravan, bearing treasures for some unknown Child, following a star that would lead them to His birthplace. Herod knew there was doom in that news. He sent for the wise men and tried to cajole them. He hoped they would find the Holy Child who was to be the new king of the Jews and pretended that he would go with them to kneel and worship.

But the wise men kept their own counsel and did not return to Herod. The craven king was left on his throne, with his ulcers and cancer, to confront a new world that was being born. The Old Testament was finished and the New was beginning in the stable of Bethlehem toward which the wise men moved under the star in the east.